FEMINIST PHILOSOPHY

Feminist Philosophy: An Introduction provides a comprehensive coverage of the core elements of feminist philosophy in the analytical tradition. Part 1 examines the feminist issues and practical problems that confront us as ordinary people. Part 2 examines the recent and historical arguments surrounding the subject area, looking into the theoretical frameworks we use to discuss these issues and applying them to everyday life.

With contemporary and lively debates throughout, Elinor Mason provides a rigorous and yet accessible overview of a rich array of topics including:

- feminism in a global context
- work and care
- reproductive rights
- sex work
- sexual violence and harassment
- sexism, oppression, and misogyny
- intersectionality
- objectification
- consent
- ideology, false consciousness, and adaptive preferences.

An outstanding introduction which will equip the reader with a thorough knowledge of the fundamentals of feminism, *Feminist Philosophy* is essential reading for those approaching the subject for the first time.

Elinor Mason is a Professor of Philosophy at the University of California, Santa Barbara, USA. She is the author of *Ways to be Blameworthy: Rightness, Wrongness, and Responsibility* (2019), and a co-author of *Philosophy for Everyone* (Routledge, 2nd edition 2016).

'In this engaging and well-crafted introduction to feminist philosophy, Elinor Mason offers us a helpful contemporary map of a perpetually contested intellectual terrain. Mason guides the reader through a range of debates that display the continuing vivacity and urgency of feminist thinking.'

Miranda Fricker, *City University of New York Graduate Center, USA*

'The book is wonderfully clear and engaging. It provides an introduction to a diverse range of topics such as sex work, objectification and intersectionality. The philosophical debates within each topic are explained with attention to detail and rigour that will be rewarding for students and teachers alike.'

Natalie Stoljar, *McGill University, Canada*

FEMINIST PHILOSOPHY

An Introduction

Elinor Mason

Routledge
Taylor & Francis Group

LONDON AND NEW YORK

First published 2022
by Routledge
2 Park Square, Milton Park, Abingdon, Oxon OX14 4RN

and by Routledge
605 Third Avenue, New York, NY 10158

Routledge is an imprint of the Taylor & Francis Group, an informa business

British Library Cataloguing-in-Publication Data
A catalogue record for this book is available from the British Library

Library of Congress Cataloging-in-Publication Data
Names: Mason, Elinor, author.
Title: Feminist philosophy : an introduction / Elinor Mason.
Description: 1 Edition. | New York City : Routledge, 2021. |
Includes bibliographical references and index. |
Identifiers: LCCN 2021002989 (print) | LCCN 2021002990 (ebook) |
ISBN 9781138215948 (hardback) | ISBN 9781138215955 (paperback) |
ISBN 9781315406626 (ebook)
Subjects: LCSH: Feminist theory. | Women's rights. | Sex crimes. | Sexism.
Classification: LCC HQ1190 .M37747 2021 (print) | LCC HQ1190 (ebook) |
DDC 305.42-dc23
LC record available at https://lccn.loc.gov/2021002989
LC ebook record available at https://lccn.loc.gov/2021002990

ISBN: 978-1-138-21594-8 (hbk)
ISBN: 978-1-138-21595-5 (pbk)
ISBN: 978-1-315-40662-6 (ebk)

Typeset in Interstate
by SPi Global, India

CONTENTS

Preface and Acknowledgements   vii

Introduction   1

1   **Feminism in a global and multicultural context**   14

PART 1
Practice   31

2   **Work and care**   33

3   **Reproductive rights**   53

4   **Pornography**   68

5   **Sex work**   85

6   **Sexual violence and harassment**   101

PART 2
Theory   121

7   **Sexism, oppression, and misogyny**   123

8   **Intersectionality**   138

9   **Ideology, false consciousness, and adaptive preferences** 151

10   **Objectification**   167

11   **Consent**   181

12 Knowledge and ignorance   196

13 Speech acts and silencing   212

Glossary   225
Bibliography   231
Index   240

PREFACE AND ACKNOWLEDGEMENTS

This book is dedicated to my students, and to my daughter and my son.

The largest debt I owe by far is to my students: this book has developed from our classes and conversations. I would like to thank my students at Edinburgh University, and also at Dartmouth College, the University of Colorado, Boulder, and the University of California, Santa Barbara for rewarding discussions and challenges. I could not have written this without you.

I have benefited from help and advice from lots of people at different stages of the writing of this book. I owe particular thanks to Bob Pasnau and to Aidan McGlynn, whose very detailed comments on the entire first draft were extremely helpful. I would also like to thank Sophie Grace Chappell, Rachel Fraser, Bridget Harris, Federico Luzzi, Maggie O'Brien, Flora Page, Chao-Ying Rao, and Lee Wilson for reading sections of previous drafts. Routledge commissioned very helpful readers' reports, and I am grateful to those anonymous readers for their suggestions. I have also benefited enormously from the editorial skills of Tony Bruce, and the rest of the team at Routledge, especially Lusana Taylor. My final thanks goes to the most important feminist in my life, my husband Eric.

Introduction

"Feminism is the struggle to end sexist oppression."

bell hooks, *Feminist Theory: From Margin to Center*

> Chapter overview: In this introduction I lay out what I mean by 'feminism' and 'feminist philosophy', and introduce my general approach to the topics. I explain some foundational concepts, such as patriarchy, structural sexism, and the distinction between sex and gender.

What is feminism?

We should start with the obvious question, 'what is feminism?' Feminism, as bell hooks says, is the struggle to end sexist oppression. It is a political and social movement, aimed at change. Being a feminist entails accepting two claims. The first is a moral one, that sexist oppression is wrong, that being a woman does not disqualify someone from any rights, opportunities, or freedoms. The second claim is a factual one, the claim that women are currently subject to sexist oppression. Feminists argue that women's lives are shaped and limited by structural forces, that keep women less free and less safe, give them fewer opportunities and less money, and prevent them from having or exercising power and authority.

I accept both of those claims, but I am not trying to convince anyone to be a feminist. Instead, I am taking my audience to be broadly in agreement on the two claims, and to be interested in a philosophical approach to the details. Feminists (including feminist philosophers and feminist theorists in other academic disciplines) do not always agree on the details. There are complicated issues about how to understand sexist oppression, and how to remedy it. In this book I will explain and critically discuss the arguments of feminist philosophers. My aim is to provide a critical overview, which can be read alongside the texts I examine, or on its own. I present the arguments themselves as neutrally as possible, but there are places where I state my own view too.

Let's begin with some empirical facts. The 2018 Global Gender Gap Report, published by the World Economic Forum, measures not just pay, but four broad areas: Economic Participation and Opportunity, Educational Attainment, Health and Survival, and Political Empowerment. The findings are summarized as follows:

- Globally, the average gender gap is 32%. (Women have only 68% of what men have in terms of the values identified).
- The largest gender disparity is on Political Empowerment, which shows a gap of 77.1%. (Women have only 22.9% of the political power that men have, or, to put it another way, a man has about four votes to a woman's one vote). The Economic Participation and Opportunity gap is the second-largest at 41.9%, while the Educational Attainment and Health and Survival gaps are significantly lower at 4.4% and 4.6% respectively.
- Across the 149 countries assessed, there were only 17 that had women as heads of state, while, on average, just 18% of ministers and 24% of parliamentarians globally are women. Similarly, women hold just 34% of managerial positions across the countries where data is available, and less than 7% in the four worst-performing countries (Egypt, Saudi Arabia, Yemen, and Pakistan).
- In terms of broader economic power, gaps in control of financial assets and in time spent on unpaid tasks continue to preserve economic disparities between men and women. Women have as much access to financial services as men in just 60% of the countries and to land ownership in just 42% of the countries assessed. Also, among the 29 countries for which data is available, women spend, on average, twice as much time on housework and other unpaid activities as men.
- Although average progress on gender parity in education is relatively more advanced than in other aspects, there are still 44 countries where over 20% of women are illiterate. Similarly, near-parity in higher education enrolment rates often masks low participation of both men and women. On average, 65% of girls and 66% of boys have enrolled in secondary education globally, and just 39% of women and 34% of men are in college or university today.
- Projecting current trends into the future, the overall global gender gap will close in 108 years across the 106 countries covered since the first edition of the Report. The most challenging gender gaps to close are the economic and political empowerment dimensions, which will take 202 and 107 years to close respectively.
- Similarly, if current rates were to be maintained in the future, the overall global gender gap will close in 61 years in Western Europe, 70 years in South Asia, 74 years in Latin America and the Caribbean, 124 years in Eastern Europe and Central Asia, 135 years in Sub-Saharan Africa, 153 years in the Middle East and North Africa, 165 years in North America, and 171 years in East Asia and the Pacific.[1]

For philosophers, the initial question is, what explains these disparities? One possible answer is that disparities in outcome are all explained by biological differences. A very common view is that men and women are fundamentally different in psychological and physical ways, that men and women have different talents, and different needs, and so it is inevitable that their social positions will differ in systemic ways. Feminists usually object to the claim that men and women have different talents, and argue that the explanation for the disparities between men and women is that our social world is structured by patriarchy. So feminist theorists work to understand patriarchy, and to show that this is indeed the correct explanation for the inequalities that we observe.

Patriarchy is the name given to a hierarchical social system which disadvantages women in systemic ways, not because of any relevant qualities of women, but just because they are women. The term does not denote something monolithic or easy to define. Rather, it names a pattern of advantage. In particular, in a patriarchal system, being a man is deemed necessary (though not sufficient) to have power and authority. Patriarchy does not advantage men over women in every area (women may be better off than men in some), and it does not automatically advantage men (for example, race may undo the benefits of being a man in some contexts). The point of talking about 'patriarchy' is to indicate that sexism works in systemic ways; it is pervasive in our institutions and our ideas.

This is often expressed by saying that sexism is a 'structural issue'. The relevant structures are things like institutions (such as schools and healthcare systems), practices (for example, marriage and divorce), and customs (which can be strict and involve social enforcement, such as gendered modes of dress, but can also appear trivial, like 'gender reveal parties', which celebrate the sex of an unborn child). To say that sexism is structural, or that the system is patriarchal, is to say that these structures work in ways that disadvantage women. Sometimes this is obvious: if girls and women are excluded from formal education (as is still the case in many places), they are structurally disadvantaged. If women are firmly expected to be the primary childcarers, their opportunities outside of that realm will be limited.

Sometimes patriarchal structures are less obvious. Our gendered customs may seem to have no serious effects, but small things can mount up, or have effects we do not see at first. Furthermore, we can be surprised by sexism in structures that we take for granted. In her recent book, *Invisible Women: Exposing Data Bias in a World Designed for Men*, Caroline Criado Perez documents the myriad ways in which things are designed for men, and the disadvantages women face as a result. For example, crash test dummies are shaped like and weighted as male bodies. As a result, safety tests protect men, but not women, who on average have smaller and lighter frames. Criado Perez documents several other examples of safety equipment that fits men's bodies but not women's, and many other cases where data about men is used to the detriment of women.

It is worth stressing that in talking about patriarchy or patriarchal systems I am not saying that sexism is the only axis of oppression. The world we live in is structured so as to disadvantage other groups too, and these disadvantages are systemic just as sexism is. For example, healthcare outcomes in Western countries vary by race, which suggests that there is structural racism in our healthcare systems. In the chapter on intersectionality, I examine the complex ways that these various different sorts of oppression relate to each other and interact. It is not always possible to disentangle sexism from other oppressive systems. But we shouldn't take that to imply that there is no such thing as sexism.

In order to assess the idea that the differences we observe between women's lives and men's lives are down to our social systems, we need to look at the situations both up close and from a distance, and theorize about the mechanisms behind inequalities. Feminist activists and feminists from all academic disciplines have contributed to this work. In this book, I focus on philosophy, but I often refer to work that originated in other disciplines that provides an important foundation, and even where that is not explicit, it is implicit. In thinking about the different social roles that men and women occupy, we need to draw on a wide range of knowledge and evidence, and we need to think carefully about what to make of the evidence.

Mary Wollstonecraft cautions against taking evidence about gender difference at face value in her 1792 book, *A Vindication of the Rights of Woman*. Wollstonecraft objects to the idea that we can deduce that women are not as intelligent as men from the fact that all the great books are written by men. Wollstonecraft points out that if women are not educated, and instead are socialized to be concerned with their appearance rather than their minds, of course they are not going to write great books. Here is a contemporary example: why are there so few women in STEM (Science, Technology, Engineering, and Mathematics) subjects? One persistent idea is that women are less good at science (I come back to that below and in the chapter on work and care). But there are lots of other possible explanations, and we should look at those: perhaps our school systems encourage boys into STEM subjects more. Perhaps there are biases in university entrance requirements and in hiring practice. Perhaps STEM environments seem unattractive to women in some way, so that they are not likely to choose associated jobs, not because they are not good at the subjects in question, but because the environment feels hostile.

What about the gender pay gap? In both Britain and America, women earn, on average, only about 80% of what men earn. To some, this claim looks like feminist propaganda. This statistic is sometimes denied outright. More commonly, detractors argue that although there is a gender pay gap, it is not explained by any sort of injustice. The reason women earn less than men, it is suggested, is that *they choose to*. The idea is that women choose lower paying jobs, and that they choose to take time off to have children, and that they choose to work part time. But what should we make of such choices? Are our choices always free and unconstrained? Is it not possible that our choices are structured by the options that are available to us? If a woman is given a choice between a low paid job and no job, it is likely that she will take the low paid job. If she has been encouraged since early childhood to think that she is only capable of a small range of things, and that education is a waste of time for her, it is likely that she will give up on education. If she has a child with a man, and paternity leave is not an option, then she will take maternity leave rather than make a greater income sacrifice. If childcare is not affordable she will have to go part time. Or perhaps part time work is all that is available to her. And so on. So the question becomes, 'are these constraints on her choices just?' And the feminist answer is usually, 'No, we should change the constraints'.

Women all over the world, to varying degrees, are underpaid and disempowered. It is often easy to see how political and social structures restrict women's power and freedom, and sometimes the injustices are very obvious. But other issues, both empirical and moral, are more complex. What do we say about sex work? On the one hand, the choices of sex workers are often constrained by poverty, lack of education, and violence. But on the other, we should be wary of moralizing about sex, demonizing sex workers, and failing to respect the autonomous choices of adult women. And pornography is a similarly complex issue. Does it degrade and disempower women, encouraging a view of women as sex objects? Or is it, under the right conditions, a healthy expression of human sexuality? And even if pornography is sexist, does that matter? Perhaps there is a right to make and consume pornography that survives feminist worries about the content.

Questions about pornography and sex work intersect with broader questions about sex, sexuality, and sexual violence. Rape and other forms of sexual violence are globally endemic. How can we understand the relationship between sexual violence and patriarchal culture? Some feminists argue that sexual violence is an enforcement mechanism, that the threat of sexual violence is a way to keep women down. Furthermore, feminists argue that patriarchal culture normalizes a lot of sexual violence and treats it as normal sex. For example, in many jurisdictions, if a man rapes his wife, it is not a crime, it is not rape. Of course, feminists do not always agree on how we should understand various oppressions, or on what should be done. What makes a philosophical account of these issues feminist is not that a particular answer is given, but that the focus is on the interests of women. In the first part of the book I examine many of these real world issues and discuss the arguments that feminist philosophers have offered.

In the second part of the book, I focus on theoretical foundations. What is sexism? What is misogyny? What is the difference between harm that befalls men under patriarchal power structures, and harm that befalls women? We need to think about what oppression is, and what it is to suffer disadvantage as a result of structure. We need a clear account of intersectionality, the way that different sorts of oppression can intersect to create new forms of oppression. If we want to understand the way that people internalize the narratives and ideologies of their culture, we need an account of false consciousness and adaptive preferences. We need to be able to explain the way our language – our speaking, our listening – can be affected by oppressive structures and, indeed, be part of those structures. Feminist philosophy can help to illuminate and sharpen these ideas, and in that way plays a part in the political struggle to end sexist oppression.

What is feminist philosophy?

As I see it, feminist philosophy is a subject matter, not a methodology. Historically, philosophers study everything. The field has narrowed as other subjects found ways to define themselves independently. Philosophers no longer study everything; rather, we study the things that call for a particular method: a method we might roughly characterize as non-empirical investigation. That can be applied to language, to ethics, to what exists, to knowledge, and so on. Philosophy is the methodology, and we can take a more or less broad view of what counts as 'philosophy'. My own inclination is to be fairly liberal about what counts as philosophy. We might allow some historical reflection, some sociological or psychological data, some cognitive science, some speculation, as well as strict logical deduction. So feminists philosophers do that, whatever it is, applied to questions about the standing of women, and with concern that women are not excluded or marginalized by a focus that may appear neutral on the surface but is actually skewed towards men.

This is not a universally shared view about what feminist philosophy is. Some philosophers have assumed that feminist philosophy must be a methodology, a special female or feminine way of doing philosophy. One version of this idea has its genesis in Carol Gilligan's 1982 book, *In a Different Voice*. In it, Gilligan criticizes the conclusions of Lawrence Kohlberg's research on moral development. In brief, Kohlberg argued that girls develop moral faculties more slowly than boys and do not reach as high a level. Gilligan argues that the girls were reasoning in a different way but not necessarily a worse way. She points out that the boys were using universal principles, but the girls' thinking also had a form, one that Gilligan characterizes as being chiefly concerned with personal connection.

This gave rise to care ethics, which is often characterized as a 'feminine' ethics. Philosophers such as Nel Noddings developed fully fledged philosophical accounts of care ethics, and endorsed the idea that this is an essentially female way of thinking that had been unfairly ignored in philosophical theorizing about ethics.[2] Other thinkers have made even more radical claims about different ways of thinking, suggesting that 'masculine' norms of objectivity, rationality, and logic should be distrusted by feminists. In fact, there may be fewer defenders of such views than is generally thought, at least in philosophy. It is rare for feminist philosophers to reject rationality and objectivity; rather, they argue that our ideas about which things are rational and objective are often flawed. We may dispute the patriarchal orthodoxy about which things are objectively true, or what it is rational to believe, but if we give up on the very idea of objectivity or rationality, we cannot communicate our arguments and then we cannot expect to convince anyone.

This is related to a common misunderstanding of Audre Lorde's oft quoted line, that the master's tools will never dismantle the master's house. That is sometimes understood to mean that reason and logic are the master's tools, and feminism must eschew them. But when seen in context, it is clear that this is not what she means. Lorde is addressing a conference on feminist theory, and she points out that only two women of colour were invited. She says, "the tools of a racist patriarchy are used to examine the fruits of that same patriarchy".[3] Middle-class heterosexual white women are only one group, and if they ignore the other groups – poor women, Black women, lesbians, disabled women, trans women – they are playing into the hands of the racist patriarchy. The patriarchy can easily resist or even accommodate demands from isolated sub-groups of women while maintaining power overall. It is the categories of patriarchy that are the master's tools, not the tools of analytic philosophy.

What then, of the idea that women have a particular feminine way of thinking? There is, of course, an empirical issue here. What innate differences are there between the sexes? Gilligan herself does not claim to have established that the differences she sees in moral thinking are innate differences. But the idea that there could be, even that there surely must be differences between men and women at a psychological level is a common one. The psychologist Cordelia Fine has recently done a lot of work debunking this idea. What Fine points out is that again and again the studies that are commonly cited turn out to be very problematic. One of her targets is Simon Baron-Cohen, the author of several well publicized studies that purport to show that there are innate sex differences. Baron-Cohen believes that testosterone makes you good at maths, and that females are less focussed on abstract issues and more on other people. By this logic, Baron-Cohen argues that autism is the 'extreme male brain'. These theories have done well in the market-place of ideas, in that sense lots of people know about them and take them to be very plausible. They may even be reaching the status of 'common knowledge'. And that is not surprising, as Fine points out. Many of these theories accept and amplify old stereotypes about women, that they are submissive, emotional, not rational.

One of Baron-Cohen's studies, done with his graduate student Jennifer Connellan, purports to show that infants a day and a half old already exhibit gender differences. At such a young age, the thought is that they cannot have been socialized, so any differences we see are innate, or at least not caused by external influences. The babies were shown a mobile and a female human face. As Baron-Cohen predicted, the boy babies were more interested (looked longer) at the mobile, and the girl babies looked longer at the face. This seems to confirm Baron-Cohen's account of the differences between girls' and boys' psychology.

But Fine points out myriad flaws in the experiment. First, the babies were shown the objects one after the other, and the time they spent looking was measured. But infant attention span is very short in the first few days, so showing objects one after the other is not the best way to judge which the infant finds more interesting. The objects should be shown simultaneously. Second, newborns do not have well developed vision. In this study, some of the babies were on their backs, while some were propped up in a parent's lap. So the objects would have looked different from those different positions. Third, the babies were visited in the maternity ward. As is always the way in a maternity ward, the sex of the baby would have been apparent to the experimenter: colour coded gifts and congratulation cards revealing, 'It's a Boy!' And to compound that, the fourth problem: the experimenters knew exactly what they were looking for, and we cannot rule out the possibility that they affected the babies' attention. The female face in question was Jennifer Connellan's.[4]

Louise Antony addresses the issue of differences between men and women in her discussion of the under-representation of women in philosophy.[5] One explanation that has been mooted (by Kant and many since) is that women are less rational then men, and philosophy requires advanced rational capacities. The view is usually dressed up in slightly less critical terms, perhaps women are less interested in arcane abstract pursuits and more grounded in things that really matter. Perhaps men's aggression in male-dominated fields like philosophy is intolerable to the gentler sex. But, however we dress it up, the claim is committed to some sort of intrinsic difference between men and women. This may not be used in an explicitly sexist way, indeed, what Antony calls the 'different voices model' has been adopted by many feminists. But Antony argues that we should not accept the different voices model: like Fine, she thinks that it is not empirically sound, but she also suggests that it is dangerous for women.

Antony argues that claims about the differences between men and women will almost always end up being used to disadvantage women. First, differences are taken as natural and immutable, so that if women are more family oriented, they must be like that by nature, and it must be something that cannot change. But, of course, observed differences need not be natural or immutable – they could be acquired (by socialization in a very gendered society) and changeable (for example, if we moved to a less gendered society). But the view that nurturing and motherhood are natural for women leads to political conservatism: why introduce paternity leave when it is right and good for women to stay at home with children?

This illustrates a point that Antony puts in terms of 'generics'. There can be true general statements (what philosophers call 'generics') where it is not immediately clear what makes the statement true. Take the general claim, 'women are nurturing'. We could take this to be made true by the fact that women are essentially like that. The claim would be that it is a part of their nature and possibly immutable. Or, we could think that it is true as a matter of *social* reality: women in our society have been socialized to be nurturing, and so they tend to be. Consider the claim that boys are rough. It could be heard as a claim that men are by nature violent, or as a claim that boys are socialized to be rough. Furthermore, there is subtlety in how to interpret the statistical claims inherent in generics. Take the claim that ticks carry Lyme disease. Not all ticks carry Lyme disease, and yet it is true that ticks carry Lyme disease. Enough do, and we are concerned to avoid Lyme disease, so this is what matters to us. What if someone says, 'men are violent'? They usually don't mean that *all* men are violent, and we usually understand that the implication is not supposed to be that all men are violent. (The hashtag #notallmen is rightly mocked for its flat-footedness in not recognizing this). Rather, the claim is probably that violence is more common in men than women, and that it is in some important (though not innate) way connected to masculinity. Feminists need to be able to use generics to say important things about the way that men and women are socialized and stereotyped without being committed to universal or innateness claims.

Antony's point, going back to the different voices model, is that generics about gender differences may be true if understood as claims about socialization, but are dangerous for women if heard as claims about nature. They reinforce the very stereotypes that feminists aim to banish. I have little sympathy for the different voices model for the reasons that Fine, Antony, and many others give. The empirical evidence that men and women are fundamentally psychologically different is weak at best. And we do not want to buy into the old and damaging stereotypes about men and women. So, naturally, I do not take feminist philosophy to be a different voice, a different way of thinking. Rather, it is just a different subject matter. Feminist philosophers talk about topics that concern women, and in particular the oppression of women. But the philosophy is just philosophy.

Let's return briefly to care ethics. I think we should be suspicious of the idea that women have a particular way of thinking that is innate. But that is not to say that we should abandon care ethics altogether. One possible view is that care ethics is the right approach to ethics and that it can be applied equally to men and women. That view is compatible with rejecting the claim that women innately have a different way of thinking. Care ethics originates in observations about gender differences, but we needn't think those differences are innate. If it so happens that women have been raised to be more nurturing and have developed different ways of thinking, we could decide that insights gained from this should now be applied universally.

This thought can be applied more generally. Men and women are socialized in different ways. Sometimes the way that women are socialized is preferable and should be applied to men too. For example, it doesn't take much thought to see that in Anglo societies it is very common for men to be socialized to avoid real intimacy with anyone but their immediate family. (Have a few beers and talk about the game last night by all means, but please don't talk about the deep loneliness inside you). But equally, sometimes the way that men are socialized is preferable. For example, men tend to be more comfortable with their bodies and their appearance than women. When it comes to particular elements of our social and cultural practices, feminists do not always agree about what is worthwhile and should be shared amongst everyone and what should be jettisoned. But the general point is an important one, that the patriarchal gender rules have apportioned goods unfairly in both directions.

Sex and gender

The traditional distinction between sex and gender is a distinction between characteristics that are biological, and characteristics that are socially constructed. A simplistic way to put the distinction is to say that sex is biological and gender is socially constructed, but it is worth saying a bit more about what that means.

Sex is biological in that it depends on things like chromosomes, reproductive organs, and secondary sex characteristics. That does not imply that our ways of characterizing sex are independent of social forces. As is well documented, biological sex characteristics do not fall neatly into two categories. Anne Fausto-Sterling argues that the biological facts as we know them are compatible with recognizing five or more sexes.[6] Which biological features are focussed on, and how many sexes are recognized, can and does vary. An emphasis on reproductive roles leads to thinking of two sexes, corresponding to two different roles in sexual reproduction, with intersex categories seen as exceptional. But a more socially oriented classification system may recognize intersex categories as categories in their own right. This does not mean that sex is not biological, it just means that the biological facts can be categorized in different ways. Compare classification systems for celestial bodies: Pluto is out there, and it is whatever it is, whether we call it a planet or not.

We may say then, that sex is biological, but sex categories are partly socially constructed. As Fausto-Sterling points out, this is politically important: intersex conditions should not be seen as a problem, as they often have been. In Western societies, infants are routinely and unnecessarily surgically altered to fit into the sex binary. Intersex people face misunderstanding and prejudice. Fausto-Sterling argues that we should change attitudes, change our account of sex, rather than change people's bodies.

By contrast with sex, I take gender to be a thoroughly social construction. By that I mean that being a man or a woman (as opposed to male or female) is a matter of social customs and practices, rules and norms that have developed and evolved through social processes. Compare money: money represents exchange value, and we have quite deliberately invented it and imbued physical objects with social meaning in order to serve a useful purpose. The use of money is regulated in accordance with its purpose, which is clearly defined. Other social constructions are less deliberate and evolve more organically. The informal set of politeness rules, for example, has a purpose (to ease our social interactions), but the customs evolve in sometimes random and possibly counterproductive ways.

Whether a construction is fully independent of empirical facts also varies. Hysteria, the disease in which the uterus breaks free and moves around the body, is completely invented. But other social constructions are tied to independent reality. Take, for example, different ways of characterizing stages of development. Talk of toddlers, terrible twos, terrible threes, children, adolescents, and teenagers varies across cultures. These ideas are socially constructed, in that the attributes of a teenager, for example, are understood differently in different times and places. Being a teenager is socially constructed as more than merely being a certain age. But being 13, as opposed to 30 or 3, is an independent fact, not a socially constructed fact.

Furthermore, when a social construction is tied to a person, there will be a feedback loop, as Ian Hacking calls it, which reinforces the construction.[7] Thirteen-year-olds will respond to the expectations that are placed upon them. If one thinks of oneself as a teenager, one behaves in ways that are expected, one follows the script, thus reinforcing the idea that being a teenager is a thing. Sally Haslanger adds that social constructions are reinforced without conscious internalization too. Being thought of as a teenager affects what opportunities are available and may have other wider ranging effects that we do not even have names for. Haslanger's example is widowhood. Like 'teenager', 'widow' is a social construction that goes beyond the mind-independent facts. How much further varies: in some cultures, being a widow is not a big deal; in others it is associated with considerable loss of status and rights. A widow in a culture that imposes hardships on widows will suffer as a widow no matter what her self-conception is.[8]

One reason to talk about social construction is to argue that accepted ideas about a particular thing should not be taken for granted. Feminists argue that much of what has evolved in the case of gender is deeply problematic, shot through with oppressive restrictions. Woman, or femininity, is constructed as nurturing, communicative, emotional (but not very rational), intuitive (but not very clever), and so on. And we might even observe that in the world. But this is a social construction of gender, and it could have been different. As Simone de Beauvoir puts it, "One is not born, but rather becomes woman".[9] The framework of social construction gives us another way to put the points I argued for in the previous sections, that our ideas about what women are like are a product of patriarchy, they do not reflect a deep truth about women.

In this book I focus on women, understood as the group of people that are the main target of patriarchal oppression. This book is a book about how to understand and how to resist that oppression. Sometimes that involves investigating the details of the common social construction of woman, for example, in discussions of the construction of heterosexuality that are relevant to the issues of sexual violence and rape. It is worth pointing out that the mainstream social construction of gender is very complex and can be self-contradicting: women are expected to be both competent and responsible, but are also told that they are helpless and dependent on men. Sometimes this can be explained by subtle differences in interactions between different stereotypes, but other times there are simply contradictions. The construction of gender is not a careful process. But the descriptive task of mapping actual constructions of gender is not a project that I undertake in any systematic way.

There is another, different, project that I do not cover in this book: an ameliorative project, as Haslanger terms it, concerned with redefining 'woman' so that it remains a politically useful tool but loses the problematic baggage of the patriarchal construction.[10] Different theorists give different accounts of what we should say about what it is to be a woman, with some arguing that we should abandon the concept altogether. That project, often referred to as the metaphysics of gender, has produced its own literature and controversies. I do not have space to address that literature here, although some of the issues come up in the chapter on intersectionality.

My assumption in this book is that we can deal with the main concerns of feminism without giving a definition of 'woman'. Instead, we should look at the oppressions that people – all people – face as a consequence of patriarchal power structures. We can use a deflationary account of 'woman' when we argue that violence against women is endemic, or that women are paid less than men.[11] Of course, the term 'woman' is used in different ways. But we do not need to resolve the boundary disputes in order to identify sexist oppression. The power system that I refer to as 'patriarchy', the system that oppresses people on the basis of gender, is oppressive to those it takes to be women but also to anyone who disobeys the gender rules, including gay people, and trans and non-binary people. The topics I discuss in this book apply variously to different groups, and to the intersections of different groups. Some apply to all women, but some apply directly only to some women. The topic of abortion, for example, is only directly relevant to women who might get pregnant. And it is not only relevant to women, it is relevant to some trans men too. The point is that philosophical questions about how to define woman need to not be answered in advance of the much more urgent issue of understanding and addressing the sexist structures and forces that are damaging to people.

Aims and audience

This book is primarily intended for philosophy students, but I hope that it is sufficiently accessible for it to be of interest to the general reader too. It is, however, a book about philosophy. I do not attempt to cover all the other various academic and non-academic contributions to the feminist movement. And, of course, it is not exhaustive. There are many issues I do not deal with. I have tried to cover enough ground for the reader to come away with a sense of the major issues, and a clue for where to start further exploration. But obviously this is only an introduction, and I have had to omit whole topics and important strands within topics. The focus of this book is on the practical and political issues that arise from sexist oppression.

I start the book with a chapter on the difficulty of applying feminist arguments across different contexts and cultures. My own situation, as a privileged white woman working in academia in Britain and the USA, limits my experience, and also my understanding: what I notice; what I take to be important. Who am I to talk about a feminism that applies beyond my own sphere? There are serious difficulties here, but I argue that feminists can and should theorize about situations other than their own. It is important to be aware of the limits, to listen to others, to be open to correction. But we should not think that each person only has the authority to speak about their own oppression. Feminists should be concerned with all women and should be willing to risk stepping outside of their comfort zone.

The chapters in Part 1 of the book focus on some real world problems. I talk about the things that are working badly for women (not necessarily only women), and analyze the nature of that problem. The first part of the book could be understood as focussed on practical issues, topics to which the question, 'what should we do about this?' applies. Philosophers usually address the 'what should we do' question by answering a different question: 'how should we think about this?' Philosophers are concerned to identify what is at stake - is this a matter of rights? Of fairness? Of equality? From there we can move towards assessing practical steps.

In the second part of the book I talk in more detail about the concepts, the theoretical tools that feminist philosophers have introduced in order to better talk about the real world. One of the inevitable results of an oppressive system is that the very terms and concepts that we need to analyze what is going on will be missing or marginalized. Take the term 'intersectionality'. This is an invaluable conceptual tool for understanding the way that different oppressions interact with each other. Yet many, including mainstream analytic philosophers, are entirely ignorant or suspicious of the term. At the same time, it has become a 'buzzword', used often in mainstream feminism, but in such a vague way that it does not contribute anything of value, and, indeed, fuels the mistrust of people who want to think carefully and clearly. Ideas like sexism, misogyny, false consciousness, and so on call out for a clear analysis. In the chapters in Part 2 I look at and explain the various conceptual tools of feminist philosophy.

The two parts of the book, and indeed the individual chapters, can be read in any order. Readers should choose which order to read the chapters in based on their own concerns and learning style. Some people prefer to get clear on all the theoretical questions and terms before thinking about practical problems. For them, Chapter 7, on sexism and oppression (the first chapter in Part 2) will be the obvious place to start. But for those who are new to philosophy, it can be better to jump in to the practical issues and return to examine the theoretical framework in more detail later. For others (and this is how I design my own courses), it is good to switch back and forth, to read about a practical issue and then to learn more about the concepts that are used to discuss it. Where it seems useful, I have previewed theoretical issues in the chapters in Part 1, so that there is at least a very basic primer on the relevant theoretical tools. And, of course, it is not always easy to distinguish between or separate practical and theoretical issues, so the division should be taken as very rough and slightly artificial. I have also provided a glossary of the main technical terms. I hope that this helps in allowing the reader to choose their own path through the chapters.

Marx complained that philosophy has only interpreted the world, but the point is to change it. Many of us do hope to change the world, but we aim to interpret it first. If we understand how our practices and institutions, our language, our science, our laws are sexist, we can work on change. That was Marx's approach too: he had a theory of how capitalism works, and he took that to be the first step in dismantling it. Feminist philosophy similarly starts with interpretation. The hope is that through a better understanding of patriarchal systems, we can dismantle them. But not every step in feminist philosophy is directly a step towards a practical aim. Sometimes the aim is more purely philosophical, just to make sense of something in more illuminating terms; to show how something relates to other areas of philosophy; to say something that is true, if not immediately useful.

Notes

1 'The Global Gender Gap Report 2018', pp. vii–viii, www3.weforum.org/docs/WEF_GGGR_2018.pdf.
2 Noddings, *Caring: A Feminine Approach to Ethics and Moral Education*.
3 Lorde, 'The Master's Tools Will Never Dismantle the Master's House', in *Sister Outsider: Essays and Speeches*.
4 Fine, *Delusions of Gender*, pp.112–117.
5 Antony, 'Different Voices or Perfect Storm: Why Are There So Few Women in Philosophy?'
6 Fausto-Sterling, *Sexing the Body*.
7 Hacking, *The Social Construction of What?*
8 Haslanger, *Resisting Reality*, p.126.
9 de Beauvoir, *The Second Sex*, p.330.
10 Haslanger, 'Gender and Race: (What) Are They? (What) Do We Want Them to Be?', in *Resisting Reality: Social Construction and Social Critique*.
11 For arguments along these lines see Antony, 'Feminism Without Metaphysics', and Mikkola, *The Wrong of Injustice: Dehumanization and Its Role in Feminist Philosophy*, pp.105–106.

Other introductory books and collections

Adichie, Chimamanda Ngozi (2014) *We Should All be Feminists*. Fourth Estate. (Accessible and eloquent argument for why we should all be feminists).

Botts, Tina Fernandes and Tong, Rosemarie (2017) *Feminist Thought: A More Comprehensive Introduction*. Routledge. (5th edition of this text, an introduction which classifies feminist theories by tradition, e.g., liberal feminism, radical feminism, and Marxist and socialist feminism, care-focussed feminism, psychoanalytic feminism, and ecofeminism).

Buxton, Rebecca and Whiting, Lisa (2020) *The Philosopher Queens*. Unbound. (Collection of short, accessible pieces on neglected women philosophers from Hypatia to the present day).

Crasnow, Sharon and Superson, Anita (eds.) (2012) *Out of the Shadows: Analytic Feminist Contributions to Traditional Philosophy*. Oxford University Press. (Collection of essays in the analytic tradition).

Finlayson, Lorna (2016) *Feminism: An Introduction*. Cambridge University Press. (Accessible and opinionated introduction).

Fricker, Miranda and Hornsby, Jennifer (2000) *The Cambridge Companion to Feminism in Philosophy*. Cambridge University Press. (Collection of essays by well-known feminist philosophers).

Garry, Ann, Khader, Serene, and Stone, Alison (2017) *The Routledge Companion to Feminist Philosophy*. Routledge. (Collection of articles representing and discussing a wide range of traditions).

Hackett, Elizabeth and Haslanger, Sally (eds.) (2000) *Theorizing Feminisms*. Oxford University Press. (Collection of many classic pieces in feminist theory from a range of academic fields).

Hay, Carol (2020) *Think Like a Feminist*. W.W. Norton & Company. (Accessible and sometimes irreverent short introduction).

Jaggar, Alison and Young, Iris Marion (2000) *A Companion to Feminist Philosophy*. Wiley Blackwell. (Large selection of articles from both analytic and Continental philosophy, and including many from non-Western traditions).

Saul, Jennifer (2003) *Feminism: Issues and Arguments*. Oxford University Press. (Introductory discussion of the main themes in analytic philosophy).

Stone, Alison (2007) *An Introduction to Feminist Philosophy*. Polity. (Introductory discussion of feminist philosophy, focussed on figures in Continental philosophy such as de Beauvoir, Irigaray, and Butler).

1 Feminism in a global and multicultural context

"Let woman's claim be as broad in the concrete as the abstract. We take our stand on the solidarity of humanity, the oneness of life, and the unnaturalness and injustice of all special favoritism, whether of sex, race, country, or condition. If one link of the chain is broken, the chain is broken."

Anna Julia Cooper, *A Voice from the South*

Chapter overview: This chapter addresses concerns the reader may have about the complexities of applying feminist arguments across different cultures. I briefly introduce the idea of intersectionality, and go on to discuss Martha Nussbaum's account of universal values. I cover Uma Narayan's examination of the dangers of imperialist assumptions and misguided interventions, as well as defences of the possibility of speaking for others despite these difficulties. I discuss Susan Okin's worries about multiculturalism; the issue of adaptive preferences; and Iris Marion Young's social connection account of responsibility for justice.

Introduction

In 1963, Betty Friedan argued that the lives of North American middle-class white women were stunted by the demands of being a housewife. Except, of course, she didn't always put it quite like that. She often writes as if she is talking about women in general, not the very specific geographical, class- and race-defined group of her peers from Smith College, an elite women's college in Massachusetts. The problems that Friedan identifies were (and to a large extent remain) real problems, but they are problems for only a tiny sub-section of the world's women. Other women: poor women, uneducated women, women in the global south, immigrant women, women of colour, LGBTQ+ women, disabled women, for example, are not primarily oppressed by the tyranny of the messy suburban house.

In this chapter I focus on the question of how academic feminism should approach questions about women in the third world and in multicultural contexts in Western societies. Before

I go further, I should note that the terminology here is disputed. I follow Serene Khader and others in avoiding the term, 'developing world'. As Khader points out, that term implies that income is the most important indicator of flourishing. Khader defends her use of the term 'third world women', arguing that it accurately captures the hierarchical geopolitical situation of the people being discussed. Like Khader, I will talk about the third world, because of, rather than despite, the hierarchical nature of the term. This is not to say that all third world women suffer the same problems and disadvantages: of course the third world is culturally diverse, and there are varying levels of deprivation.

What can feminism say about all of these women, all of these different problems? And how should comparatively privileged women think of their own disadvantages in the context of the far worse problems of other women? Feminist philosophers have said various things, and in this chapter I will explore some of the territory, but this is by no means a complete picture. The first thing to say, though, is that I think that there are important factors that all instances of women's oppression have in common. As well as the differences, there are common experiences: women everywhere are more likely to suffer sexual and domestic violence, are more vulnerable to poverty, are less in control of their own destinies, and are deprived of power and authority.

So how should we deal with the differences in different women's situations? As feminists, we should stand in solidarity with each other. As philosophers, we need to think about how the differences in our situations might affect the way we see things, and work to avoid narrow or inaccurate understandings of how things are for women in different situations. This applies across the various differences between women.

It is common to hear the term 'intersectionality' used in both academic and non-academic feminist circles. The term 'intersectional feminism' is often used to mean feminism that includes all women and respects their differences. In philosophy the term has a very specific meaning that is slightly more complex, but also more useful than the broader common usage. I discuss the idea in more detail in Chapter 8, but it is worth a quick explanation in the context of the discussions of this chapter.

The term 'intersectionality' was introduced by American legal theorist Kimberlé Crenshaw (the idea appears in the work of other Black feminist theorists, such as that of bell hooks, a bit earlier). Crenshaw argued that Black women suffer a sort of oppression that cannot be captured by talking simply about either sexism or racism. Crenshaw gives the example of a discrimination case brought by a group of Black women against their employer. They argued that they were being discriminated against in not being promoted. The employer responded that it couldn't be sexism, because lots of women had been promoted, and it couldn't be racism, because lots of Black people had been promoted. But all the women who were promoted were white, and all the Black people who had been promoted were men. Crenshaw argues that the employer's argument misses something crucial: Black women are at the intersection of those axes of oppression, and so they are discriminated against not as women, or as Black, but as Black women.[1]

Intersectionality is relevant in thinking about global feminism. We need to be able to recognize the ways in which the lives of some third world women are affected by the intersections of different axes of oppression. And the axes of oppression that are relevant may be unfamiliar to first world feminists. As Elizabeth Spelman says, it is crucial to sustain a lively regard for the variety of women's experiences. On the one hand, what unifies women and justifies us in talking about the oppression of women is the overwhelming evidence of the worldwide and historical subordination of women to men. On the other, while it may be possible for us to speak about women in a general way, it also is inevitable that any statement we make about women in some particular place at some particular time is bound to suffer from ethnocentrism if we try to claim for it more generality than it has.[2]

This leads to a related point that has been very important in recent philosophical discussions of global feminism: how should Western feminists deal with their own unfamiliarity with the cultures they are talking about? There is a tension here. On the one hand, there is a justified pressure to respect difference, to keep out of other people's business, and not presume to know better than them how to organize their lives. On the other hand, practices such as genital cutting seem to be objectively wrong, and to refuse to criticize them on grounds of cultural difference seems overly deferential. How to resolve that tension is not clear, and much of the discussion of this chapter is focussed on that question.

Universal values

If we are to talk about injustice across different cultural contexts, we need a robust account of universal values. Perhaps we should be relativists about morality, about value, about cultural practices. I will not spend long arguing against relativism, but I will make a few brief remarks.

First, the philosophical landscape is very complex here. Let's start with a distinction between cultural relativism and moral relativism. In one sense, cultural relativism is an uncontroversial and obvious stance. Customs and etiquette vary from culture to culture, and the right way to do things in one culture is not necessarily the right way to do them in a different culture. So long as the variations do not impact on more serious matters, being a relativist – agreeing that the right way to do things differs from culture to culture – is unproblematic. However, cultural relativism is much more difficult to defend if it shades into moral relativism. A moral relativist doesn't stop at superficial customs and etiquette, but claims that what is *morally* right also varies from culture to culture. In that case, if a culture's dominant moral code condones slavery, or genital cutting, or animal cruelty, the moral relativist is committed to accepting that in that society, those things are morally permissible.

Very few philosophers accept moral relativism, but that does not commit us to an ambitious form of realism. Many philosophers take a position that we might call 'modest objectivism'. This is the view that there are objective values, moral standards that apply universally, but the ground for them is not something metaphysically ambitious. Rather, there is some account of moral values that is compatible with a naturalistic worldview.

The appeal to some sort of objective morality seems essential to the feminist project. Feminists claim that certain structures and institutions are morally criticizable because they are bad for women. It would be odd to say that this applies only to women in the speaker's own culture. That would appear to exclude some women from concern. Do those women matter less? Is it not morally problematic for them to suffer? If the underlying thought is that women in the third world (or elsewhere) are *not* suffering, then this is not relativism: the claim would be an empirical one, that the conditions are not as bad as they appear. This sort of view may also rely on an epistemological claim, that feminists from one culture are not good at judging what is going on for women in another. These points can be made without appealing to relativism.

The philosophical commitment to universal values is explicitly defended by Martha Nussbaum. Chapter 1 of Nussbaum's 2001 book, *Women and Human Development*, is called, 'In Defense of Universal Values'. Obviously, any critique of cultural practices must assume that there really is a right or wrong of the matter. Nussbaum recognizes that this may invite suspicion. As she puts it,

> The suspicion uneasily grows that the theorist is imposing something on people who surely have their own ideas of what is right and proper. And this suspicion grates all the more unpleasantly when we remind ourselves that theorists often come from nations that have been oppressors, or from classes in poorer nations that are themselves relatively privileged. Isn't all this philosophizing, then, simply one more exercise in colonial or class domination?[3]

Nussbaum argues that we can formulate an account of universal values that respects various differences between people and between cultures. She argues for a version of political liberalism which allows people to choose their own path, where that path might involve commitment to traditional cultural or religious values. However, no way of life should be compulsory, there should always be freedom to choose other options. Nussbaum argues that we should measure this, not by asking about well-being or by asking about income (often how development agencies try to measure progress), but by looking at capabilities, what people are able to be and do.

This is a familiar line of thinking in political philosophy, and Nussbaum's view has a close relative in Amartya Sen's account as well as John Rawls' account of primary goods.[4] The idea is that there are certain things that all humans need, and that is supposed to be true no matter what other variations among people there are. Liberals tend to give a fairly minimal list – the idea is not to valorize a particular way of life, but to list the goods that are necessary for any sort of decent life. Nussbaum, an American, came to her list through interviewing women in many different parts of the world, as well as by the traditional philosophical method of solitary reflection. Much of her field work was focussed on India, but she also consulted people from other countries.

Nussbaum's list of capabilities (which she does not think is necessarily definitive) is as follows:

1. Life: being able to live to the end of a human life of normal length.
2. Bodily health: being able to have good health, including reproductive health; to be adequately nourished; to have adequate shelter.
3. Bodily integrity: being able to move freely from place to place; having one's bodily boundaries treated as sovereign.
4. Senses, imagination, and thought: being able to use the senses, to imagine, think, and reason – and to do these things in a "truly human" way, a way informed and cultivated by an adequate education.

5. Emotions: being able to have attachments to things and people outside ourselves; not having one's emotional development blighted by overwhelming fear and anxiety, or by traumatic events of abuse or neglect.
6. Practical reason: being able to form a conception of the good and to engage in critical reflection about the planning of one's life.
7. Affiliation: being able to live with others, being able to recognize and show concern for other human beings, being able to engage in various forms of social interaction, and having the social bases of self-respect and non-humiliation, being able to be treated as a dignified being whose worth is equal to that of others.
8. Other species: being able to live with concern for and in relation to animals, plants, and the world of nature.
9. Play: being able to laugh, to play, to enjoy recreational activities.
10. Control over one's environment: both political, being able to participate effectively in political choices that govern one's life; and material, being able to hold property (both land and movable goods), not just formally but in terms of real opportunity.[5]

Nussbaum points out that these goods are not independent. Education will promote the other goods (such as health and political participation). Control over one's environment promotes the capacity to maintain bodily integrity, and so on. Importantly, they cannot be traded off against one another, having more of one will not make up for lack of another. The government, of course, cannot necessarily provide these goods; it cannot guarantee health. But Nussbaum's argument is that governments should seek to provide the social and material conditions that make these things possible. This is why she refers to her approach as the 'capabilities approach': the point is not to make sure that people do these things, it is to make sure that people have the capabilities necessary for these things. The government's job is to provide the conditions that enable exercise of these capabilities up to a certain threshold. The idea is that these are the things that together make a good life possible, and Nussbaum aims for this list to apply cross-culturally. As Nussbaum says, "Certain basic aspirations to human flourishing are recognizable across differences of class and context".[6]

So we should work with the assumption that there are universal values, and that if suffering is bad for women in one culture, it is bad for women in other cultures. That doesn't detract from the need to be humble about making cross-cultural judgments about what *causes* suffering. And at the same time, as we shall see below, too much humility may be destructive.

Epistemic humility

Some feminist philosophers, such as Uma Narayan and Seyla Benhabib, argue that the first step to a better way of thinking about third world women is to be critical of the use of the term 'culture', and the idea of 'cultural differences'.[7] Narayan argues that those who use these terms are prone to various mistakes of simplifying and idealizing. Writers about the third world can fall into the habit of presenting a simplistic narrative that doesn't take account of counterexamples. For example, 'Western culture' is often presented as committed to values like liberty and equality, which ignores Western civilization's propensities for slavery and colonization. Another mistake is 'totalizing', that is, ignoring diversity within a culture. For example, saying that Indian culture holds women to be goddesses, while ignoring the poor regard for women of low caste.

The origins and complexities of cultures are forgotten in these simple narratives. Westerners write as if they assume that the cultures they critique pre-date the colonial era, and are independent of contact and conflict between cultures. Narayan suggests that struggles related to colonialism have affected both conceptualizations and self-conceptions of what counts as culture and how it works. As she argues:

> In these conflicts, Western colonial powers often depicted indigenous practices as symptoms of the 'backwardness and barbarity' of Third-World cultures in contrast to the 'progressiveness of Western culture.' The figure of the colonized woman became a representation of the oppressiveness of the entire 'cultural tradition' of the colony . . . Male-dominated Third-World elites often responded by constructing these very practices as sacred and longstanding traditions that were constitutive of their values and world views, and as practices that were tied to the spiritual place of and respect for women in their cultures.[8]

These battles often left women by the wayside, or divided their loyalties between their feminism and their allegiance to their colonized nation. When they espouse feminism, they are accused of disloyalty to their nation, of having accepted Western values. Narayan, speaking as a third world feminist, argues that third world feminists should not position themselves as outsiders within, but should embrace their commitment to universal values such as education and argue for instantiation of those values. Culture, as Narayan argues, is complex, and women who argue for feminist aims are not necessarily unrepresentative or culturally alien.

One of Narayan's central examples concerns the practice of 'sati', or widow immolation, in which a widow throws herself into her husband's funeral pyre. Narayan is responding to Mary Daly's account of the issue, which Narayan accuses of inadvertently taking a colonialist stance. Daly writes about *sati* without contextualizing it in Indian history and society. She writes as if it happens now (as opposed to being virtually extinct, like witch-burning in Europe, which Daly does write about in a historical context), and she writes about it as if it happens across Indian cultural and class groups. Furthermore, Daly conflates *sati*, a historical practice, with dowry murder, a modern phenomenon, in which women are murdered by their husbands (often by fire in 'kitchen accidents' after a campaign of harassment aimed at extracting more dowry from their families). This simplification buys into a picture of a homogenous, uncivilized culture that can be blamed for all ills. One might think that, 'in India, they are always burning women, savages that they are'. Narayan argues that this inattention to the real complexities of the case colludes with both the colonialist powers and with the anti-woman religious fundamentalists.

Narayan's own analysis of the practice of *sati* throws doubt on its status as a 'traditional practice'. There are complex influences on what comes to be thought of as a cultural tradition, particularly in colonial contexts. In the nineteenth century, the British rulers in India were generally concerned to intervene in Indian people's lives only if it would consolidate or, at least, not undermine their power. The question of *sati* was thus a strategic one – could it be abolished without de-stabilizing power? That in turn seemed to rest on the question of whether it was mandated by scripture. And that question was not easily answered, particularly in a context where authority to answer it (being a religious official) was bestowed by British officials. Thus, Narayan argues, the verdict of cultural authenticity ended up being invented rather than arrived at through a process of discovery. Furthermore, the importance of the practice was amplified by the attention given to it, and it became a powerful symbol of the cultural values of the colonized nation.

Third world women are seen as victims of their culture, not as individuals. Narayan uses the example of dowry murder to show how asymmetric the focus of Western feminists can be. Narayan points out that dowry murder is seen as a cultural problem, whereas domestic violence in the US is seen as a problem that is down to a few individuals, bad apples, and whereas 'dowry murder' has a name, 'domestic violence murder' does not. This lack of true investigation, and prejudging the issue as 'death by culture', impedes progress.

Narayan worries that Western attention to third world feminist issues (and the same point applies to issues facing women in sub-groups within Western nations) is limited by a fascination with the exotic, with seeing third world women as 'Other'. Narayan stresses that viewing someone as exotic may appear harmless, even positive, but it masks a tendency to ignore and override the welfare and interest of the people who are seen in this way. The woman in a different culture is seen as so foreign and exotic that it is imagined that she does not suffer in the way that a Western woman would suffer in the same situation.

These worries have huge practical implications. The wrong sort of intervention can result in worsening conditions for women. Alison Jaggar describes the case of Amina Lawal, who was sentenced to death by stoning under Sharia law in Nigeria. Her crime was to have had a baby outside of marriage. In 2003 Amnesty International launched a global petition to stop the sentence being carried out. But two Nigerian lawyers representing Lawal, Ayesha Imam and Sindi Medar-Gould, launched a counter campaign to stop the Amnesty letter. They argued that the petition was full of factual errors and imperialist assumptions, and that it would, paradoxically, make the carrying out of the sentence more likely rather than less likely. Jaggar quotes the letter, which pleads with Western media to stop presenting Islam and Africa as "the barbaric and savage Other". [9] In the end, Lawal was freed by the Sharia Court of Appeal in September 2003.

As Jaggar argues, Western criticism of Nigerian culture is self-servingly selective. It is common to see supposedly feminist critique, which sensationalizes the horrors faced by African women, being used to justify policies that have no genuine respect for the people who live in these countries. Westerners are carried away by the seductive appeal of being the white saviour, of 'saving brown women from brown men', as Gayatri Spivak puts it, in her account of the silencing of third world women.[10] Meanwhile, as Jaggar points out, poverty and injustice in Nigeria are mostly linked to international tolerance and support for regimes which will enable access to mineral resources. Feminist groups in Nigeria struggle against these and other injustices, and feminist activists from other countries ought to make themselves aware of these local movements. Most importantly, Jaggar's point is that, "Rather than simply blaming Amina Lawal's culture, we should begin by taking our own feet off her neck."[11]

Despite their critiques of the pitfalls, writers such as Jaggar and Narayan do not think that Western feminists should remain silent on the situation of third world women. The point is rather that they should make sure that they are properly informed. Narayan argues that there are deep problems with the idea that only those within a culture should be allowed to talk about it. She observes that women with third world connections are often expected to be experts on their 'culture' and to be able to convey the situation to Westerners. But that is unsatisfactory in various ways. First, it is an unfair burden on the speaker, and is also a form of stereotyping, limiting what she can do and say: she becomes a witness with limited mandate rather than a full participant. Second, the idea that there is an 'authentic insider' (as Narayan terms it) allows the Western audience to refrain from critical engagement. Narayan argues that this handicaps rather than aids the project of feminist solidarity across cultures.[12]

Linda Martín Alcoff puts the issue in terms of 'speaking for others'. The idea that we should not speak for others, she says, has two sources: First, the worry that a speaker cannot transcend their own position – they may miss crucial facts about the position of the person they are speaking for. Thus, a certain amount of epistemic humility is required. Second, speaking for others can be harmful: it can reinforce the subordinated position of the person spoken for. Alcoff grants both of these points, but she is concerned that speaking for others is sometimes a political good, and that we should not foreclose that possibility.

Indeed, Alcoff argues that sometimes closing off the possibility of speaking for others is not noble self-effacement, but rather something distastefully self-centered, a desire to avoid criticism, which is clearly morally and politically objectionable. Alternatively, someone might avoid speaking for others in order to avoid making errors. But that too is a bad strategy and may reveal self-centered motives. As Alcoff puts it,

> The desire to find an absolute means to avoid making errors comes perhaps not from a desire to advance collective goals but a desire for personal mastery, to establish a privileged discursive position wherein one cannot be undermined or challenged and thus is master of the situation. From such a position one's own location and positionality would not require constant interrogation and critical reflection; one would not have to constantly engage in this emotionally troublesome endeavor and would be immune from the interrogation of others. Such a desire for mastery and immunity must be resisted.[13]

To sum up the advice of both Alcoff and Narayan, respect is crucial, but first world feminists should not interpret that as a requirement to remain silent. To stand back entirely from engagement on issues of third world feminism is cowardly. Mistakes are inevitable, but, as in all areas of enquiry, there will not be progress without mistakes. Alcoff agrees that all speakers should, of course, try to avoid the pitfalls of speaking for others. Someone in a more privileged position should sometimes 'move over', as Alcoff puts it, and allow the relevant person to speak for herself. We should be aware of our privilege and how it might colour our perceptions, we should be open to criticism, and we should think about our words in context, about what effect they will have, given the speaker, the location, the historical situation. But with all that in mind, it seems permissible, indeed, obligatory, for feminists in the Western world to think about the situations of women in the third world.

Multiculturalism

It is interesting to explore how these lessons apply to the case of Susan Okin's feminist critique of multiculturalism. Okin, writing in 1998, argues that 'multiculturalism', understood as a term of art used to refer to the endorsement of rights for a cultural group within a larger different culture, has become the norm, and that feminist issues have been ignored.[14]

Okin argues that cultures are often treated as monolithic, and differences in the situations of men and women are occluded. Further, as Okin argues in detail in her book *Justice, Gender, and the Family*, the private sphere has been neglected in political theory. [15] Okin points out that important differences in cultural practices are often located in the private sphere, the home and family, where women are situated. Different cultures have different norms regarding marriage, child rearing, inheritance, and property owning. So tolerating or ignoring cultural practices will impact disproportionately on women and girls. The examples that Okin discusses in her various articles on the topic fall into four categories: forced marriage (often of minors), violence in the name of honour, genital cutting, and restrictive dress codes for women.

Okin prefaces her discussion with an acknowledgement of the difficulties of speaking for others. But she is also aware of faults in the other direction. She cautions against excessive deference to the differences between women, and against hyper concern to avoid cultural imperialism, which can lead to a problematic form of cultural relativism. These are points that both Narayan and Alcoff make too. Excessive deference to difference can be a form of Othering, and thus underestimating the suffering of women in other situations. Cultural imperialism – that is, assuming that the speaker's culture has all the answers – is certainly to be avoided, but as Narayan says, feminism is not merely a Western value.

Okin examines three cases of cultural groups within other nation states, and argues that the notion of group rights cannot be used to justify unfair treatment of women and girls. Okin uses the examples to show that arguments for group rights tend to overlook the fact that the group rights would benefit the men but harm the women. In the first example, she addresses Margalit and Halbertal's argument that ultra-orthodox Jewish communities in Israel should have state subsidies. Okin argues that some of the gendered practices of community being defended are damaging to both girls and boys. Boys are expected to be Torah scholars, while girls are expected to be wives and mothers. This narrowing of options is damaging to all children. This, Okin says, cannot be defended on the grounds that it is a cultural tradition. We could sum her view up by saying that justice matters more than culture.

Her second case is Chandran Kukathas's argument that an immigrant group with a tradition of choosing marriages for daughters should be allowed to 'try' to maintain that tradition, but that the daughter has legal recourse if she objects. Kukathas argues that if group members acquiesce to a group's customs, then the larger society should tolerate the customs. Okin objects that acquiescence is not a good guide to what is just, as it is often caused by powerlessness. Her main point, again, is that the fact that something is a cultural tradition does not override the objection that it is unjust for women. Okin argues that if coerced marriage is bad for people, it should not be made difficult for girls to protest coerced marriage, and the fact that it is a cultural tradition does not make it any less problematic.

Finally, Okin engages with Kymlicka's argument for group rights. Kymlicka argues that culture and community are vitally important, and so we should countenance group rights. However, he agrees that the fundamentally important unit is the individual: it is because individuals need communities and culture that those things are important. Kymlicka argues that only liberal cultures, ones that do not discriminate on the basis of sex, should have group rights. Okin objects that this is not helpful in practice. First, she points out that almost all cultures are sexist, and that in reality none would pass his 'no sex discrimination' test. Second, illiberal practices are often hidden. Even where there is no overt sex discrimination, there are subtle indoctrinations, expectations, restrictions, narratives, and so on that reinforce the subordination of women. If we focus only on overt discrimination we will miss these.

Okin's central argument is that there is no good justification for allowing fewer rights and protections to women who happen to be part of a sub-culture that is more patriarchal than the surrounding nation. Kymlicka and other group rights sympathetic philosophers argue that cultures will be eroded if they are not afforded special protections. Okin's response is to argue that, ultimately, if culture matters, it is because it matters to individuals. And to ignore the way a culture harms women is to focus only on the male individuals, which is not justifiable.

Okin's work on the tensions between multiculturalism and feminism has received a great deal of attention. The article I summarize above was published in a revised version in the *Boston Review* with responses, and, eventually, a book with various responses and a reply from Okin was published. One criticism, pressed by several responders, is that Okin's view of other cultures is over-simplistic at best, and xenophobic and Othering at worst. Despite Okin's own awareness of these tendencies of defenders of cultural practices, critics accuse Okin of taking cultures as monolithic, as static, and as uniformly patriarchal. Critics suggest that the practices she criticizes may be more complex than she allows. Veiling, for instance, is seen by some Muslim feminists as liberating, allowing them to move around freely, as Leila Ahmed argues.[16] Furthermore, it is a mistake to put all individual crimes down to culture ('death by culture' as Uma Narayan calls it). If we do that we are failing to see the perpetrators as individuals and are guilty of seeing foreign cultural practices through a racist lens.

It is important to distinguish between two slightly different criticisms here. One is the worry that analysis of the practices of other cultures is missing something, that there is more going on in these cases than is visible from a very limited perspective. This is an epistemological worry, that it is easy to be misled by the racism and imperialism that permeate Western culture into misunderstandings of other cultures.

The other worry is a more practical one, that criticism of other cultures has effects beyond those that are intended. First, as Anne Phillips stresses in her work on legal reforms relating to feminism and multiculturalism, feminist justifications could be (and have been) used to enact racist policies. For example, many have argued that legislation in France to ban the wearing of religious clothing and symbols is not what it appears to be on the face of it (a move towards gender equality), but is actually a law that is designed to be used disproportionately against the Muslim population. The tension between feminism and multiculturalism means that the feminist argument can be co-opted into the service of xenophobic and repressive regulation.[17]

In the 1990s, when Okin was writing, it seemed to her and to other feminists who shared her concerns, that multiculturalism had won the day. However, the world has changed between then and now. Recent years have seen a rising tide of anti-immigrant sentiment in wealthy nations, particularly focussed on Muslims, and bound up with fears of terrorism. Religious and cultural tolerance has reduced, and multiculturalism has fallen by the wayside. These historical facts make the context of feminist objections to multiculturalism even more delicate.

Both of these points, the epistemological one and the practical one, are raised in Alcoff's advice about speaking for others: we should be aware of our privilege and how it might colour our perceptions; we should be open to criticism; and we should think about our words in context, about what effect they will have, given the speaker, the location, the historical situation. Okin herself, and other writers who defend her position, readily admit that these are important guidelines, and that they are not always easy to follow. They do not undermine Okin's main point, which is that group rights should not obscure women's rights.

Another issue that arises explicitly or implicitly in many criticisms of Okin is the fact that a lot of the supposedly oppressive practices seem to be consented to by the women involved. This does not automatically mean that there is no injustice. People sometimes consent to things that are unjust. The fact that something is chosen is not a guarantee that it was chosen freely, or that it would be chosen had the circumstances been different. Women are often in very poor choice conditions, so that either they have to choose between very bad options or they have internalized the values of an oppressive system, and we cannot take their choice at face value. This is the problem of 'false consciousness', or 'adaptive preferences', which I discuss further below. On the other hand, it is important not to be too quick to assume that a choice is problematic. Perhaps there are features of the situation that are not immediately obvious to someone looking at it from a different standpoint. It might be that Okin and other white Western feminists are sometimes too quick to accuse third world women of being 'dupes of patriarchy', as Narayan puts it, and are unaware of their own false consciousness.

Autonomy and adaptive preferences

One problem for any critique of social conditions is that poor conditions are sometimes *chosen*. Women might actively choose to conform to gender rules, or they may simply submit without protest. Either way, it is hard to justify criticism and even harder to justify intervention. Criticism and intervention seem patronizing and undermining of autonomy, particularly in the case of Western feminists talking about third world women. Yet, it does appear that people sometimes embrace things that they should not put up with, and that it is reasonable to analyze the situation as one in which an oppressed person has 'adaptive preferences', or 'deformed preferences', preferences that they would not have if it were not for their limited choice situation. I examine adaptive preferences in more detail in Chapter 9, but I will discuss the issue here in the context of the challenge of cultural differences.

Uma Narayan argues that there is a tendency in feminist analysis to oversimplify matters, either seeing third world women as 'prisoners of patriarchy', completely unwilling victims, or at the opposite extreme, as 'dupes of patriarchy', totally brainwashed participants.[18] Narayan complains that a lot of feminist writing about the situation of third world women presents a view of patriarchal ideology as completely engulfing, so that there is no room left for women's agency – they are portrayed as being capable only of 'zombie-like acquiescence.'[19] But, Narayan says, it is important to understand the way women's agency is at work even in bad choice situations. Sometimes what looks like an adaptive preference may be a case of 'bargaining with the patriarchy'. The women are aware of the constraints they are under and of the compromises they have to make. They have stakes in the situation, and so they make rational choices.[20]

This still leaves the need to distinguish autonomous choice from adaptive preferences. Marilyn Friedman argues that we should take a content neutral view of autonomy: we should think that someone's choice counts as autonomous when they have had the opportunity to reflect on it and endorse it, they have not been coerced, and when it reflects their deeply held values. Friedman does not think that this imposes any restrictions on what sort of thing someone might end up choosing. Someone could end up choosing a life of submission and subservience to men, for example. Friedman accepts that consequence of her view, and in the context of group rights and multiculturalism, she argues that so long as women choose the conditions of a culture, their choice should be respected.

She concludes:

> Thus, a liberal culture should respect and tolerate the practices of cultural minorities in its midst even when those practices violate the rights of females in those minority groups, but only so long as the females themselves choose to participate in those practices and do so under conditions that facilitate autonomy. Those conditions must include the presence of genuine alternatives for the women's choosing, the absence of coercive and manipulative interferences with the women's reflections on their cultural practices, and socialization that is capable of developing in the women real autonomy competency.[21]

It is not easy to see how far this argument takes us in the multiculturalism debate. For one thing, it does seem that in many of the cases that feminists worry about (genital cutting most obviously, but also severe restrictions on women's freedom), it is fairly obvious that women's options are limited and their choices coerced. So the actual class of cases where women autonomously consent to sexist norms may be very small indeed. Furthermore, it is very difficult to diagnose autonomy (no matter what definition we give of it). How can we tell that someone is acting on their deep values and not on values that have been inculcated by manipulative influences? This is one of the hard problems in understanding false consciousness and adaptive preferences.

Martha Nussbaum takes a different view, one that makes diagnosing a problematic preference easier. Nussbaum offers an account of adaptive preference (of a non-autonomous preference, to put it in Friedman's terms) that is *not* content neutral. She thinks that a crucial feature of adaptive preferences is that they impede flourishing, and that if a preference impedes flourishing, we should be suspicious of it. For Nussbaum, the grounds for intervention are lack of capabilities. If women do not have the capabilities that are crucial for flourishing, then there are grounds for intervention, even if the women themselves express a preference to remain as they are. Once the capabilities are enabled, then choice is once more politically valid: so a woman can choose to wear a veil, but she should not be forced to wear one.

Serene Khader agrees with Nussbaum that we should allow some substantive content into the idea of what counts as a properly autonomous preference, and that flourishing is crucial. Khader adds that what is distinctive about adaptive preferences is that they were formed in circumstances not conducive to flourishing, and would not have been formed had the circumstances been better. We can sometimes end up with preferences that are self-destructive even though we had every opportunity to form better ones. Thus an adaptive preference is one that is detrimental to the agent's flourishing and is causally related to the poor circumstances in which it was formed.

Echoing the worries about cultural imperialism and insensitivity to cultural variations and complexities, Khader argues that there are various difficulties in assessing real world situations. First, we cannot always assume that people have adaptive preferences from their choices. In other words, their revealed preferences may not reflect their desires but instead their limited options. She illustrates the point by citing Brooke Ackerly's objection to one of Nussbaum's examples. Nussbaum argues that the success of a literacy program in Bangladesh was impeded by women's lack of interest in education. Ackerly points out that the women may in fact be making the best use of a limited resource, choosing for their children to be educated rather than themselves. Thus their preference structure is fine; it is only their situation that is problematic.[22] As Narayan puts it, they are bargaining with the patriarchy rather than being dupes of patriarchy.

Second, women who make choices that negatively affect their flourishing may be in a situation of imposed trade-offs. Khader discusses the findings of sexual health studies that show that even in areas of very high HIV infection, women do not ask their partners to wear condoms. She postulates that the women may be facing a trade-off: they fear angering their partner and losing access to resources that are essential to life, far less flourishing. Again, a woman in this situation does not have adaptive preferences. She may be quite rational in fearing her partner's anger.

Finally, development practitioners may 'mistake difference for deprivation' – that is, they may lack an understanding of the culture they are looking at, and thus misidentify some preferences as adaptive due to missing some important benefit the preference enables. Perhaps female seclusion has the advantage of allowing women a safe and free environment from which they can critically assess the norms of their society.

In a later article, Khader points out a further possible source of misunderstanding: it may be that someone has made a factual mistake, overestimating the penalties for non-compliance, for example, or may be unaware of the benefits of non-compliance. Khader cites a study that showed that women who complied with genital cutting practice were unaware that there were health risks associated with genital cutting. Once they knew that, their participation in the practice decreased.[23]

However, Khader is committed to the view that in some cases, women have problematic adaptive preferences, and that we can make this diagnosis without being patronizing. Khader argues that a view according to which adaptive preferences are a result of a false view about the subject's own value and entitlement is too global. It is in danger of being patronizing, and of making mistakes in interventions, by assuming that such women are unable to form *any* authentic preferences. Khader argues that an account of adaptive preferences need not assume that the subject suffers a 'global self-entitlement deficit'. Adaptive preferences in some areas are compatible with a well-developed sense of self-worth in other areas. So saying that someone has adaptive preferences is not saying that the agency of the person with adaptive preferences is deeply flawed.

Khader argues that when people do have some sense of self-worth, deliberative processes can help to rid them of adaptive preferences and live a life that is more in line with their actual values. She describes a project in Zambia, where women were asked to draw pictures of and discuss violence in their lives. Khader reports that "At the close of the workshop, participants often say, 'I have learned that what I used to think of as normal is actually violence against women'".[24] Khader suggests that so long as we leave room for a 'way in' in our theorizing about adaptive preferences, development practitioners can work within local practices to build on existing conceptions of positive self-worth.

Khader claims that consciousness raising is not patronizing or imperialistic. She agrees with other writers on third world feminism that non-intervention is not a noble option, but rather, a sort of cowardice dressed up as cultural sensitivity. Careful intervention is sometimes the more respectful option. "To engage a person with a seeming [inappropriate adaptive preference] in deliberation is to engage her at the level of her reasons for her behavior – to engage her as the type of being who has a conception of the good worth respecting."[25]

Responsibility

So far, I have interpreted the worry that first world feminists should stay out of other people's business as epistemological (they don't know enough about what they are taking about) and practical (intervention can backfire). Another way to approach these issues is by thinking about responsibility. One might try to argue (quite generally as well as in the case of feminism) that third world issues should be dealt with by people in the third world, that it is not the responsibility of anyone else.

In the philosophy of global justice there are two main ways to reach the conclusion that people in wealthier nations have duties to the third world. The first is Peter Singer's well known argument, that if we saw a child drowning in a shallow pond and could save them at minimal cost, we would all agree that we ought to save the child. Singer generalizes to the conclusion that when helping others could be done without enormous sacrifice, then of course we should help.[26] The second approach points out that, due to global structures, those in the first world are in some way complicit in, or at least beneficiaries of, third world poverty, and so have a duty to help that is not a duty of charity, but is based on a duty not to do harm.

Iris Marion Young argues for an account of responsibility that is in the second family. She defends a 'social connection model of responsibility', according to which our responsibility for remedying the suffering of others is based on our social connections to them. We sometimes participate in shared social systems and institutions that are structurally unjust. Even if this is not deliberate or knowing, it is enough to make us responsible.[27]

Young examines the functioning of the global garment industry to explain her account of the way that shared responsibility for global injustice works. Young points out that many of the clothes worn in rich countries are made in sweatshops, in which the workers are predominantly women, often very young, frequently subjected to sexual harassment, and who lack basic employment rights and are often paid less than a living wage. A significant part of the industry functions by employing women who work in their own homes, where conditions are not much better and in some ways are worse. There are, of course, some individuals who can be held responsible in the traditional ways, but things are not that simple. Factory owners and managers function under the constraints of the global market. And the people who benefit from that market are people from wealthy nations who buy these cheap clothes.

Young focusses on the garment industry partly because she recognizes that this is an area where there is already a growing awareness of the structural injustices at play. Collective action and pressure groups have made some difference. So we should not be overwhelmed by the expansion of responsibility that Young's theory implies. Furthermore, Young argues that what we ought to do depends on our social position. This varies along several dimensions: power, privilege, interest, and collective ability.

Those who have more power have a greater responsibility, and so the anti-sweatshop movement has quite rightly focussed on the major multi-nationals, such as Nike, Calvin Klein, and Benetton. Those who have more privilege should also take more responsibility. For example, consumers with more financial privilege have more responsibility to avoid cheap sweatshop produced clothing than those who are poor. Young argues that her social connection model, unlike a liability model of responsibility, allows responsibility to be shared by the victims of injustice too. And here her account connects up with the worries about being patronizing or imperialistic that we explored earlier: Young argues that sharing responsibility with the victims allows them a voice and avoids implementation of solutions (such as closing down factories) that can make things worse for the victims of structural injustice. Finally, what we should do depends on what collective abilities we have. Young uses the example of campus groups pressuring universities to adopt no-sweatshop policies for their branded apparel to illustrate the way in which collective action is necessary and effective.

One lesson for the feminist discussion here is that, as we talk about issues that arise for women in the third world, we must be cognizant of the global structures that contribute to third world poverty and to the gendered nature of that poverty. These global structures are ones that first world people are complicit in to some extent, as Iris Marion Young argues. And as Uma Narayan and Alison Jaggar point out, it is easy to lose sight of the global forces and focus on local cultural practices as the main oppressive forces.

Summary

Feminists should be concerned with all women, and the various issues that women face wherever they live. Accounts of injustice need to rely on universal values. Martha Nussbaum offers an account of the human capabilities that she thinks are the best way to judge whether a good life is possible. This list is designed to apply across cultures and so can be used to criticize any society.

However, thinking about appropriate intervention and modes of analysis is complex and delicate. The debate about tensions between feminism and multiculturalism illustrates this difficulty. On the one hand, as Okin argues, it seems that cultural groups should not have rights to oppress women. On the other hand, Western feminists should not charge in with patronizing and imperialist ideas about how other people should live.

Feminists writing about these issues generally agree that remaining silent or backing off altogether is not a good strategy. Instead, as Narayan argues, a careful and sensitive engagement is called for, one that pays attention to the complexity and variety within the culture in question, avoids Othering, and avoids reifying and simplifying the practices that are foreign to the investigator.

We may need to rely on accounts of adaptive preferences to explain the choices that women in oppressive situations make. Serene Khader offers a thorough analysis of adaptive preferences, which she argues can be applied without falling into the vices of being imperialistic or patronizing.

Finally, feminists who are interested in global justice need to rely on a more general argument to show that inhabitants of wealthy nations have a duty to engage with the problems of poorer nations. Iris Marion Young argues that this duty can be defended by relying on a 'social connections model of responsibility', according to which we are responsible for doing something to help when we are participants in a social system or institution that gives rise to injustices.

Notes

1 Crenshaw, 'Demarginalizing the Intersection of Race and Sex: A Black Feminist Critique of Antidiscrimination Doctrine, Feminist Theory, and Antiracist Politics'.
2 Spelman, *Inessential Woman*, p.131.
3 Nussbaum, *Women and Human Development*, p.35.
4 Rawls, *A Theory of Justice*; Sen, 'Capability and Well-being'.
5 Nussbaum, *Women and Human Development*, pp.78–80.
6 Op. cit., p.31.
7 Narayan, *Dislocating Cultures*; Benhabib, 'The Liberal Imagination and the Four Dogmas of Multiculturalism'.
8 Narayan, *Dislocating Cultures*, p.17.
9 Jaggar, '"Saving Amina": Global Justice for Women and Intercultural Dialogue', p.73.
10 Spivak, 'Can the Subaltern Speak?'
11 Jaggar, '"Saving Amina": Global Justice for Women and Intercultural Dialogue', p.75.
12 Narayan, *Dislocating Cultures*, p.148.
13 Alcoff, 'The Problem of Speaking for Others', p.22.
14 Okin, 'Feminism and Multiculturalism: Some Tensions'. See also Okin, *Is Multiculturalism Bad for Women?*
15 Okin's arguments are discussed in Chapter 3 of this book.
16 Ahmed, *Women and Gender in Islam: Historical Roots of a Modern Debate*.
17 Phillips, *Multiculturalism Without Culture*.
18 Narayan, 'Minds of their Own: Choices, Autonomy, Cultural Practices, and Other Women'.
19 Op. cit., p.422.
20 Op. cit., p.421. The phrase comes from Deniz Kandiyoti's article with the same name.
21 Friedman, *Autonomy, Gender, Politics*, p.201.
22 Khader, *Adaptive Preferences and Women's Empowerment*, pp.55–56.
23 Khader, 'Identifying Adaptive Preferences in Practice: Lessons from Postcolonial Feminisms', p.318.
24 Ibid., p.133.

25 Op. cit., p.153.
26 Singer, 'Famine, Affluence, and Morality'.
27 Young, *Responsibility for Justice*.

Further reading

Anzaldúa, Gloria E. (1987) *Borderlands/La Frontera: The New Mestiza*. Aunt Lute Books. (Prose and poems exploring oppression from the position of a Chicana lesbian).
Benhabib, Seyla (2002) *The Claims of Culture: Equality and Diversity in the Global Era*. Princeton University Press. (Examines the issues that arise for feminism in the context of globalization and multicultural societies).
Chambers, Clare (2007) *Sex, Culture, and Justice: The Limits of Choice*. Pennsylvania State University Press. (An account of how to approach the fact that all our choices are culturally conditioned).
Khader, Serene J. (2019) *Decolonizing Universalism: A Transnational Feminist Ethic*. Oxford University Press. (Explores the nature of transnational feminism).
Narayan, Uma and Harding, Sandra (eds.) (2000) *Decentering the Center: Philosophy for a Multicultural, Postcolonial, and Feminist World*. Indiana University Press. (Collection of essays on multicultural and post-colonial feminism).

Part 1
Practice

2 Work and care

"Men may cook or weave or dress dolls or hunt humming birds, but if such activities are appropriate occupations of men, then the whole society, men and women alike, votes them as important. When the same occupations are performed by women they are regarded as less important."

Margaret Mead, *Male and Female*

Chapter overview: I examine feminist responses to a gendered division of labour, beginning with a discussion of the idea of innate differences in aptitude, moving on to alternative explanations, including implicit and explicit bias. I cover Susan Okin's classic account of gendered cycles of vulnerability, and solutions such as affirmative action, and parental leave policies, as well as more radical interventions.

Introduction

One of the most resilient myths about men and women is that they are fundamentally suited to different activities, and that a gendered division of labour is natural and just. In this chapter I discuss feminist challenges to that idea and survey some of the practical solutions that feminists have suggested.

The worlds of men's work and women's work have been segregated in different ways in different cultures, but there is almost always some sort of segregation. It often goes along with a division of labour, such that labour associated with the family, and caring responsibilities, falls chiefly on women. These patterns are not universal, and there is much variation in what counts as women's work and what counts as men's work. But in general, women's work, whatever it is, is less well paid than men's. In Britain and America, non-native speakers and women of colour earn even less. Estimates vary, but there is broad agreement among research organizations (such as the World Economic Forum) that in Britain and in America, the median pay for women is around 80-83% of what the median pay for men is for comparable work. Not only that, but women are often expected to do the bulk of care work on top of wage labour. Furthermore, women are excluded from many of the most desirable roles, either through formal or informal measures. Thus the interconnected realms of work and family are feminist issues.

Before launching into the discussion, it is worth saying more about what work is, and what it means to us. Karl Marx, looking around at the miserable condition of factory workers in Victorian Britain, argued that in being underpaid and exploited, workers are not just being treated unfairly, they are being deprived of one of life's great goods: the good of productive labour. According to Marx, productivity, working, and producing things is a central part of human life. Commodification of labour, that is, working simply for money, is destructive to the self. Marx imagines that in an ideal world, where centralized control of production ensured that supply and demand were always in tune, we would be free to work in truly productive labour, seeing and being able to use the end product. In this romantic vision it would be possible "to hunt in the morning, fish in the afternoon, rear cattle in the evening, criticise after dinner, just as I have a mind, without ever becoming hunter, fisherman, herdsman or critic." [1]

Marx may have been overly optimistic, and the regulation of production that he imagines may not be possible, but his analysis points to something important to the feminist argument. Work can be a desirable thing, a source of satisfaction. One of the things that feminists want is access to the best sort of work – work that is a source of status, self-worth, and fulfilment. Middle-class white feminists have been criticized for focussing on this and ignoring the reality of most women's lives, where work is not a luxury but a grim necessity, and where the feminist struggle is for basic rights, such as a safe working environment and fair pay. As bell hooks points out, seeing work as a privilege is a very white middle-class perspective: "Attitudes towards work in much feminist writing reflect bourgeois class biases."[2]

In thinking about feminist approaches to work, we need to take the reality of a non-ideal world seriously. Take first, the intersectionality of oppression, the way that oppression affects those in different groups differently. bell hooks argues that focus on high paid professional work gives a distorted picture of how much progress has been made. In America, well-educated white women have certainly made enormous progress in the workforce, but this may have been at the expense of Black people. hooks points out that affirmative action programs often group race and gender together, so that employers can meet affirmative action targets without hiring any non-white people. Furthermore, the idea that work is 'liberating' implies that women who work are already liberated. hooks argues that this sends a message to Black women that the feminist movement is not for them. Finally, hooks argues that the phrase 'the feminization of poverty' only came into use when middle-class white women started to get divorced and to face poverty. Women of colour have always struggled with poverty in America, and so again it is clear that their plight has not been the focus of the feminist movement.

Moreover, we need to think about priorities in a non-ideal world. If, for example, sex workers are being assaulted and murdered at high rates, we need to think about how best to keep them safe, and that seems more urgent than thinking about ideal forms of work. On the other hand, if sex work is a form of work that is seriously problematic in itself, as some philosophers claim, the priority might be to eliminate sex work. In general, if we focus only on emergencies, we can lose track of ultimate justifications. What feminists want, in the end, is not just for men and women to have equal rights, but for everyone to be able to flourish. Feminists want to move towards a society in which the best forms of work are as available as possible and equally available to all.

A closely related point is that, in thinking about work, we should be willing to 're-think the nature of work', to borrow the title of bell hooks' chapter on the topic. We should not take for granted the framework that we have been handed and merely try to tinker with the distribution. hooks argues that feminists should not be agitating simply to share the domestic labour more equally with men, but to change our conceptions of domestic labour. It need not be drudgery. She says:

> By learning housework, children and adults accept responsibility for ordering their material reality. They learn to appreciate and care for their surroundings. Since so many male children are not taught housework, they grow to maturity with no respect for their environment and often lack the know-how to take care of themselves and their households. They have been allowed to cultivate an unnecessary dependence on women in their domestic lives, and, as a result of this dependence, are sometimes unable to develop a healthy sense of autonomy. Girl children, though usually compelled to do housework, are usually taught to see it as demeaning and degrading. These attitudes lead them to hate doing housework and deprive them of the personal satisfaction that they could feel as they accomplish these necessary tasks.[3]

This is a hugely important point. We have been taught to value the work that is traditionally done by men, and to denigrate the work that is traditionally done by women. Yet, much of women's work, not just child rearing but also housework, does have intrinsic satisfactions, and we need to throw off the misconceptions that a sexist society forces on us to be able to see that clearly. So feminists want to achieve a situation where labour is distributed more evenly, and where it is as fulfilling as it can be. We need to change our structures radically for this to happen, and we need to keep both our ideal and non-ideal world models in mind to do that.

Different aptitudes or different circumstances?

As I said, women worldwide tend to do more care work than men. And, women are underrepresented in jobs that involve power, responsibility, and better salaries. Is it possible that women are simply less well suited to those roles, and that men are less well suited to care work? It is certainly possible, but it is unlikely. I spent some time in the introduction discussing the idea that men and women have different aptitudes. It's a very persistent idea, but the evidence for it is questionable. We do need an explanation for why women cluster in different jobs to men, but plenty are available that do not rely on the different aptitude view.

A recent study by Haines, Deaux, and Lofaro compares data on gender stereotypes collected in the USA in the 1980s with data collected in 2014, and finds depressingly little change.[4] Since the 1970s, gender stereotypes have been assessed in terms of clusters of characteristics, broadly categorized into 'agency' and 'communion'. The agency category includes competence, instrumentality, and independence. The communion category includes expressivity, warmth, and concern with the welfare of others. Obviously, our stereotypes have it that men do better on agency traits and women do better on communion traits. Haines et al. designed a study using a similar sample size, demographic, and questionnaire as a 1983 study that showed that perceptions of men tend to the agentic and perceptions of women tend to the communal. The 2014 results show virtually no difference in people's ideas about gender traits.

This suggests that our ideas about gender are very resilient. The representation of women in various fields has changed during the last 30 years, and although this ought to undo some of our stereotyping, it seems that other mechanisms step in to neutralize the effect of that evidence. Haines et al. point out that there is a wealth of other theories in psychology that can make sense of our resistance to giving up our stereotypes. For example, we are subject to confirmation bias (we pay more attention to confirming evidence). As an anecdotal illustration of this: parents often notice the way that children conform to gender stereotypes, but do not notice the ways in which they don't. A boy who sometimes likes to play rough and tumble will be held up as a traditional boy, even though he also plays with dolls and loves cuddles. It is likely that a girl with the same traits will be noticed for her dolls and cuddles, not for her rough and tumble.

Additionally, status incongruity theory finds that women who step outside their expected roles engage in other feminine behaviour to minimize backlash against them. Women can signal their conformity to patriarchal rules by dressing in a very feminine way, wearing traditional make-up, and speaking in soft tones and using non-confrontational styles. Women can also 'apologize' for their success by highlighting their failures in other areas. This is well illustrated by the fictional case of Liz Lemon, the high achieving head writer of a TV sketch show in the NBC show *30 Rock*. Liz is extremely smart and capable, but she is presented as chaotically disastrous in other areas of her life. She is unhappily single, self-loathing, and a periodic binge eater. Of course, we don't know what the intent of the writers is. Is Tina Fey, the show's creator, apologizing for her fictional character's successes? Or is she pointing out that such an apology is expected? Either way, it is interesting to analyze the presentation of the character through the lens of status incongruity theory.

Another finding in social psychology that Haines, Deaux, and Lofaro appeal to is that counter-stereotypical behaviour is often framed as exceptional. When a woman does well at something in a traditionally masculine field, she is explicitly and implicitly seen as the exception to the rule. We are subtly taught that a woman who succeeds must really be something special (and, most likely, have 'masculine' traits). This is related to a phenomenon that is familiar to women in academic fields, and probably other professional areas: a very small number of women are permitted to succeed in the field on roughly the same terms as men, but the women who do are held up as being exceptionally talented. Resistance to other women, women of normal talent levels, remains just as strong. And of course, frustratingly, the presence of the 'exceptional' women is taken as proof that there is no sexism.

These points are all useful in thinking about the under-representation of women in fields related to STEM subjects (Science, Technology, Engineering, and Mathematics). Women are also under-represented in academic philosophy, which bears some resemblance to STEM subjects as an academic discipline. In the USA, only 21% of full-time professional philosophers are women,[5] in the UK the number is slightly better at 24%.[6] The view that women are simply less good at these things is extremely common. For example, in 2005, the president of Harvard University suggested that the reason that women are under-represented is that there are biological differences, and that women do not face other barriers.[7] But we should look at the potential barriers before we accept that claim.

In plain terms, women are discriminated against in traditionally male areas. It is hard for women to find positions in these areas in the first place, and women who try to step outside of their assigned gender role will be discouraged and punished. Women face what Marilyn Frye calls a 'double bind': if women show strong leadership and decision-making characteristics, they are denounced as aggressive and difficult to work with. But if they stick to more feminine traits, they are deemed incompetent. Furthermore, women's achievements and their potential are judged less charitably than men's.[8]

Research on implicit bias shows that people on hiring committees (both men and women) make more negative judgments about women candidates without even realizing that they are doing it. The well-known CV study repeatedly shows that CVs with female sounding names must be considerably more impressive in order to be judged as good as a CV that is attached to a male sounding name.[9] Another study indicates that in a science lab, both men and women judge that the candidate they assume to be a man merits higher pay and that they would be happy to mentor him more.[10] People with female sounding names are less likely to get grants, awards, and invitations to speak at conferences. Furthermore, another study shows that men in STEM fields judge the research that shows that there is bias in their fields as less meritorious than women do.[11]

Since the 'replication crisis' in social psychology (there has been a worrying failure of many experimental results to replicate, suggesting that the original methodology was flawed), it is easy to argue that these results do not show much. But we should be careful not to allow the replication crisis to be weaponized. It is true that we should always be aware of the possibility that a study is flawed. As Cordelia Fine argues, many of the studies that purport to show innate gender differences are flawed in obvious ways (I discussed her arguments in some detail in the introductory chapter).[12] But we should also be aware that some distrust is ideological. As I argued in the introduction, and as is clear from my brief discussion of stereotypes above, oppressive structures tend to adapt to ensure their own survival. So, assuming we agree that there is currently some sort of patriarchal power structure operating, we should not be surprised that there is backlash against any research that would destabilize the system. What else would we expect? That the men in power would read the research on implicit bias and say, 'Oh no, who knew? We will immediately work to rectify this injustice!'?

Jules Holroyd and Jennifer Saul offer a robust and detailed defence of the notion of implicit bias in response to criticism of the empirical data.[13] They start by making an important independent point, which is that measures to improve under-representation in philosophy and other fields do not generally depend on the existence of implicit bias for their justification. Most of the sensible measures, such as anonymous marking, anonymous refereeing, various forms of affirmative action, agreeing on criteria in advance, reducing reliance on letters of reference, and so on, are justified simply by the fact that there is under-representation, and the fact that they do, or *might*, help alleviate it. We don't need to know if they work by circumventing implicit bias. Perhaps they work by circumventing explicit bias. It doesn't matter.

Holroyd and Saul address various worries about the research on implicit bias. First, one criticism has centered on the Implicit Association Test (IAT). This test looks at the speed (and so, ease) with which people associate ideas. For example, being slower to match the pair 'woman' and 'leadership' than the pair 'man' and 'leadership' suggests that the first pairing seems unnatural to the subject, that they have some gender bias. One apparent problem with the test is that people's scores change, suggesting that what is being measured is not a stable attitude. Holroyd and Saul argue that that is not a genuine problem. The test measures very fine-grained response times, which will vary according to background factors. In fact, that is one of the things that is taken into account in recommendations for avoiding bias: make sure you have plenty of snacks, as hungry decisions are more likely to be biased. Second, they suggest that we should not worry too much about individual variations, but instead think of the test as being useful over large populations. The results do seem to be stable over large numbers.

Another worry about the IAT is that it does not predict behaviour in other areas. The point of the IAT seems to be that it measures something, bias, that will then emerge in other behaviours. Recent meta-analysis seems to undermine that. Holroyd and Saul argue that there are serious problems with the meta-analysis. First, the study ignored complexities in what was taken to be predicted. The idea was not that (for example) a monolithic thing, 'racial bias', could be discovered and that it would predict all racist behaviours. Rather, particular sorts of association will correlate with behaviour related to judgments of competence, and other associations will correlate with behaviours related to warmth and friendliness. The study ignored that, and so the results included low predictive power in cases where the original studies would have agreed that there would be low predictive power.

Furthermore, Holroyd and Saul argue, even if the predictive validity is low, it can still be important. The predictive validity for *explicit* beliefs is pretty low, yet we still think that they are important. We want to know that people harbour these attitudes. And even if there is only a small risk of such beliefs being acted on, a small risk justifies preventative measures. Finally, even if predictive validity at the individual level is low, it can be significant when applied to large groups, which is how Holroyd and Saul argue we should be seeing the IAT.

So, one explanation for the under-representation of women in STEM fields is that they face various forms of discrimination. It is simply much harder for them to complete their training, to get jobs, and to get promoted. But notice that prejudices have indirect effects as well direct ones. It is not hard to believe that if girls and women are discouraged from doing these subjects and told that they are not good at them from an early age, they will opt for different directions. Again, this is backed by research (much replicated!), on what psychologists call 'stereotype threat'. The term was coined by Claude Steele and Joshua Aronson in 1995.[14] Research since has repeatedly confirmed their findings, that if a task is framed in terms of some stereotype that the subject is aware applies to them, the subject's performance will be impacted by their awareness of the stereotype. For example, it is commonly held that women are better than men at social sensitivity (at picking up what is going on in a situation without explicit verbal cues). Men generally do worse in tests for social sensitivity. But the gender gap disappears when the test is reframed as a test of 'information processing'.[15]

Again, these points apply to philosophy as well as to STEM subjects. Philosophy is very 'male coded' (think about the image that comes to mind when you imagine 'a philosopher' – is it an old bearded white man?). Cheshire Calhoun takes this as very important in her discussion of the reason that philosophy is so male dominated. Calhoun argues that our cultural tendency to think of philosophers as men means that women feel marginalized from the very start of their undergraduate experiences of philosophy, and will tend to experience the environment as hostile to them. A bad experience will seem like confirmation of what they knew all along, that philosophy is for men and not for them.[16]

Philosophy is male coded in ways that reflect deeply held sexist stereotypes. It is very much a subject that we think of as requiring raw talent, genius, even. To be a philosopher is to be wise but distracted, disengaged from the real world (certainly from dirty nappies and school bake sales). This stereotype fits men, but not women. Research by Sarah Jane Leslie et al. shows a correlation between lower percentages of women and fields that are thought to require 'brilliance' and 'genius'. Crucially, these are agentic traits, not communal ones. It is difficult for women to be taken as having agentic traits.[17]

Another barrier to success for women in fields like STEM and philosophy, or in the army or other male coded and male dominated areas, is the pervasiveness of sexual harassment. Feminists argue that sexual harassment is a way of putting women in their place, as it creates a hostile environment, not by accident, as a result of the out of control libidos of individual men, but as its hidden purpose. If women enter male realms, they will be punished. Male violence against women is systemic; it has a sort of purpose, even if that purpose is not clear to the perpetrators.

Here is just one example, borrowed from Ann Cudd's discussion of oppression. Cudd describes the Tailhook scandal, where 26 women were sexually assaulted at a convention of naval aviators. As Cudd points out, what is shocking is not just that the assaults happened, but that the men who were not involved went to great lengths to protect the ones who were.[18] And this is not a unique incident. I come back to these issues in the chapters on sexual violence and on ideology, where I discuss the ways that narratives about sexual harassment and rape as individual failings support a patriarchal structure.

Yet another possible explanation for under-representation of women in high paid jobs and positions of power is that these jobs tend to be unsuited for people who have caring responsibilities. High paid jobs, and promoted positions (such as partnership in a law firm), often require late nights and weekend work, and are low on flexibility. It is rare for top executives to dash home from work at 11am because the school has called about a sick child. Promotion in academia usually requires 'an international reputation' and the chief way to prove that you have an international reputation is to show that you have been invited to and attended international events. This is much harder for those with major caring responsibilities. Given that people with caring responsibilities tend to be women, this structure disadvantages women.

If the idea that women are less good at being rational and working in important and high paid jobs is common, the idea that men are not good at domestic and care work is even more so. Men are under-represented in early years education, in caring professions and those that are perceived that way (such as nursing), and in care work their own homes. Thus the traditional family can seem like a good and necessary division of labour. But should we accept that men are not naturally suited to care work?

As many feminist philosophers have pointed out, men and women are socialized to think that parenting is the woman's realm, and little boys are not taught how to parent. Worse, boys are socialized to aim for a model of masculinity that ranks childcare as an aberration for a man, a lowering of himself to a feminine task. Recent writing on masculinity highlights the disadvantages to men inherent in this division. Traditional masculinity excludes men from genuine childcare, and this is to the detriment of men, who miss out on the joy and the richness of nurturing.

Larry May and Robert Strikwerda argue that not only traditional masculinity, but also more recent cultural models, are bad for men.[19] They identify three models of fatherhood: 'traditional fatherhood' in which the man works outside the home and has little to do with the kids; 'augmented traditional fatherhood', in which the man 'babysits' from time to time, but the woman is still the primary emotional and physical nurturer; and most recently, 'the sensitive new age guy'. May and Strikwerda's analysis of the new age guy is that although superficially it is an improvement, it is still not a good model of nurturing parenting. On this model, the man is emotionally involved and spends time with his children, but he is not the responsible adult. He seeks emotional connection from his children, but more as an equal, not as a nurturer.

May and Strikwerda's point is that our culture makes it very difficult for men to be good fathers. Apparent advances disguise a more sinister reality, that men are still cast as Homer Simpson, or at best, Peppa Pig's dad, basically incapable of taking proper responsibility. Men are socialized into pre-defined roles, and their own expectations of fatherhood are limited accordingly. But there is no evidence that things *must* be like that. Both men and women can unlearn these habits, and if we did, it would be better for all of us.

In sum, there are many possible explanations for under-representation of women in some fields (and under-representation of men in others). Our gender stereotypes are deep and resilient. Men and women trying to enter and succeed in occupations that are not traditional for their gender face both subtle and unsubtle discrimination, and must also manage their own self-conceptions. We do not need to think that any of this is natural or innate.

The family and gendered cycle of vulnerability

One of the most influential philosophical accounts of these issues is Susan Okin's. In *Justice, Gender, and the Family* (1989), she argues that "the family is the linchpin of the gender structure".[20] Okin argues that the division of labour in which men work for money and women look after children is deeply unjust and disadvantageous to women. Okin insists that none of this is innate. Rather, women are socialized, incentivized, and coerced into these gender roles. She points out that girls are treated differently from boys from an early age, and socialized to be caring, gentle, and domestic – in effect, to be good wives. Meanwhile, the world of work is structured so as to suit someone who has a wife at home, someone to do the cooking and cleaning and childcare. Okin argues that we need to change both our ideas about gender and our social and political institutions.

Okin is responding to a tradition of thinking about political arrangements that ignored family structures altogether. John Rawls, the dominant figure in modern liberalism, proposed that a just situation is one that would be chosen from a position of ignorance about one's place in society. The core idea is that if you didn't know that you were going to be from a rich or a poor family, your race, what your talents are, you would not choose a society that discriminated against people on those grounds. Those attributes do not entail deserving more or less, they are just a matter of luck. So, Rawls argues, we should imagine what society would be chosen from behind a 'veil of ignorance'. The problem is that Rawls imagined the people choosing societies as 'heads of families', implicitly men, and simply assumed that the family itself was just.[21]

Okin argues that the system where women are expected to be primarily wives and mothers perpetuates a cycle of vulnerability for women. It "involves women in a cycle of socially caused and distinctly asymmetric vulnerability. The division of labour within marriage (except in rare cases) makes wives far more likely than husbands to be exploited both within the marital relationship and in the world outside the home".[22] Her point is that the family is not an independent realm. The way the family works is affected by and affects the way that the world of waged labour works.

Women in the traditional Western family work hard, but their labour is unpaid. The husband is taken to be the more important labourer, and he is granted more power and status by society. This leaves women vulnerable to abuse and exploitation. If women get divorced, they are often even worse off. Women do not gain the skills and training they need to be independent, and so are dependent on their husband for alimony and child support, and thus still vulnerable to him. They raise their children to accept their assigned gender roles as inevitable, and so the cycle continues.

Okin might be criticized for her limited scope. She was writing in particular about women in the USA in the 1970s and 80s. However, despite the huge increase in women in the workforce since then, especially in Western countries, it is plausible that her critique remains valid. Women still get paid less than men, and work in more precarious jobs. Divorce is still a financial risk for women much more than it is for men. As the lower earner in a heterosexual relationship, women have often made income sacrifices for a joint enterprise that the man has not. When finances are separated, he has a bigger pension and a higher salary. The man is also less likely to take custody of children, and less likely to have caring obligations to the generation above, and these fall on daughters more than on sons.[23]

In her recent book on these issues, Gina Schouten surveys the latest empirical work on the gendered division of labour and argues that it shows that women are still doing most of the housework and most of the childcare, even when they are in full-time employment. Even if women don't do the housework, they are in charge of managing it and have overall responsibility. The same applies to childcare.[24] Women are still doing what sociologist Arlie Hochschild termed 'the second shift'. It is also worth noting that the second shift is not just housework, but emotional labour and kin work too. In heterosexual couples, women do most of the work related to emotional support of the whole family, and most of the work related to keeping the family together. Schouten argues, just as Okin before her, that the pervasive gendered division of labour that persists and has been internalized as natural and normal contributes to a situation of gender injustice.

Okin was writing about the vulnerability of predominantly middle-class women in relatively wealthy Western societies, but she takes her analysis to apply to women in other societies too.[25] Iris Marion Young takes up that issue, and argues that Okin's account can be applied to the situation of women in the third world.[26] Young argues that gendered division of labour always creates vulnerability for women. In almost all societies, women do more of the domestic work, and do it on an unpaid basis. But the relationship between this work and power structures is ignored in our public norms and narratives. As Young puts it, "Nearly every society . . . assumes and relies on unpaid domestic work. Despite this reliance, the public norms of nearly every society affirm a separation of public and private. They function as though the power relations, economic opportunities, and social projects of non-familial institutions operate independently of the family and that family relations are independent of them. In nearly every society, however, there are systematic structural relations of mutual influence between family relations and the dynamics of costs and benefits, power and domination, opportunity and obstacle, in non-family institutions."[27] And it is not a coincidence that this situation is brushed under the carpet. State institutions and private enterprises both benefit from the gendered division of labour. Work done for free by women is work they do not have to pay for.

Young argues that this pattern is global. She discusses a study by Saba Gul Khattak of women working in their homes or in small factories in three industries – garments, carpets, and plastics – in urban areas in Pakistan. The women work because they have to: it is not empowerment, but necessity. These women, like American women, usually have childcare and domestic responsibilities on top of the need to earn money. One reason to prefer taking paid work into the home is that it is compatible with cooking and childcare. It also avoids some social stigma attached to women working, and risks of sexual harassment or rape. But working at home makes women particularly vulnerable to exploitation. Wages are very low, there is no job security, and the employer takes no responsibility for hours or conditions. Again, as in America, women who do not have husbands or whose husbands die or leave are even more vulnerable, for now they must earn a man's wage while still doing all the woman's work.

Young agrees with Okin that a multitude of factors converge to render women vulnerable. Okin and Young both argue that part of what maintains the gendered division of labour is ideology: widely held beliefs about how things naturally are and ought to be. Young argues that we should include the ways that ideology about sexuality interact with the supposed public and private spheres. Norms of sexual modesty, and risks of sexual harassment and rape, often serve to keep women in segregated forms of labour. This was one of the findings of Khattak's study: women reported that work at home was preferable because of those factors.

Alison Jaggar, building on both Young and Okin, adds another area where Okin's basic structure can be applied.[28] Jaggar discusses the transnational markets in gendered labour, particularly care work and sex work. There is a huge international trade in domestic labour. Migrant women, especially if they are undocumented, are vulnerable in many ways that women in their own homes are not. However, Jaggar argues that although there are important differences between women doing their own domestic labour and the women who are paid to do it, there are important similarities too. Women who work in their employer's home are especially vulnerable to exploitation in the form of low wages and long hours. If the woman's own children have been left behind at home, care for them increases the burden on female relatives there, thus reinforcing the gendered cycles of vulnerability at home.

Similarly, there is a huge transnational market in sex work, including women who are trafficked, who voluntarily migrate, or who migrate as 'mail order brides'. On top of various similarities to domestic labour, the work is often illegal, which adds to the potential for exploitation. Jaggar argues that despite important differences in the circumstances of women in different cultural situations, it is crucial to understand global gender disparities as caused by our practices and institutions, and not to fall into the trap of thinking that similarities are coincidences.

The gendered division of labour is a cross-cultural phenomenon, with wide-ranging consequences. It is supported both by institutions and by ideology, making undoing it a vast and complex task. Feminists have suggested various interventions, ranging from minor to radical. In the following sections I examine some of these proposed policies.

Affirmative action

Affirmative action is an umbrella term for policies that aim to increase the representation of under-represented groups by some direct measure. This can be contrasted with indirect measures, measures that aim to increase representation by making things easier or providing opportunities, and hoping for uptake. Affirmative action policies include quotas, lower barriers for candidates in the under-represented group, using group membership as a tie breaker, and more complex measures such as active recruitment.

There are, broadly, three justifications for affirmative action. First, it might be seen as a compensation for past wrongs. Judith Jarvis Thomson was one of the first to make that argument.[29] In her 1973 article, she argued that preferential treatment for African Americans and women would in some way make up for their unjust treatment in the past. This is a very complex argument and rests on issues in compensatory justice that I cannot spend long on here. The obvious objection to a defence like Thomson's is that affirmative action does not compensate the right people, and does not compensate them in the right way. But as soon as we move away from cases of individual harms, it is impossible to compensate the exact people harmed and to give them back what they lost. So compensatory justice must deal in substitutes. The question – a hard question – is which ones are appropriate.

Second is a forward-looking argument for affirmative action, that we are justified in aiming for a more equal distribution of desirable positions and power, and an effective way to do that is to make sure that there are people from under-represented groups in those places. This is a consequentialist argument: the policy is justified by it having good consequences overall.

Third is the argument that affirmative action programs simply compensate for bias on the part of selectors. Requiring a selection committee, for example, to give at least some roles to women forces them to allocate on merit rather than on gender. On this account, affirmative action doesn't favour less-qualified candidates; rather, it makes sure that the qualified candidates are the ones favoured.

These different justifications invite different objections. I will focus on the second and third justifications, and on the objections that have been levelled against them. The objections to a forward-looking justification for affirmative action are: first, that it will not be effective after all (that it will result in backlash, for example), and second, that it is unjust to those candidates, who, but for the policy, would have been successful. The backlash argument is in danger of a sort of circularity: if we are in a situation where women are discriminated against and employers are swayed by a sense that women are inferior to men, then we seem to need some sort of policy to correct for that. But if we introduce an affirmative action measure, there will be backlash against it: people will think that the women in those positions do not deserve them, and have taken them from people who did deserve them. This is illustrative of the tough problem of ideology. Attempts to undo it will always strike those in the grip of the ideology as wrong-headed. Nonetheless, if it is an empirical fact that affirmative action policies would be counterproductive, that is a good argument against the forward-looking justification for them.

As Marilyn Frye points out, in the real world, affirmative action policies can become a strategy of "assimilation, co-optation and tokenism".[30] Talking about academia in particular, Frye observes that affirmative action programs are used to recruit the most assimilable candidates, those who are already similar to the people recruiting them. Thus the reach and influence of such programs are limited: the academy can claim to be progressive while actually maintaining the status quo. Frye also points out that those who are recruited into academic and other professional careers from under-privileged groups are then less likely to pay attention to change in the group they came from. They are co-opted into a new loyalty system.[31] Finally, policies of affirmative action can work to maintain the status quo by making it permissible to have a token 'woman' and a token 'minority'. If this is accepted as sufficient for justice to be done, the battle is lost.

A different problem is that affirmative action inevitably focusses on groups, and that can create rivalries between different groups and controversies about who is in what group. These tensions are what give 'identity politics' (the term used to describe a political focus on oppressed groups) a bad name. For example, Floya Anthias and Nira Yuval-Davis argue that various race-based policies in Britain, policies that were on the face of it designed to help people in those groups, actually did more harm than good by co-opting identity politics and turning groups against each other.[32] As Patricia Hill Collins puts it in her summary of the worry, "When state distribution of social rewards in relation to group membership fosters a situation of group competition for scarce resources, policing the boundaries of group membership becomes much more important."[33] This is a tricky problem: it is important to be able to talk about group membership as a cause of oppression, and solutions to the injustices must focus on members of the relevant groups. But this can result in lack of solidarity and, worse, active hostility between sub-groups.

Relatedly, a focus on groups as a target of political action risks a reification of the group: making group membership appear to be marking innate difference. If women receive special treatment in one arena, it can be used to legitimate other special treatment, treatment that is not positive or welcome. The feminist justification for paying attention to group membership is not that there is any important innate difference between group members and other people – the point is not that women are weak and need an extra leg up. But of course, if that's what affirmative action policies make people think, there is a problem.

Let's return to a different sort of objection to affirmative action, which is not that such policies are counterproductive, but that they are *unjust*. The idea is that if some people are treated preferentially due to group membership, other people will miss out on something that they were entitled to. This objection has been addressed by Ronald Dworkin.[34] He discusses a particular case, that of Allan Bakke, who was denied admission to a University of California medical school although his scores were better than many of the successful applicants. Bakke sued, alleging that the 'reverse discrimination' was still discrimination, and so illegal. Dworkin frames the issue in terms of rights: does Allan Bakke have rights that conflict with a policy of affirmative action? Dworkin's answer is 'no'. He argues that public institutions like medical schools do *not* have a duty to judge each candidate on their merit, where that is understood as desert. How *deserving* the candidate is is irrelevant. Rather, medical schools have a duty to judge candidates on the basis of how effective they will be as doctors. Dworkin argues that in a racist world, race can be relevant to how effective someone is as a doctor. Indeed, this was one of the justifications given by the UC Davis medical school for their policy, that increasing the number of African American medical students would increase the number of doctors serving those communities. By moving away from Bakke's rights and what he deserves to what society needs, Dworkin reframes affirmative action programs as social goods rather than individual harms.

Iris Marion Young makes a slightly different point in response to the injustice objection. She argues that although affirmative action is indeed a way of discriminating against members of the dominant group on the basis of their group membership, we should not shy away from that.[35] Young points out that the primary wrong done to the relevant groups is not discrimination (treating different people differently is not always a problem), it is *oppression*. When we think about solutions, we need to be able recognize the groups that have been the focus of unfair treatment. Young stresses the importance of recognizing social differences to ensure just outcomes. She also argues that we cannot think of justice as a matter of distributing goods according to merit: we have to start by looking at patterns of domination and oppression.

The injustice objection is entirely sidestepped by the third way of defending a policy of affirmative action, which is to argue that affirmative action does not really give preferential treatment to some, it merely attempts to see *through* the damaging effects of institutionalized oppression. Luke Charles Harris and Uma Narayan argue along these lines.[36] First, they argue that the idea that it is fair to admit people on the basis of test scores is seriously flawed. They point out that a simple test score approach to admission does not reflect true talent. Standardized tests are not good predictors: they record the past not the future. If someone is from a deprived educational background they will have lower test scores than someone who is the beneficiary of an elite primary and secondary education. But their future potential can depend on the next step: tertiary education, for example.

Harris and Narayan also stress that recruitment techniques are often based on word of mouth and prior knowledge, which of course limits the candidate pool to the same demographic as the recruiters. The 'old boy network' works to keep non- 'old boys' out. Additionally, of course, selection committees are often biased, implicitly and explicitly, in the ways we discussed above. So, current procedures do not evaluate members of disadvantaged groups fairly. Harris and Narayan argue that affirmative action programs aim to make up for this. If that is right, if affirmative action merely corrects for discrimination in the appointment process, then there is no argument from injustice.

Parental leave

Okin argues for wide-ranging changes to our laws, including about marriage (she argues that laws should not assume sex or gender, and that divorce laws should ensure fair outcome). She also argues that paternal responsibilities should be enforced. Workplace policies should not disadvantage primary childcarers, and should not assume that the primary childcarer is always the woman. Parental leave after the pregnancy period should be distributed equally, it should be assumed that any worker may have childcare responsibilities, and workplace flexibility should be the norm.

Since she wrote *Justice, Gender, and the Family*, employment policies worldwide have moved in the direction Okin urged (though the USA is among those places where there has been very little progress). The traditional model of parental leave is as 'maternity leave', with the biological or adoptive mother being entitled to some small amount of paid leave on the birth of the child, and a longer amount unpaid (with employers offering various packages to supplement the statutory pay). Since 2015 in the UK, parental leave entitlement can be shared between both parents, and in Nordic countries this has been the case for a long time. Yet it is still often the woman who actually takes the leave in situations where either parent can.[37] It makes financial sense for the lower earner to take time off, and that is often the woman. And of course, there are cultural pressures, ideals of masculinity, and so on, that put pressure on men to stay at work while women take time off. Thus perhaps we need to move from flexibility to mandatory (or heavily incentivized) paternity leave, as is the case in Finland, Norway, Sweden, and Germany, where some of the time is reserved for fathers (if they don't take it, the time cannot be transferred to the mother).

Gina Schouten argues that we have good evidence that state intervention can decrease gendered division of labour.[38] But it is important to get the policies right. A badly designed policy can easily make things worse and further entrench problematic gender roles. Schouten argues that if we are serious about changing the gendered division of labour, the state needs to be inflexible and intrusive. The state needs to provide powerful incentives for men to take parental leave, provide subsidized childcare, and improve the conditions for part-time work.

The difficulties and risks inherent in designing incentives are pointed out by Anca Gheaus and Ingrid Robeyns.[39] They criticize a proposal by Harry Brighouse and Erik Olin Wright, who argue for a radical change in parental leave policies.[40] Recognizing that men often do not take parental leave, even when it is incentivized, Brighouse and Wright argue that commitment to gender egalitarianism requires that the state makes extended parental leave for the mother conditional on her co-parent also taking parental leave. A mother would be entitled to one month of leave no matter what, but her entitlement beyond that would depend on her co-parent taking the same amount. Brighouse and Wright argue that this would be a sufficiently strong incentive for men to take an equal amount of parental leave, and that the effect would be that society would move more quickly to a gender egalitarian situation.

Gheaus and Robeyns agree that men should be incentivized to take parental leave, but they are skeptical about the effects of a policy like the one proposed by Brighouse and Wright. First, they worry that the policy leans too far in the direction of limiting individual freedom in the service of a social goal. As they point out, there is an inherent tension here: they accept the liberal principle that it is good to allow people to choose to live the way they would like to. However, they also accept the feminist aim of gender fairness. As things stand, people's choices perpetuate gender injustice, so feminists argue for interfering with those choices to some extent, for example through state organized incentives. But, Gheaus and Robeyns argue that those interventions should not go so far as to be a serious suppression of individual freedom.

Gheaus and Robeyns' second objection is that Brighouse and Wright's proposal would be bad for women and is likely to further entrench, rather than eliminate, gender injustice. For one thing, it assumes that couples are always harmonious units, but that is not always the case, and this policy makes the mother dependent on her not necessarily cooperative partner. Furthermore, the policy may perversely create an incentive for women to drop out of the labour market and move into full-time childcare. As they put it, people are often 'gender conservative': they are attached to the gender ideology that mandates gendered division of labour; they believe that young children must be nurtured by their mothers rather than their fathers. Consider a situation in which a gender conservative couple must decide what to do about childcare when the mother cannot take more leave without the father doing so, but the father will not take leave. It may be that the rational option is for the mother to quit her job and go into full-time domesticity – exactly the trend the policy aims to counter.

Finally, Gheaus and Robeyns point out that the illiberal character of the policy could easily fuel an anti-feminist backlash. It would be perceived as a feminist assault on freedom and would alienate many people who might otherwise be in favour of more gender justice. The point here is not that such a backlash would be justified (although Gheaus and Robeyns do think that the policy is overly restrictive). The point is that if the aim of a policy is gender justice, it is important to take into account the effects it would actually have.

Both Gheaus and Robeyns support the gender egalitarian aims of Brighouse and Wright's proposal, but they argue that it is possible to achieve a better balance of egalitarianism and individual freedom. They propose that parental leave policies should work on a default basis, so that the default situation is that men take parental leave, and in order to opt out they must take active steps. They also point to evidence showing that people are more likely to take an option if it is the default. For example, if organ donation is the default, more people remain registered as donors. Thus a policy of having both parents take parental leave as the default is likely to increase the rate of fathers taking parental leave without imposing any actual restrictions on their freedom, and without disadvantaging women.

Workplace flexibility is another area where it is a delicate matter to design a policy that is not counterproductive. It is important not to confuse workplace flexibility with variable hours that are set by the employer. A worker who must work different hours each week and has no or little choice over that schedule will be much worse off in terms of childcare arrangements. The rise in jobs with variable hours is not a victory for feminism. But even more sincere attempts to design good policies can backfire. As Schouten points out, improving the conditions for part-time work may just encourage women who would have worked full time to work only part time, thus harming their promotion prospects, incomes, and pensions in comparison with men's. With that danger in mind, legal theorists Vicki Schultz and Allison Hoffman argue that the state should mandate a shorter working week for everyone.[41] This would ensure that men and women are able to participate equally in both work and childcare.

The fact that policies aimed at gender equality can easily misfire is a symptom of the deep enculturation of our gender norms. As Okin argues, it is essential to dismantle the ideology that mandates that women must do the care work. Okin also argues that as well as policies aimed at enabling women to work, we need to take action to reduce our adherence to gender stereotypes. We need to focus on the way that children learn what their gender roles are, and design careful interventions in early years education in children's books, television, and so on.

Gheaus and Robeyns' proposal addresses this. The fact that people are psychologically affected by a policy being the default illustrates what social creatures humans are. We tend towards the option that seems 'normal', least disruptive, and reflective of our society's values. Most people don't want to rock the boat. So policies that play on that tendency, and make the feminist option the normal option instead of the exceptional and difficult option, are more likely to succeed in their long-term aims.

Radical solutions

Indirect measures, such as incentivizing men's uptake of parental leave, or direct ones, such as affirmative action, may change the gendered of division of labour, but some feminists have argued that more radical change is needed. One obvious danger with overhauling the current system is that it leaves too much in place. The problems with our systems of labour and consumption may run deeper than gendered divisions of labour. bell hooks suggests that this is the case. hooks accepts that in the short term, measures such as a shorter working week will improve the situation, but she urges a longer-term view, that in the end we need to overthrow capitalist patriarchy. hooks argues in a Marxist vein that capitalism depends on the exploitation of an underclass. According to hooks, Western culture is permeated by an ideology of domination, and that that must be undone. A feminist movement comprised of white women seeking equality with white men will never achieve that.[42]

hooks points out that race plays a large role in the patterns of the gendered division of labour. She argues that white middle-class feminists have oversimplified things in arguing that motherhood is a barrier to freedom and entry into the workforce. hooks reminds us that many Black women work outside the home in a situation that is "stressful, degrading and dehumanizing".[43] hooks argues that, by contrast, parenting is fulfilling and valuable work, and it should be celebrated. However, we need to move away from the idea that only women can do it, that the traditional family is natural and inevitable. Further, hooks argues that revolutionary parenting is already happening in ways that white feminists have missed:

> Childrearing is a responsibility that can be shared with other childrearers, with people who do not live with children. This form of parenting is revolutionary in this society because it takes place in opposition to the idea that parents, especially mothers, should be the only childrearers. Many people raised in Black communities experienced this type of community-based child care.[44]

Other feminist writers have suggested other radical possibilities. Shulamith Firestone's book, *The Dialectic of Sex* (1970), focusses on the female role in reproduction. She takes the idea that women need to be freed from domestic labour to extremes, arguing that technology could free women from reproductive labour, and that that is what is required for true emancipation. Firestone argued that we should be working to develop artificial wombs, and that ideally, children would be raised by collectives, rather than in the traditional family.

Adrienne Rich presents a different view of motherhood and technology. According to Rich (and to many other feminists, such as Sarah Ruddick), mothering is undervalued and under-theorized, and we should be seeking to expand mothering type bonds and relationships, not to limit them. Rich argues that controlling reproductive technology and birth is a way of controlling the one thing that is clearly women's realm, and that women should be distrustful of more reproductive technology.[45]

Firestone's argument, like the original argument that women need to be freed from domestic labour, struck many Black feminists as being very focussed on the perspective of middle-class white women. At the time that Firestone was writing about the need to free women from reproductive labour, Black women in North America were being sterilized against their will. As Angela Davis, and, more recently, Shatema Threadcraft argue, Black women's rights over their own bodies, rights to bear and nurture their own children, to control access to their bodies, have always been limited by a racist patriarchy.[46] Thus for Black women, liberation is not always saliently in freedom from motherhood, but sometimes in freedom to be mothers.

Parallel issues arise in considering gay and lesbian theorizing about the family. Cheshire Calhoun argues that whereas heterosexual women have traditionally wanted a way out of the traditional family, lesbians want a way in: lesbians and gay men want the right to have a family, to be married, to have parental rights and responsibilities and so on. Calhoun cautions against conflating lesbianism with resistance to patriarchal male–female relationships. Calhoun stresses that the system of patriarchal dominance is in principle separate from the system of heterosexual dominance. As Calhoun puts it,

> unlike the heterosexual woman, including the heterosexual feminist, the lesbian experience of the institution of heterosexuality is of a system that makes her sexual, affectional, domestic, and reproductive life unreal. Within heterosexual society, the experience

between women of sexual fulfillment, of falling in love, of marrying, of creating a home, of starting a family have no social reality. Unlike the heterosexual feminist, the lesbian has no socially supported private sphere, not even an oppressive one.[47]

Claudia Card is more skeptical about the wisdom of gaining entry to traditionally heterosexual structures.[48] She argues that marriage and the traditional family are terrible institutions, and that lesbians and gays should not be fighting for the right to marry, but for abolition of marriage. The state should not be involved in intimate relationships. Card argues that it would be better to have more choice about ways of living and romantic partners. Card cites both bell hooks and Patricia Hill Collins and applauds their advocating for a more communal way of raising children where they are less at their parents' mercy. Similar ideas about the problems of traditional marriage are developed by more recent feminist writers, including Elizabeth Brake and Clare Chambers.

Other feminists have advocated for political lesbianism, a chosen identification with other women and avoidance of heteronormative relationships. Adrienne Rich points out that heterosexuality is an institution, and that as such heterosexuality is compulsory, enforced, and policed. As Marilyn Frye puts it,

> Female heterosexuality is not a biological drive or an individual woman's erotic attraction or attachment to another human animal which happens to be male. Female heterosexuality is a set of social institutions and practices defined and regulated by patriarchal kinship systems, both by civil and religious law, and by strenuously enforced mores and deeply entrenched values and taboos.[49]

Summary

All over the world there is a gendered division of labour. We do not have very good reasons to think that there are innate differences between men and women, or that women are not fitted for intellectual or high-powered jobs and men are not fitted for caring responsibilities. Rather, there are lots of reasons to think that women are discriminated against in subtle and unsubtle ways, and that our social norms and ideologies reinforce the gendered division of labour.

As Susan Okin argues, women face a gendered cycle of vulnerability. Domestic division of labour makes women more vulnerable to exploitation and violence both inside and outside the domestic sphere. Iris Marion Young points out that although Okin was primarily writing about Western women, the same is true globally.

Changing that situation is not easy. We need a careful empirically informed approach, looking at the actual effects of various policies. Feminists have argued for affirmative action programs, more equal parental leave arrangements, subsidized childcare, and flexible working hours. The devil is the details, and these policies can easily backfire or fail to work if not designed carefully.

There is a rich tradition of more radical responses, which I have not done full justice to here. Feminists have argued that technology could free us, and others that it could enslave us further. Most feminists agree that the traditional family is toxic, but there are different views about what should replace it. Some argue for a completely different way of thinking about intimate associations, others for less dramatic change.

Notes

1 Marx and Engels, *The German Ideology*, p.47.
2 hooks, 'Rethinking the Nature of Work', in *Feminist Theory: From Margin to Center*, p.96.
3 Op. cit., p.105.
4 Haines, Deaux, and Lofaro, 'The Times They Are a-Changing . . . Or Are They Not? A Comparison of Gender Stereotypes, 1983–2014'.
5 Norlock, 'Update on Women in the Profession'.
6 Beebee and Saul, 'Women in Philosophy in the UK: A Report by the British Philosophical Association and the Society for Women in Philosophy UK'.
7 www.theguardian.com/science/2005/jan/18/educationsgendergap.genderissues.
8 Frye, 'Oppression', in *The Politics of Reality*.
9 Steinpreis, Anders, and Ritzke, 'The Impact of Gender on the Review of the Curricula Vitae of Job Applicants and Tenure Candidates: A National Empirical Study'.
10 Moss-Racusin et al., 'Science Faculty's Subtle Gender Biases Favor Male Students'.
11 Handley et al., 'Gender-Biased Evaluations of Gender-Bias Evidence'.
12 Fine, *Delusions of Gender*.
13 Holroyd and Saul, 'Implicit Bias and Reform Efforts in Philosophy'.
14 Steele and Aronson, 'Stereotype Threat and the Intellectual Test Performance of African Americans'.
15 Koenig and Eagly, 'Stereotype Threat in Men on a Test of Social Sensitivity'.
16 Calhoun, 'The Undergraduate Pipeline Problem'.
17 Leslie et al., 'Expectations of Brilliance Underlie Gender Distributions Across Academic Disciplines'.
18 Cudd, *Analysing Oppression*, p.96.
19 May and Strikwerda, 'Fatherhood and Nurturance'.
20 Okin, *Justice, Gender and the Family*, p.14.
21 Rawls, *A Theory of Justice*.
22 Op. cit., p.138.
23 For some data on this see the recent Chartered Institute of Insurers Report on 'Women's Risks in Life', www.cii.co.uk/media/7461333/risks_in_life_report.pdf.
24 Schouten, *Liberalism, Neutrality, and the Gendered Division of Labor*, p.34.
25 Okin, 'Gender Inequality and Cultural Differences'.
26 Young, 'The Gendered Cycle of Vulnerability in the Less Developed World'.
27 Op. cit., p.228.
28 Jaggar, 'Transnational Cycles of Gendered Vulnerability: A Prologue to a Theory of Global Gender Justice'.
29 Thomson, 'Preferential Hiring'.
30 Frye, 'Getting it Right', in *Wilful Virgin*, p.19.
31 See also Jennifer Morton's recent book, *Moving Up Without Losing Your Way: The Ethical Costs of Upward Mobility*.
32 Anthias and Yuval-Davis, *Racialized Boundaries: Race, Nation, Gender, Colour and Class and the Anti-racist Struggle*.
33 Collins, *Fighting Words: Black Women and the Search for Justice*, p.206.
34 Dworkin wrote many articles and opinion pieces on the topic. The main arguments are found in section V of *A Matter of Principle*.
35 Young, 'The Myth of Merit', in *Justice and the Politics of Difference*.
36 Harris and Narayan, 'Affirmative Action and the Myth of Preferential Treatment: A Transformative Critique of the Terms of the Affirmative Action Debate'.
37 Moss and Deven, 'Leave Policies in Challenging Times: Reviewing the Decade 2004–2014'.
38 Schouten, *Liberalism, Neutrality, and the Gendered Division of Labor*, p.50.
39 Gheaus and Robeyns, 'Equality Promoting Parental Leave'.
40 Brighouse and Wright, 'Strong Gender Egalitarianism'.
41 Schultz and Hoffman, 'The Need for a Reduced Workweek in the United States'.
42 hooks, *Feminist Theory: From Margin to Center*.
43 'Revolutionary Parenting', in *Feminist Theory: From Margin to Center*, p.134.

44 Op. cit., p.144.
45 Rich, 'Compulsory Heterosexuality and Lesbian Existence'.
46 Davis, *Women, Race, and Class*; Threadcraft, *Intimate Justice: The Black Female Body and the Body Politic*.
47 Calhoun, 'Separating Lesbian Theory from Feminist Theory', p.581.
48 Card, 'Against Marriage and Motherhood'.
49 Frye, 'Wilful Virgin, Or Do You Have To Be a Lesbian To Be a Feminist?', in *Wilful Virgin*, p.132.

Further reading

Beeghly, Erin and Madva, Alex (2020) *An Introduction to Implicit Bias: Knowledge, Justice, and the Social Mind*. Routledge. (Collection of essays from philosophy and social sciences on implicit bias).
Chan, Sarah and Cutas, Daniela (eds.) (2012) *Families: Beyond the Nuclear Ideal*. Bloomsbury Academic. (Collection of essays on forms and limits of the traditional family structure).
Hutchison, Katrina and Jenkins, Fiona (eds.) (2013) *Women in Philosophy: What Needs to Change?* Oxford University Press. (Collection of essays on under-representation of women in philosophy).
Williams, Joan (2000) *Unbending Gender: Why Family and Work Conflict and What to Do About It*. Oxford University Press. (A sustained argument for workplace reforms that takes account of caregivers' needs).

3 Reproductive rights

"The decision whether or not to bear a child is central to a woman's life, to her well-being and dignity . . . When government controls that decision for her, she is being treated as less than a fully adult human responsible for her own choices."

Ruth Bader Ginsburg, *Senate Confirmation Hearings for her Supreme Court Appointment, 1993*

Chapter overview: The main topic of this chapter is moral and legal questions about abortion, but I also discuss forced sterilization, contraception, and emergency birth control. I explain Judith Jarvis Thomson's defence of abortion, and put it in context with other feminist approaches to abortion, including arguments about the nature of pregnancy and virtue ethical approaches. As well as the argument that there is a moral right to abortion, I also consider the weaker claim that, given sexist oppression of women, a legal right to abortion is crucial.

Introduction

Women's bodies are controlled and policed in many ways, but there is no interference as common, or as political, as interference with women's capacities to bear a child. Feminists have been arguing for the right to control their own bodies, including a right to safe, legal abortion, for centuries, but progress is patchy. Hard-won victories can be undermined with the stroke of a pen, and even where practices such as forced sterilization are illegal, they still happen.

One of the major battlegrounds is abortion. According to the Center for Reproductive Rights, 26 countries prohibit abortion altogether, and 39 allow it only in cases where the woman's life is at risk. The rest allow abortion in varying circumstances, from threat to mental or physical health, to more or less on demand. But the situation is in flux. In the United States, abortion on demand is protected by a federal law, known as *Roe v Wade* (after the case that established the law in 1973). But as I write in 2020, 13 states of the USA have introduced restrictive abortion laws, and it is widely thought that there is a swell of support for repeal of *Roe v Wade*. Of course, political movements are hard to identify, so perhaps this is a mere blip. In 2018, Ireland held a referendum on repealing the abortion ban, and a substantial majority (over 66%) voted in favour of legalizing abortion. Northern Ireland, which is part of the UK, has historically had much stricter abortion regulations than the rest of the UK, but Westminster legislation of 2019 is set to bring Northern Ireland's regulations in line with the rest of the country's much more liberal laws.

At the same time, feminist protests against restrictive abortion laws in Poland seem to be falling on deaf ears. Poland has the most restrictive laws in Europe. The Polish government (the right-wing Law and Justice party) proposed a blanket ban in 2016, but backed down in the face of mass protests. However, despite apparent public opinion in favour of a more liberal stance, the government wants to make the laws more restrictive, and is pressing on in the face of ongoing protests. Law and Justice party leader Jarosław Kaczyński, speaking in 2018, the same year that the abortion referendum took place in Ireland, said, "We will strive to ensure that even in pregnancies which are very difficult, when a child is sure to die, strongly deformed, women end up giving birth so that the child can be baptized, buried, and have a name."[1]

In places such as Poland and Ireland, which have strong Catholic traditions, it is clear that anti-abortion laws have a religious foundation. The idea is not so much that the foetus has a right to life as that it has a soul, and that soul must be treated with all the respect and care due to all immortal souls. This religious argument, taken at face value, transcends feminist worries, as Kaczyński's remarks clearly indicate. If abortion is forbidden by divine will, then it doesn't matter that women may suffer. But feminists sometimes worry that what is behind anti-abortion movements in other places, such as the USA, and perhaps lurking behind some religious arguments, is a more general patriarchal aim. The concern is that political movements that seek to restrict abortion are not coincidentally restricting the freedom of women; rather, it is partly *because* reproductive control is so important for women that these groups are against abortion. Restricting abortion, and access to contraception, is a way of controlling women. Repeal of *Roe v Wade* would have a symbolic meaning and practical ramifications that go way beyond the actual cases of women who are denied abortions.

This brings us to forced sterilization. There is a long history of women being sterilized against their will across the globe. Sterilization policies in America in the twentieth century, often designed by 'Eugenics Boards' at state level, were chiefly used against racialized groups: many Puerto Rican, Black, Latina, and Native American women were sterilized with coerced consent or no consent at all. Even where consent for the procedure was obtained, it was often obtained on false grounds, for example, by misleading women into thinking that tubal ligation is easily reversible, a temporary contraceptive measure. In the 1970s, after pressure from women's rights groups (particularly organizations of women of colour, such as the National Black Feminist Organization), new laws designed to ensure that consent to sterilization was informed and genuine were introduced.[2] Despite that, institutional forced sterilization has continued. In 2013, a report on California's prison conditions found that nearly 150 illegal (non-consensual) sterilizations had been carried out on inmates between 2006 and 2010.[3]

The United States is not unique in having enacted sterilization policies. In the twentieth century, up until the 1980s, Japan, Canada, Sweden, Australia, Norway, Finland, Estonia,

Slovakia, Switzerland, and Iceland all had laws allowing non-consensual sterilization. It is not easy to separate out the different elements of oppression (see Chapter 8 on intersectionality for more on this), but it seems fair to say that eugenics programs were primarily racist. However, this does not mean that they are not of feminist concern. Black feminist theorists have stressed that a focus on abortion rights alone ignores the struggles of Black women, who were victims of forced sterilization policies at a much higher rate than white women. From a feminist point of view, the issues of abortion and enforced sterilization are closely related: women are not taken to have a right to control their own reproductive lives.

Moral arguments against forced sterilization are, or should be, uncontroversial. Even if there is a valid reason for population control, it is obvious that a government should not sterilize people against their will. The work for feminist theorists with regard to enforced sterilization is not so much arguing against it, as showing that it happened, that it continues to happen, and illuminating the social conditions that lead to it and obscure it. Abortion, however, is trickier to debate. Like forced sterilization, abortion restrictions deny women the right to control their own bodies. But abortion involves killing a foetus, and so the case is more morally complex than that of forced sterilization. It is *not* obvious that abortion is morally permissible.

For many, the issue of contraception is closely related to the moral question of abortion. As with abortion, the view that it is wrong is often based on religious codes. Empirical questions arise in relation to what exactly the religious code forbids. Some methods of contraception prevent fertilization of the egg (such as the pill, which prevents ovulation, or barrier methods, which prevent the sperm reaching the egg). Others allow fertilization, but prevent implantation (such as the IUD). Perhaps the most controversial form of contraception, the morning after pill (commonly an emergency measure) works by preventing ovulation. There is a common misconception that the morning after pill is essentially an early abortion, that it works to undo an early pregnancy. In fact, it works just like the regular pill, in preventing an egg from being released.

From a feminist point of view, the pressing ethical issue is availability of contraception. If access to contraception is limited by a religious or moralistic state, or by poverty, women face enormous hardships in unwanted pregnancy and the risk of sexually transmitted diseases. It is naïve to think that women can control whether they become pregnant without contraception. Some can, but for many women, the choice to refuse sex is not a simple matter. There may be no choice at all, or it may involve heavy costs in terms of their relationship to men they are dependent on.

Before I get on to the main arguments, I will make a few brief remarks about the relationship between law and morality, and the nature of legal rights. First, it might be that something is morally problematic in some way and yet should not be illegal. Some have argued that the purpose of the law is to enforce morality, and this is given as a justification for criminalizing abortion, for example in the Catholic countries I mentioned. The idea is that (religious) morality forbids abortion, and so the law must forbid it too. But we needn't think that the purpose of the law is to enforce morality, and I think we ordinarily don't. Even many people who accept religious codes that, for example, forbid masturbation, or adulterous relationships, would say that this is not a sufficient reason for making such activities illegal. Rather, it is a reason for those who accept such codes to avoid them (and perhaps to preach and proselytize). One way to defend this sort of approach is to argue that there is some zone of behaviour that the law has no business governing. This is often justified using something like John Stuart Mill's famous harm principle. He argued that if a behaviour does not harm others, the state should not interfere.

However, it is *not* clear that abortion does not harm others: that is what makes the debate about the morality of abortion so difficult. Nonetheless, even if we think that there are moral problems with abortion, it is coherent to argue that it should be legal. The argument here does not use the harm principle; rather, it is a consequentialist, or forward-looking argument. The claim is that if abortion is illegal, then women will still have abortions, but they will be backstreet abortions, dangerous and expensive, supporting a criminal network. So, even if abortion is immoral, a pragmatic response is that it should be legal and carefully regulated. It is important to note that whether the bad effects of prohibiting abortion would be sufficient to justify allowing it depends on how bad abortion is, so this does not sidestep the moral argument entirely. For those who think that abortion is murder, no number of bad consequences of it being illegal would justify legalization. The point here is that law and morality do not *necessarily* go hand in hand. Whatever we think about the details of the issue in this case, the question of what the law should be is different to the moral verdict.

Having said that, if there is a moral right to abortion, then there should be a legal right. The relationship between law and morality is not symmetrical. We do think (and there are good reasons for thinking) that some immoral activities should not be prohibited by law. But what about the other direction? Obviously, some otherwise morally innocuous and morally permissible activities should be forbidden by law if that is necessary for coordination (for example, driving on the right in the UK, driving on the left in the USA). But when we ask whether some things we have a moral right to may be forbidden by law, the answer seems to be 'no'. If we have a moral right to abortion, the law should allow it.

Unfortunately, the notion of rights is not a simple one. In particular, there is an important complication here about the extent to which a right entails duties for others. A right obviously entails some duties: if you have a right to free speech, I have a duty not to silence you. But it is not at all clear that I have duties that go beyond that. In particular, it does not seem that a right entails a duty to help the person get the thing they have a right to. You may have a right to free speech, but I don't need to rush out and provide you with a sound system to broadcast your views. Universities must respect free speech rights, but that does not mean providing a platform to all those who request it. So, having a right is not having a right that others help you use that right. On the other hand, we should recognize that some rights are futile if the conditions do not allow them to be exercised. These issues come up in Chapter 13, on silencing, where I discuss the idea that women are permitted to speak in some merely formal sense, but in fact their speech is not heard.

The question of what a right to abortion means in practice comes up in policy. Do women have a right to financial or medical assistance to obtain an abortion? Do doctors have a right to refuse to perform abortions? As that example illustrates, the rights of others may limit a person's exercise of their rights. If the rights of others rule out them having duties to aid us in exercising our rights, our rights may not be very powerful. This turns out to be an important point in Judith Jarvis Thomson's argument about abortion, which I will get to shortly. Rather than arguing that a foetus has no right to life, she focusses on the way that a foetus's right to life might be limited.

The right to life

Traditional arguments about abortion start with the question, 'does the foetus have a right to life?' But we need to know what qualifies a being for a right to life, so the question becomes, 'is the foetus the sort of thing that has a right to life?' We might understand that as being a question about whether the foetus is a human, or a question about what qualities the foetus has (does it feel pain? Does it think?). Philosophers usually dispense with the first interpretation quickly. A foetus is certainly a human, that is, a member of the species *homo sapiens*, but merely being a member of a species is not enough for moral status. To think otherwise is the mistake that Peter Singer dubs 'speciesism'.[4]

So what matters is what intrinsic qualities the being has. It seems intuitively compelling that a conscious, sentient, emotional alien has more rights than a living but brain-dead human. (Imagine you can only save one of two creatures from a burning building – one is a human with irreversible brain death, the other is an intelligent alien, such as Spielberg's E.T.). Philosophers usually express this in terms of personhood: a creature that has the right set of qualities is a *person*, regardless of whether they are a human. If a creature is a person, then it has rights.

The question, then, is whether or not a foetus is a person. Mary Anne Warren suggests that there are five traits that are central to the concept of personhood. These are consciousness, including the capacity to feel pain; reasoning capacity; self-motivated activity; communication; and self-awareness.[5] Warren is not claiming that it is necessary to satisfy all of these to be a person. Rather, her claim is that something that satisfies none of these is not a person. She takes it as obvious that an embryo satisfies none of these and is therefore not a person. Warren recognizes that we may have strong emotions about unborn babies, particularly in the later stages of pregnancy, and the relationship between an embryo or foetus and the moral community can be relevant. However, the pregnant woman is a full moral agent, with a right to control her own body. Warren's point is that an embryo could not possibly have rights that would compete with the rights of an adult woman.

We need to think about whether it matters that there is no sharp dividing line between the non-person and the person. A bundle of cells slowly develops into a person. Someone might say, 'it is not permissible to kill babies, there is no sharp line between a baby and an embryo, so it is not permissible to kill embryos'. But that would be a bad argument. There may be a grey area between permissible and impermissible, but that does not change the fact that at one end there is a period when the foetus is not a person, and at the other end, a period when it is. Compare this argument: 'adults should be allowed to vote. But there is no sharp line between adults and children, so children should be allowed to vote too'. Clearly, when we are making laws, we just have to pick an arbitrary cut-off point. We can be more or less cautious in choosing our cut-off point. If the issue is voting, we might want to err on the side of letting people vote too young. If the issue is the age of consent, or consuming alcohol, we might want to err the other way, make the cut-off point later than it really could be. The cut-off point is arbitrary in one sense, but it is not completely arbitrary. When we are making laws, we need a line, and it needs to be somewhere, so approximately right is as good as it gets. The law is thus as good as it can be; it is not arbitrary. The moral situation is more complex. We do not need a cut-off point. So, if we are going to focus only on the morality of the situation, we can directly reflect the indeterminacy in the development of the foetus into a person and say that abortion is morally permissible for some period after conception, then it is morally unclear, and then it becomes impermissible.

Talking of personhood as the essential condition for a right to life leaves early term abortions as permissible. But some philosophical opponents of abortion have made a different suggestion, that what is important about a foetus is that it is a *potential* person. Left to its own devices, it will grow into a person. Michael Tooley gives a vivid example in his argument against that view. He imagines that there is a special serum that when injected into a kitten will turn it into a supercat, a cat that has all the qualities essential to personhood. Tooley points out that before the kitten has turned into a supercat, it is just a kitten like all the other kittens (Tooley assumes that kittens do not have a right to life). So it would not be wrong to refrain from injecting the serum and killing the kitten instead. And likewise, if the kitten has been injected, but has not yet developed into a supercat, it would not be wrong to kill it. The point is that a *potential X* is *not* an X: it does not have the qualities that are important. An acorn is not an oak tree.[6]

Warren also considers the possibility that potential persons have a right to life. Her response is more concessive than Tooley's. She acknowledges that there might be something morally important about a potential person, and that perhaps, other things being equal, we should not wantonly destroy them. But, she argues, the rights of a potential person couldn't possibly be strong enough to compete with a woman's right to abortion. Her thought here is the same as Tooley's: a potential X is not an X.

As Warren points out, the intrinsic properties of the foetus are not the only thing that is relevant to the morality of abortion. Feminists emphasize the point that pregnancy happens to women, and that the experiences of pregnancy and motherhood are life changing. As Margaret Little puts it,

> when entertaining the possibility that the foetus is a person, we have no way of acknowledging the kind of relationship that holds between the pregnant woman and this person: it turns up in the literature as either a relationship between strangers or with the woman dubbed a ready-made mother who is blithely assigned responsibilities of a kind and level unmatched by any other citizen.[7]

The reality of pregnancy, what it is like for women, should not be in the background. It is of central importance.

The moral right to abortion

One of the most famous articles on abortion is Judith Jarvis Thomson's 'A Defense of Abortion'. She argues that even if the foetus is a person, the woman has a right to abortion because she has a right to defend herself. What Thomson recognizes is that, at the very least, there is a conflict of rights. Even if foetuses have moral standing, we have to accept that the mother's life is impacted by pregnancy and birth, and that that matters. Other feminists have argued that issues around abortion are even more subtle and complex, and that we need to think, not just about rights, but about virtue, and love, and the nature of motherhood.

Thomson starts her argument by acknowledging that the issue of whether a foetus is a person is a tough one. She is prepared to allow (for the sake of argument) that a foetus is a person and even that it has a right to life. Her overall point is that women also have rights, and that the foetus's right to life does not necessarily override the woman's rights. Thomson uses an analogy:

The violinist example
You wake up one morning to find that you have been attached to a famous violinist and his body is currently surviving by using your kidneys. The Society of Music lovers kidnapped you. The doctors are very apologetic, but explain that if you were to disconnect yourself now, the violinist would die. If you stay connected, the violinist will be cured, and you can safely unplug after 9 months and walk away.

Thomson wants us to agree that if we woke up one day to find ourselves attached to a famous violinist, we would have the right to detach ourselves, even though the violinist has a right to life. The point is that the violinist does not have a right to use my body. Thomson is trying to get us to see that whether or not the foetus has a right to life is not decisive. A woman has a right to self-defence that trumps it. Thus, she concludes, abortion is permissible.

Of course, in this example, you have done nothing to bring about the situation where you are attached to the violinist. So the analogy might work for cases where a woman is raped, but it does not apply to pregnancy brought about through consensual sex. In that case, it seems that the women knowingly risked bringing another person into existence, and so is morally responsible for the outcome in a way that Thomson's violinist example does not capture.

Thomson recognizes that, and gives two more analogies to show that responsibility for another person's life cannot be acquired so easily. She asks us to think about whether opening the window on a hot day is equivalent to inviting a burglar in and giving him the right to stay. Thomson argues that it is not, even if a burglar getting in is something we knowingly risk when we open a window. But of course, you should be careful with windows. Insurance companies will not pay up in cases where a house has been left unsecured. They are saying, effectively, 'yes, you did invite the burglar in, now you must take the consequences!'

Thomson has another example, this time more fanciful, but perhaps a better analogy. She asks us to imagine that human reproduction works rather differently than it does. People seeds float about in the air, and, if they have the opportunity, will implant themselves in soft furnishings and grow into people. Of course, you could rid your house of any soft furnishings, but it seems fair to say that soft furnishings are a reasonable thing to want to have, so instead, you can put screens up over your windows to prevent the people seeds drifting in. Very occasionally, a people seed gets through even the best quality screens. So, let's imagine you had the best quality screens, and you used them carefully, following the instructions to the letter. You are unlucky, and a people seed gets in. Are you responsible? Does the person have a right to live in your home and be cared for by you? Thomson thinks not.

The major point behind Thomson's examples is that a right to life is not necessarily a right for others to take care of you. This is why she can grant that the foetus has a right to life. As Thomson puts it,

> In some views having a right to life includes having a right to be given at least the bare minimum one needs for continued life. But suppose that what in fact is the bare minimum a man needs for continued life is something he has no right at all to be given? If I am sick unto death, and the only thing that will save my life is the touch of Henry Fonda's cool hand on my fevered brow, then all the same, I have no right to be given the touch of Henry Fonda's cool hand on my fevered brow.[8]

Mary Anne Warren resists Thomson's attempt to circumvent the issue of whether the foetus is a person. Warren argues that pregnancy, except in cases of rape, is something that the woman has *risked*. She has engaged in voluntary behaviour that she knew could result in pregnancy. Warren is clearly right that when we take risks, we must take into account how bad the outcome might be. If the possible bad outcome is very bad indeed, then we should not take the risk, even if the chances of the bad outcome coming about are very small. For example, imagine that 1% of avocados are contaminated, and there is a chance that a contaminated avocado could kill you. There is no way to know which avocados are contaminated, so most of us would simply stop eating avocados, even though the chances of an avocado being fatal are pretty small. On the other hand, if the avocado would only make you slightly sick, it may well be rational to continue eating them.

The point about abortion is that if a foetus is a person, then abortion is murder. It would be grossly morally irresponsible to carry on having sex in conditions that risk pregnancy with the thought that the pregnancy could be terminated. We don't risk having to commit murder. If people seeds were actually tiny little people, just like us but smaller, we would not kill them when they implanted in our soft furnishings. In other words, it is only because the foetus is not a person that Thomson's argument is at all convincing.

Towards the end of her article, Thomson brings up another issue, one that is not expressible in the language of rights. She says that although the foetus's right to life does not impose duties to keep it alive on the mother, there may be a different sort of issue here. It may be sometimes morally *indecent* for a woman to have an abortion. Thomson has in mind cases where the costs of carrying to term or the benefits of termination are not great. Imagine that pregnancy only lasted an hour. Or imagine that someone wants an abortion at seven months pregnant in order to avoid the inconvenience of rescheduling a holiday. In such cases, Thomson argues, there is a still a right to abortion. But to have an abortion for trivial reasons, such as postponing a holiday, would be very bad indeed.

It is worth expanding on the difference between decency and rights, as it is not a completely straightforward issue and is often overlooked in discussions of Thomson. Moral rights are complex things, and philosophers have argued about them a lot. But here is one thing that seems fairly clear: if you have a right to do something, you are morally permitted to do it.

This is a very minimal assessment. It says nothing about whether it would be a good thing for you to do it, or whether it would be a virtuous thing. There is room for moral criticism even when one is acting within one's rights. Thomson has yet another analogy to make that point: imagine that a boy is given a box of chocolates. They are his chocolates, and so (other things being equal) he does not have to share them with his brother. He has the right to eat them all. But it would not be generous of him to eat them all. It would be mean.

Thomson's appraisal in terms of decency is designed to capture these other sorts of assessment. She argues that women always have a right to abortion. But it could be morally criticizable to have one in some circumstances. I stress this aspect of Thomson's view to emphasize that her approach may have anticipated, and may be consistent with, some of the later feminist discussions of abortion.

Pregnancy

Rosalind Hursthouse, arguing that virtue ethics can provide useful moral guidance, applies a virtue ethical framework to the question of abortion. Hursthouse says that "whether women have a moral right to terminate their pregnancies is irrelevant within virtue theory, for it is irrelevant to the question, 'In having an abortion in these circumstances, would the agent be acting virtuously, or viciously, or neither?'."[9] Hursthouse proceeds to give a very rich and subtle account of the various considerations a virtuous person would take into account. Hursthouse emphasizes that killing a foetus is never going to be something undertaken lightly, something that a purely rights-based analysis does not focus on. But the different situations that women find themselves in make a difference to what sort of considerations make abortion the best answer to an unwanted or complicated pregnancy. And even when it is the best answer, the moral situation may be more complex than the permissible/impermissible framework allows. Perhaps the woman lacks the virtues required to raise a child, and so although having an abortion is sensible, it is not entirely virtuous. Or perhaps she is somewhat responsible for the pregnancy (perhaps she was careless).

One could see Hursthouse's approach as an alternative to Thomson's. But one could also see it as a development of some of Thomson's remarks about decency. Thomson agrees that there can be moral issues beyond rights. The circumstances, the reasons for doing what you have a right to do, are morally important too. As philosophers, we want to talk about morality and law, and we want to deliver some clear conclusions about those things. There are important black and white questions: Is abortion morally permissible? Should it be legal? But there are also hard questions about other moral assessments, and about what these experiences mean for people like us, and we should leave room for those.

Margaret Little develops the thought that is foundational in Thomson's article, that it is crucial for the woman that the foetus is *in her body*. As Little explains this, the issue is not just that the foetus is a passenger; the important point is that to be pregnant is to be in an intimate relationship with another being. Little starts by pointing out that there is something odd about the rights argument, which sets up a conflict between the foetus's right to life and the mother's right to do what she wants with her body. If someone seriously thinks that a foetus has an absolute right to life, inconvenience and discomfort for the mother would be irrelevant.

Indeed, some people do take that extreme position. However, the argument usually proceeds by investigating the limits of a right to life, just as Thomson argues is appropriate. And if the right to life has limits, Little argues, we need a discussion of the sorts of concern that make a difference. Given that the nature of pregnancy is clearly what makes a difference, that should be playing a central role in arguments about when a pregnancy can be terminated.

Little argues that an unwanted pregnancy is a serious harm. There are, of course, harms and health risks in pregnancy, and there can be harms associated with the subordination of women (I return to that below), but the harm that insufficient attention has been paid to, Little argues, is the harm of an unwelcome intimacy. The fact that a wanted pregnancy can be so joyous illustrates this point: pregnancy is a major change, and so it can be a wonderful intermingling. But it can also be "an invasive occupation in which the self feels subsumed".[10]

Little rejects the claim that a pregnancy that results from voluntary sex is very different to a conception that was non-consensual. Little points out that consenting to sex knowing that there is a risk of pregnancy is not the same as consenting to a pregnancy. In general, consenting to one thing is not consenting to another thing that may or may not follow from the consented-to thing. And even if one has consented to a risk of pregnancy, that does not entail that one has consented to gestate rather than have an abortion. Thus there is no simple argument from voluntary sex to the impermissibility of abortion.

Little argues that in thinking about a possible duty to gestate, we should keep the realities and complexities of pregnancy and parenthood in mind. She suggests that the best framework for thinking about these things is relationship ethics, thinking about the special obligations and permissions that arise in the context of personal relationships. Women who become pregnant find themselves in some sort of relationship with a foetus, but the sort of relationship that it is varies with the circumstances. Sometimes the relationship is motherhood in a rich sense from the start, at other times it is not. This, Little says, makes sense of the way that the duty to gestate strikes us as varied and underdetermined. There is no general rule about abortion, but, rather, particular and varied relevant relationships in each case.

The broader context of oppression

It is important to keep in mind that control of women's reproductive capacities is not isolated from more general conditions of oppression. The reality is that in most, if not all places, women are not fully in control of their own sexuality, their own contraception, or their own future. On the contrary, access to contraception is often difficult or impossible, women are generally subordinated, and in particular they are raped, and the reality of having a child is that the child will be the woman's responsibility, and that the world will not be a helpful place; women can face unemployment, homelessness, and other enormous hardships as a result of motherhood. We are not in a situation where it is easy for women to avoid pregnancy, and we are not in a situation where a child is always a blessing. These issues are compounded by racism. As Angela Davis points out, Black women's relationship to the struggle for abortion rights was different to white women's, in that Black women often sought abortions because they did not want to bring a child into poverty, rather than because they did not want a child.[11]

Alison Jaggar focusses on the wider oppressive conditions in considering the morality of abortion.[12] She argues that the fact that the burdens of motherhood will fall on women means that women have authority to make a decision about abortion. Her point is not that all abortions are morally permissible; her point is that in an already unjust situation, it is crucial that women have a legal right to terminate pregnancies. She readily admits that this argument is not an argument for an absolute moral right to abortion. Rather, it is an argument about the social situation we are actually in, in most parts of the world. The fact is that bearing and raising a child is much more likely to be a damaging burden for women than fathering a child is. If the world were different, then women would be less badly impacted by pregnancy, and perhaps there would be fewer abortions.

Sally Markowitz objects that Jaggar's account is like the traditional approaches to abortion, in being very focussed on personal autonomy. Markowitz agrees that the patriarchal conditions we are actually in make a difference to what we should say about abortion. She argues more directly that abortion rights are needed to end sexism. Markowitz proposes a principle, the 'impermissible sacrifice principle', according to which "When one social group in a society is systematically oppressed by another, it is impermissible to require the oppressed group to make sacrifices that will exacerbate or perpetuate this oppression".[13] In other words, women should not be required to bear children in a situation where that will make sexist oppression worse. Markowitz takes it as a virtue of this proposal that it talks about groups rather than individuals, and that it does not focus on individual rights. This raises an issue that I discussed in the introduction to this book, about whether feminists should be concerned with autonomy and individual rights. But even if we think (as I do) that women's autonomy and rights should be the primary concern for feminists, we could agree with Markowitz's principle as a way of adjudicating between competing moral demands.

Practical issues about reproductive rights

As I acknowledged in the introductory section, the idea of a right is not a simple one. Most feminists argue that women have a right to abortion, and the public discussion is usually framed in terms of 'abortion rights'. However, a lot hangs on how we understand this right in law and policy. Is it a robust right, which entails that the state ensure that it can be exercised? Or is it instead merely a right not to be interfered with?

The feminist legal theorist Catharine MacKinnon argues that *Roe v Wade* is formulated in problematic ways and does not grant a very robust right. She explains that *Roe v Wade* falls under a constitutional right to privacy. Abortion is conceived of as a private matter for a woman to decide: a personal choice. As MacKinnon puts it, abortion is granted as a private privilege, not a right. This means that *Roe v Wade* does not mandate that state funding be provided for abortion. This was decided in a later case, *Harris v McRae* (1981), in which the court stated (as reported by MacKinnon) that "although the government may not place obstacles in the path of a woman's exercise of her freedom of choice, it need not remove those not of its own creation".[14] MacKinnon argues that this approach, non-interference, does not protect the autonomy of women. Rather, privacy laws only protect the autonomy of people who already have power: men. MacKinnon's point here meshes with the feminist slogan, 'the personal is political'. As many feminist political theorists have pointed out, the idea that there is a realm of behaviour that the government should not interfere in has not helped equality, but left women vulnerable in the 'private' spheres of family and sex. (I discussed some of these issues in the chapter on work and care).

The reality for women seeking abortion in the United States is that the government does not recognize a duty to help. If women are already in a position of vulnerability – if they are poor, or in an abusive relationship, geographically isolated, not a native speaker of English – they may, in reality, not be able to get an abortion. Susan Sherwin's discussion of abortion takes these practical points very seriously.[15] Sherwin argues that it is not enough to legalize abortion. Abortion providers should be accessible for everyone, and the experience should be dignified and should respect the woman's autonomy in deciding on an abortion. The current situation is often far from that, even in places where abortion is legal.

In the US, federal law mandates abortion on demand for a non-viable foetus, and further, forbids regulation that puts an 'undue burden' on women seeking an abortion. Yet many states have passed restrictive laws that require women considering an abortion to undergo an ultrasound, and, in some cases, the regulations require that the woman view the ultrasound.[16] As of 2020, these laws are still going through the courts. Some have been struck down but have been reallowed by a court of appeal. State decisions to close abortion clinics are likewise being tested in court. The current Supreme Court is majority opposed to *Roe v Wade*, so the future for abortion rights in the United States is very uncertain.

The same points apply to the availability of contraception. It is one thing not to ban contraception, but for many women that does not mean that contraception is readily available. If we think that contraception is a right, then it seems that the state should make sure that it is a right that women can avail themselves of without hardship, and with dignity. Access to contraception can be limited in various ways. Education about contraception is the first step: without that, young people are unable to make informed choices. Second, whether or not contraception is publicly funded makes an enormous difference to many women.

For public health policy about both abortion and contraception, an interesting question arises about the choices of individual healthcare providers not to offer birth control on the basis of their own religious or moral beliefs. On the one hand, it could be argued that the state must decide whether these things are public goods, and, if they are, compel all providers to offer them. On the other hand, it might be argued that these things are a matter of private conscience, and that if some providers do not wish to offer them, that does not infringe on the rights of patients. Most bioethicists writing on the topic advocate a compromise position, which allows that there is a right to conscientious objection, but that certain conditions should be met, for example, that a referral is made to another non-objecting provider nearby.

Carolyn McLeod takes a stronger line, arguing on feminist grounds that the right of conscientious refusal should be extremely limited in practice.[17] She acknowledges that conscientious refusals can be morally important. McLeod contrasts refusal to provide abortion or contraception with refusals that target particular groups, for example, refusing reproductive healthcare to LGBTQ+ people. As McLeod points out, such refusals are clearly discriminatory, and the right to conscientious objection does not extend to that sort of case. But a conscientious objection to abortion is itself non-discriminatory. However, McLeod points out that conscientious objections to abortion and contraception are related to sexist views about women's rights and autonomy.

McLeod argues that in a patriarchal society, refusals are more than mere inconvenience for a patient – they are actively harmful, even if a patient can access the same service somewhere else. Focussing on emergency contraception, she points out that there is considerable stigma attached to requesting this kind of contraception, often related to oppressive stereotypes of 'loose' or 'irresponsible' women. A pharmacist or other healthcare provider refusing to dispense it can reinforce that oppressive view. Further, a society that permits conscientious refusals sends a message to patients who seek abortion or contraception, that they are not respected, that their autonomy over their own body is not an important value. In the end, McLeod concludes that conscientious objection should be severely restricted, and that healthcare providers should prioritize patients over their own conscience.

McLeod's observation, that we should not ignore the sexist and oppressive background of conscientious refusals to provide birth control, takes us back to an idea I floated in the introduction to this chapter. What is really going on behind today's anti-abortion movements? As pro-choice campaigners often point out, the pro-life supporters exhibit many hypocrisies and inconsistencies. They (by 'they' I mean officials of the political parties and anti-abortion lobbyists) argue for the sanctity of the foetus's life, but do not support providing mothers or children with healthcare or welfare support. They often argue for cutting funds for contraception for low income women. They pay no attention to miscarriages, which, if a foetus is a human life as sacred as any other, would seem to be a great tragedy and something that would perhaps require significant research funding. They do not always respect the life of the woman (the most extreme anti-abortionists argue that abortion is impermissible even when the woman will die), and they are often cavalier about the lives of innocent adults in other contexts, for example, the lives of refugees or undocumented immigrants.

Hypocrisies and inconsistencies do not undermine the isolated argument against abortion, but they do undermine the platform. As feminists often point out, there is some reason to think that the anti-abortion movement is not about the rights of the foetus. So what is it about? It is not implausible that it is about controlling women. Now this, of course, is what philosophers call an 'ad hominem' argument. It is an accusation of cynical motives. I am arguing that we should not trust the people who argue against abortion. It is not about their arguments in themselves, and so, in that sense, this is not a philosophical argument. But there are philosophical issues here: the nature of oppression, false consciousness, how ideology works. Part of the task of feminist philosophy is to look beyond particular issues and to try to understand what the patterns of oppression are.

Summary

Feminists have argued that we need to broaden our focus from a narrow view of what rights the foetus has to looking at the mother's rights too. Thomson argues that even if the foetus does have rights, these are not rights to use the woman's body, and the woman has a right to defend herself. Thus Thomson argues, there is a moral right, and there should be a legal right to abortion.

We can add to that that the language of rights may not capture all that there is to be said about the morality of the situation; we need to look at the nature of pregnancy, and at the moral complexities surrounding a woman's decision to continue a pregnancy or not. Margaret Little argues that the experience of pregnancy is an experience of a special sort of intimacy, and that this should not be imposed on people without their consent. Rosalind Hursthouse argues that abortion is morally complex, and the situation cannot be fully explored using only the framework of rights: even if there is a right to abortion, it is not always a virtuous thing to do.

But perhaps we need to go even further, and look at the context that surrounds pregnancy and motherhood. Feminists are concerned to identify structural issues, ways that societies are arranged, both formally and informally, to disadvantage women. We should take into account that women's options are often limited, and that, in a patriarchal society, the experience of bearing and raising a child can be extremely costly to the mother. In a patriarchal society, limiting women's control of their reproductive capacities compounds their oppression. These are contextual – and so variable – facts, but they are the actual context for many women.

Finally, feminist theorists such as Catharine MacKinnon and Susan Sherwin have pointed out that talk of abortion rights must be made more precise. We need to know what sort of right it is, whether it is a right merely to non-interference, or if it is a more robust right: a right to assistance and dignity. In practice, even when abortion and contraception are not banned, they may be difficult to access, and that practical issue raises important questions of justice.

Notes

1 www.theguardian.com/world/2018/jan/11/polish-mps-reject-liberalised-abortion-laws-but-back-new-restrictions.
2 See Threadcraft, *Intimate Justice: The Black Female Body and the Body Politic*, ch. 1 for a brief history of forced sterilization in the United States.
3 As reported by the Center for Investigative Reporting.
4 Singer, *Practical Ethics*.
5 Warren, 'On the Moral and Legal Status of Abortion', p.55.
6 Tooley, 'Abortion and Infanticide'.
7 Little, 'Abortion, Intimacy and the Duty to Gestate', p.296.
8 Thomson, 'A Defense of Abortion', p.55.
9 Hursthouse, 'Virtue Theory and Abortion', p.235.
10 Op. cit., p.303.
11 Davis, *Women, Race, and Class*, p.204.
12 Jaggar, 'Abortion and a Woman's Right to Decide'.
13 Markowitz, 'Abortion and Feminism', p.7.
14 MacKinnon, *Feminism Unmodified*, p.96.
15 Sherwin, 'Abortion Through a Feminist Ethics Lens'.
16 According to the Guttmacher Institute: www.guttmacher.org/state-policy/explore/requirements-ultrasound.
17 McLeod, *Conscience in Reproductive Health Care: Prioritizing Patient Interests*. See also her earlier paper, 'Referral in the Wake of Conscientious Objection to Abortion'.

Further reading

Boonin, David (2002) *A Defense of Abortion*. Cambridge University Press. (Liberal defence of abortion focussing on the status of the foetus).

Kamm, F.M. (1992) *Creation and Abortion: A Study in Moral and Legal Philosophy*. Oxford University Press. (Deontological account of the principles involved in killing a foetus).

Shrage, Laurie (2003) *Abortion and Social Responsibility: Depolarizing the Debate*. Oxford University Press. (Focusses on the practical and political issues related to *Roe v Wade* and argues for alternative legal strategies).

Steinbock, Bonnie (2012) *Life Before Birth*. Oxford University Press (2nd ed.). (Examination of the moral and legal status of foetuses).

Tooley, Michael, Wolf-Devine, Celia, Devine, Philip E., and Jaggar, Alison M. (2009) *Abortion: Three Perspectives*. Oxford University Press. (Contrasting accounts of the morality of abortion).

Warren, Mary Anne (2000) *Moral Status: Obligations to Persons and Other Living Things*. Oxford University Press. (A comprehensive account of moral status and correlated rights, defending the view that moral status comes in degrees).

4 Pornography

"Pornography as a mirror shows us how men see women. Not all men, of course – but the ways in which many men who accept the conventional conception of masculinity see women. It is unsettling to look into that mirror."

Robert Jensen, *Getting Off: Pornography and the End of Masculinity*

Chapter overview: In this chapter I examine pornography as a legal and political issue (for philosophy of language approaches, see Chapter 13 on silencing). I discuss Andrea Dworkin and Catharine MacKinnon's argument that pornography is a grave harm to women, and examine whether there may nonetheless be a free speech or moral right to pornography. I examine the harm claim, asking whether pornography is harmful to women and what sort of harm that might be (including how men may be harmed by pornography). I close by looking at the possibility of feminist pornography.

Introduction

Sexually explicit material has been a part of human culture as far back as we know. Since the late 1990s the internet has made pornography available to more people than ever, and it seems that pornography consumption has increased accordingly. According to Pornhub, one of the major internet porn sites, 2019 saw over 42 billion visits to the site, which means there was an average of 115 million visits per day. As Pornhub itself says, "One-Hundred-Fifteen Million – that's the equivalent of the populations of Canada, Australia, Poland and the Netherlands all visiting in one day!"[1] Pornhub reports on its traffic, search terms, and user statistics in jaunty tones. For example, in their account of the top search terms for 2019 they say,

> Cosplay was another popular search for this year . . . 2019 seemed to be a year for dressing up and partaking in all those other-worldly desires everydayness doesn't afford us! Mature searches also defined 2019, with the rise of GILF porn and categories people are now free to indulge in their aged-to-perfection fantasies. Bisexuality was also a definitive term, why choose when you can have both?[2]

Pornhub presents pornography as joyful expression of human sexuality. And sometimes, surely, that's just what it is. However, feminists worry that some pornography is disturbingly misogynist, and that it is harmful to women in both direct and indirect ways. Feminist philosophers have tried to pin down what the problem is with certain depictions of women in pornography. It is not immediately obvious that something that is intended to be merely fantasy, a masturbation aid, should be criticized for being misogynist. But of course, sexual fantasy does not always stay in the realm of fantasy. Moreover, pornography might have a role in creating and reinforcing ideas about women that result in real harms. Even if the harms of pornography can be elaborated, it is a further question what should be done. These are hard questions, and feminists do not agree about the answers.

One of the central arguments in the feminist discussion of pornography is Catharine MacKinnon's claim that pornography subordinates and silences women. In this chapter I examine those claims as issues in political philosophy. What sort of harm is done to women, and what political action is justified? In the chapter on silencing in Part 2 I examine a rather different way of approaching these issues. Rae Langton, Jennifer Hornsby, and others have deployed a philosophy of language framework to make sense of the subordination and silencing claims, and there is a large literature discussing that approach. In this chapter I focus on political and legal theory.

We need to think about how to define pornography. The simplest definition says that pornography is sexually explicit material that is primarily designed to produce sexual arousal. This is a broad definition, which includes anything that we think of as pornography. People sometimes try to make a distinction between erotica and pornography, according to which erotica is tasteful, or artistic, or subtle, or something along those lines. Some pornography is certainly more aesthetically valuable than other pornography, but, on its own, that is not an important distinction. As porn actor Gloria Leonard is said to have proclaimed, "the difference between pornography and erotica is lighting."

I suspect that the aesthetic claims about pornography are really grasping towards a moral distinction, between pornography that is morally acceptable and pornography that is morally bad. The idea that aesthetic merit can redeem pornography has its roots in obscenity laws, which make artistic merit a defence against an obscenity charge. But aesthetic distinctions won't necessarily map onto moral distinctions. Something that is aesthetically stunning can be morally bad, and something that is aesthetically offensive can be morally pure.

Some feminist philosophers, notably Catharine MacKinnon, make a distinction between pornography and erotica that is a *moral* distinction. In their anti-pornography civil ordinance, which became law briefly in Indianapolis in 1984 (but was subsequently overturned as unconstitutional), Andrea Dworkin and Catharine MacKinnon define pornography as:

> the graphic sexually explicit subordination of women through pictures and/or words that also includes one or more of the following:
>
> a. women are presented dehumanized as sexual objects, things or commodities; or
> b. women are presented as sexual objects who enjoy humiliation or pain; or

c.   women are presented as sexual objects experiencing sexual pleasure in rape, incest, or other sexual assault; or

d.   women are presented as sexual objects tied up or cut up or mutilated or bruised or physically hurt; or

e.   women are presented in postures or positions of sexual submission, servility, or display; or

f.   women's body parts - including but not limited to vaginas, breasts, or buttocks - are exhibited such that women are reduced to those parts; or

g.   women are presented being penetrated by objects or animals; or

h.   women are presented in scenarios of degradation, humiliation, injury, torture, shown as filthy or inferior, bleeding, bruised, or hurt in a context that makes these conditions sexual.

The use of men, children, or transsexuals in the place of women in (a)-(h) of this definition is also pornography for purposes of this law.[3]

It could be objected that this definition begs the question: if we define pornography like that, of course it is problematic. But Dworkin and MacKinnon are not trying to argue that sexually explicit material in the sense above is sexist; they take that as obvious. Rather they focus on that sort of material, which they take to be very common, and argue that it is harmful enough that it ought to be taken seriously as an issue of public good. It is not just a private matter.

Feminists who argue against pornography allow that sexually explicit material that is *not* sexist is conceptually possible, if not common. Their objection is to what we can call 'inegalitarian pornography'. But it is usually taken as a matter of empirical fact that the mass of material that is consumed, the material that is widely available in print, on the internet, and in live shows, is pornography in something approaching Dworkin and MacKinnon's sense.

Is this an accurate assessment of the content of popular pornography? A 2010 study claims that 88% of popular pornographic films contain physical aggression against women.[4] A more recent study is much more conservative in its estimate, but for some reason excluded spanking and gagging from physical violence.[5] That raises the question: when is spanking physical aggression and when is it not? Despite these problems, it is fairly safe to say that a lot of mainstream pornography depicts the subordination of women, whether that is subordination through violence, or subordination in more mundane ways, such as showing men in the dominant role, showing women as submissive, focussing on penetration as the definition and the male orgasm as the aim of sex.

This conclusion is shared by Robert Jensen. Jensen has spent over 20 years studying pornography. His 2007 book, *Getting Off: Pornography and the End of Masculinity*, includes detailed content and textual analysis of mainstream pornography. He argues that mainstream pornography relies heavily on increasingly extreme mistreatment of women, a fact that we try to ignore. As he puts it, "People routinely assume that pornography is such a difficult and divisive issue because it's about sex. In fact, this culture [the USA] struggles unsuccessfully with pornography because it is about men's cruelty to women, and the pleasure men sometimes take in that cruelty. And that is much more difficult for people - men and women - to face."[6]

I accept MacKinnon and Dworkin's empirical claim that most mainstream pornography is inegalitarian. However, in what follows I will use a more neutral definition of pornography than MacKinnon and Dworkin do. I will simply mean 'sexually explicit material designed to arouse'. I focus on complaints about inegalitarian pornography, leaving open the possibility that feminist pornography could or does exist.

The possibility of feminist pornography illustrates the important difference between the feminist objection to pornography and moralistic objections. One account of what is wrong with pornography is that it is immoral in itself, that there is some moral rule, religious or secular, that forbids sexually explicit material. Pornography is, of course, designed to aid masturbation, and masturbation has a long history of being outlawed by various different sorts of moral code. So it is easy to see how pornography can end up classified as immoral. I will not spend long on this idea, which tends not to be endorsed by feminists. The feminist argument against pornography is not that it is immoral because it is sexually explicit, but that it is harmful to women.

Alternatively, pornography might be thought to be immoral because it is obscene. The idea of 'obscenity' is an obscure one, usually explained in equally obscure terms, such as prurience or lewdness. One of the earliest definitions of obscenity is from the British case *Regina v Hicklin* (1868). The Hicklin rule provided the following test for obscenity: "whether the tendency of the matter . . . is to deprave and corrupt those whose minds are open to such immoral influences, and into whose hands a publication of this sort may fall." Later definitions in US laws are based on 'appealing to prurient interests' (*Roth v United States*, 1957). The definition that still stands says that obscene material must appeal to prurient interests or depict offensive sexual acts, and also includes as a necessary condition that the material lack artistic value. In Britain, a new obscenity act in 1959 also introduced the public good as a defence. In other words, if the material could be shown to be "in the interests of science, literature, art or learning, or of other objects of general concern", it could not be banned under the obscenity act. Famously, Penguin Books was tried under the new act for the publication of *Lady Chatterley's Lover*. The book was deemed to have sufficient artistic merit to escape the obscenity charge.

In Canada in 1992, as a result of the case *R. v Butler*, the obscenity law was changed so that the definition of obscenity was not based on public decency, but on harms to women. Very recently in the UK (2019), the Obscenity Act has been amended so that there is no longer a list of obscenities. The items that were dropped (and so no longer necessarily count as obscene) include depictions of sadomasochism, torture with instruments, bondage, and activities involving 'perversion', such as urinating or defecating. Instead, the emphasis is put on harm and consent. The new guidelines say that so long as the activities depicted are consensual and do not involve serious harm, they are unlikely to be prosecuted.

This movement in law is reflected in and reflects a more general attitude shift that I think is gradually (though not uniformly) happening in Western and many non-Western countries. First, the liberal idea that what we do consensually, in the privacy of our own homes, is nobody else's business, has gained traction in public opinion, law, and policy over the last 50 years. As I explain below, this is one of the classic principles of liberalism.

Second, a more general tolerance seems to be growing. Obscenity laws were often used disproportionately against forms of sexuality that were considered deviant, particularly gay and lesbian sexualities. In other words, the very idea of obscenity is morally laden in ways that are objectionable to liberal egalitarian sensibilities.

Furthermore, as Kimberlé Crenshaw points out, obscenity laws have also been deployed in ways that are clearly racist. She uses the example of the 1990 prosecution of the rap group, 2 Live Crew, for obscenity. Crenshaw does not deny that 2 Live Crew's lyrics are misogynistic. Her point is that, "Even the most superficial comparison between 2 Live Crew and other mass-marketed sexual representations suggests the likelihood that race played some role in distinguishing 2 Live Crew as the first group ever to be prosecuted for obscenity".[7]

For these reasons, feminists are unlikely to avail themselves of the idea of obscenity in criticizing pornography. First, it implies commitment to a rigid and illiberal moral view. Second, even if the laws are formulated in acceptable ways, the application of the law is very prone to abuse.

The right to pornography

If obscenity is a morally loaded idea, often used to oppress marginalized groups, then it might seem that pornography should be permitted, that we do not have the right to interfere with each other's sexual preferences. John Stuart Mill's famous harm principle, presented in *On Liberty*, says that the only justification for interfering with freedom is harm to others. According to Mill, we should not interfere with someone's freedom for their own good (he is anti-paternalist), or for the sake of what we think is morally right.

Clearly, if harm can justify interference, the liberal defence of pornography does not extend to child abuse images, or pornography that involves real as opposed to simulated violence. In what follows, I will focus on pornography featuring adult actors, in which any violence depicted is simulated. So the question is whether that sort of material is harmful. Obviously, we need to know what counts as harm. This is a complicated question. Mill himself discusses two difficult cases, mere offence, and harms due to fair competition, both of which he thinks can be permissible. Fair competition is not relevant here, but 'mere offence' is. The history of obscenity laws in Britain can be read as a shift from taking pornography to be a harm, something that would 'deprave and corrupt', to taking it to be a mere offence.

If pornography merely causes offence, then it seems that it is protected by a right to free speech. Indeed, in the United States, the first amendment, which grants the right to freedom of speech, has been used to defend the rights of pornographers against censorship. It is a cherished principle of free societies, that citizens have the right to say what they want, even if that offends others. Of course, it is somewhat odd to say that pornography is speech, but the idea behind the free speech defence of pornography is clear enough: some people may be offended by pornography, but that does not justify censorship.

However, the right to free speech is not absolute, either morally, or in law. The legal exceptions to the presumption in favour of free speech include: words that will bring about clear evils, fighting words, libel, obscenity, false advertising, advertising of dangerous products. These exceptions demonstrate a recognition that speech can be harmful, and harmful in ways that make it impermissible. So the question is whether pornography is harmful in these impermissible ways. Susan Brison argues that degrading and violent pornography is not protected by free speech principles because it is harmful in exactly the impermissible ways laid out in the exceptions to free speech protection. In particular, she argues that pornography is sometimes 'group libel'. It says false things about women, and is thereby harmful.[8] The free speech defence of pornography thus depends on the cogency of arguments about the harms of pornography.

There is a different way to argue that there is a right to pornography that does not depend on it falling under a right to free speech. Ronald Dworkin's suggestion is that people have a right to pornography based on a right to moral independence. Dworkin's point is that other people's moral disapproval is not sufficient grounds for limiting freedom. As he puts it, "a right not to suffer disadvantage in the distribution of social goods and opportunities, including disadvantage in the liberties permitted to them by the criminal law, just on the ground that their officials or fellow citizens think that their opinions about the right way for them to lead their own lives are ignoble or wrong."[9]

It is clear from that quote that Dworkin takes objections to pornography to be based on moral offence, rather than more serious harms. Dworkin's argument takes pornography to be a neutral sexual preference, one that is as a matter of fact disapproved of by a puritanical moral majority, but probably should not be. (It is worth pointing out that Dworkin was writing in 1981. Attitudes may have changed.) Dworkin does not rule out the idea that non-moralized harm (that is to say, physical, emotional, or other actual harm) could justify restrictions on pornography. Feminists argue that, in reality, the pornography that is out there is in fact harmful, and so that it is not the sort of thing that people have a right to, even on Dworkin's own conception. So the issue is, what sort of harm does pornography do? Is the harm sufficient to overturn the freedom of pornography makers and consumers to do what they want?

I come to the question of what sort of harm pornography might do in the next section, but it is worth making one more preliminary point. We should not assume that the only possible response to concluding that pornography is harmful is to favour censorship. There might be other legal solutions, such as the one that Andrea Dworkin and Catharine MacKinnon suggest, which is to allow civil action against pornographers for harms done. It is also worth noting that we need not think of censorship as part of an Orwellian dystopia, nor as an impossible and unwieldy criminalization. The British Advertising Standards Authority recently banned sexist stereotypes in advertising. This is not a legally enforceable ban, but a ban introduced as a self-regulatory move. Something similar in the pornography industry seems at least possible. There are also non-legal solutions, such as education, counter speech, and protest. Societal change sometimes comes about from the bottom up rather the top down, through public awareness rather than through legislative action.

Harm to women

There are various ways that pornography might be harmful. First, it might be that women are exploited in the making of pornography. If the production of pornography always, or usually, hurts women, then that is obviously good grounds for worrying about it. Historically, it seems highly likely that the production of pornography has been very problematic, and this is confirmed by testimony of actors in pornographic films.[10] However, this is a purely contingent fact. There doesn't seem to be any principled reason why pornography could not be made with fair pay and good working conditions. (Some of the same issues will arise that I cover in the chapter on sex work). This is not to say that working conditions for porn actors is not a real issue: it is a real and important issue. Pornography is big business, and like most big business, it has a seedy underbelly. In the pornography industry, the seedy underbelly is a larger proportion of the business than in non-sex based industries. Thus the harms of production are pressing. The solutions here are in some ways the same solutions as apply to any exploitative working conditions: unionization, regulation, and so on.

Another feminist argument against pornography is independent of the way that pornography is made. The worry is that consumption of pornography may cause harm. Pornography, it is said, objectifies women (I discuss objectification in Chapter 10), and consuming pornography may cause men to have sexist attitudes, to think of women as sex objects, or as having secondary status. It may shape male and female sexual desire – in particular, shape male desire in a way that is problematic for women. Pornography presents an unrealistic picture of arousal and satisfaction, and young people who learn about sex from pornography risk developing a distorted set of expectations. Finally, pornography may cause men to rape women, for example by trivializing rape, or by making it seem that women welcome rape.

MacKinnon's influential account of the problems with pornography argues that all of these harms happen. She also makes another claim that is harder to get to grips with, that pornography *is*, as well as causes, the subordination of women. This claim on its own is not easy to parse, but various feminist philosophers have tried in different ways to defend it. I discuss Langton and Hornsby's philosophy of language approach in Chapter 13 on speech acts and silencing. In this chapter I discuss an alternative understanding of MacKinnon's subordination argument.

Let's start with the causal claim, that pornography causes the subordination of women. MacKinnon does not think that such harms are easily quantifiable. Her picture is a complex one, about the role that pornography plays in our society. She complains that,

> The dominant view is pornography must cause harm just as car accidents cause harm, or its effects are not cognizable as harm. The trouble with this individuated, atomistic, linear, exclusive, isolated, narrowly tort like – in a word, positivistic – conception of injury is that the way pornography targets and defines women for abuse and discrimination does not work like this.[11]

MacKinnon urges us to think about the way that sexuality is formed. We like to think of it as coming 'from the stork', but, MacKinnon argues, we should be suspicious of that view, which in the end serves the patriarchy. She says, "A theory of sexuality becomes feminist to the extent it treats sexuality as a social construct of male power: defined by men, forced on women, and constitutive in the meaning of gender."[12] In other words, our ideas about sex, and about men and women, are not natural or innate; rather, they come from our society, and as our society is a sexist one, the ideas about gender and sexuality that we have are bound to be sexist.

MacKinnon criticizes the 'neo-Freudian sexual revolution' of the 1960s for what she saw as its ill thought out, and ultimately sexist, 'sex positivity'. MacKinnon complains that the 'derepression movement', encouraging women to become less sexually repressed, was not really about liberating women's sexuality, but about improving men's access to sex with women.

Sex is defined on the model of male sexuality as primary (more important) and dominating. The sex act is penetration, the end of the sex act is male orgasm. These conceptualizations, MacKinnon says, are not liberating to women. The idea of the liberated woman that comes out of the sexual revolution is not good for women – it does not liberate them sexually or any other way, it is rather a construct of patriarchy.

Pornography plays a crucial role in this story. According to MacKinnon, "pornography is a means through which sexuality is socially constructed".[13] Pornography makes gender inequality socially and sexually real: "pornography sexualises gender and genders sexuality". Pornography creates a picture of sexuality in which sexuality consists of female submission to the male. The forms vary from soft core to hard core, but the basic structure is always the same.

MacKinnon emphasizes the continuity between 'ordinary sex' and rape: a continuity that is usually strenuously denied. She approvingly quotes her co-author, Andrea Dworkin, saying that rape is a defining paradigm of sexuality (in that it is paradigmatic male power over women), rather than a deviant form of sexuality, or violence, as is often claimed. In sum: heterosexual sexuality valorizes and eroticizes male dominance.

Male dominance is not the only problematic theme in pornography. Patricia Hill Collins argues that examining the intersecting forces of racism and sexism is crucial to understanding pornography. Collins argues that white women and women of colour are treated differently in pornographic representations. Representations of Black women often refer to slavery: Black women are depicted in submissive positions of bondage, with the 'trappings' of slavery, chains, whips, neck braces, wrist clasps. She argues that the objectification and enslavement of Black women is a central force in the origins of pornography: "African-American women's experiences suggest that Black women were not added into a pre-existing pornography, but rather that pornography itself must be reconceptualized as a shift from the objectification of Black women's bodies in order to dominate and exploit them, to one of media representations of all women that perform the same purpose."[14] Collins argues that pornography functions as ideology, in that it contains a subtle justification of sexist and racist power relations. The objectification and commodification of Black women in pornography echoes the sale of Black women in slavery, and reinforces their oppression.

It should be noted that it is not part of the feminist claim that *only* women are at risk of harm from pornography. Harry Brod argues that pornography is damaging to both men and women. Mainstream heterosexual pornography perpetuates ideas about male sexuality that are very damaging to men. Brod identifies two dimensions of the alienation of hetero men's sexuality: the objectification of the body, and the loss of subjectivity. Men are objectified by being presented as sexual acrobats with oversize penises – a standard few real men could live up to. Men are portrayed as being 'always up for it', so that men who are not always up for it are by definition inadequate. Under 'loss of subjectivity', Brod discusses the tendency of pornography to play into a narrative in which men are only interested in emotion-free sex. It presents sex as a sort of competitive sport of masculinity, thus rendering it emotionless and unsatisfying. It creates a hierarchy of sexual conquests, dictating the shape that male desire must take, telling men which women are desirable. Women are trophies, and men must compete for the ones that are marked as desirable in the patriarchal system. Thus men are limited by the pornographic scripts for desire and sexual experience.

It is important to point out that Brod is not denying that the problems of pornography stem from patriarchy, or that pornography reinforces men's power over women. His point is that the power structures of patriarchy are damaging to everyone. Brod approaches the topic from a Marxist point of view, aiming to analyze the problematic social conditions that create damaging hierarchies. As Brod argues, echoing Marx's analysis of capitalism, the suffering that results from a hierarchical system should not be attributed to the bad behaviour of individuals, but to problems of the system. As Brod puts it, "Just as capitalist exploitation is caused not by capitalists' excess greed but rather by the structural imperatives under which capitalism functions, so men's violence is not the manifestation of some inner male essence, but rather evidence of the bitterness and depth of the struggles through which genders are forged."[15]

Brod's philosophical arguments about alienation are supported by work by sociologists. For example, Michael Kimmel details the perils of the dominant conception of masculinity in his book *Guyland*. Kimmel discusses multiple ways in which pornography sets men up for failure, creating "a toxic brew of entitlement and despair".[16] Gail Dines describes her interviews and conversations about pornography with men as giving her the sense that they feel like "sexual losers . . . they worry they're not good-looking enough, smooth enough, or masculine enough to score, and since the porn view of the world suggests that women are constantly available, these men are bewildered by rejection. They often express deep shame about their inability to hook up, and this shame morphs into anger at their female peers who, unlike porn women, have the word 'no' in their vocabulary."[17]

The pornography debate in feminism takes us to the heart of a complex and difficult issue about sexuality. Most feminists agree that women's sexuality has been repressed, exploited, misconstrued, and commodified by sexist power structures. The disagreement is over how to make progress. MacKinnon's point is that the 1960's version of progress, the so-called sexual revolution, was very problematic. And this is not very surprising, when we think about the nature of oppression. Oppressive structures tend to adapt to ensure their own survival, and one effective way to do that is to provide illusory liberation to the oppressed, enough to stop them from revolting. MacKinnon thinks that this is what the idea of the sexually liberated women is: an illusion of freedom that is actually compliance.

This view attracted the contempt and hostility of enemies of feminism, but it also alienated many feminists. Many feminists reacted with the thought that (to paraphrase Emma Goldman), 'if I can't have sex, I don't want to be part of your revolution'.[18] It seems that there must be some way to have sex, even heterosexual sex, that is truly fun and free. MacKinnon does not deny that, though she does not think it is simple. For the record, Andrea Dworkin does not deny it either, although she is often quoted as saying that 'all sex is rape'. Dworkin's style is often polemical, but she didn't say that. Nonetheless, Dworkin was villainized, and contrasted with a new direction, of sex positive 'fun feminism'.

We should be careful of reading these cultural polarities back into philosophical writings on sex and pornography. There is (usually!) a lot more nuance in arguments against pornography, and, of course, there are different sorts of pornography. MacKinnon and Dworkin are explicitly talking about material that depicts the subordination of women. MacKinnon is prepared to countenance the idea that there could be egalitarian pornography: 'erotica' as she calls it. So, the anti-pornography feminist line need not be seen as ruling out fun. But it raises complex issues about what can be retained from our current cultural pornographic repertoire. What we find fun is not a good guide to what is 'truly' feminist. Mainstream pornography has a firm grip on our collective sexual imagination.

Assessing the causal claim

MacKinnon and others are convinced that pornography, in depicting the subordination of women, causes the subordination of women. As I said, there are various harms that feminists have thought are correlated with pornography, including things that should be relatively easy to investigate, such as increased violence against women. But even for the more nebulous issues, we might think we need more than MacKinnon gives us. MacKinnon does not tell us very much about how the causal connection between pornography and harm is supposed to work. Hers is a speculative account of what pornography is, what explains the form it takes, and how it plays a role in constructing sexuality. But, it might be thought, what we need is a clear causal story: about how exactly pornography causes violence against women, for example.

One account is that pornography has a message about what women are like, and what they are for. It is not simply that it depicts subordination, but it endorses that subordination; it tells men and boys that this is the appropriate way to treat women. Helen Longino argues for this way of understanding the harms of pornography. She recognizes that this puts pornography in the category of speech, and thus makes it eligible for a free speech defence. Her point is that pornography is the sort of speech that is not protected by free speech laws: it is libellous. As Longino puts it,

> Pornography lies when it says that our sexual life is or ought to be subordinate to the service of men, that our pleasure consists in pleasing men and not ourselves, that we are depraved, that we are fit subjects for rape, bondage, torture, and murder. Pornography lies explicitly about women's sexuality, and through such lies fosters more lies about our humanity, our dignity, and our personhood.[19]

The construal of pornography as speech focusses on the portrayal of women as subordinate and the uptake of that on a cognitive level. Alternatively, we could think of the effect of pornography as being a sort of conditioning. Masturbation with pornography creates a deep association of subordination of women with sexual pleasure. Just as early exposure to different foodstuffs forms tastes in later life, so exposure to pornography may shape sexual tastes. Our public sex education is often, for bad reasons, woefully inadequate. For many young people, pornography is the way they find out about sex, and offers their first experiences of sexual excitement. Pornography may work in both ways, as a set of instructions, gleaned from the background picture of sexuality, and as conditioning.

Guesses about how pornography might affect attitudes are explanatory stories, and the thing they are trying to explain is an alleged harmful effect on women. The important claim is that pornography causes attitudes *that lead to harmful behaviour*. That is an empirical claim, and we should be able to assess the evidence. Unfortunately, although much has been published on possible links between pornography consumption and harm to women, there is no clear consensus. It seems that theorists can cherry pick the evidence that suits them.

However, as Anne Eaton points out, there are some obvious pitfalls to avoid.[20] Studies on sex crime and pornography look for correlations between more or less prohibitive pornography laws and crime rates. These studies seem to contradict the feminist claim that there is a causal connection between pornography and rape. It is often claimed that countries with permissive pornography laws have a lower rape incidence than countries with more restrictions. And some places with very restrictive laws, like Singapore, have a comparatively higher incidence of sex crime. Countries that have changed their laws seem to show that liberalization has a good effect. Denmark liberalized its pornography laws in 1969, and the rate of sex crimes dropped.

Eaton points out that these studies are flawed in various ways. First, the Danish study ignores the fact that the legal definition of a sex crime was changed at the same time, so that although the number of minor sex crimes reduced, the number of rapes actually rose. And the studies ignore the complex relationship between what the law prohibits, and what is actually available. Censorship enacted incompetently can of course result in black market pornography, which may be worse than legal pornography. It is also hard to know what to make of crime statistics. Rape is underreported in many places for complex reasons, including fear of reprisal, shame, and fear of or skepticism about the effectiveness of the legal system. One of the places that is cited as demonstrating a correlation between high pornography use and low crime is Japan. But for various reasons, it is plausible that Japan is one of the places where rape is not always reported.

Perhaps the most powerful objection that Eaton has is that these studies do not take account of other factors. Countries that have liberal pornography laws may instantiate other conditions that make sex crime less likely. They may have a better education system, more of a welfare state, more gender equality in general, and so on. Just as the link between smoking and lung cancer is dependent on other factors – some people smoke without getting lung cancer – so pornography does not always cause pornography consumers to be rapists. Maybe in societies with good education systems and gender equality, pornography's power is reduced. But that doesn't mean that pornography is harmless. As Eaton puts it, the claim is that pornography is a salient risk factor.

Another problem is that these studies, of necessity, focus on crimes. But the harms done to women are not always recorded in that way. Part of the feminist critique of pornography is that it affects men's attitudes to women overall. So the harms that we are concerned with are not just rape, but forceful seduction, bad sex, sexual harassment, objectification, and so on. These things are much harder to study. They are not reported, not kept track of, and often not even recognized by the victims due to the deep enculturation of gender and sexual norms. The very problem we are trying to get to grips with makes it harder to prove that there is a problem. This is one of the challenges of understanding oppression.

Relatedly, it is worth comparing uses of empirical evidence here to the example I discussed in the introduction to this book, of studies on innate sex difference. First, studies do often end up showing what the experimenter expects them to show. It is not always deliberate bad science, but it is bad science nonetheless. Second, studies that purport to show innate differences are often well publicized. Perhaps this is not always the author's doing. For some reason, people have an appetite for that sort of thing, and psychologists tell us that we are prone to 'confirmation bias': we favour evidence that supports what we already believe. So when journalists pick up on press releases that will sell papers, they are feeding into our appetite for confirmation. As philosophers, we are not well placed to make a final determination on the evidence of the harms of pornography, but we are well placed to be suspicious of ideology, to look out for bad methodology, and selective reporting.

Expanding the causal claim

Perhaps we don't need to show that there is a robust causal connection between consumption of pornography and a tendency to misogynistic violence. Perhaps it is enough to point out that inegalitarian pornography is a part of a sexist and patriarchal structure. I think that is one way to read MacKinnon (perhaps it is a way of understanding her claim that pornography *is* subordination), but of more concern here is that it is a plausible view.

Compare a feminist critique of literature. Most literary fiction written by white men in English before about 1990 (and much more since) is, subtly or unsubtly, sexist and misogynistic. It would be very hard to prove that it is harmful. Most readers are self-aware and critical, perhaps they can abstract away from the sexism, and effects would be small and hard to measure anyway. Nonetheless, these novels are problematic from a feminist point of view, and although they should not be banned, they should (perhaps) not be taken for granted on syllabi, not be the first point of comparison for new writers, and so on. Perhaps pornography viewers can critically bracket the sexist content and focus on the sexual stimulation. Nonetheless, it seems worth pointing out that the depiction of the subordination of women in order to produce sexual pleasure is problematic.

Perhaps this is simply a way of restating the claim that such things might be harmful, and so we ought to minimize them just in case. This would not be a bad argument: risk of harm can justify restrictions if the harm is severe enough and the loss in what is restricted not enormous. Arguably, that is the case with pornography (again, bearing in mind that this is not an argument for restricting *all* pornography). But there may be a subtler argument in the background. It may be that the manner in which inegalitarian pornography is symbolic is problematic from a feminist point of view in ways that cannot be expressed in terms of straightforward cause and effect.

Deborah Cameron and Elizabeth Frazer present an argument to this effect. They suggest that there are complex connections between pornography use in society and sexual violence, but argue that these cannot be understood on a causal model that takes pornography consumption to cause (even probabilistically) violent behaviour. They identify two causal models: the copycat model, according to which viewing pornography inclines people to copy what they see, and the addiction model, which characterizes pornography use as an addiction, with users seeking more and more extreme pornography in order to reach the same 'high'.

Cameron and Frazer focus on sexual murders, examining in particular the case of serial killer Ted Bundy, who was executed in 1989. Bundy portrayed himself as having been badly affected by pornography, on both the copycat and addiction models. Cameron and Frazer argue that we should be cautious of taking this at face value. As they point out, the murderer's story about his own acts does not come from an epistemically privileged place, but "from a finite repertoire of cultural clichés which the murderer, like everyone else, has come across in case histories, pop-psychology, newspapers, films and ordinary gossip with family, friends and workmates".[21]

Cameron and Frazer compare the 'porn-blaming' cliché with an older and less fashionable cliché: the mother-blaming cliché. The idea that inadequate mothering produces murderers became common currency in the 1950s and 60s, not so much through psychoanalytic expertise, but through movies such as Hitchcock's *Psycho*. Real life killers then began to cite the explanation as applicable in their own case. These narratives involve what sociologists call a 'vocabulary of motive', and part of the purpose they serve is in providing a sort of excuse.

Cameron and Frazer argue that the addiction model of pornography, far from being a feminist advance, undermines feminist aims. The cultural availability and plausibility of this narrative means that violent men have a sort of *excuse* for their crimes against women. Furthermore, the addiction model paints a picture of the addict as the unlucky deviant, the one who couldn't manage the addictive substance as most people can. This puts all the focus on the individual and takes it away from the patriarchal structures that feminists have long argued should be seen as a big part of the problem of sexual violence against women.

Even worse, theories about the connection between pornography and sexual murder may contribute to the incidence of sexual murder. Cameron and Frazer suggest that the existence of sexual murder as a culturally recognized category might increase the number of sexual murders. At the time of Jack the Ripper there was no obvious way to understand those crimes. Now there is, and so, Cameron and Frazer say, the sexual murder is a cultural category with social significance, and as such it can be chosen. That is not to say that it is chosen fully consciously, rather that sexual murder, like school shootings, is 'a thing', and is available to a frayed consciousness as a possible course of action.

Cameron and Frazer are making causal claims in a sense, but not the sort that are easily subjected to empirical study. The claim is that pornography produces new meanings, and that those meanings become part of our culture and affect our decisions. This is an indirect causal story: pornography causes changes in our culture, and that enables violence against women. This general picture could be used to defend variations on Cameron and Frazer's story. Perhaps we should see pornography as primarily creating meaning, producing ideas. How those ideas come to affect reality is always going to be a complex story.

The move that Cameron and Frazer make provides a link between the causal claim, that pornography causes subordination, and MacKinnon's apparently stronger claim, that it *is* subordination. A related argument comes from Katharine Jenkins, who argues that we can make good sense of MacKinnon's claim that pornography subordinates (as opposed to indirectly causing subordination) by understanding the claim in terms of social construction.[22] Jenkins appeals to John Searle's account of social construction, according to which the existence and nature of some objects are explained by their role in our social world. Take money, for example, which exists because humans invented it, and they invented it for a particular purpose. In order to understand what money is, we must understand its role and function. It seems plausible, Jenkins argues, that pornography *portrays* women as having a certain function (they are there to please men), and that thereby constructs social reality: for all intents and purposes, women are there for sexual use by men.

If the causal claim is given less prominence, it is harder to fit the feminist objection to pornography into the liberal framework, which insists that the only justification for restrictions on freedom is harm to others. Again, it could be argued that what justifies restrictions is *risk* of harm, that, given the very high rate of violence against women worldwide, we have good grounds for taking precautionary measures, even when we are not certain about cause and effect. Alternatively, we could shift to a more paternalistic style of argument and accept that restrictions on misogynistic pornography are aimed at creating a better society for everyone.

Feminist pornography

Is feminist pornography possible? There is certainly a lot of self-described feminist pornography. The Feminist Porn Awards (a Toronto-based organization that functioned from 2006 to 2015) defines feminist pornography as pornography in which:

- Actors are treated with respect, paid fairly, given choice and ethical working conditions, empowered in their work.
- Directors collaborate with and incorporate the actor's own sexual desires and fantasies (makes for better scenes too!).
- It expands the boundaries of sexual representation on film and challenges stereotypes, especially of women and marginalized communities.
- Realistic pleasure is depicted.

Feminist pornographers such as Candice Vadala (formerly Candida Royalle), Tristan Taormino, Courtney Trouble, and Erika Lust have been making feminist pornography since the 1980s, and there is a wealth of feminist pornography sites (though nothing compared to the number of mainstream sites). Philosophers such as Anne Eaton and Ann Garry have written about the need for feminist pornography, and the shape it might take. There is even a journal, *Porn Studies*, produced by Taylor & Francis since 2014, which publishes serious articles discussing issues such as 'deepfakes' (apparently real footage of a famous person saying or doing something that is, in fact, created by clever technology), condom use, the political meaning of queer pornography, and so on.

If the feminist worries about inegalitarian pornography are valid, and pornography can affect us in deep and serious ways, then presumably feminist pornography can have a *good* effect. It can say true things, or important things, it can condition people towards healthier sexualities, and it can infuse a culture with beneficial meanings and ideas. Perhaps good pornography can break down ingrained assumptions about roles, and change our responses to race, gender, body shapes, and disability. If inegalitarian pornography can shore up the patriarchy, egalitarian pornography can undermine it.

However, there are practical and theoretical hurdles to overcome. First, it is not easy to define feminist pornography. Those who are involved in making feminist pornography are often guided by the aim of making something that women would enjoy. But it would obviously be a mistake to think that feminist pornography should represent what women want, where we think of that as the stuff of paperback romances. This, of course, just accepts many of the stereotypes of women that feminists aim to disrupt. However, there are more subtle mistakes we could make, and it is harder to recognize them. Our actual desires may have been formed by inegalitarian pornography and inegalitarian social conditions, so that we are, as a matter of fact, turned on by the tropes of feminine submissiveness and masculine power. So, we may have to move away from what actually turns us on. And it's not easy to see how to do this. If the sexual preferences of both pornographers and consumers have been formed to find power differential sexy, how can egalitarian pornography be sexy? Do we have to start again with a new generation of pornography consumers? Or is it possible to subvert these tropes, as feminist pornographers have argued? These are hard questions, requiring both theorizing and experimentation in the pornography market-place.

Furthermore, the very idea of egalitarian pornography may seem unsexy, and not just because we are already steeped in the eroticization of gender power differentials. What seems unsexy is the virtue, the worthiness, implied in egalitarian pornography. Sex, and so pornography, sometimes gets its thrill from being 'naughty' or 'dirty' in some way. That's an easy point to grant, but it is much harder to navigate the line between naughtiness that is egalitarian, and nastiness that simply comes from the familiar playbook of mainstream misogynistic pornography: gagging, slapping, choking, and so on.

Second, there are difficult practical questions about how best to encourage feminist pornography. Given the difficulties in defining it, it may not be easy to draw the line, and as with obscenity laws, the risks of badly written laws being applied in unfair ways should be taken seriously. Perhaps a better way to go is to think of feminist pornography as a protected category, to be encouraged by affirmative action style measures. But what would that involve? Formulating a politically viable plan for encouraging feminist pornography and discouraging misogynistic pornography would involve an in-depth examination of how the pornography industry actually works. Given that most internet pornography is free, much of the revenue must come from advertising. Advertising is already a fairly heavily regulated business, so perhaps one way in is to regulate advertising, perhaps through taxation, perhaps through tax incentives.

In her recent book investigating the pornography industry, Shira Tarrant points out that currently one company, MindGeek, controls the production and distribution of the vast majority of pornography made today. In that situation, there is not much scope for independent feminist pornography to flourish. Governments try to limit monopolies in other areas, precisely because of the harms to employees and consumers. MindGeek has been subject to antitrust lawsuits already, but its virtual monopoly is such that its grip on the industry remains tight. A serious political effort to change our pornography might start by looking at our antitrust regulations.[23]

Summary

Arguments that there is a free speech right, or a more general freedom right to pornography, depend on the assumption that the objection to pornography is that it is immoral. However, the feminist objection to pornography is that it is, or might be, harmful to women.

The thought is not that all pornography (where we understand pornography as sexually explicit material designed to titillate) is harmful, but rather that a common sort of mainstream pornography, and much 'extreme' pornography, is deeply sexist and misogynistic, portraying and endorsing the degradation of women. This is the stuff that feminists object to. Some feminists make a distinction between pornography and erotica to capture this difference; others refer to inegalitarian pornography and allow the possibility of egalitarian pornography.

The issue of how harm is caused by pornography is complex, and various suggestions have been offered as to how to cash out that claim. Pornography might present sexist ideas in such a way that they are accepted as truths. It might condition sexuality in a way that is bad for both men and women. Or, perhaps it is just part of patriarchal structures in a way that cannot be explained in terms of simple causal links to harm.

This leaves open the possibility of feminist pornography, but there is much more to be said about how that would work, and how legal and state structures should respond to the various types of pornography.

Notes

1 www.pornhub.com/insights/2019-year-in-review.
2 www.pornhub.com/insights/2019-year-in-review. The 'G' in GILF stands for 'Grandmother'.
3 MacKinnon and Dworkin, *In Harm's Way: The Pornography Civil Rights Hearings*.
4 Bridges et al., 'Aggression and Sexual Behavior in Best-Selling Pornography Videos: A Content Analysis Update'.
5 Klaassen and Jochen, 'Gender (In)equality in Internet Pornography: A Content Analysis of Popular Pornographic Internet Videos'.
6 Jensen, *Getting Off: Pornography and the End of Masculinity*, p.14.
7 Crenshaw, 'The 2 Live Crew Controversy', p.218.
8 Brison, 'The Autonomy Defense of Free Speech', p.314.
9 Dworkin, 'Is There a Right to Pornography?', in *A Matter of Principle*, p.194.
10 See, for example, Linda Marchiano's account of her experiences making the film *Deep Throat*. Shira Tarrant discusses these issues in Chapter 4 of her book *The Pornography Industry*.
11 MacKinnon, *Toward A Feminist Theory of the State*, pp.207–208.
12 MacKinnon, 'Sexuality, Pornography, and Method: "Pleasure under Patriarchy"', p.316.
13 Op. cit., p.327.
14 Collins, *Black Feminist Thought*, p.149.
15 Brod, 'Pornography and the Alienation of Male Sexuality', p.266.
16 Kimmel, *Guyland: The Perilous World Where Boys Become Men*, p.172.
17 Dines, *Pornland*, p.89.
18 The quote often attributed to Goldman, "If I can't dance I don't want to be part of your revolution", is in fact a paraphrase of some remarks she makes in her autobiography (*Living My Life*, p.56).
19 Longino, 'Pornography, Oppression, and Freedom: A Closer Look', p.156.
20 Eaton, 'A Sensible Antiporn Feminism'.
21 Cameron and Frazer, 'On the Question of Pornography and Sexual Violence: Moving Beyond Cause and Effect', p.245.
22 Jenkins, 'What Women Are For: Pornography and Social Ontology'.
23 Tarrant, *The Pornography Industry*.

Further reading

Altman, Andrew and Watson, Lori (2019) *Debating Pornography*. Oxford University Press. (Altman argues that there is a right to sexual autonomy that protects pornography, while Watson argues that pornography is harmful to women and develops the MacKinnon/Dworkin line that civil action is justified).

Coleman, Lindsay and Held, Jacob (2014) *The Philosophy of Pornography: Contemporary Perspectives*. Rowman & Littlefield. (Wide-ranging collection of articles).

Cornell, Drucilla (ed.) (2000) *Feminism and Pornography*. Oxford University Press. (Collection of reprinted articles and extracts including several cited in this chapter).

Mikkola, Mari (2019) *Pornography: A Philosophical Introduction*. Oxford University Press. (Clear introduction to the debates, heavy focus on silencing).

5 Sex work

"The strangest question I have been asked by a client so far (and note he is talking about himself) is 'How can I go home and be on my own, knowing what I now know about myself?' Sex is deep stuff, saturated with meaning. Humans touch each other here. Lives change in my Whoring Room. I wonder about sex work under a non capitalist non patriarchal system, as if that ever existed. I would be perhaps sacred, and valued. I would be a healer and an educator. Perhaps I am already."

Clio Magnum Rossi, 'Not About the Heart of Darkness:
Whoring as a Profession at the End of Capitalism'

Chapter overview: The chapter covers the morality and legality of sex work. I contrast the liberal feminist position, defended by Martha Nussbaum, Debra Satz, and others, that sex work is wage labour like any other and should be destigmatized, with the essentialist view that sale of sex cannot be compared to other jobs. I explore the relationship between moral arguments and policy suggestions, and look at the policy options: criminalization, legalization (regulation), the Nordic model, and decriminalization.

Introduction

Sex work is an umbrella term, covering prostitution (which I use in a morally neutral sense, to refer to sexual intercourse for money), and other forms of consensual sex work, such as stripping, lap dancing, phone sex, pornographic film acting, or BDSM (Bondage-Discipline, Dominance-Submission, and Sadomasochism) work. According to estimates, around 40 million people worldwide work as sex workers of one sort or another, although precise numbers are difficult to verify because sex work is often illegal, and therefore official figures are hard to come by.

The term 'sex work' does not include those who are trafficked, that is, those who are forced into sexual services for money against their will. It is important to keep these two things distinct. First, the two are morally distinct: it is an open question whether sex work is morally acceptable, whereas trafficking is obviously wrong. Second, it is politically important not to conflate consensual and non-consensual sex markets. Focussing on prosecuting participants in a consensual market can distract from the more urgent work of stopping trafficking, and focussing on trafficking may unfairly demonize consensual sex work.

Feminist thinkers are not in agreement about sex work. On the one hand, some feminists argue that sex work is not morally wrong in itself, and has been unfairly stigmatized. These thinkers argue that feminists should be fighting to make the working conditions for sex workers, who are predominantly women, better and safer, and to remove the stigma that is associated with sex work. In that sense, sex work is like other forms of work that have been traditionally done by women, for example domestic labour and care work. These jobs are disproportionately precarious, badly paid, and exploitative. We should be working to change the conditions of the job rather than working to abolish it.

But, on the other hand, many feminists have argued that sex work is not wage labour like any other. Selling sex has seemed to some to be inherently alienating, and they argue that it is no coincidence that sex work is often a last resort for women who do not have better options. Some feminists have argued that the problems with sex work, particularly prostitution, are deeper than the cultural context, and that prostitution would not exist at all in an egalitarian society. In this chapter I shall examine both of these positions.

One idea that I shall not spend time on is what we might call 'old-fashioned moralism'. I call this 'moralism' because it stakes a fairly extreme and inflexible moral position, usually based on traditional morality, and then insulates that particular moral judgment from criticism and reflection. For example, I take it to be a moralistic position to claim that sex has a reproductive purpose, and that non-reproductive sex is unnatural and morally bad. On this account, morally acceptable sex is a very small domain. That sort of view, though once widely held, is an anathema to feminism, and no longer very relevant except as an explanation for residual prejudices.

Even without precise figures, it is clear that, globally, most sex workers are women, who sell sexual services to men. This is not to say that sex workers who are not women are not part of the feminist concern. The ways that gender affects our practices harms people of all genders, and in the broadest sense, feminists are concerned with the oppression and suffering that is caused by patriarchal power structures. Different genders are differently situated with respect to those power structures, and so being a sex worker will have different social meanings depending on gender. Perhaps there is even *more* stigma associated with a man being a sex worker, as he has 'fallen' further, it is less suited to his 'natural role'. And a man who sells sex to other men is flouting the rules of heterosexual masculinity. However, in some ways, men selling sex will likely retain some of their male privilege. As Debra Satz points out, the asymmetry of power and status in a sexist society means that, whereas female prostitution reinforces women's inferiority, male prostitutes are taken as individuals; their personal debasement is not taken as debasement of all men.[1] In general, men's status is more robust than women's status.

Non-binary and trans people who sell sex may also be even more stigmatized than women who sell sex, and that stigma is likely to be closely related to their being outside of accepted gender binaries, and the way that their gender identity is unacceptable to mainstream moralism. Trans people are marginalized in general, and that means that police and legal protection is even more precarious for them than for other sex workers. For example, in the Philippines in 2014, sex worker Jennifer Laude was murdered by a US marine. The jury allowed the 'trans panic defence' – murdering her was not his fault, because he had not realized that she was trans.[2]

In other words, we need to take account of intersectionality in understanding the ways that different groups will be stigmatized and victimized for being sex workers. How people are seen and treated varies according to the ways that different aspects of perceived identities intersect (see Chapter 8 for a more detailed account of intersectionality). So the feminist claim is not that women suffer uniquely in being sex workers; the claim is rather that sex work is bound up with our hierarchical ideas about gender and gender roles, and the vulnerability of sex workers is related to gender hierarchies.

In thinking about prostitution, we should take care to be clear whether we are talking about the morality of it or the legality. As I note in my introductory discussion in the chapter on reproductive rights, these things can come apart. One might think that prostitution is morally problematic, but that criminalization is extremely harmful and so our best strategy is something other than criminalization, perhaps criminalization only of the buyers and not of the sellers of sex. It seems fairly clear that full criminalization is very bad for sex workers, and so for most feminists, even those who think sex work is inherently problematic, criminalization does not seem like a good option. Criminalization means that sex workers are unable to rely on police protection, because they risk their own arrest if they call the police. Thus they are vulnerable to violence and exploitation by pimps and clients, and are also vulnerable to police corruption and brutality. It also means that sex workers cannot rely on institutional protection of other kinds, such as health and safety regulations and unions, and, of course, means that prostitution is further stigmatized.

The morality and legality of prostitution can come apart in the other direction too. One may think that prostitution is morally acceptable in itself, but in the actual world, which is riven with sexist ideology, it would be a good idea to minimize it. It may be that in an ideal world sex work would be respected, taken as a form of therapy, and safe and healthy for both worker and client. However, it could be argued that we are so far from that world that the best option is to limit sex work in some way.

Furthermore, there are lots of different options for regulation of prostitution: there are different forms of decriminalization, and there are different ways to enact legalization. There is not simply a choice between 'legal' and 'illegal'. Broadly, there are four options:

1. **Criminalization**. Criminalizes the sale and purchase of sexual services, along with related activities, such as soliciting or operating a brothel. This can be more permissive, as in the UK, where selling sex is not itself illegal but everything associated with it is (such as street solicitation), or less permissive, as in most of the USA (Nevada is an exception) where both selling and buying sexual services is illegal.
2. **The Nordic model**. Involves criminalizing only the purchase of sexual services, along with related activities such as curb crawling or procuring. Prostitutes themselves are not acting illegally. This can be more or less permissive depending on the exact formulation of the laws.

3. **Regulation**. Makes sex work legal, but involves governmental licensing and regulating of sex work businesses. This is the policy in parts of Nevada, as well as Germany, the Netherlands, and a handful of other countries. Again, this can be more or less permissive.
4. **Decriminalization**. Involves removing criminal prohibitions but does not make special regulations for the sale of sex, instead treating it as governed by employment and labour laws like any other line of work.

So, a realistic political plan needs to consider many possible options, some of which have been tried, and others which have not. It would be important to examine what has happened in the various places that have tried out different policies, despite the huge complexities in comparing how policies work out in different conditions.

It is often said that prostitution is the world's oldest profession. That's very unlikely to be true, and the source of the phrase, a short story by Rudyard Kipling (*On the City Wall*, 1889), does not present it as a serious claim. But sex work is certainly an old profession, existing in a multitude of forms and contexts throughout human history. The idea that it is the world's oldest profession resonates because it captures a widely held belief: that sexual desire is a powerful driver, particularly in men, and that there will always be a market for sexual services.

We should be cautious about such sweeping statements. It is very difficult to disentangle the sale of sex and sexual services from other social conditions. We should ask what sex work would look like in a non-patriarchal society. Perhaps it would be completely unrecognizable. In thinking philosophically about sex work, we should bear that in mind: that the history of sex work as we know it is rife with its own mythology and narratives, many of them sexist. Part of the theoretical work here is to think about sex work without taking anything about it for granted.

On the other hand, we need to think about the reality of sex work, the actual conditions in which it takes place, at this moment in time. There is no point in an entirely abstract approach, which ignores the patriarchal background of the conditions of sex work. Even if there is an ideal world in which sex work is not dangerous or stigmatized, we need to think about what to do in the actual world.

Consent and coercion

As I said above, it is important that we distinguish between trafficking and sex work. Trafficking is coercing or forcing someone into commercial sex acts against their will, and often involves kidnapping and imprisonment. Trafficking of women and children is real and urgent. However, the focus on trafficking can end up being problematic. If all sex work is lumped in with trafficking, and sex work and trafficking are treated the same way in law enforcement, sex workers will suffer. Ironically, sex workers may be made more vulnerable by attempts to shut down trafficking. In the USA, recently introduced laws, SESTA and FOSTA (the Stop Enabling Sex Traffickers Act and the Fight Online Sex Trafficking Act), have attracted the ire of sex workers, who complain that these laws have done nothing but harm. In closing down online spaces where sex workers could find clients safely and share information about them, these laws have made things *less* safe. The rhetoric and the reality are very different.

Another problem with the discourse around trafficking is the way that it racializes the issue. Many of the images used in awareness campaigns feature a young white girl with a dark hand over her mouth, or a dark figure looming behind her. These images conjure a world where 'white innocence' is under threat from dark-skinned villains. This feeds a racist and sexist ideology about immigration and sex work. The focus is put on individual villains instead of on the structures that cause chaos at our borders. Laws are then used to victimize the already marginalized, the dispossessed and displaced, and, of course, sex workers.

In this chapter I will discuss issues about the morality and legality of consensual sex work, in particular prostitution, not trafficking and child exploitation. But of course, the question of consent is a vexed one, and any discussion of sex work should recognize the constraints that inform choices to work in the sex industry. Sometimes, people make choices because they have terrible options, and when that is happening, the right response is to change the options. On the other hand, people, particularly women, sometimes make genuine choices that others don't take seriously. It is disrespectful of autonomy, and can be a classic sexist manoeuvre, to say, 'you chose that, but you don't know your own mind, you are deprived and suffering in ways you don't even see'. This dilemma dogs discussions of oppressive circumstances. I discuss these issues in more detail in Chapter 9, on adaptive preferences and false consciousness, and in Chapter 11, on consent.

In their 2018 book about sex workers' rights, *Revolting Prostitutes*, Juno Mac and Molly Smith recognize this dilemma, and stress the complexity and variety of the experience of sex workers. They object to the tendencies on both sides of the prohibition debate to oversimplify and polarize things. On one extreme, anti-prostitution activists, such as Andrea Dworkin, paint a picture of harm and degradation in lurid terms. On the other side, pro sex work organizations sometimes portray the prostitute as a character that Mac and Smith label the 'erotic professional', joyfully expressing her sexuality and helping her clients overcome disadvantages or disabilities to reach sexual fulfilment. Just as the first portrayal unfairly vilifies the work, so the second unfairly romanticizes it. In order to understand the reality of sex work, we need to try to see through these ideological oversimplifications and examine what actually happens.

As Lorelei Lee puts it, in her essay on her experiences as a sex worker and pornography actor,

> In the radical narrative, all sex trading is understood as trafficking and our ability to consent does not exist. In the competing liberal-libertarian narrative, those of us who have been publicly described as having "consented" to our work are categorically characterized as "empowered," as "choice feminists." Under these constructs, we have only two options: to be victims, which means we need to be rescued from our work – even if that rescue happens in handcuffs – or to be empowered sex workers, which means saying we've never experienced violence or constrained choice, that we love our jobs all day every day, and to be free we only need access to the free market.[3]

The reality, of course, is that some sex workers are in the line of work because they had no better options. Others are in it because they have freely chosen it. For most, the truth lies somewhere in between. Even for those who are in it because they want to be, there are difficult moments, problematic clients, dangers and vulnerabilities. As sex workers' organizations continually remind academics, it is crucial to listen to the voices of sex workers when speculating about the conditions of sex work.

The liberal feminist argument

There is no well-defined school of thought called 'liberal feminism'. In fact, there are no well-defined 'schools of thought' within feminism at all; rather, there are general approaches that we can sometimes usefully identify by important features of their starting points. Liberal feminism, loosely understood, starts by accepting many of the tenets of liberalism as the term is used in political philosophy. One such tenet is the idea that if an activity does not harm others, the state should not interfere. This is John Stuart Mill's harm principle.[4] The harm principle implies that so long as sexual activity does not harm the participants or others, it should be allowed by law. Sexual practices are often disapproved of for moralistic or religious reasons. But according to the harm principle, this is not a good reason for banning these practices.

Liberal feminism, then, is just a feminist position that starts with a presumption in favour of liberty. Applied to issues where there is a history of censorship and moralism, liberal feminists tend to apply the harm principle: is there a harm to others here? If not, the practice should be allowed by law. Of course, the harm question is not simple when we take into account the subtle ways that sexist practices can be harmful. I discuss this in detail in the chapter on pornography, where the question is whether pornography harms women. This is complicated, because harms can be indirect and long term. Many of the same complexities apply to the question about whether sex work is harmful to women. And perhaps even more so than in the case of pornography, we must consider whether banning sex work could be more harmful.

Many feminist philosophers have argued that, from a feminist point of view, the problem with prostitution is not inherent, but rather in the sexist social practices that surround and define sex work. The first step is an anti-moralistic argument: there is nothing wrong with selling sex in itself, and those who have argued otherwise are in the grip of moralistic thinking about sex that liberal feminists reject. Many feminist philosophers have argued that sex work itself is not morally problematic. However, in the real world, sex work does cause harms to women. Thus the second step in the liberal feminist approach is to identify the ways that prostitution in the real world functions to harm women, and to identify structural and legal solutions to those problems.

Debra Satz and Martha Nussbaum both compare prostitution to other forms of labour, and argue that prostitution is no worse in itself. Other jobs involve similar downsides, such as low wages, health risks, ceding autonomy, ceding bodily control, and so on.[5] As Satz puts it,

> Many forms of labor, perhaps most, cede some control of a person's body to others. Such control can range from requirements to be in a certain place at a certain time (e.g., reporting to the office), to requirements that a person (e.g., a professional athlete) eat certain foods and get certain amounts of sleep, or maintain good humor in the face of

the offensive behavior of others (e.g., airline stewardesses). Some control of our capacities by others does not seem to be ipso facto destructive of our dignity.[6]

Likewise, Nussbaum compares a range of jobs to prostitution, including some that are related to capacities that are central to our identities, and are sources of joy and fulfilment, as sex is. Yet, Nussbaum argues, in the case she examines (nightclub singer and philosophy professor), these capacities can be commodified without harm. These jobs do not, at this moment in history, attract stigma, and are not dependent on inegalitarian gender norms. Nussbaum's suggestion is that the real difference between those jobs and prostitution is in the external conditions: the way the job is perceived.

Of course, one aspect of prostitution that seems central is that it involves the body in an intimate way. Nussbaum considers two more jobs that involve more bodily interaction and yet do not have the stigma that prostitution has: massage therapy, and the invented job, colonoscopy artist. A colonoscopy artist is someone who has colonoscopy instruments tested on her for a living. That job is not real, but there are similar jobs that are real. We might even think of giving blood as involving 'bodily invasion' in the way that prostitution does. Yet, these jobs are not stigmatized, so Nussbaum argues that bodily engagement itself cannot be the crucial factor.

Nussbaum concludes that disapproval of prostitution involves something irrational, something moralistic. Nussbaum goes through the various arguments that are standardly offered, and tries to show that they are either arguments that only apply because prostitution is illegal, or that they are arguments for better regulation and fairer practices, and apply to jobs other than prostitution.

Take first the worry that prostitution poses health risks and risks of violence. Nussbaum and others point out that these risks are really caused by the fact that prostitution is illegal. If it is illegal, it is underground, and prostitutes cannot call the police, or rely on health services as they could if it was legal and regulated. We can compare the argument here to arguments about the legalization of drugs. Proponents of legalization of drugs point out that when drugs are legal they are much less likely to be contaminated with other substances, users are more likely to be in a safe environment when taking them, and there are no incentives for criminal activity. The same arguments apply to prostitution. The dangers come from the fact that sex work takes place in a criminal underworld. Nussbaum's arguments are echoed by health experts, such as the World Health Organization, and the UN commission on HIV and the law, which recommends decriminalization of sex work as a major way to prevent the spread of HIV.

Liberal feminists often argue that the extrinsic harms of prostitution in its current form affect people beyond those who work in the sex industry. That is because the sale of sex is shaped by and contributes to gender inequality. As Laurie Shrage puts it, although it is possible that prostitution could have other meanings, in our culture it "epitomizes other cultural assumptions – beliefs which, reasonable or not, serve to legitimate women's social subordination."[7] Satz argues that prostitution, as in all labour markets that are disproportionately occupied by one gender, reinforces stereotypes. Traditional sexist prostitution affects the way that men and women think about sex, it reinforces the idea that men have uncontrollable sex drives that must be satisfied, and reinforces the idea of marriage as an ownership contract. She points out that female prostitutes are represented as being sexual servants of men, and that this echoes and reinforces the more general idea that women are the sexual servants of men. Satz is not very optimistic that our ideology about sex and prostitution can be changed easily or quickly. Shrage argues that the sort of change that would be required to make the actual practices of prostitution egalitarian would be radical, transforming it into something more like sex therapy.

It is worth reiterating here that the worry is not that something about selling sex is inherently dangerous. The dangers are external. I discuss a different style of argument, which I term the 'essentialist argument', in more detail in the next section. The essentialist position argues that there is indeed something essentially harmful about selling sex, and that selling sex would be harmful no matter what the legal position. The idea is that sex is not the sort of thing that can be bought and sold.

Those who are broadly in the liberal camp often acknowledge the force of the essentialist argument, even though they argue that sex work is not inherently wrong. Satz, for example, agrees that there is something problematic about treating persons as things, but she thinks that the more urgent problems are with the conditions of work for most prostitutes: the lack of power and autonomy. Satz points out that there may be variations; for some people, selling sex may be too emotionally complex to be done without psychological damage; for others it may be just fine. Similarly, Nussbaum points out that there can be different sorts of sex and different sorts of love, and argues that they need not impinge on one another. Nussbaum argues that someone who sells sex still has her sexuality, she can still do what she likes with it in her own time. Perhaps romantic sex cannot be sold, but the sex that the prostitute is paid for is not romantic sex.

Other liberals are firm in their rejection of the idea that sex is not the sort of thing that can be bought and sold. Jason Brennan and Peter Jaworski argue that if something is permissible, then it is permissible to ask for money for it.[8] It is permissible to have sex, so it is permissible to have sex for money. They argue, against those who say that sex cannot be bought and sold, that the interesting issues are all about what sort of limits and regulations can be put on how sex is bought and sold. It might be important to have careful regulations and limits on the sale of sex, but that does not entail that sex cannot be sold at all. Jessica Flanigan, in her defence of decriminalization, endorses this position, arguing that there is a right to sell sexual services, and a right to buy sexual services, and that others are not morally permitted to interfere.[9]

To sum up the liberal feminist argument: it is an anti-moralistic argument that prostitution is not wrong in itself. In particular, liberal feminists claim that sex work is not wrong for reasons of old-fashioned morality, such as that any extramarital sex is wrong. Furthermore, prostitution is not inherently wrong on grounds of being inherently degrading, or alienating, or impeding flourishing. And finally, it is not wrong on the grounds that sex is not the sort of thing that can be bought and sold. However, liberal feminists acknowledge that in the current situation, due to a confluence of social and historical factors, sex work is very problematic for women. This leads to the question, what should be done? The contemporary practice of prostitution is deeply intertwined with gender hierarchy, and as a result is harmful to women in ways that cannot easily be ameliorated. It is thus not obvious that the liberal feminist position points to legalization.

Liberal feminism and policy

Given that they are skeptical about intrinsic harms of prostitution and other forms of sex work, liberal feminists focus on the various extrinsic harms that come about in different scenarios, and propose policies that minimize harm. Satz's answer is that criminalization is worse for women than some form of legalization. Nussbaum agrees, and her argument has the same underlying form. Nussbaum argues that even if prostitution is not ideal and not a fully free choice, it is better to have it legal and safe than criminalized. If we are concerned with the welfare of women in these situations, we should fight for regulation and measures to help them.

This is effectively a consequentialist argument, and as such is distinct from the anti-moralistic argument. The anti-moralistic argument says that prostitution is not morally problematic in itself, but is unfairly stigmatized because of our cultural ideology about sex and gender. The consequentialist argument is neutral on the morality of prostitution: the point is that in terms of harm, criminalizing it is worse than the alternatives. Note again the parallel with drug laws here. Whatever we think about the morality of taking drugs, we could argue that it is better if drugs are not criminalized. It may be true that taking a lot of drugs is not the morally ideal lifestyle; it may be true that those who take them are in positions where they are not really making clear informed choices. But given that criminalization is so disastrous for both users and bystanders, some form of regulation or decriminalization seems preferable.

Debra Satz, who argues that although prostitution is not wrong in itself it is very harmful to women in the current context, suggests that a system of regulation is probably the safest approach. She recognizes that the effectiveness of any policy in both changing attitudes and keeping women safe will be hard to predict, but she thinks that there are a few obvious measures, a sort of bill of rights for women performing sex work. The principles she suggests are (slightly abridged):

1. No woman should be forced to have sex against her will.
2. No woman should be denied access to contraception or to treatment for sexually transmitted diseases, particularly AIDS, or to abortion (at least in the first trimester).
3. The law should ensure that a woman has adequate information before she agrees to sexual intercourse. The risks of venereal and other sexually transmitted diseases, the risks of pregnancy, and the laws protecting a woman's right to refuse sex should all be generally available.
4. Minimum age of consent laws for sexual intercourse should be enforced. These laws should ensure that women (and men) are protected from coercion and do not enter into sexual relationships until they are in a position to understand what they are consenting to.
5. The law should promote women's control over their own sexuality by prohibiting brokerage (pimps).[10]

This bill of rights (as Satz is aware) expresses an idealistic aim. If sex work could be governed by these principles, it would be well on the way to being a safe profession. However, it is difficult to see how to enforce this bill of rights in practice. I talk about practical problems with regulating sex work in the last section of this chapter.

The essentialist argument

The essentialist argument is that there is something essentially harmful or degrading about prostitution. Some philosophers have argued that selling sex is inherently problematic, that sex is too personal, too private to be sold. These philosophers argue that the liberal feminist position misses something important about what sex essentially is. This is not usually presented as an argument for prohibition; it is an argument about the *morality* of prostitution. At most, the thought is that there may be *prima facie* grounds for prohibition.

It is also worth stressing that the essentialist argument is not a moralistic position. The view is not an entrenched and non-reflective acceptance of traditional morality. Rather, defenders of the essentialist position give an argument for why prostitution is morally problematic.

One such argument was referred to in the previous section: the argument that sex is not the sort of thing that can be bought and sold. For example, Margaret Radin argues that there are some very personal things that can be given away or shared, but they cannot be sold, they are 'market inalienable'. She says that sex is one of those things. She argues that there is a sort of domino effect of commodifying things that should not be commodified, where they come to be valued in the wrong way. The non-commodified version of the good thing comes to be degraded by the existence of the commodified version. About commodifying sex, she says, "we do not wish to unleash market forces onto the shaping of our discourse regarding sexuality and hence onto our very conception of sexuality and our sexual feelings."[11]

To illustrate her point, Radin asks us to imagine a situation in which prostitution is legalized, and the stigma has been removed as the liberal feminist argument urges. Radin says,

> What if sex were fully and openly commodified? Suppose newspapers, radio, TV, and billboards advertised sexual services as imaginatively and vividly as they advertise computer services, health clubs, or soft drinks. Suppose the sexual partner of your choice could be ordered through a catalog, or through a large brokerage firm that has an "800" number, or at a trade show, or in a local showroom. Suppose the business of recruiting suppliers of sexual services was carried on in the same way as corporate headhunting or training of word-processing operators.

Similarly, Scott Anderson imagines various policies that could be suggested if prostitution were legal and destigmatized: sexual work could attract a bonus in an otherwise non-sexual job, unemployed people could be asked to do sex work rather than being given benefits, and sexual contracts would be legally enforceable.[12] He imagines that sex workers, as legal employees, could be subject to objectionable control: sex workers' own sexual practices might be controlled by their employers, they would have to adhere to non-discrimination laws (i.e., not reject clients), and the government could control sex workers' sexual activities on health and safety grounds. Finally, Anderson suggests, if sex work were destigmatized, there is no reason why sex could not be aggressively marketed, or why sex work could not be a high school course.

Anderson admits that this is not very likely to happen if prostitution were decriminalized (and, in fact, it has not happened in New Zealand, where sex work has been decriminalized; there, job seekers' benefits are explicitly protected in the face of a preference not to do sex work). Anderson's point is that if we take seriously the claim that prostitution is wage labour like any other, we should be willing to countenance these policies. The fact that they seem so unattractive, Anderson argues, is evidence that we do not really think that sex work is like other work. His argument is an argument against the normalization of prostitution.

Elizabeth Anderson argues along similar lines that prostitution is an inappropriate com-modification. She says, "prostitution is the classic example of how commodification debases a gift value and its giver."[13] She argues that sex must involve a special sort of reciprocity, each partner offering her sexuality in the same spirit. When a man pays a woman for sex, he is treating her as an object to be used for his sexual purposes, not as a sexual agent.

Anderson recognizes that this is not an argument for making prostitution illegal. But Anderson argues that commodification of sex would have broader effects, and that those effects may well justify restrictions. Anderson, following Catharine MacKinnon, points out that ideas about heterosexuality and masculinity go deep in our cultural narratives, and have effects on all women, not just the women who sell sex. Anderson illustrates the point by arguing that if sex is commodified, the wrong of rape is hard to distinguish from the wrong of theft. In other words, we begin to think of sex as something that can be detached from a woman's real self, and not as an integral part of selfhood for women as it is for men.

A slightly different argument for essentialism comes from Jeffrey Gauthier. He argues that prostitution is damaging in a way that other modes of selling one's labour are not. He quotes Carole Patemen's verdict, that it involves selling *oneself* in a very real way.[14] Gauthier argues that comparisons between other jobs and prostitution fail to establish that prosti-tution is no more damaging than other jobs. He argues that with most jobs, there can be authentic and degraded versions of the work, and that prostitution is comparable to the degraded version, not the authentic version. He takes up Nussbaum's example of the phi-losophy professor and uses it to argue that prostitution involves a problematic exchange. In the unproblematic case, a worker finds meaning in her own work. Her work is self-creative and self-directed. Philosophy professors work very hard and are paid, but payment does not demean them. However, being a philosophy professor could be alienating if the conditions were altered. If the professor was in a repressive regime, writing only what they were told to write (tracts to justify corporate interests, for example), an aspect of work that should be self-directed becomes commodified. The worker must pretend that there is still self-directed activity, but there is not. This is professional extortion.

Gauthier argues that prostitution meets the conditions for professional extortion. It engages a potentially self-creative capacity, but the prostitute must feign self-expression. Her success depends on her client thinking that she is genuinely enjoying herself and expressing her sexuality. At the very least, the client must be engaging in some sort of double think, in that he thinks the prostitute works for money *and* for a sexual motive. So being a prostitute is like being a philosophy professor forced to write for corporate interests, and not like the phil-osophy professor who exercises her creative capacities autonomously in exchange for pay.

Other thinkers appeal to empirical evidence. Catharine MacKinnon cites various studies that show that prostitution results in mental and physical harms, including post traumatic stress disorder.[15] Peter de Marneffe draws on work by historians, sociologists, and journalists, and the testimonies of prostitutes themselves. According to de Marneffe, the verdict is clear:

prostitution is psychologically damaging. He quotes criminologists Cecilie Hoigard and Liv Finstad: "Every trick is a scratch on the women's minds; as the sum of scratches increases, the consequences become increasingly destructive."[16] Further, de Marneffe argues that working as a prostitute damages capacities for a healthy relationship, and that it limits a woman's future social and employment opportunities. For all these reasons, he thinks that sex work is not 'work like any other', and that if we are concerned with the welfare of sex workers we must acknowledge this.

Lori Watson stresses the empirical evidence that suggests that women who go into prostitution go into it as a last resort. She argues that these choices are not meaningful choices, but rather are made under coercive and exploitative conditions. She compares the choice to go into prostitution to the choice to sell a kidney, or to work in a sweatshop.[17] Watson argues that liberal positions, such as Satz's, are overly optimistic about the chances of a better system of the sale of sex. Watson argues that prostitution cannot meet basic health and safety requirements, and the work is inevitably unhealthy and dangerous. Sex itself involves exposure to risk, and the nature of sex work creates vulnerabilities to violence and exploitation. Watson appeals to empirical evidence from places where sex work has been decriminalized to support her argument that even with careful regulation and support, sex work is bad for women.[18]

It should be noted that the appeals to empirical evidence about the harms of prostitution are vulnerable to the objection that the evidence is gathered in an environment where prostitution is part of a sexist system, where it is stigmatized and often illegal. Even evidence about places where sex work has been decriminalized is questionable: decriminalization still takes place in a context where there is sexism, and deep social problems. It is at least possible that selling sex would be harmless in a different situation.

Considering this point shows us that the liberal feminist position and the essentialist position can begin to converge. They agree that in its current form, prostitution is very bad for women. The issue is how much would have to change for prostitution to be benign. Both liberal feminists and essentialists agree that a lot would have to change. Some, such as Laurie Shrage and Debra Satz, who take the view that sex work is morally neutral in principle, accept that in fact it would be very hard to change things so that it was safe and egalitarian.

Liberals and essentialists may also converge on policy. Given that criminalization is so undeniably harmful, the other options should be judged on their effectiveness in achieving their aim. The big difference between the liberal feminist position and the essentialist position is on what the *aim* of a policy should be. Liberal feminists think a policy should aim at safe and egalitarian sex work as an ongoing feature of society; essentialists think that a policy should aim at safety while minimizing and decreasing the practice as far as possible. This tends to lead to a divergence in what policy is favoured, with liberals favouring decriminalization and essentialists more likely to argue for regulation or the Nordic model.

Essentialism and policy

Thinkers who find that selling sex is inherently problematic – essentialists, as I have termed them – are faced with a dilemma. On the one hand, it is obvious that criminalization is very harmful, and if the aim is to prevent harms, a policy of full criminalization is likely to be counterproductive. On the other hand, if selling sex is inherently harmful, then policy should not normalize sex work, on the contrary, it should aim at abolition of sex work.

Elizabeth Anderson argues that although commercial sale of sex should be restricted (she makes an exception for cases where the economic situation is so dire that it is the best option for many women), there are other ways that sex might be sold without the problems of commodification. Anderson argues that there could be a worthwhile practice of professional sex therapy, particularly in a context where sexuality has been corrupted and deformed by inegalitarian norms. Professional sex therapy, as Anderson imagines it, would not be governed by market norms, but by professional ideals.

Essentialists inevitably face this difficulty in recommending a policy: given the harms of criminalization, they are pushed towards some sort of compromise. But it is worth pointing out that the idea that prostitution may be someone's best option is in tension with the essentialist argument that prostitution is inherently harmful. As Margaret Radin points out, the argument that selling sex is someone's best option is not an argument that selling sex is fine; it is an argument that the circumstances in which sex is sold are very problematic, and so we must work to change that. In the meantime, we need a transition strategy, and that is complex, but, essentialists insist, we should not let go of the important fact that selling sex has a negative impact on personhood.

Peter de Marneffe focusses on that point and defends restrictions of prostitution on paternalist grounds. A paternalistic argument is an argument that defends restrictions on freedom for the sake of the person whose freedom is restricted. In other words, paternalism endorses laws that are for your own good. Motorcycle helmet laws, for example, are paternalistic. A paternalistic argument for prohibition says that selling sex is mentally or physically damaging in some way, and so other things being equal, we should prevent people from doing that. De Marneffe's point is that some sort of regulation is justified by a paternalistic concern for the well-being of prostitutes.

Other essentialists, such as Catharine MacKinnon and Lori Watson, argue instead for the Nordic model, which criminalizes the buyer of sex with the express intention of discouraging men from buying sex from women. The Nordic model aims at minimizing prostitution, while avoiding the harms of criminalization. Lori Watson justifies criminalizing the buyer by citing research into the psychology of men who buy sex, showing that they have sexist and misogynistic attitudes to women, in particular the women they are buying sex from.[19] These men score highly on two of the strongest predictors of sexual aggression: 'hostile masculinity' and 'impersonal sex'. Hostile masculinity consists of attitudes of distrust and disrespect towards women, for example, rape myth acceptance, and also hyper sensitivity to rejection by women. Impersonal sex is just what it sounds like: a tendency to have sexual relationships without emotional relationships. Watson argues that criminalization of buyers is an effective deterrent and should be enacted along with more rehabilitative measures.

In general, those who think that selling sex is inherently harmful to the seller do not favour full decriminalization. Catharine MacKinnon is scathing about the potential of decriminalization to reduce harm, for, as she puts it, "everyone supports less harm to the woman. But harm *elimination* is not part of the sex work agenda because it is not compatible with sex for sale."[20]

Policies in practice

There are numerous sex workers' rights organizations, many of which have been active since the 1970s. Sex workers' rights advocates aim to have their voices heard in the context of law-making: in other words, their interventions have primarily practical rather than academic aims.

Juno Mac and Molly Smith, writing from the point of view of sex workers, examine the various possible policies and talk about the effects on real people. They confirm the liberal feminist suspicions of criminalization. Complete criminalization, as practised in the USA (and South Africa, Kenya, Uganda, Russia, Iran, Pakistan, and China) is, in their words, a "brutal, clumsy and unjust system".[21] Mac and Smith describe the cycles of harm that befall women whose work is criminalized: their work is driven into more private and thus more dangerous places; they are vulnerable to exploitation from clients, managers, and police; they cannot rely on legal or police protection; and, of course, these issues are often compounded by other criminalizations, such as drug use and immigration status, and by prejudices and oppressions about class, race, and gender.

The Nordic model doesn't fare much better. On this model, the activities of clients and managers are criminalized, but the prostitute herself is not guilty of any crime. The idea is to discourage the sex trade, while protecting the prostitute. But Mac and Smith argue that criminalizing clients is not good for prostitutes. First, it deters customers, particularly the nice ones, and so there is less and possibly more dangerous business to go round. This makes the prostitute vulnerable, less able to work on her own terms. Deterring customers is, of course, the aim of the Nordic model. But if the policy mainly deters the decent customers then it does not seem like an effective policy.

Mac and Smith argue that criminalizing clients is a bad idea because the fear of arrest for the client will impact badly on the prostitute. She will have to cater to his need for privacy, and for her, privacy is danger. As Mac and Smith put it,

> As for having a conversation before getting into his car, that is the time when he is *most* visible to the police as a client, and therefore he will be keen to speed that process up. Instead of having a conversation about services, prices and condom use while still on the street, he'll ask you to hop into his car and have that conversation while you're already speeding away. Because you need to keep his custom in order to get the money you need, you say yes. But that means you have no chance to reach a verbal agreement about prices and condoms before getting in the car, let alone assess his demeanour or even establish whether he has a friend hiding in the back seat.[22]

The Nordic model is supposed to be supplemented by 'exit services': support systems designed to help women find alternative means of support. Mac and Smith argue that even if such services were both well-funded and non-judgmental enough to work (which they are often not in the places that have piloted them), pushing prostitutes into exit services by making their working world intolerable is cruel and unjust.

Mac and Smith also argue against legalization, which they also term 'regulationism', as it inevitably comes with a suite of regulations and restrictions. Their argument is a pragmatic one. What actually happens in places where prostitution is legalized is that a two-tiered system is created, where some sex work is legal and some, the sex work that takes place outside the related zones, is illegal. For all sorts of reasons – including being trans, being undocumented, being married, drug use, having HIV – some sex workers cannot work legally, and will end up working illegally. The people who end up working illegally are usually the ones who were most vulnerable in the first place, and so suffer the familiar cycles of harm that result from criminalization.

The model that Mac and Smith favour is decriminalization. This has been tried in New Zealand and in one Australian territory, New South Wales. Prostitutes are protected by regular labour laws, and can work together, from ordinary premises or in managed brothels without fear of arrest. The system is not perfect, as criminalization in other areas, such as drugs and migration, affects many sex workers. But, Mac and Smith argue, decriminalization is the model that best protects the rights of sex workers.

It is fair to say that this is a widely shared conclusion. Decriminalization is also the solution favoured by Amnesty International, the World Health Organization, UNAIDS, the International Labour Organization, the Global Alliance Against Traffic in Women, the Global Network of Sex Work Projects, the Global Commission on HIV and the Law, Human Rights Watch, the Open Society Foundations, and Anti-Slavery International. A law review committee, comprised of people from a wide range of fields, is very positive about the effects of the 2003 New Zealand Prostitution Reform Act. The stated purpose of the PRA was "to safeguard the human rights of sex workers and protect them from exploitation; promote the welfare and occupational health and safety of sex workers; contribute to public health; and prohibit the use in prostitution of persons under 18 years of age."[23] In a summary of their findings, the review committee says, "The PRA has been in force for five years. During that time, the sex industry has not increased in size, and many of the social evils predicted by some who opposed the decriminalisation of the sex industry have not been experienced. On the whole, the PRA has been effective in achieving its purpose, and the Committee is confident that the vast majority of people involved in the sex industry are better off under the PRA than they were previously."[24]

Summary

There are two opposing views on the morality of prostitution. First is the liberal view that there is nothing wrong with it in itself, and that all the harms that are associated with prostitution are either related to criminalization, or to stigma, which comes both from vestigial remnants of old-fashioned morality, or aspects of our sexist and misogynist culture. On the other side, the essentialist view says that there is something inherently harmful about selling sex, that it is inevitably alienating and distressing in some way.

Neither view leads to an automatic conclusion about legalization. The options for legalization are complex, and range from full criminalization to full decriminalization with various options for regulation in the middle. Most feminist writers on these topics recognize that full prohibition can be counterproductive, hurting women working as prostitutes more than it helps them. But there are a wide range of positions on what should actually be done, and facts about what the actual effect of different legal policies would be are crucial.

Essentialists often defend a position known as the Nordic model, which criminalizes the buyer but not the seller. This policy is expressly aimed at minimizing prostitution, while avoiding the harms of criminalization. Liberal feminists, meanwhile, usually favour legalization or decriminalization. Legalization has the drawback of leaving open the possibility of a criminalized sector: those sex workers who, for one reason or another, cannot or choose not to conform to the regulations. Decriminalization is the option most often favoured by sex workers' rights advocates.

Notes

1 Satz, 'Markets in Women's Sexual Labour', p.80.
2 The case is discussed in this context in Juno Mac and Molly Smith, *Revolting Prostitutes*, p.24.
3 https://nplusonemag.com/issue-35/essays/cashconsent/.
4 Mill, *On Liberty*.
5 Nussbaum, '"Whether From Reason Or Prejudice": Taking Money For Bodily Services', in *Sex and Social Justice*; Satz, 'Markets in Women's Sexual Labor'.
6 Satz, 'Markets in Women's Sexual Labor', p.73.
7 Shrage, 'Should Feminists Oppose Prostitution?', p.352.
8 Brennan and Jaworski, *Markets Without Limits: Moral Virtues and Commercial Interests*.
9 Flanigan and Watson, *Debating Sex Work*.
10 Op. cit., p.84.
11 Radin, 'Market Inalienability', p.1922.
12 S. Anderson, 'Prostitution and Sexual Autonomy: Making Sense of the Prohibition of Prostitution'.
13 E. Anderson, *Value in Ethics and Economics*, p.154.
14 Gauthier, 'Prostitution, Sexual Autonomy, and Sex Discrimination', p.168, quoting Pateman, *The Sexual Contract*, p. 207.
15 MacKinnon, 'Trafficking, Prostitution, and Inequality'.
16 de Marneffe, *Liberalism and Prostitution*, p.13.
17 Flanigan and Watson, *Debating Sex Work*, pp.50–56.
18 Op. cit., p.92.
19 Op. cit., pp.143–149.
20 MacKinnon, 'Trafficking, Prostitution, and Inequality', p.286.
21 Mac and Smith, *Revolting Prostitutes*, p.115.
22 Op. cit., p.145.
23 English Collective of Prostitutes, 'Report of the Prostitution Law Review Committee on the Operation of the Prostitution Reform Act 2003', p.13. The report can be found here: https://prostitutescollective.net/wp-content/uploads/2016/10/report-of-the-nz-prostitution-law-committee-2008.pdf.
24 Op. cit., p.168.

Further reading

Dewey, S. and Kelly, P. (eds.) (2011) *Policing Pleasure: Sex Work, Policy, and the State in Global Perspective*. New York University Press. (Collection of articles presenting data and ethnographic research on sex work policies worldwide).
Satz, Debra (2010) *Why Some Things Should Not Be for Sale: The Moral Limits of Markets*. Oxford University Press. (Expands on the arguments presented in the earlier article discussed in this chapter).
Spector, Jessica (ed.) (2006) *Prostitution and Pornography: Philosophical Debate About the Sex Industry*. Stanford University Press. (Collection of articles, including several that are cited in this chapter).

6 Sexual violence and harassment

"Women are raised to work with dexterity, to keep their nimble fingers ready, their minds alert. It is her job to know how to handle the stream of bombs, how to kindly decline giving her number, how to move her hand from the button of her jeans, to turn down a drink. When a woman is assaulted, one of the first questions people ask is, *Did you say no?* This question assumes that the answer was always yes, and that it is her job to revoke the agreement. To defuse the bomb she was given. But why are they allowed to touch us until we physically fight them off? Why is the door open until we have to slam it shut?"

Chanel Miller, *Know My Name*

Chapter overview: In this chapter I look at the role that sexual violence plays in oppression. I examine Catharine MacKinnon's arguments about the social construction of sexuality in society and law, and Susan Brownmiller's argument that sexual violence is systemic. The chapter also covers issues arising from consensual but unwanted sex, the nature of sexual harassment, and the #MeToo movement.

Introduction

Susan Brownmiller, in her ground breaking 1975 book, *Against Our Will: Men, Women and Rape*, argues that sexual violence is integral to patriarchal power structures, that it both supports and results from a system where men have power over women. As Brownmiller puts it, "[Rape is] nothing more or less than a conscious process of intimidation by which *all* men keep *all* women in a state of fear."[1] To put the point in more sober terms: the threat of sexual violation and/or violence is constant; it is systemic, in that it is supported by our culture and institutions, and it is an effective way of limiting women's power and freedom.

This understanding of sexual violence contradicts a narrative that is still repeated and defended in law courts, media, and policy decisions, as well as in popular imagination. The narrative is that rapists and other sexual offenders are individual bad apples, acting alone, suffering from some sort of mental illness, and they will be dealt with swiftly when caught.

Feminists argue that the reality is that sexual violence against women is culturally condoned and normalized, and that sex crimes against women are not taken seriously by the police or legal systems.

In this chapter I focus on issues of sexual violation as they apply to cases structured by traditional gender roles and heterosexist assumptions. There are closely related phenomena that are beyond the scope of this book, particularly domestic violence and child abuse. There are also practices of sexual violence against men (for example, in prisons) that I do not examine here. Other groups are also targets of sexual violation in a systematic way: for example, gay people, trans and non-binary people, older people, and disabled people. These groups overlap with women, and they are vulnerable in ways that are related to the vulnerabilities of women. Again, although in some cases what I say here is applicable, I cannot do justice to the varying issues raised in all of these cases.

It is hard to get accurate figures about sexual violence because there is such stigma attached to being a victim of rape or sexual assault. UN Women, the United Nations organization dedicated to women's issues, estimates that 35% of women worldwide have experienced some form of sexual violence.[2] RAINN (Rape, Abuse & Incest National Network) estimates that one out of every six American women will be the victim of attempted or complete rape in her lifetime.[3] Women are much more commonly victims of sexual assault than men, and the vast majority of perpetrators are men, usually a man that the victim knows.

Yet the idea that rape is a rare crime, and that the only real rape is a violent attack by a stranger persists. This myth, and other rape myths, contribute to a climate where acquaintance rape is not taken seriously, and women are blamed for being victims. For example, provocative dress and flirtatious behaviour are often believed to invite rape ('she asked for it'). Other common rape myths include the idea that women are likely to lie about rape; that real rape is when a stranger attacks violently; that women often say 'no' when they mean 'yes'; that women welcome rape in some circumstances; that they will enjoy it in the end; that rape is a trivial event; that only young, attractive women are raped; and so on. Meanwhile, stereotypes of men make it seems that rape is inevitable, and that men cannot be held responsible, because their urges are unstoppable.

Other feminists have shown that these narratives vary with other factors, such as race and class. Patricia Hill Collins points out that Black women's sexuality is often stereotyped as voracious and primal.[4] Divisions of class and race are used to categorize women into the sexually pure, the sexually available, and the sexually disposable. This ideological story makes room for deviant women, women who want to have sex, and they are demarcated by race or class, and treated as being lower down the hierarchy accordingly. The feminist thought is that all of these constructions are just that: constructions. That is to say, they are invented, they do not reflect any deep reality. And these particular constructions are problematic, they are a form of ideology. Feminists argue that dominant understandings of sexual violence take for granted this ideological background, and so are flawed.

As Kimberlé Crenshaw points out, the ideal of the chaste women applies to white women, and the law does not treat Black women the same way.[5] Crenshaw argues that rape statutes generally do not reflect male control of female sexuality, but *white* male regulation of *white* female sexuality. Black women, she points out, are not assumed to be chaste, and to this day the likelihood of a white man being prosecuted for the rape of a Black woman is shockingly low. The converse, the rape of a white woman by a Black man, is implicitly part of the story about what rape essentially is: a violent Black man attacking a chaste white woman. The 1989 case of the 'Central Park Jogger' illustrates these racist tropes. The case was spectacularized by the media, including (then, local businessman) Donald Trump taking out full page ads in the New York newspapers demanding the death penalty for the group of young Black men who were arrested for the crime. The men were later exonerated when the actual perpetrator confessed.

Another notorious case is that of Brock Turner, the Stanford student who sexually assaulted an unconscious woman and was sentenced to only six months in jail. He served just three months. The judge's remarks in justifying the short sentence suggested that his focus was on the negative impact on Turner of a lengthy sentence, rather than on the impact of the assault on Chanel Miller, the woman whom he assaulted.

This case was not forgotten, as so many others are. Chanel Miller read out her own eloquent and powerful 7,000 word statement about the events at the sentencing, and her statement was later read aloud in the house of representatives. California voters recalled the judge and the law was changed so as to mandate a minimum sentence in sexual assault cases. Miller's book about the events, *Know My Name*, was published in 2019, and in it she talks about her own experiences, as well as those of other women, and the #MeToo movement. There are grounds for hope, that cultures and legal systems are changing, and that recognition of sexual violence as pervasive and systematic is growing.

Sexuality

One of the huge questions underlying any discussion of human sexual practices is the question of what is natural, or innate. As I argue in the introductory chapter, views about what women are innately like are often simply false. It is not true that women are less good at maths, or emotionally unstable. Yet it can be hard to unpick the deeply embedded assumptions and ideologically driven scientific views that inform our cultural norms and practices.

Throughout history and cross-culturally, women have been punished for expressing sexual feelings in anything but narrow acceptable ways (usually penetrative sex with a man), and this has often correlated with ideologically flawed scientific ideas about female sexuality. In the nineteenth century, conditions such as nymphomania and hysteria were serious diagnoses, with brutal treatments prescribed, such as being sent to an asylum, or clitoridectomy. Distrust and disdain for female sexuality are seen even in contexts where some level of sexuality is admitted as normal: Freud notoriously thought that the clitoris was an infantile organ, and that true orgasm must come from a 'vaginal orgasm' brought on by penetrative sex.

We may think ourselves more enlightened now, but young women are often ignorant about their bodies and how their sexual responses work. For example, for many years scientific orthodoxy was that the clitoris is a pea-sized nub, and that's what many people are taught to this day. However, as long ago as 1981 the Federation of Feminist Women's Health Clinics published a guide to women's sexual health, using an anatomically correct model of the clitoris, which shows that the clitoral organ is not a tiny nub, but a 10cm long wishbone-shaped mass of tissue that extends into the pelvis on both sides of the vagina. Yet this remains largely unknown and undiscussed. Our mythology about clitoral orgasm is almost as misguided as mythology about vaginal orgasm: we are telling women a falsehood about how they should be experiencing sexual pleasure.

Freud's ideas are typical in prioritizing male sexuality and particularly the penis. Feminists argue that these ideas are not 'pure science', rather they reflect and reinforce social roles. Social roles are defined for us by our society, and, as social beings, we end up conforming to those roles. As philosophers and social scientists put it, much of human interaction depends on things that are 'socially constructed'. Social construction is the process of inventing a social reality for ourselves. For example, money is socially constructed: a mere piece of metal comes to have exchange value. Social roles and identities are also socially constructed. This does not mean that they are not real. Gender roles may be invented by us, but, like money, they are hugely influential. Ideas about what men and women are like, and what roles are appropriate, are often very powerful and can be self-fulfilling.

Feminists such as Catharine MacKinnon argue that male sexuality and female sexuality are constructed in different ways, so that we see male sexuality as inherently dominating and aggressive, and female sexuality as weak and submissive. Men are the agents in sexual encounters, their desire determines what happens, and their orgasm determines what counts as sexual intercourse. These narratives affect our sense of what is normal and natural in sexual relations. We assume that men want sex more than women do. We take male sexual aggression and forcible seduction to be normal. We expect women to accommodate men's appetites, and to safeguard themselves against their excesses. As Ann Cahill puts it, this is the problem of the 'heteronormative continuum': sexual assault and supposedly 'normal' heterosexual sex are conceptually and politically related.[6]

Rape and sexual assault in law

The legal definitions of rape and sexual assault vary. Rape was originally defined as non-consensual 'penetration of the vagina with a penis'. The definition has been expanded in many places to include other orifices (which means that men can count as being raped) and other penetrating objects. Often, but not always, sexual assault is defined as non-penetrative sexual violence. The ways these terms are used sometimes indicate an assumption that rape is a more serious crime than sexual assault. I do not accept that: non-penetrative sexual assault can be as serious as penetrative sexual assault. In what follows I use 'sexual assault' as an umbrella term, which includes rape as a penetrative assault. Men are sometimes raped and sexually assaulted, and women are sometimes guilty of these crimes. But the vast majority of rapes and sexual assaults are done by men, to women.

It used to be that the only sort of non-consensual sex that the law recognized as truly non-consensual was physically forced sex. But, of course, there are other ways that non-consensual sex can happen: the victim can be under threat, under pressure, deceived, or incapacitated by sleep, drink, or drugs. And as feminist legal theorists have pointed out, requiring that a woman 'resist to her utmost' before the event counts as rape ignores the fact that women who resist a credible and serious threat are more likely to be killed. Thus the utmost resistance law asks women to value their chastity above their own lives. Feminist legal theorists and philosophers argue that rape laws were originally designed to protect male interest in their property.[7] English common law originally treated marriage as a property contract. As Joan McGregor points out, a woman who has had sex with someone other than her husband is less valuable than a chaste one, and so chastity is an extremely important value to men.[8]

Women are no longer legally the property of men, and legal reforms, mostly due to the work of feminist legal theorists such as Susan Estrich, have removed the force requirement and changed the definition of rape to non-consensual sex in many places, including the UK and the USA. But there are many places where force is still an essential part of the definition of rape. In the rest of this chapter I will take it for granted that non-consensual sex need not involve force. (I discuss the notion of consent as it appears in both philosophy and law in more detail in Chapter 11.)

Another problematic area of law is the 'marital rape exception'. It used to be the case in the UK and USA, and is still the case in most countries in the world, that rape within marriage is not a crime. On one interpretation of the history of the law, this is based on the idea of woman as property. In marrying a woman, a man comes to own her, and as she is his property, he can do what he likes with her. In that case, the man has the right to have sex with his wife, no matter what her view is. Alternatively, but with the same result, we could understand laws as being based on the feudal doctrine of coverture: on marriage, the woman's identity is subsumed under the man's, and he can no more rape his wife than he can rape himself, as Sir William Blackstone argued in 1765.[9] A more recent theory says that in marrying a man, a woman has consented to all future sex with him. This might seem a more liberal view of the issue, but in fact is no better when we consider that a man can rape his wife *at gunpoint* and yet her clear refusal counts as consent.

The marital rape exception was abolished in US states between the 1970s and the 1990s. In Scotland the marital rape exception was abolished in 1989, and in England and Wales in 1991. But the reality is that marital rape is hard to prove, and there are often loopholes that effectively legalize marital rape. In some US states the law defines rape within marriage as requiring force, so that, for example, non-consensual sexual acts with a sleeping spouse do not count as rape or sexual assault. In South Carolina, marital rape is only rape if it involves a weapon, or highly aggravated violence.

A more general way in which the law has disadvantaged women is in the evidence requirements for prosecuting rape cases. A presumption of innocence of the accused, and a presumption of mendacity in the accuser, was enshrined in the procedures for proving guilt in a rape case. As the eighteenth-century judge and legal theorist Lord Matthew Hale famously put it, a rape accusation is "easily to be made and hard to be proved, and harder to be defended by the party accused, tho' never so innocent".[10] Hale thus suggested four conditions that must be met for a conviction to be appropriate: the complaint must be immediate, the allegation must be corroborated, the victim's character must be examined, and the jury must be cautioned to be especially vigilant about the possibility of false accusation in rape cases. In other words, the courts took it that false accusations of rape were common, that there were respectable women and bad women, and that innocent men must be protected.

Again, there has been some progress here. Immediacy and corroboration requirements have been dropped in many places, and 'rape shield laws', laws that prohibit evidence about an accuser's past sexual history, have been introduced in the US states and Canada over the last 30 years. The UK introduced a rape shield law in 1999. However, it remains the case that information about a victim's sexual history is often used in court, either informally, or by legal exception.

The UK law (Section 41 of the Youth Justice and Criminal Evidence Act, 1999) states that information about sexual history was inadmissible *unless the court approved the use of such evidence*. In a now notorious case, the footballer Ched Evans was convicted of raping a 19-year-old woman in 2012. He was acquitted on appeal in 2016 after the judge allowed evidence from two men who claimed to have had sex with the accuser at around the time of the alleged rape. The case led to calls for a change in the law, but lawyers involved in prosecuting and defending in sexual assault trials defended Section 41, pointing out that there can be a valid reason for sexual history evidence. For example, if the language and signals on a previous occasion when the sex was undoubtedly consensual were sufficiently similar, the defendant has evidence for a claim of reasonable belief in consent. This example illustrates the difficulty of composing laws that can be applied to all cases. In the end, there will always be judgment calls, all the way from reporting crimes to jury instructions. How the legal system works depends on those who work in it.

Unfortunately, the reality of rape law enforcement is often problematic, starting with the first point of contact. Police procedures are haphazard at best, sexist and abusive at worst. According to a recent report by the End Violence Against Women Coalition, only 1.4% of reported rapes in England and Wales are prosecuted. EVAW describes the situation in England and Wales as "effective decriminalization of rape".[11] Women often report feeling harassed and being treated as a criminal rather than a victim, for example, in having their mobile phones seized. Rape support organizations argue that women who are raped are deterred from reporting in the first place, and, if they do report, deterred from taking the case further. The situation in the USA is similar. According to RAINN, only 5 out of every 1,000 sexual assault perpetrators will be convicted.[12]

This is the background against which feminist philosophers examine the issue of sexual violence. But law is not the only arena where it is possible to make progress. Feminist philosophers are often engaged in a more theoretical project, to situate sexual violence and sexual violation in a context of sexist oppression.

Sexual violence as a structural problem

The point of talking about 'structural problems' is to shift focus way from individual acts and individual responsibility to the more general systems and institutions that organize our lives. Social structures are things like families, schools, etiquette rules, and so on. When we are trying to explain something that happened, it is sometimes important to refer to the way that the thing that happened is enmeshed in social structures. For example, imagine that a woman, Jane, falls into poverty after her divorce. One explanation is that Jane didn't have a job in the years prior to her divorce, and so was unable to earn enough money to support herself and her children. But in order to understand the situation properly, we need to understand the social structures in play here. We need to understand that Jane was a wife in a heterosexual marriage. We need to understand how heterosexual marriage roles work.

In this section I will focus on the arguments of feminist philosophers that are aimed at understanding sexual assault as part of the general system of sexist oppression rather than as merely a crime of individuals. Susan Brownmiller, one of the first to make this argument, gives an account of the history of rape and rape tolerance, exposing rape myths and demonstrating their falsity. She emphasizes the similarities of rape in everyday life, including acquaintance rape, and rape in war. Her main claim is that rape is a weapon of subjugation.

Her arguments were a huge step forward in many ways, but were criticized by some Black feminists, despite their agreement that sexual violence is a systemic part of patriarchal power.[13] Angela Davis and bell hooks both pointed out that many of Brownmiller's examples tacitly accepted the racist rape myth that Black men are rapists, and that, in other ways, her arguments are centered on white women and do not comprehend the complex intersections of race and sex. For example, Brownmiller has a whole chapter devoted to exploring the rape of white women by Black men, yet does not spend much time at all on the rape of Black women by white men, nor on the victimization of Black men in the name of protecting white women.

Despite problems with Brownmiller's arguments, the central claim, that rape has a political significance beyond the actions of individuals, remains a crucially important one in feminist philosophy. Claudia Card, for example, argues that rape is an institution, in that it is "a form of social activity structured by rules that define roles and positions, powers and opportunities, thereby distributing responsibility for consequences."[14] Card compares the institution of rape to the institution of punishment, arguing that they are similar. When taken as a practice, punishment has certain aims and methods, and although individuals engaged in punishment may not have those aims in mind, they are nonetheless playing into the practice. Similarly, Card argues, a major task of rape is to subjugate, and it does so, just as punishment does, by threat. Those who comply with patriarchal norms of suitably meek behaviour, being a 'good girl', may not feel under threat, but they are pre-emptively surrendering. However, Card insists that those who have suffered sexual violence can resist manipulation: "Survivor rage can overcome fear".[15]

This is the context for feminist accounts of their own experiences of sexual violence. The idea is not to share a personal tragedy, but to illuminate a practice, and to undermine sexist mythology. Susan Brison's account of a violent rape examines the harms of rape and the difficulties in framing a narrative of victimhood. She discusses the way that rape is related to gender, and the way that it functions as a threat to keep women afraid and compliant.[16] Linda Martín Alcoff, in her recent book *Rape and Resistance*, integrates accounts of victims, including her own experiences, with her theoretical analyses. She argues that we must take victims' voices into account when discussing these issues. She says,

> it is the voices of victims that need to remain at the center of the fight for cultural change. It is their/our knowledge that is at stake when the problem is shrugged away, but this knowledge must be heeded to enlarge, enrich, and also complicate our understanding of the problem. Hence what we need is a new epistemology of rape, which is to

say we need a new understanding of the way in which our collective knowledge of the problem has been formed, and might be improved.[17]

It is worth stressing that the analysis of sexual violation as institutional does not imply that it is really violence, not sex. Catharine MacKinnon takes issue with a claim she attributes to Brownmiller, that rape should be seen primarily as an act of violence. That interpretation of the idea that rape is systemic, and related to patriarchal power, is understandable. We think of power struggles as using violence to subdue and subjugate. But Catharine MacKinnon argues that heterosexual sex is so bound up with the notion that men are dominant and women are submissive that rape and 'normal' sex are not so different. Rape is sexual, because sex in a patriarchal culture already embodies male dominance. As MacKinnon puts it, "The male sexual role . . . centers on aggressive intrusion on those with less power. Such acts of dominance are experienced as sexually arousing, as sex itself."[18]

MacKinnon objects that part of a problematic narrative about sexual liberation assumes that all sex is good. She worries that this is just another way of oppressing women, of making them feel that they must have sex with men, that if they don't, they are repressed.

> To say rape is violence not sex preserves the "sex is good" norm by simply distinguishing forced sex as "not sex," whether it means sex to the perpetrator or even, later, to the victim, who has difficulty experiencing sex without reexperiencing the rape. Whatever is sex, cannot be violent; whatever is violent, cannot be sex. This analytic wish-fulfilment makes it possible for rape to be opposed by those who would save sexuality from the rapists while leaving the sexual fundamentals of male dominance intact.[19]

Other feminists object that there must be a way to make sense of acceptable heterosexual sex. Ann Cahill offers such an account in her book, *Rethinking Rape*. According to Cahill, MacKinnon overstates that continuity of sex and rape. Cahill claims that most women can readily distinguish between rape and consensual sex. Cahill thinks that we can preserve the idea that rape is a crime of sex, one that is deeply bound up with sex and sexuality, and yet also that rape is a weapon of subjugation. Cahill frames her argument in terms of postmodern theories of the body, such as Luce Irigaray's. To simplify somewhat, she argues that rape is sexual just because it uses sexual body parts.

This leaves an unanswered question: why is power over women so often expressed sexually? MacKinnon's theory, that heterosexual sex is modelled on domination, solves this puzzle. In MacKinnon's view, sexual violation of various sorts is *inevitable*. It is what sex tends towards, rape is the simply the extreme. So if power needs to be demonstrated more firmly, as in war, rape is the obvious course of action. But MacKinnon's view has the consequence that heterosex under conditions of patriarchy is always problematic. She doesn't say that all sex is rape, but her view implies something close to that: that our ideas about sex have been so messed up by patriarchal ideology that it is very hard to disentangle heterosexual sex from violation. This conclusion has seemed unpalatable to many feminists, because it seems to undermine the idea that women have sexual agency.

There is a tension here that runs throughout discussions of oppression: on the one hand, women want to understand oppressive conditions, and that means seeing how pervasive they are. On the other hand, women want to throw off the false assumptions about them that justify their oppression. So, we want to complain that our sexual agency has been taken away from us, and somehow, at the same time, assert that we have sexual agency.

Bad sex

A certain strain of feminism takes the view that feminist accounts of sexual assault and harassment can undermine feminist aims by assuming that women do not have full agency, that they are at the mercy of men, and that nothing they say or do can really be taken seriously. Writers such as Laura Kipnis and Janet Halley stress that women sometimes make bad decisions about sex, they consent to sex they do not really want, but that this is just part of being an adult, and requires no special explanation or analysis in terms of oppression.[20]

Yet there is something worrying about the way that women's agency in sexual encounters is often ambivalent. The problem is that there are powerful social forces at work. As psychologist Nicola Gavey puts the domination account of sex, our cultural constructions of gender create a 'script' for heterosex, in which men are aggressive and women are passive, and this script blurs the lines between sex and rape.[21] Gavey is aware that there is a risk of reinforcing the problematic picture of women as mere victims in feminist understanding of rape, and she wants to illuminate the complexity of the 'scaffolding' of rape. Gavey examines the testimony of many women, drawing from a multitude of sources including her own empirical studies. The overall pattern is that from their earliest sexual experiences, young women feel the need to please men at the expense of their own needs.

Gavey's interviews confirm MacKinnon's worry that the sexual revolution, the promise of sexual pleasure to women, has not delivered. In fact, it just gives women an extra burden in heterosex: women feel the need to perform their own pleasure in addition to giving genuine pleasure to their male partners. Gavey frames the problem in terms of two 'organizing principles' of cultural narratives around sex. The male sex drive discourse, and the coital imperative. The convergence of these, Gavey argues, entails that it would be unfair of women to stop a sexual encounter before male orgasm. We see this idea in courts (where 'leading a man on' may still be taken as evidence that the man's belief in consent was reasonable), in the words for women who try to stop a sexual encounter before coitus ('cocktease' and so on), and in women's own acceptance of something like an obligation to please men.

Gavey goes on to examine cases where the sex, although not non-consensual, is not wanted, and where the reasons for having sex do not seem defensible in the person's own terms. Her subjects do not claim to have been raped, but report feeling uncomfortable, feeling that they were somehow made to do something they did not want to do. For example, one of her subjects reports her teenage sexual experiences as follows:

> Yeah, it wouldn't have occurred to me to have said no. (Long pause) And also that feeling of, "well, I've led them on," you know, "I've led them on this far, I've, I've done these things, I've gotten a bit drunk, I've danced in a certain way, I've got in the car, we've come to the park." And there is still, remember, very much that feeling where, you know, I mean, if you led boys on then that's what you did. Whereas, when I think about it, I think,

> well, did I, when I was sort of leading them on, did I want to have it to end in penetrative sex? I don't think I did really. I think it was just more the enjoying of the flirting, I mean I was definitely quite flirtatious and enjoying of the attention that that got me, um – but then sort of the getting in the car, it was like, well, it was like, you just had to pay your dues really, for the other three hours of flirting, you know.[22]

Gavey's point is that there is a huge weight of expectations on women to behave in a certain way, and so they end up behaving that way, even against their better judgment. It seems as though the women are trying to achieve control over the situation by faking agency, but telling themselves it was their choice.

Some of Gavey's subjects report or reveal an even more problematic reason for having sex, and that is to avoid being raped. Being raped would be more violent, more dangerous, but it would also be awkward to deal with, both personally and socially. It is easier to smooth things over, and to avoid victim-blaming, and social punishment. One of the subjects describes a situation where her flatmate unexpectedly climbed into her bed when she was asleep and started, quite roughly, forcing sex on her. She did not resist. She says,

> We just make it easier, it's like – and he doesn't have to think of it as rape. It's just what he does to women that he wants to sleep with, you know, he wants to fuck with, I mean, you know, but – He doesn't ever have to confront his behavior, or the effects of it, um, and because, you sort of protect them from it. You know. And you internalize the distressing effects of it as well so that they don't – as the victim or whatever – have to see you as the victim or whatever, so they don't even have to see the distressing effects.[23]

Gavey's interviews suggest a continuum between consensual and non-consensual sex. Women are under pressure all the time, they face many barriers to controlling their own sexuality, and the pressures are so pervasive that even women themselves can't reliably tell when they are genuinely consenting to sex. This is exactly the conclusion that writers like Kipnis object to. They insist that women should be treated as adults, capable of making both good and bad decisions. They worry that an account like MacKinnon's has the unwelcome result that consent does not matter at all, as no consent to heterosex can be assumed to be uncoerced.

Ann Cahill suggests a way of distinguishing between unjust sex and rape that may avoid that conclusion. Cahill's central claim is that what defines rape is that the agency of the woman is ignored. The rapist overrides the will of the woman. However, in unjust sex, the agency of the woman is deployed against her, it is hijacked, in that her consent is obtained, not through respect for her agency, but just in order to legitimize the encounter.

Cahill points out that in many of the cases that Gavey examines, consent is explicitly sought, in fact the man goes to great lengths to obtain consent. The problem is that the woman feels that this is the only response she is allowed to give. So, although she is being treated as properly agential in one way – a proper sexual subject, as Cahill puts it – she is not being treated as a sexual subject in the right way. The man wants her to consent to make what he does permissible; he does not want to engage with her real interests on a sexual level. Cahill's proposal aims to capture why this is problematic, without saying that consent has lost all meaning.

There are at least three sorts of unwanted sex. First, there is sex that is clearly rape, sex that was not consented to. But there are more difficult cases, where sex is consented to even though it is unwanted. These are the cases we might call 'bad sex', and it is an open question whether and to what extent the sex is unjust. We can certainly imagine sex that is unwanted but not unjust. First, as Sarah Conly argues in her discussion of coercion, one can be seduced or persuaded, and make a decision that one is not fully behind, but a decision one is responsible for.[24] For example, in a mundane case, one can be persuaded to buy a product from a mall salesperson, and although the decision seems foolish later on, the consent given was proper consent. Another sort of situation is one where the decision is made in a clear-eyed way, and is not regretted, but involves choosing something one would rather not have, other things being equal. For example, a woman might choose to have sex, not because she feels desire, but because she wants to comfort her partner, or she wants to get pregnant. That is also genuine consent. Those who object to feminist critiques of heterosexual norms for sex want to argue that all unfortunate sexual choices are cases like these two.

This strikes many as implausible. It does not seem that when women choose to have sex that they don't really want, it's always simply their mistake, or their compromise. As Scott Anderson objects to Conly's account, and as Gavey's interviews illustrate, it seems that some seduction and persuasion is not just individuals making individual choices, but men pressuring women into sex by (knowingly or unknowingly) bringing the weight of their patriarchal power to the situation.[25] Thus as well as bad sex, there is also unjust sex, sex that even if we do not think it is non-consensual, is morally problematic.

Sexual harassment

Sexual harassment was not recognized as a problem, or even named, until fairly recently. The phrase 'sexual harassment' originates with Carmita Wood's case. Wood was a 44-year-old administrative assistant in the physics department at Cornell University from 1971 to 1974. She was harassed for that entire period by her boss, who groped her, made sexual comments, and tried to kiss her. When Wood complained, she was told that 'any mature woman should be able to handle it'. When she applied for a transfer, she was refused. Eventually, she resigned and was denied unemployment benefits on the grounds that she had left the job for personal reasons. When Wood left, she sought advice from the Human Affairs Office at Cornell, and along with several other women, including Lin Farley, she founded an organization called Working Women United, which aimed to raise awareness of and fight sexual harassment in the workplace.

Another leap forward was with the publication of Catharine MacKinnon's 1979 book, *Sexual Harassment of Working Women: A Case of Sex Discrimination*, which argued for bringing sexual harassment into law and regulation. In the USA, and many other places, sexual harassment is now classified as a form of sex discrimination, and is therefore illegal in workplaces and educational institutions. Despite that, it is still rife, and often behaviour that constitutes sexual harassment is seen as normal banter, 'locker room talk', or standard seduction. The idea that a mature women should be able to handle it remains.

Under US law, which is based on MacKinnon's proposals, sexual harassment can be 'quid pro quo' (sexual attention is demanded in return for something else, such as promotion, or grades), or 'hostile environment', where the victim is made to feel extremely uncomfortable. In the UK, sexual harassment is defined as unwanted behaviour of a sexual nature which violates your dignity, or makes you feel intimidated, degraded, or humiliated, or creates a hostile or offensive environment.

One thing that feminist thinkers point out is that sexual harassment, like other forms of sexual violation, is not just something that individuals do, it is a structural issue: it depends on and feeds into existing inequalities. Anita Superson, following MacKinnon, argues that sexual harassment is a form of domination, and a harm to all women.[26] Superson argues that sexual harassment expresses the general belief that women have certain limited, inferior roles: as sex objects, or as wives and mothers, nurturers and comforters. Even mild forms of harassment, such as cat-calling, express the belief that it is permissible to rank women on their appearance. Actions that create a hostile environment, denigrating women by displaying pictures of them naked in professional contexts, for example, express a belief that women are not full participants in that professional arena. These beliefs are reinforced by sexual harassment, and continue to limit the opportunities and freedoms available to women.

The claim that sexual harassment is domination depends on it being essentially related to inequality. MacKinnon's definition of sexual harassment explicitly includes that claim: "Sexual harassment, most broadly defined, refers to the unwanted imposition of sexual requirements in the context of a relationship of unequal power."[27] As Superson acknowledges, this has the implication that men sexually harass women and not the other way around.

> When a woman engages in the very same behavior harassing men engage in, the underlying message implicit in male-to-female harassment is missing. For example, when a woman scans a man's body, she might be considering him to be a sex object, but all the views about domination and being relegated to certain sex roles are absent. She cannot remind the man that he is inferior because of his sex, since given the way things are in society, he is not.[28]

This presents a problem: what should we say about other cases, where there is something like sexual harassment, but the victim is not a woman? One option is to redefine sexual harassment so that there is no reference to oppression or dominance. We could simply say that sexual harassment is a sort of coercive sexual attention, focussed on an individual. But that ignores something that does seem crucial: that men have power over women, and that is what enables them to harass women with confidence and impunity. Harassment is often out in the open, even now: it is mainstream, it is part of the normal course of events. It differs from bullying, which is recognized as unacceptable, and is usually disguised or hidden.

An alternative interpretation suggests that although sexual harassment always involves an abuse of power, there are many complex intersections of groups, and power patterns can vary accordingly. Thus the inequality needed to make an instance of harassment qualify as structural rather than individual may be produced by gender or race, or other social hierarchies. So, for example, it is arguable that a woman could harass a man in a context where all the other social markers are in her favour: for example, a white woman might sexually harass a Black man. This preserves the idea that being vulnerable to sexual harassment is related to social position without committing us to a particular account of the hierarchies within intersecting oppressed groups. Sexual harassment, on this conception, is sexualized harassment of someone in a less powerful social group. Thus it is not sex discrimination as such, but discrimination more generally.

Elizabeth Anderson points out that there are plausible cases of sexual harassment that involve targeting a victim in a sexual way but without a sexual motive. Rather, it is a means of expressing disapproval of a woman's role in a man's world, or of her way of dressing or behaving. And again, not all victims of that sort of role policing are women: men who don't seem masculine enough, women who don't seem feminine enough, as well as gay and trans people all face this sort of harassment. Anderson argues for a definition of sexual harassment that is based on sex discrimination, as MacKinnon suggests, but that takes a more expansive definition of what male domination involves: it involves policing gender in a wide range of ways.

Anderson draws on legal theorist Kathryn Abrams' account to explain how male dominance functions through harassment:

> Gender harassment functions to maintain a male monopoly on relatively privileged jobs, and to mark femininity as inferior, because it is linked to incompetence at these jobs. Along with gender policing of women, it also functions to keep sub-ordinate female roles occupied. Both types of harassment reinforce separate spheres of work and conduct, with the female sphere inferior in esteem, prerogatives, and material rewards. Pornography and open sexual fantasizing about women marks the workplace as male space, dominated by a sexist view of women as men's sexual playthings. Harassment of lesbians and female-to-male transsexuals amounts to gender boundary policing, ensuring that women stay women and accept their role as men's sexual objects. In all of these cases, harassment of women is discriminatory because it is sexist: it asserts the superiority of men over women, the masculine over the feminine, and ensures that women stay in subordinate, feminine positions.[29]

In the end, Anderson thinks that there are cases that cannot be fitted neatly into this account. She argues that there is no single framework that can accommodate all the valid claims of sexual harassment: it is not a unified phenomenon. Jennifer Saul makes a related point in her plea to philosophers to 'stop thinking so much about sexual harassment'.[30] Saul is writing in the context of widespread condoning of sexual harassment in the academic discipline of philosophy. For several years she ran a blog called 'What it's like to be a Woman in Philosophy', and was deluged with stories of sexual harassment and other sexist and offensive behaviours, ranging from small insults and slights that added up to a hostile environment over time, to actual assaults. Saul argues that philosophers, and others in an environment where there is sexual harassment, should not make the mistake of thinking that if something is not technically sexual harassment then there is nothing we can do about it. We can react in ways that might help the victims and might stop the perpetrators, even in cases where the conduct is not officially sexual harassment.

Title IX

In American universities over the last ten years, much discussion of sexual violation and harassment has focussed on Title IX regulations. The political situation is very much in flux as I write in 2020, but it is worth spending a little time explaining the regulatory situation as it stands now, and examining the philosophical issues that arise. Title IX of the Education Amendments Act (1972) states that "No person in the United States shall, on the basis of sex, be excluded from participation in, be denied the benefits of, or be subjected to discrimination under any education program or activity receiving Federal financial assistance". In 2011 the Obama administration's Department of Education issued guidelines about how to interpret Title IX requirements. This guidance was a response to a perceived crisis on university campuses, which seemed to be facing epidemic proportions of rape and sexual harassment. The National Sexual Violence Resource Center reports that one in five women are sexually assaulted while at college.[31] These guidelines were overturned by the Trump administration, and the Title IX guidelines are currently (in 2020) being reviewed by the Department of Education.

The Obama era guidelines were designed to strengthen the Title IX regulations. They required that universities pursue investigative and disciplinary proceedings to prevent sexual harassment and assault, and mandated that the standard of proof in such proceedings should be preponderance of evidence, rather than the 'beyond reasonable doubt' standard used in criminal proceedings. Many universities and colleges have developed their own consent policies, in which they lay out the conditions for what counts as consent, often demanding that consent be a clear and verbal 'yes'.

One objection that was made to the new guidelines was that it was all slanted towards the accuser, and that the whole system might enable malicious accusations. In particular, critics objected that the 'preponderance of evidence' standard was unfair to the accused. The preponderance standard just requires that it seems more likely than not that the accused is guilty, and so is a lower bar than the beyond reasonable doubt standard. The objection is that it would be too easy to convict someone, particularly in a situation where the alleged assault has often taken place with no witnesses, and we have a 'he said/she said' situation.

First, it is important to note that the preponderance of evidence standard is the usual standard for civil cases, that is, cases where the punishment is something like a fine or expulsion, and not a custodial sentence. Criminal cases, where the punishment is more severe, use a 'beyond reasonable doubt' standard. So there is nothing very peculiar about the guidelines' suggestion that the appropriate standard for a university tribunal, a tribunal that can at most mete out a sentence of expulsion, is the civil standard not the criminal one.

A second, more difficult issue, here, is who we think is being treated unfairly in a situation where there is a risk of a mistaken verdict. The objectors argue that it is unfair to the man that women can easily make false accusations, when, for example, they simply regretted having consensual sex. Supporters of the Title IX tribunals point out that this assumes that a false accusation is more likely than a true one. That idea feeds into the common stereotype of women as deviant and mendacious, out for revenge, constitutionally unstable. It brings to mind Lord Hale's warning, quoted earlier in the chapter, that a rape accusation is easily made and difficult to prove, and that it is difficult for an innocent man to defend himself. (It also resonates with Kate Manne's expression, 'himpathy'.[32] It is common in sexual assault cases, as with Brock Turner's, for the judge and commentators to feel more sympathy for the accused than the accuser.)

But in fact it is very rare for women to make false accusations. The National Sexual Violence Resource Center reports that studies put the number of false reports between 2% and 10%.[33] And these numbers may be higher than the real number, because they do not distinguish between insincere reports and mistaken reports, that is, reports of incidents that turn out not to be a crime. For example, a third party may report something that turns out to be consensual. There may also be reports that are logged as false reports that are in fact cases where an initial report was dropped by the accuser. Furthermore, these studies cannot distinguish between cases where the accuser made a false accusation and cases where the accused was wrongly exonerated.

Another strain of objection to the stricter interpretation of Title IX regulations on American university campuses is that it limits freedom and infantilizes women in the service of a bogus sort of political correctness. Janet Halley argues that feminists like MacKinnon want to argue that the conditions of everyday life under patriarchy are equivalent to the threat of force, and so that women are not able to consent.[34] Laura Kipnis argues that the whole story of rape culture and sexual violence on campus is overblown hysteria, and that measures such as tribunals encourage women to think of themselves as weak and in need of protection. They both stress that women sometimes make bad decisions, they have bad sex, but they do it consensually, and it is not the place of the law, or of the universities, to intervene.[35]

The first part of Kipnis's claim, that there is not nearly as much sexual assault as people think, is belied by the statistics, as I have said. But it may be that Kipnis and other critics of a stricter Title IX regime have an alternative definition of sexual aggression in mind. If they tacitly or explicitly accept a patriarchal account of sexuality; if they think that forcible seduction is normal; that consent under pressure is nonetheless valid consent; and that women often bring rape on themselves by 'asking for it' in some way, then naturally the statistics will not be convincing to them. Of course, statistics like the oft-quoted finding that 20% of undergraduate women have suffered some sort of sexual assault depend on self-reporting. If someone distrusts the self-reports, thinking that young women have been encouraged to see sexual assault where there is merely seduction, they will not be convinced.

Me Too

'Me too' was originally the name for a movement started by Black feminist activist Tarana Burke, aimed at supporting victims, particularly those in marginalized communities who struggled to access official sources of support. In 2017, in the wake of the allegations against Harvey Weinstein, Hollywood actress Alyssa Milano urged women to share the hashtag #MeToo as a way of drawing attention to the magnitude of the problem, and (perhaps subconsciously) to express the philosophical idea that sexual violence is structural, that people like Weinstein are not just bad apples, but part of a patriarchal power structure. Within a day, 12 million women had shared the hashtag, proclaiming that they too had been victims of sexual violation.

A more general movement has developed since the initial social media campaign. It is not centrally organized, so it is not easy to state its aims with confidence, but the basic intention is to raise awareness and thus to stop the sort of sexual predation that, as Weinstein himself said, was taken as normal in the world he grew up in. #MeToo is not a theory; it is a political and social movement, aimed at change. However, philosophers will have things to say about its presuppositions, its methods, and its messages.

One uneasy issue for #MeToo is how inclusive it is. The original Me Too was started by a Black woman, and aimed at helping Black victims, who are disproportionately disadvantaged by sexual violence and often under-represented in mainstream feminist analysis. Thus it is ironic that the Me Too movement was popularized by very privileged white feminists. On the one hand, it can seem as though Black and working-class women are merely being paraded across the stage (quite literally, as in the case of the 2017 Golden Globes). As Tarana Burke is reported as saying to white actress Michelle Williams when Williams suggested that she take Burke to the awards ceremony, "Why? I'm trying very hard not to be the black woman who is trotted out when you all need to validate your work".[36] On the other hand, the alternative is doing nothing, as Burke is aware. The high profile of Hollywood actresses and their version of #MeToo has also raised the profile of Burke's work and her focus on vulnerable women, as Burke herself acknowledges.

Another complex question about inclusivity concerns abuse of men, and cases of same-sex violence and harassment. Around the same time as the Harvey Weinstein accusations surfaced, Anthony Rapp came forward with an account of harassment by the actor Kevin Spacey, which had taken place when Rapp was a teenager. Dozens more credible allegations followed. The issues here echo those discussed above about whether sexual harassment essentially involves a social power differential, and whether that must be related to gender. What should we say about men who complain that men who are harassed by women are left out of the #MeToo movement? One thing that could be argued is that although women do harass men, it is not at all the same sort of thing. Women do not harass men with the approval and safety net of a matriarchal power structure behind them.

The case of same-sex harassment is more complex, as I indicate in the discussion of sexual harassment earlier in the chapter. Deviations from heteronormative gender roles are a threat to patriarchal power, and sexual violence towards and within groups that do not conform to those norms may well be bound up with issues of gender. Lori Watson explores this argument in relation to harassment between women. Watson argues that masculine presenting women are targets for unwanted sexual attention as a result of various assumptions that stem from gender hierarchy. For example, masculine identified women are taken to be sexually available, as per the standard script for masculinity. Thus another woman will expect her advances to be accepted, without regard for actual desire. At the same time, the script for sexual availability has a twist: the masculine identified woman is still a woman, and so she is also subject to the femininity script, which says she must be nurturing and must attend to the needs of those around her. So her agency in the situation is suppressed.[37]

Another issue is about whether the movement puts too much pressure on victims to disclose. Disclosing a past incident can be risky for victims. Victims often know the perpetrator, so they also face potential retaliation or social ostracism. There are also serious emotional burdens for victims in revealing sexual assault, reliving it, and being forced to process it in public. Furthermore, as Miranda Pilipchuk points out, there may be an extra burden on women of colour, who, if the perpetrator is from their own community, may worry that disclosure will be used to fuel racist stereotypes. Another burden is the burden of being asked to educate others. (I discuss Uma Narayan's account of this phenomenon in the chapter on knowledge and ignorance.) Finally, as Pilipchuk argues, the possibility of disclosing can become a *de facto* expectation, and those who do not join in with a 'me too' are either assumed not to be victims, or taken as reneging on an obligation. Pilipchuk argues that #MeToo should return to the aims of the original Me Too in focussing on the survivors more, and in particular, survivors from marginalized communities.[38]

Robin Zheng addresses the methods of the #MeToo movement. She draws a contrast between structured organizing (such as union-approved strikes) and mass protest, such as the Women's March on Washington in 2016. Zheng argues that although mass protest has symbolic value and can be very effective at changing a conversation, we need more than that. As she puts it, "disruption functions to loosen the grip of unreflective ideology and subject it to questioning. But it is not sufficient. Momentary disruptions can be brushed past, and powerful elites will not be swayed unless they are under pressure, that is, unless and until their self-interest is actually at stake."[39]

Zheng points out that women are particularly vulnerable to sexual violation because of the conditions of work in a gendered division of labour. Women, particularly poor women and women of colour, often work in relative isolation (as maids, for example, or as fruit pickers, in exploitative conditions, that they have no means of exit from). Zheng cites the Fair Food Program in Latin America as an instance of organizing that has successfully cut down sexual harassment. The FFP is a contract between the farmworkers and the corporate buyers, such as McDonald's and Taco Bell. The buyers must pay an extra penny on the pound to raise wages, and must agree (on pain of penalty) to buy only from farms that are abiding by the FFP code of conduct. This code was drawn up in consultation with farmworkers and uses their knowledge of exploitative practices. It includes zero tolerance for forced labour, child labour, and sexual harassment. Zheng reports that, since 2013, there has been only one case of sexual harassment on farms signed up to the FFP.

This success is due to a combination of pressure by consumers (threats of boycotts) and the efforts of worker coalitions in proposing and implementing policies. Zheng sees the #MeToo movement as a pressure movement, one that needs to be backed up by detailed demands for change. As well as changing the ideology, we need to think about the economic conditions that render women vulnerable, and work to change those.

These criticisms do not detract from the enormously positive influence of the #MeToo movement. The sheer numbers of women participating, women from all different backgrounds, is powerful. Additionally, the movement has made people think critically about the complex issues around resisting and reporting incidents. This helps victims answer the hostile questions, 'Why didn't you just leave?', 'Why didn't you report it immediately?', and so on. In raising awareness, #MeToo makes it more likely that women will be believed. I discuss epistemic oppression and silencing in Chapters 12 and 13. In brief, the thought is that women are routinely prevented from speaking, and are not taken seriously when they do speak. Philosophers have tried to understand and map these phenomena. #MeToo aims to change the situation, to create a situation where women are taken as credible witnesses.

Summary

Rape and other forms of sexual violence are endemic. Many feminists argue that rape is accepted and normalized in our society. The history of rape law confirms this, insofar as law defines rape very narrowly and makes it very difficult to prosecute. Reforms in rape law have ameliorated some of these issues, in moving away from the requirement that rape involves physical force; in dropping the requirement that a woman must have resisted to her utmost in order to count as having refused; in dropping corroboration and immediate reporting requirements; and in abolishing the marital rape exception. However, actual legal practice remains extremely problematic, with low reporting, which may be due to a deterrence effect of sometimes brutal treatment by police and the courts, and very low conviction rates. This is the backdrop against which feminist discussions of rape and consent take place.

Susan Brownmiller's view that rape is not just accepted but an essential part of patriarchal power structures has been taken very seriously by feminist thinkers, but there is disagreement about how that works. Catharine MacKinnon argues that sexuality is socially constructed so that heterosexual sex is always about male dominance and female submission. On that view, rape and heterosex are on a continuum, and rape is an extreme form of normal sex. Other feminists worry that this picture excludes the possibility of good sex, that it is patronizing to women, in that it paints a picture of women as victims, and may reinforce their subordinate status.

The idea that heterosex inherently involves male dominance provides an explanation for the ambivalence and ambiguity of consent in many cases. 'Bad sex', as I call it, is sex that someone consents to in some sense, but does not want. If, as MacKinnon's framework suggests, women are constantly under coercive pressure to have sex, then the common experience of bad sex can be explained. As Ann Cahill argues, that does not necessarily mean that consent is never valid or important: there can be cases where consent has been given even if the situation is not morally ideal. Other feminists argue that women sometimes consent to things they do not want out of foolishness or pragmatism, and we should not undermine women's agency by assuming their consent is coerced.

This dilemma, the dilemma between understanding oppression as pervasive and granting women agency, appears in discussion of sexual harassment, where the question is whether the definition of harassment should include gender power differences. Some feminists argue that sexual harassment essentially depends on male power, others argue that the definition should be more neutral. The same basic issue appears in reactions to Title IX regulations in the US, and to the #MeToo movement. On the one hand, sexual violence against women seems to be structural: deep in the fabric of our cultures and institutions, rendering all women vulnerable at all stages of life. On the other hand, we do not want to take for granted that women are constitutionally weak or incapable of informed consent.

Notes

1 Brownmiller, *Against Our Will: Men, Women and Rape*, p.15.
2 www.unwomen.org/en/what-we-do/ending-violence-against-women/facts-and-figures.
3 www.rainn.org/statistics/victims-sexual-violence.

4 Collins, *Black Feminist Thought*.
5 Crenshaw, 'Demarginalizing the Intersection of Race and Sex: A Black Feminist Critique of Antidiscrimination Doctrine, Feminist Theory, and Antiracist Politics'.
6 Cahill, 'Unjust Sex vs. Rape', p.746.
7 See the Women's Law Project Report, 'Rape and Sexual Assault in the Legal System'.
8 McGregor, *Is It Rape? On Acquaintance Rape and Taking Women's Consent Seriously*.
9 Quoted in Anderson, 'Marital Rape Laws Globally: Rationales and Snapshots Around the World'.
10 Hale, *The History of the Plea of the Crown*, p.635.
11 www.endviolenceagainstwomen.org.uk/rape-effectively-decriminalised-womens-coalition-demand-action-from-prime-minister/.
12 www.rainn.org/statistics/criminal-justice-system.
13 Davis, *Women, Race, and Class;* hooks, *Ain't I a Woman: Black Women and Feminism*.
14 Card, 'Rape as a Terrorist Institution', pp.297–298.
15 Op. cit., p.302.
16 Brison, *Aftermath: Violence and the Remaking of a Self*.
17 Alcoff, *Rape and Resistence*, p.2.
18 MacKinnon, 'Sexuality, Pornography, and Method: "Pleasure under Patriarchy"', p.316.
19 Ibid., p.323.
20 Halley, 'The Move to Affirmative Consent'; Kipnis, *Unwanted Advances: Sexual Paranoia Comes to Campus*.
21 Gavey, *Just Sex? The Cultural Scaffolding of Rape*.
22 Op. cit., p.134.
23 Op. cit., p.152.
24 Conly, 'Seduction, Rape, and Coercion'.
25 Anderson, 'Sex Under Pressure: Jerks, Boorish Behavior, and Gender Hierarchy'.
26 Superson, 'A Feminist Definition of Sexual Harassment'.
27 MacKinnon, *Sexual Harassment of Working Women: A Case of Sex Discrimination*, p.1.
28 Ibid., p.55.
29 Anderson, 'Recent Thinking About Sexual Harassment: A Review Essay', p.307.
30 Saul, 'Stop Thinking So Much About "Sexual Harassment"'.
31 www.nsvrc.org/sites/default/files/publications_nsvrc_factsheet_media-packet_statistics-about-sexual-violence_0.pdf.
32 Manne, *Down Girl: The Logic of Misogyny*.
33 www.nsvrc.org/sites/default/files/Publications_NSVRC_Overview_False-Reporting.pdf.
34 Halley, 'The Move to Affirmative Consent'.
35 Kipnis, *Unwanted Advances: Sexual Paranoia Comes to Campus*.
36 www.theguardian.com/world/2018/jan/15/me-too-founder-tarana-burke-women-sexual-assault.
37 Watson, '#MeToo?'
38 Pilipchuk, 'Good Survivor, Bad Survivor: #MeToo and the Moralization of Survivorship'.
39 Zheng, 'Women, Work, and Power: Envisaging the Radical Potential of #MeToo', p.31.

Further reading

Burgess-Jackson, K. (ed.) (1999) *A Most Detestable Crime: New Philosophical Essays on Rape*. Oxford University Press. (Edited collection of essays on moral and legal issues).
Curry, Tommy (2017) *The Man Not*. Temple University Press. (Examines the systematic sexual abuse of Black men and boys).
Manne, Kate (2020) *Entitled: How Male Privilege Hurts Women*. Penguin. (Written for a general audience, this is an account of the various ways that male privilege works).
Teays, Wanda (ed.) (2019) *Analyzing Violence Against Women*. Springer. (Collection of philosophical essays on violence, including sexual violence against women).
Wilson, Yolonda (ed.) *Feminist Philosophers and #MeToo*. Routledge. (Forthcoming collection of philosophical essays on #MeToo).

Part 2
Theory

7 Sexism, oppression, and misogyny

"If all men are born free, how is it that all women are born slaves?"

Mary Astell, *Political Writings*

Chapter overview: This chapter offers a philosophical introduction to the major concepts of feminism, looking at accounts offered by Marilyn Frye, Iris Marion Young, Ann Cudd, and others. I explain the term 'patriarchy', and examine the concepts of sexism, oppression, and misogyny.

Introduction

In Part 1 of this book I examined a range of practical issues that affect women in today's world. Some of these issues affect men too, and even harm them. But it has been implicit that oppression is a more complicated notion than harm, and that women are the oppressed group, and men are the oppressor group. This is the nature of a sexist and misogynist patriarchy. All of these terms need some explaining. In this and the following chapters, which make up Part 2, I look more closely at the terms and concepts that we need for talking about feminist issues.

I use the term 'patriarchy' a lot, as a name for the hierarchical social system that deprives women of power and authority, and takes being a man to be an essential qualification for those goods. The term 'patriarchy' is not a very precise one: the idea is not to describe a very fine-grained organization of power, but rather to capture a general pattern. Crucially, a patriarchal system is one that functions at a structural level. Our social lives are organized by institutions, such as education and healthcare systems, and formal and informal practices, from marriage to table manners. These structures are governed by internal rules, including rules about who can do what, and under what circumstances. A patriarchal system is one in which those structures tend to hand power to men.

In theory, one could imagine a benign patriarchy, as there might be in a family with a father and children. Sometimes, power is differentially distributed in a way that benefits everyone.

Patriarchal norms are often presented as if they are there to protect women, but feminists argue that they are deeply problematic. An important feature of the patriarchal systems that feminist philosophers see and critique in the actual world is that they are sexist, misogynistic, and oppressive. As I use the term 'patriarchy' in this book, patriarchy is a system of power that enacts sexist oppression.

The first question then is: what is sexism? Sexism is discriminating against someone on the basis of sex. But is it always sexist to take sex into account? Compare the same thought about race. Critical race theorists point out being 'colour-blind' is not being anti-racist or even non-racist: only the racially privileged can ignore race. We need to think about the history of oppression based on race, even if ultimately we don't think that race is a deep biological category. Race may be a social construction, and perhaps we would be better off without it, but we have to recognize disadvantages and vulnerabilities that arise from racism. Similarly, given the history of oppression based on sex, the widespread belief that sex indicates deep and important differences, we need to talk about sex. This implies that some discrimination, as in noticing that the category is relevant, is permissible. So, sexism is not simply discrimination based on sex – it must be a certain sort of discrimination.

Clearly, we also need to know what oppression is. Philosophers define oppression in various different ways, but they agree that it is not just harm – it is a special sort of harm, a harm related to power structures. So, to be a randomly selected victim of an internet fraud is not to be oppressed, although it is to be harmed. More controversially, we will see that many feminist philosophers argue that to be harmed due to bad effects of being in the more powerful group does not count as oppression. Patriarchal power structures are bad for everyone, but not in the same way, and philosophers such as Marilyn Frye argue that it is important to recognize those different sorts of harm.[1]

Finally, the term 'misogyny' is used in various ways. Traditionally, 'misogyny' is defined as a hatred of women, a hostile gut reaction often expressed in lurid representations of women. As Andrea Dworkin argues in *Woman Hating*, misogyny provides a way to read cultural practices across the globe, from fairy tales to pornography, from witch hunts to foot binding, but is also a plausible interpretation of many depictions of women in mainstream film and television (for example, in the frequent representations of naked and semi-sexualized female corpses). Recently, Kate Manne has argued that we should see misogyny not as a personal attitude, but as an indispensable part of the patriarchal power structure. She argues that misogyny is the enforcement wing of the patriarchy, which steps in to punish women who step out of line.[2]

So, all three of those terms – sexism, oppression, and misogyny – need some explanation. They mean different things, and it is not always clear how the terms are being used. In everyday usage, this doesn't matter much. But feminist philosophers aim to give more precise accounts of these notions, accounts that can be used to illuminate the complexities of the issues.

Sexism

The term 'sexism' is commonly used to refer to ways of thinking and acting that underestimate or deny benefits to women just because they are women. So, for example, it is sexist to deny women the right to vote, because there is no good reason to deny them that right; it is just denied on the basis of being a woman. It is sexist to exclude women from certain areas of professional life. It is sexist to treat or think of women as sex objects. These are all ways of discriminating against women.

But there might be other ways of differentially treating men and women that are not sexist. Take for example programs of affirmative action. Is it sexist to insist that 50% of people on a shortlist be women? Some people object that it is, on the grounds that it is acting on the basis of the fact that someone is a woman or a man, and if that is sexist in other contexts, it is sexist in this one too. However, as I point out in the discussion of affirmative action in Chapter 2, the justification for treating women differently is not just that they are women. There are various different justifications given for affirmative action, but none of them rely simply on the fact that someone is a woman. It is not, 'we should include her on the shortlist because she is a woman'. Rather, it is something along the lines of, 'we should pay special attention to this candidate because she is a member of a group that is historically and currently oppressed'. Affirmative action programs do not focus on being a man or a woman for its own sake, but on the relevance of group membership for fairness, given a history of discrimination against that group.

What about treating group membership as important due to differences between groups? What if there are differences in the average capacities of men and women, for example? Would it be sexist to differentiate between men and women on the basis of those differences? Yes, it would be. Here, group membership is not relevant in the same way. In the affirmative action case, the point is that group membership is relevant even if the issues of oppression and dis-advantage do not apply to the individuals who are affected. Different accounts of affirma-tive action defend that claim in varying ways. For example, forward-looking accounts of affirma-tive action might argue that because women have been excluded from STEM careers, and we want to have more women in STEM positions, it is important to provide role models who are women. Obviously, this woman, the one who gets the job, need not have been excluded pre-viously – the point is that her being a woman is relevant to justifiable social aims. Contrast, for example, exclusion of women from the military. The justification for that might be that women are not as strong as men. But even if that is true on average, it is not true for every man and every woman. For a particular woman who wants to join the military it would be unfair to exclude her on the basis of being a woman. If strength matters, the military selec-tion procedure should test for strength, not for being a woman.

This point is put slightly differently by Marilyn Frye. In her chapter, 'Sexism' in her 1983 book, *The Politics of Reality*, she discusses her original definition of sexism, which defined sexism as irrelevant differentiation between the sexes. She refines that definition because in one sense, sex is often relevant. It is relevant because people are sexist. So for an employer looking to hire a supervisor who will supervise men, perhaps it makes sense to hire a man: the employees will be more cooperative with a man boss. But that does seem sexist. We need to recognize sexism, but then try to counteract it, not pander to it. This is why we must be careful in formulating the goal that is to be met, and be sure that it is justifiable. Refusing to hire a woman to supervise men seems to be pandering, and not justifiable. Having said that, of course it is important to recognize that hiring a woman in that sort of situation will throw up issues, and that perhaps preventative actions should be taken. Again, it is not sexist to recognize sexism.

Frye stresses the importance of seeing sexism as a structural phenomenon rather than something that occurs in particular acts. This is crucial: the point is not to identify and label particular acts or people as sexist. The point is that our whole social world is structured by gender, and that this is sexist, because gender is not in fact relevant. As Frye points out, we are under enormous pressure to identify ourselves along a gender binary through our dress style and self-presentation.[3] This may be less true now than it was in 1983 when Frye was writing, but it is still true. And the reason that we must identify ourselves as a (heterosexual) man or woman is in order to easily be assigned the appropriate gender role. But these different roles are not justified by any real or relevant differences between men and women, though they pretend to be.

It is worth noting that sexism is premised on (and enforces) a strict correlation between biological sex and social role. Feminist theorists since the 1970s have made a distinction between sex and gender to point out that biological sex is one thing, the social role a separate thing, and that the two are not necessarily connected. Complex issues arise about trans identity, which I do not cover in this book. But one thing is not in dispute: the sexist system will not tolerate any divergence between biological sex and binary gender roles. Talia Mae Bettcher, in her account of transphobia, argues that the mandatory system of public gender presentation is there to force us to declare our genital status, and that in turn is supposed to reveal deep and important features of our being.[4]

On the broader view of sexism suggested by Frye's and Bettcher's work, sexism is the system of sex marking, the system of thinking that being male or female has far-reaching consequences, and that it is therefore crucial that we declare our biological sex unambiguously and stick to our assigned roles. This allows us to say that affirmative action is not sexist, as that is about moving *away* from the sex-marking system. It recognizes the history but does not endorse it. Whereas pandering to the system by refusing to hire a woman to supervise men implicitly endorses the system.

Oppression

What is 'oppression', and what distinguishes it from other forms of wrongful harm? The gender rules - the system of sex-marking - affect both men and women in negative ways. Both men and women are restricted by patriarchy. Women are restricted in all kinds of ways, which I discuss in the chapters in Part 1. But men are restricted too, for example, in their mode of dress, their employment options (it is still the case that very few men go into caring professions, far less stay at home to parent children), and their permitted range of emotional expression. Famously, 'boys don't cry'. And some of these are areas where men are restricted and women are less so: women are permitted to wear a wider range of clothes, they are permitted to work or stay at home, and they are allowed to cry, to be emotional, to admit it when they are weak.

Marilyn Frye argues that, nonetheless, men are not oppressed by patriarchy. Frye takes the phenomenon of the 'double bind', where all the options result in penalties, as fundamental to oppression. There is pressure on women to be cheerful and accommodating. If women conform to that, they signal that they are compliant and so participate in their own erasure, as Frye puts it. But if women show their anger or annoyance, they are seen as difficult, bitter, problematic. There is no way to win. There is pressure on women to be heterosexual, and attractive according to feminine norms of appearance. But it is very difficult to find a happy medium: if a woman is obviously sexually active, she is labelled a slut and not taken seriously. If she is not, she is labelled a prude, frigid, or a lesbian. If a woman dresses up, she is advertising her sexual availability; if she doesn't, she has let herself go. All the options lead to censure. Men do not face the same double bind. Like women, they are penalized for transgressing the relevant gender rules, but, unlike women, they are rewarded for conforming.

Frye's point is that the ways that women are restricted are systematic, part of an overall structure that limits and restricts them. If you look at one small part of the picture, the fact that men hold doors open for women, for example, it will not look like a serious restriction. But if you step back and look at the whole picture, it becomes clear that women are trapped by a combination of elements. She uses the analogy of a birdcage:

> Consider a birdcage. If you look very closely at just one wire, you cannot see the other wires. If your conception of what is before you is determined by this myopic focus, you could look at that one wire, up and down the length of it, and be unable to see why a bird would not just fly around the wire . . . it is only when you step back, stop looking at the wires one by one, microscopically, and take a macroscopic view of the whole cage, that you can see why the bird does not go anywhere; and then you will see it in a moment.[5]

If we look at only one aspect of women's experience – one bar of the cage – we will not see that any particular aspect of the structure counts as oppression rather than just something harmful, or even something that is not harmful at all. Frye points out that the practice of men holding doors open for women seems harmless considered on its own, indeed, it seems helpful and respectful to women. But Frye argues that it is merely symbolic: women do not *need* help getting through doors, and what it symbolizes is "female dependence, the invisibility or insignificance of women, and contempt for women."[6] The false gallantry of holding doors open is part of a structure where women are disempowered, not respected as agents, and not allowed true freedom.

The various ways in which men are harmed by patriarchy do not count as oppression in Frye's account: men may be restricted, but they are restricted as a by-product of a system that privileges them overall. Frye also uses an example concerning race: a white person may complain that they are not free to enter a Black ghetto. As Frye points out, this restriction of freedom needs to be looked at in the broader context: a system that systematically privileges white people over Black people. The same applies to harm: there may be ways that men are harmed (they are undoubtedly emotionally harmed by the rules of emotional expression), but this harm does not count as oppression. It is important to point out that patriarchal structures hand men *power*. Patriarchy does not necessarily hand men happiness.

Harry Brod discusses an example of the way that men can suffer under patriarchy in his account of pornography. Feminists urge us to consider the ways that pornography's depictions of women provide a script for, and reinforce, male dominance. Brod points out that men are harmed by pornography too: it creates an unrealistic standard and unrealistic

expectations that men can never live up to. But Brod is not saying that this means that pornography is not sexist and oppressive. As he puts it:

> an aspect of an oppressive system, patriarchy, operates, at least in part, to the disadvan-
> tage of the group it privileges, men. This claim does not deny that the overall effect of
> the system is to operate in men's advantage, nor does it deny that the same aspect of the
> system under consideration, that is, male sexuality and pornography under patriarchy,
> might not also contribute to the expansion and maintenance of male power even as it
> also works to men's disadvantage.[7]

Brod uses a Marxist model to argue that capitalism has evolved so that individual capitalists
have had to rely more and more on centralized management, and have thus become dominated by impersonal market forces. Brod suggests that, similarly, individual patriarchs of the
pre-capitalist era have much less power in the current system. Men still have collective power
over women, but in the late capitalist phase of patriarchy, individual men are themselves
dominated by the same patriarchal powers. Brod diagnoses the 'crisis of masculinity' that we
often hear about as a struggle between two patriarchal systems: the older individualistic one,
and the newer one, in which patriarchal power is primarily institutional.

Iris Marion Young builds on Frye's account of oppression. Like Frye, she argues that men
are not oppressed, although they are often harmed by patriarchy. Like Frye she emphasizes
the importance of seeing oppression as structural, as being about groups and group membership.[8] Young also emphasizes that oppression can come about without a clearly identifiable
oppressor. She argues that we tend to see oppression as an exotic problem, in which a powerful despot oppresses a people. But, citing Foucault on the nature of power, Young stresses
that power is embedded in everyday structures, and can operate through the actions of well-
meaning people. Oppression does not happen primarily through the conscious actions of
individuals, but through the structures within which they operate.

Young argues that oppression is complex, and recognizing the interlocking nature of it
is crucial (I discuss intersectionality in Chapter 8). We thus need a pluralistic account of
oppression, one that recognizes that people can be privileged in some ways and oppressed
in others, and that the ways that different oppressions intersect can throw up new varieties
of oppression. Young identifies five faces of oppression, which constitute what she argues is
a comprehensive account of oppression.

First is *exploitation*. The idea of exploitation is thoroughly explored by Marx, but as Young
points out, Marx's account of oppression deals exclusively with class exploitation – one group
owns the means of production and exploits the group that does not. But Young focusses on
what she takes to be the central insight in Marx's concept of exploitation: "oppression occurs
through a steady process of the transfer of the results of the labor of one social group to
benefit another."[9] Young points out that the fruits of women's labour are routinely transferred
to men: first, the fruits of their material labour, but also, the fruits of their emotional labour,
and their nurturing and sexual energies.

Second is *marginalization*, where a member of the relevant group is excluded from the
workforce on group grounds (i.e., because the person is from a particular racialized group).
This results in material deprivation, dependency on social services in a mode that suspends

basic rights to privacy, respect, and individual choice, and exclusion from opportunities for social cooperation and recognition (and hence from exercising important capacities). Thus, Young says, marginalization is perhaps the most dangerous form of oppression.

Third, is *powerlessness*. Young points out that American society is firmly segregated between 'professionals' and 'non-professionals', or the middle class and the working class. This is a new development in the structure of capitalism, and so does not appear in Marx's theory. But, Young argues, it is an important mode of oppression. The middle class are comparatively privileged, even if their labour is exploited by the capitalists, but the working class are powerless. "The powerless have little or no work autonomy, exercise little creativity or judgment in their work, have no technical expertise or authority, express themselves awkwardly, especially in public or bureaucratic settings, and do not command respect."[10]

This last point is a point about cultural respectability norms. Young says that the privilege of respectability is assumed to belong to white men, and everyone else must fight to be taken seriously, to be afforded basic respect. This has grave practical results – in seeking loans or jobs, or housing, for example. But it is also something that is discernible in everyday interactions. Young says,

> The privilege of this professional respectability appears starkly in the dynamics of racism and sexism. In daily interchange women and men of color must prove their respectability. At first they are often not treated by strangers with respectful distance or deference. Once people discover that this woman or that Puerto Rican man is a college teacher or a business executive, however, they often behave more respectfully toward her or him.[11]

The term 'microaggression' was not in use when Young wrote this in 1990, but that is part of the phenomenon she identifies here. There are small mechanisms that can escape notice if looked at individually, but collectively form a pattern of disrespect and oppression.

Fourth is *cultural imperialism*. The experience of the dominant group is made to seem 'normal', and anything else is 'Other' – deviant and inferior. The oppressed groups are reduced to stereotypes, not seen as individuals. These stereotypes limit what people can actually be: the fact that the stereotypes are applied by the group with power means that the powerless cannot escape them, cannot be anything other than what the stereotypes dictate.

This is the same point that sociologist and Black feminist theorist Patricia Hill Collins is making when she talks about controlling images of Black women, as the 'Mammy', the 'Matriarch', the 'Welfare Mother', and the 'Jezebel'.[12] Collins argues that these stereotypes are the ideological justification of oppression. The idea also appears in Uma Narayan's work on third world feminism, where she identifies three roles that are imposed on third world feminists, the 'Emissary', the 'Mirror', and the 'Authentic Insider'.[13] Rosabeth Moss Kanter identifies four possible roles for women in the public domain in America: 'the Pet', 'the Mother', 'the Battle-axe' (or 'Iron maiden'), and 'the Seductress'. She terms the phenomenon 'role traps'.[14] (I discuss ideology in Chapter 9 and explore several issues related to Young's account of cultural imperialism in Chapter 12 on knowledge and ignorance.)

Fifth is *violence*. Young points out that theories of justice do not usually pay attention to violence, because violence is not usually understood as social injustice. But the violence Young is talking about is not one-off, not randomly perpetrated by individuals. It is directed at group members simply because of their group membership. Violence against groups is systemic – a social practice. It is tolerated and normalized. It is taken for granted that violence like this will occur, and, Young argues, the line between expecting and tolerating is a fine one:

> Group violence approaches legitimacy . . . in the sense that it is tolerated. Often third parties find it unsurprising because it happens frequently, and lies as a constant possibility at the horizon of the social imagination. Even when they are caught, those who perpetrate acts of group directed violence or harassment often receive little or no punishment.[15]

This is the point made by many feminists writing about sexual violence: that rape is normalized and tolerated, taken as an inevitable fact. I discuss the structural character of sexual violence in Chapter 6.

Ann Cudd, in her book-length examination of oppression, aims to give an account of oppression that is broadly consistent with those of Frye and Young, but captures the concept more precisely. Cudd gives four conditions for oppression:

1. The harm condition: There is a harm that comes out of an institutional practice.
2. The social group condition: The harm is perpetrated through a social institution or practice on a social group whose identity exists apart from the oppressive harm in 1.
3. The privilege condition: There is another social group that benefits from the institutional practice in 1.
4. The coercion condition: There is unjustified coercion or force that brings about the harm.[16]

As Cudd acknowledges, the first three conditions are more or less the same as Frye's, but the coercion condition is important to capture the injustice in the way that inequalities between groups come about. Cudd assumes that it is possible that some group could become disadvantaged relative to another through entirely voluntary and justifiable processes, and if that happened, it would not be a case of oppression. But group inequalities in the actual world are usually oppressive, and are brought about and maintained coercively. Cudd argues that the major coercive mechanisms are violence and economic deprivation, or the threat of violence and economic deprivation.

For all of these writers, the aim is to distinguish between accidental or coincidental harms and the harms that come about as an essential part of unjust and oppressive systems. This is not always easy, as Sally Haslanger stresses. Group membership may be targeted indirectly, in such a way that it is not obvious that it is being targeted. Haslanger uses the example of the racism of child welfare policy, as discussed by Dorothy Roberts.[17] The policies are not explicitly racist; they do not say, 'we will take children away from Black families'. Yet child welfare policy disproportionately affects the Black community, reinforcing negative stereotypes, undermining the autonomy of Black families, and weakening their ability to challenge discrimination. Haslanger points out that it is not easy to see where the racism is. To see that this is racist oppression we have to look beyond the official explanation for taking children away from their families (that the children are at risk) and see how the policy actually works (it is disproportionately applied to Black people, and applied in a punitive way), and how the underlying causes of poverty and deprivation are themselves racist.

The concept of oppression is crucial for feminist aims. As Frye says, we should not allow it to be stretched too thin, overused, so that it applies to any sort of harm. Oppression is essentially related to power. The powerful group maintains their power by keeping the oppressed group down. That doesn't mean that the powerful group does this deliberately, or that all members of the oppressed group are happy and are fulfilled. Systems of oppressions are bad for everyone. Yet they are strangely resilient. As we see in the chapter on ideology, some of this is explained by the tendency of people, both the oppressors and the oppressed, to internalize ideologies that justify and disguise oppression.

Mechanisms of oppression

There are various ways that oppression is enforced and maintained. As many writers on oppression point out, one of the main forms of control is violence. Ann Cudd points to the prevalence of sexual and domestic violence to support her claim that violence is the main foundation of gender oppression. Cudd argues that women across social groups suffer a threat of violence, and so it is fair to say that women as a social group are targeted: the violence is systemic. She points to the high incidence of rape in previously all-male environments, like the military, to argue that rape is sometimes a quite deliberate tool of oppression, a signal that women are not welcome. More generally, as we saw in the chapter on sexual violence, many feminists have argued that rape and the threat of sexual violence are a way in which men control women.

Cudd argues that women are in a 'social threat situation': men (as a group) pose a threat to women (as a group).[18] Actual violence against women is not merely random, and so there is always a credible threat of more, keeping women in a state of fear and submission. Women are harmed both materially and psychologically by violence and the threat of violence. Furthermore, violence against women is often hidden: it takes place out of the public eye, and it is normalized, so it is difficult to recognize and address. These issues have been discussed by many feminist philosophers and feminist theorists. The ubiquity and normalization of violence against women remain shocking.

The second major force that Cudd identifies is economic deprivation. Cudd puts her argument in terms of segregation: where there is segregation by social group, one group is deprived of opportunities that are reserved for the other group. Segregation can be *de jure* (enforced by law) or *de facto* (socially practised and informally enforced). Globally, there is a significant history of *de jure* segregation by race, and in places where legal segregation has stopped, as in the USA, there is still rampant *de facto* segregation. Similarly with gender, although even more so than racial segregation, there remain a large number of places with *de jure* gender segregation of various sorts. I examine many of these issues in the chapter on work and care, under the description, 'the gendered division of labour'. Cudd is making the same point: the gendered division of labour harms women; it keeps them dependent on men.

Another mechanism of oppression is ideology. Oppressive systems maintain themselves by getting people to believe that the system is just, or inevitable, or natural, or all three. In other words, by inculcating and nurturing false consciousness: internalization of the ideology that justifies the system. Both men and women come to accept the stories about what men and women are, and what the suitable roles are for them. Thus oppressive conditions are apparently accepted voluntarily, and then it seems that it is not fair to characterize the conditions as oppressive. If she *chose* it, how can it be a problem? That cry is often heard in discussion of the gender pay gap, as I point out in the chapter on work and care.

But choice is not a simple notion. We can choose things under coercive conditions. These are clearly not free choices. We can also choose under conditions where, in some sense to be defined, we are not fully autonomous, our choice does not come from our own will, but from distortions caused by oppressive systems. Take, for example, someone who has been brainwashed into a cult, and insists that their bearing children for the cult leader is a free choice. We will tend not believe them and will not take their words at face value, because we think that the conditions of that choice are distorting. The sort of false consciousness that we see under patriarchy is generally more subtle and harder to define than the brainwashing of a cult, but the basic idea is the same. The person believes that they are acting freely and not against their own interests, but from the outside it is clear that they only think that because they are in the grip of a compelling but problematic worldview that they have been fed by someone who benefits from the lie.

Ideology and false consciousness are complex issues, and have their own chapter. Other major mechanisms of oppression are also examined further in the chapters of Part 2. In Chapter 10, on objectification I discuss the various ways in which women are objectified, treated as less than human, as the 'Other' as Simone de Beauvoir puts it. In the discussions of knowledge and ignorance (Chapter 12) and silencing (Chapter 13) I examine the ways in which women are not permitted to have a voice, or their voices are not listened to, or not heard.

Recent theorists have identified other, apparently trivial, things that happen to members of oppressed groups as mechanisms of oppression. I have already mentioned role traps. The way that women politicians are pilloried and mocked by their opponents and the media makes it harder for them to succeed. Men in public life are mocked too, but it is instructive to see that whereas men are mocked as individuals, women are mocked on the basis of role traps. Whether it is in the workplace, seeking accommodation, or simply shopping for clothes, women have roles imposed on them. They are in a double bind: if they conform to the role they are obediently limiting themselves, if they rebel they are disapproved of.

Another case where it is crucial to look at the overall pattern is the case of 'microaggressions'. A microaggression is a small insulting act that gets its importance from being part of a pattern. Regina Rini, in her discussion of microaggressions, points out that the idea has been around for a while, although it has only come into common usage recently. She quotes Harvard psychologist Chester Pierce, writing in 1970:

> Even though any single negotiation of offense can in justice be considered of itself to be relatively innocuous, the cumulative effect to the victim and to the victimizer is of an unimaginable magnitude. Hence, the therapist is obliged to pose the idea that offensive mechanisms are usually a micro-aggression, as opposed to a gross, dramatic, obvious macro-aggression such as lynching.[19]

Microaggressions need not be insults on the face of it, and they need not be deliberate. One common example of a microaggression is a compliment, 'you are doing very well in graduate school!' to a woman student, or a question to a person of colour, 'where are you from originally?' What they have in common is that the background assumption behind the remark or action accepts and applies oppressive stereotypes. One microaggression is not oppressive on its own, but a slow and constant drip of microaggressions contributes to undermining status and self-confidence, and indicating low status to others.

Another useful term that has relatively recently come into usage is 'gaslighting'. The term is from the 1944 movie *Gaslight*, in which a husband tries to make his wife believe that she is going insane by doing various things to her or her surroundings (including causing the gaslights to dim) and then denying it. In common usage the term refers to emotional or cognitive manipulation designed to get someone to distrust their own perceptions of things. As Kate Abramson points out in her discussion of gaslighting, the current usage does not entail that the gaslighting is deliberate, or that it has a clear purpose.[20] So, for example, the powerful might deny the existence of microaggressions, not in order to make the victim think they are insane, but simply because they believe it to be true, given their perspective and because they want to preserve their own power and comfort. However, this counts as gaslighting: a denial of the agent's perception of things.

Gaslighting is relevant to oppression because it is a way of silencing complaints, denying that there are any grounds. Gaslighting is closely related to epistemic injustice, which I discuss in more detail in the chapter on knowledge and ignorance. Abramson argues that gaslighting as a tool of oppression is perfectly suited to sexist oppression:

> There's one particular sexist norm that warrants special highlighting in this context. Call this the sexist norm of self-doubt. We encounter this under various guises every day. One form of it is the normative expectation that men will be forthright and confident, while women who are equally so get called foul names. Another variety shows up in our classrooms, when women hesitate to speak, and later say, "I didn't think it was important". Another form is gendered-deference, as when women in our classes defer to male voices, affording those men unjustified excesses of credence. And so on. It's part of the structure of sexism that women are supposed to be less confident, to doubt our views, beliefs, reactions, and perceptions, more than men. And gaslighting is aimed at undermining some-one's views, beliefs, reactions, and perceptions. The sexist norm of self-doubt, in all its forms, prepares us for just that.[21]

These mechanisms of oppression are both cause and symptom. They are ways of keeping women in their place, but they are also effects of a system in which women are oppressed. For example, the casual everyday objectification of women could not happen if women were not already in a subordinate position. In a world where children grow up to take it for granted, however, it seems normal. And so it continues – those children grow up to think it is normal, and to enact it. And then it serves to maintain the status quo.

Misogyny

The traditional understanding of misogyny is as 'woman hating', a visceral hostile reaction to women. As Andrea Dworkin argues, there is evidence for a deep and hostile attitude to women in much of our culture. Our stories, our films, our pornography, our dress codes, and other cultural practices often treat women as sex objects, but also as something disgusting, dirty, dangerous, worthless. The statistics about violence against women paint a depressing picture, one that calls for an explanation in terms of hatred and anger against women.

Kate Manne does not dispute that misogyny is hostile, but she argues that the traditional definition (the 'naïve conception', as she calls it) is not particularly helpful.[22] Manne resists what she takes to be individualistic and psychologistic aspects of the traditional understanding. She argues that misogyny is not primarily a matter of individuals' attitudes; it is structural, a functional part of patriarchy. Policies and institutions can be misogynistic, not just people. This is the same point that Frye and Young make about sexism and oppression: we should not see sexism as something that resides in individuals, but as something that permeates our social world, and is not necessarily in the minds of individuals at all.

Second, Manne suggests misogyny is not primarily a matter of how someone feels, but of what they do, of the attitudes *expressed*, rather than the attitudes held. For example, imagine that someone displays a picture of a woman being degraded. That is a misogynistic thing to do, even if the person had no idea their act was problematic, and had no personal hatred for women. The anti-psychologistic feature is also familiar from accounts of sexism and oppression. As Ann Cudd argues, in her account of the psychological harms of oppression, "the crucial factor in assessing group status and harm is the effect on the victim, not the intention of the perpetrator. This is true for two reasons: first because intention is difficult to assess, and second, because intentions may not be consciously admitted."[23] Manne takes the general use of the term 'misogyny' to imply that the misogynist hates women and intends to express that hatred. Manne wants to give an anti-psychologistic account of misogyny, one that locates it in observable and objective features of an act or structure rather than in individual psychologies.

These amendments to the traditional account mesh well with feminist analyses of sexism and oppression. First, we can see misogyny as part of the system; it is not just down to individuals. This is a standard line about sexist oppression in general. As feminists point out, seeing things on an individual basis hides the truth, which is that sexism is deeply entrenched in our systems and our institutions. So Manne is arguing for misogyny to be included as part of an account of structural oppression.

Manne goes further, and offers an account of the function that misogyny plays in the patriarchal structure. She argues that misogyny is the enforcement branch of the patriarchy: women who do not conform (or are suspected of planning disobedience, or are taken to symbolize non-conformers) are punished by various forms of harsh treatment. We could put this in terms of mechanisms of oppression: Manne wants to use the word 'misogyny' as an umbrella term for the enforcement mechanisms of a patriarchal system. On this account, violence, microaggression, gaslighting, silencing, role traps, and so on are all misogyny. They are 'down girl moves' as Manne puts it.

Manne insists that it is important to recognize that misogyny is directed only at some women: those who do not comply with patriarchal norms. This aspect of her view has been criticized by Susan Brison. Brison argues that misogyny *is* directed at all women, including women who have not disobeyed or stepped out of line. Brison argues that misogyny is directed at women no matter what they do. It is a classic double bind:

> If misogyny is punishment for something, it is for the original sin of being born female. Under patriarchy, to be fully human is to be male; therefore, women are out of line – dehumanized – to the extent that they fail to conform to the male norm. But they are also out of line if they threaten male dominance by "acting like men." This is the mother of all double binds.[24]

Brison goes on to note that misogyny could exist in a system in which there was total compliance, and therefore no need for an enforcement branch. We might imagine a Stepford wives style society, in which women are docile and compliant (*The Stepford Wives* is a novel in which the perfect wives are so compliant that the protagonist suspects that they are robots created by their husbands). Brison points out that this society could be full of misogyny, in the sense that there could be all sorts of hostility to women, expressions of hateful attitudes, and even violence. We have no reason to think that all this would die away with total compliance.

Brison's argument suggests a rehabilitation of the traditional account of misogyny, taking on board Manne's two amendments. Perhaps we should see misogyny as primarily structural and as residing in meaning not emotion. But it is nonetheless fair to characterize it as 'hatred of women': it is just that the hatred is not a psychological state of individual men, rather it is something that is expressed by systems and institutions. On this account, Dworkin's analysis of woman hating in popular culture captures central cases of misogyny. Hers was never intended to be an account of the emotional reactions of individual men.

And, it is worth stressing that insofar as individual men are misogynist in the woman hating sense, we needn't think that this must mean they hate *all* women. Clearly, some misogynists love their mothers and sisters. Manne takes that as an objection to the traditional view: she points out that accusations of misogyny are often rebutted by the claim that the alleged misogynist loved *some* women. In Manne's view, according to which misogyny applies only to some women (the transgressors), an accusation of misogyny cannot be rebutted in that way. But even if we think that misogyny is best described as woman hating, it need not imply that a misogynist hates all women.

Manne uses an analogy: imagine someone who has been disappointed by all the restaurants he has ever been to. Manne argues that we cannot conclude he hates restaurants. There might be one perfectly suited to him somewhere.[25] But we can turn this analogy around: the fact that someone hates restaurants doesn't preclude him from liking some. Perhaps he makes an exception for the one he has been going to since childhood. Or perhaps he is conflicted, and that some restaurants both attract and repel him, inducing self-loathing insofar as they attract him. We can think of individual misogyny like that: an attitude of hatred for women that is complex, and not monolithic, an attitude that the holder can struggle with, and make exceptions to.

The first two aspects of Manne's account of misogyny, that it is structural, and that it is in the meaning of acts or systems, not in the attitudes behind them, are uncontroversial. However, the idea that misogyny is limited to this particular function is more problematic. Manne's aim is to revise the concept, so as to make it more useful. We might question whether this is a more useful concept than something like the naïve conception, according to which misogyny goes beyond enforcement, in being a sort of hatred, and is not necessarily useful for enforcement.

To some extent we simply have a disagreement over the best use of the available terms here. The phenomenon Manne identifies, the enforcement branch of the patriarchy, is worth theorizing and naming. But the older definition of misogyny as hatred of women may be something worth having a name for too.

Summary

It is important to make sense of the various terms that are centrally used in feminist theory. 'Sexism' refers to a system where biological sex is taken to justifiably determine social role. So long as we are clear about that, it is not necessarily sexist to take the fact that someone is a man or a woman into account in some contexts, for example, where the aim is to subvert the sexist system.

Oppression is the particular sort of harm and inequality that comes about when social groups are taken to have hierarchically defined essential qualities, and one group is dominant over another. Philosophers have given various accounts of exactly what oppression involves, but there is broad agreement that although men suffer under patriarchy, they are not oppressed. The damage they suffer is a side effect of power, not a result of powerlessness.

Oppression is brought about and maintained through various mechanisms: violence and the threat of violence, economic deprivation and the threat of economic deprivation, a suite of small mistreatments and hostilities, and through internalization of ideology, or false consciousness, which I discuss in Chapter 9.

The term 'misogyny' is used loosely in common parlance, and is ripe for careful philosophical treatment. Kate Manne argues that we should see misogyny as structural and as residing in social meaning, not the motives of the speaker. She also argues that misogyny is 'the enforcement wing of the patriarchy', there to deter and punish transgressors. This captures one important phenomenon, but perhaps it leaves the older sense of misogyny as woman hating in search of a new term.

Notes

1 Frye, 'Oppression', in *The Politics of Reality*.
2 Manne, *Down Girl: The Logic of Misogyny*.
3 Frye, 'Sexism', in *The Politics of Reality*.
4 Bettcher, 'Trapped in the Wrong Theory: Rethinking Trans Oppression and Resistance'.
5 Frye, 'Oppression', in *The Politics of Reality*, pp. 5-6.
6 Op. cit., p.6.
7 Brod, 'Pornography and the Alienation of Male Sexuality', p.267.
8 Young, 'Five Faces of Oppression', in *Justice and the Politics of Difference*.

9 Op. cit., p.49.
10 Op. cit., pp.56–57.
11 Op. cit., p.58.
12 Collins, 'Mammies, Matriarchs and Other Controlling Images', in *Black Feminist Thought: Knowledge, Consciousness, and the Politics of Empowerment*.
13 Narayan, 'Through the Looking-Glass Darkly', in *Dislocating Cultures: Identities, Traditions and Third World Feminism*.
14 Kanter, *Men and Women of the Corporation*.
15 Young, 'Five Faces of Oppression', in *Justice and the Politics of Difference*, p.62.
16 Cudd, *Analyzing Oppression*, p.25.
17 Haslanger, 'Oppressions: Racial and Other', in *Resisting Reality: Social Construction and Social Critique*, p.329.
18 Op. cit., p.90.
19 Pierce, p.266, quoted in Rini, 'How to Take Offense: Responding to Microaggression', p.334.
20 Abramson, 'Turning up the Lights on Gaslighting'.
21 Op. cit., p.22.
22 Manne, *Down Girl: The Logic of Misogyny*.
23 Op. cit., p.156.
24 Brison, Remarks in Boston Review Forum on *The Logic of Misogyny*.
25 Manne, *Down Girl: The Logic of Misogyny*, p.48.

Further reading

Beeghly, Erin and Madva, Alex (2020) *An Introduction to Implicit Bias: Knowledge, Justice, and the Social Mind*. Routledge. (Collection of essays from philosophy and social sciences on implicit bias).
Butler, Judith (1990) *Gender Trouble: Feminism and the Subversion of Identity*. Routledge. (Butler's account of gender, including her influential idea that gender is a social performance.)
de Beauvoir, Simone (2011) *The Second Sex* (first published 1949). Translated by Constance Borde and Sheila Malovany-Chevallier. Vintage Books. (Classic feminist text, introducing many central ideas in feminist thought).

8 Intersectionality

"What I really feel is radical is trying to make coalitions with people who are different from you. I feel it is radical to be dealing with race and sex and class and sexual identity all at one time."

Barbara Smith, *Across the Kitchen Table*

> Chapter overview: I explain Crenshaw's account of intersectionality, and distinguish intersectionality from closely related notions such as inclusivity, with which it is often confused. I explore the role of privilege, the notion of solidarity, and the relationship between structural identity and subjective identity as those notions arise in intersectionality theory.

Introduction

Intersectionality is a conceptual framework that illuminates the interactions of different axes of oppression. Examples of intersectionality come up in virtually every chapter of Part 1. It comes up in Chapter 1, in looking at the complexities of global feminism and multiculturalism. In Chapter 2, on work and care, and in the chapter on sex work, intersectionality is relevant to the ways that varying stereotypes of women affect their working conditions and their vulnerabilities. In the chapter on pornography, and in my discussion of sexual violence, I examine the way that race, sexuality, and gender identity play a part in how women are categorized as sex objects. It is crucial to recognize that different women are affected by oppression in different ways depending on the various social groups they are part of.

Sexism is one axis of oppression, but race, sexuality, gender conformity, class, religion, immigrant status, disability status, and so on all affect how sexist oppression manifests. The point of intersectionality theory is that these different axes of oppression cannot be understood on a simple additive model. That is, we can't simply say that being a woman can be added to being Black, and conclude that a Black woman suffers both sorts of oppression. The interactions of different harmful stereotypes result in new stereotypes, and new modes of oppression. 'Intersectionality' refers to the way in which different oppressions interact.

So a Black woman will face discrimination not simply as Black and as a woman, but as a Black woman, and that may be different to sexism faced by white women and to racism faced by Black men.

The term 'intersectionality' comes from legal theorist Kimberlé Crenshaw, who coined it in order to criticize discrimination law, which she saw as problematically focussed on only one axis of oppression at a time. The idea appears earlier in the work of Black feminists such as Audre Lorde, Angela Davis, bell hooks, and Patricia Hill Collins, among others. The earliest appearance of the idea is possibly 1892, in Anna Julia Cooper's *A Voice from the South by a Black Woman of the South*. She says, "[T]he colored woman of to-day occupies, one may say, a unique position in this country . . . She is confronted by both a woman question and a race problem, and is as yet an unknown or an unacknowledged factor in both".[1]

The earliest naming of the idea, as 'interlocking systems of oppression', might be in the Combahee River Collective Statement. The Combahee River Collective was a group of Black feminists, and their 1977 statement is a laying out of the conceptual tools needed to critique and change the various oppressions facing Black women in the US. The statement begins,

> The most general statement of our politics at the present time would be that we are actively committed to struggling against racial, sexual, heterosexual, and class oppression, and see as our particular task the development of integrated analysis and practice based upon the fact that the major systems of oppression are interlocking. The synthesis of these oppressions creates the conditions of our lives. As Black women we see Black feminism as the logical political movement to combat the manifold and simultaneous oppressions that all women of color face.[2]

The term 'intersectionality' is now in wide circulation, but it is not always used in a very precise way. First, intersectionality is not the same as 'inclusivity'. The confusion arises because feminism should clearly be inclusive, and part of inclusivity is recognizing that there are many different sub-groups of women, and that different women experience oppression in different ways. One important reason that oppression is different for different women is that women can be members of other oppressed groups as well as being women, and membership of those other groups affects how sexism works. But only this last point, that other group memberships may alter the manifestation of sexism, is properly understood as intersectionality. To put it another way, intersectionality is not the action of including different groups, it is the theoretical move of working to understand the interaction of different group memberships.

Another confusion about intersectionality that should be avoided is over whether it is a theory of subjective identity, that is, a theory about how people do or should identify themselves. As Brittney Cooper argues, intersectionality should be understood as being about identity only in a structural sense. That means that the sort of identity at issue here is the identity recognized by the oppressive system. As Cooper puts it, "The law conceptualizes people through the structural identities of gender, race, sexual orientation, or national origin. These kinds of identities are different from personal identities of the sort that refer to personal taste, personality traits, gender performativity, or intimate and filial relationships."[3] Cooper stresses that Crenshaw's account of intersectionality is bound to fail if understood as an account of subjective identity, an account of what we take ourselves to be. But Crenshaw is explicit that that is not what intersectionality is. It is merely an account of how the world positions people according to perceived categories, and it makes no attempt to make sense of how people position themselves. It is fundamentally a theory of systems of power.

As I say, the idea of intersectionality originated and has been most thoroughly developed in work by American Black feminists, but as a theoretical framework it is not limited to describing the experience of American Black women. As Patricia Hill Collins and others argue, the application of intersectionality extends to any relevant oppression, and to exploring the complexities of global feminism.[4] Some Black feminists have worried that the 'travelling' of the theory will undermine its power as a tool for understanding the oppression of Black women. Nikol Alexander-Floyd, for example, worries that as theorists focus on other, more privileged groups, the oppression of Black women is forgotten and marginalized again.[5]

One issue here is that one of the classic moves in an oppressive society is to conveniently forget the cultural and intellectual contributions of oppressed groups, or to reattribute their contributions to white men. As Sirma Bilge notes, as the notion of intersectionality becomes more mainstream, it is more and more often referred to as the brainchild of feminism instead of as the brainchild of Black feminism.[6] The worry that intersectionality's roots in Black feminism will be occluded is a valid one. Further, the worry that focus will move from the intersectional oppressions Black women face to intersectional oppressions faced by people who are overall much more privileged is also valid. But these are worries about what is likely to happen given the unjust social conditions of the world, and do not suggest limits on intersectionality as a theoretical framework.

Another, related issue is that it might seem that *any* intersection is an interesting site of new forms of oppression. So, for example, while race and gender intersect, and are combined with other axes of oppression, such as sexuality, disability, and class, to complicate the forms of oppression that the subject may face, there may be some categories that, when combined, do not create new oppressions. It may be that being red haired and being a lesbian does not create any new form of oppression – that is, a red-haired lesbian will suffer discrimination as a lesbian, and as a redhead, but those two categories are not sensitive to each other in the way that race and gender are. In theorizing about oppression, we must rely on an intuitive sense of what makes a difference, at the same time as being open to the possibility that an intersection is relevant.

Finally, the framework of intersectionality does not imply that all axes of oppression are equally severe. It is certainly true that redheads face discrimination, but not on the scale of racism or sexism. As Patricia Hill Collins urges, we must not accept 'the new myth of equivalent oppressions'. The denial of a simply additive model is not the denial of different weights. As Collins points out, "in a situation in which far too many privileged academics feel free to claim a bit of oppression for themselves – if all oppressions mutually construct one another then we're all oppressed in some way by something – oppression talk obscures actual unjust power relations."[7] As the discussion of the nature of oppression in Chapter 7 illustrates, not all harms are unjust. A privileged academic may complain, for example, that he is oppressed at work because he does not have children, and so is expected to take on tasks that are difficult for those with children, or he may complain that he is oppressed because, although white, he is not a native speaker. These may not count as oppressions at all: they may be mere inconveniences, depending on the wider system of which they are a part.

Crenshaw's account

In a pair of articles published in 1989 and 1991, Kimberlé Crenshaw argues that we need to make sense of the intersection of different sorts of oppression, and develops an account of intersectionality. She starts by describing the way that discrimination cases in law have failed Black women.

Crenshaw examines three legal cases, which in different ways fail to recognize the complexity of the intersection of race and gender, and thus marginalize Black women. In the first case, *DeGraffenreid v General Motors* (1976), five Black women brought a suit against General Motors, complaining that they were facing discrimination in the promotion policies. The court insisted on looking for sex discrimination and race discrimination independently. They found that women had been hired and promoted, so there was no sex discrimination, and Black people had been hired and promoted, so there was no racial discrimination, and hence no case. In that situation, all the women who were hired or promoted were white, and all the Black people who were hired or promoted were men. Discrimination against Black women was thus rendered invisible.

This case neatly captures the importance of recognizing intersectional oppression. A Black woman who faces discrimination may not be facing the same sort of racism that Black men face, nor the same sort of sexism that white women face. But it would be a mistake to conclude that she is not facing sexism and racism. Rather, she faces a combination, and that combination should be recognized as a sort of discrimination.

The second and third cases that Crenshaw discusses are more complex, and she uses them to make a more subtle point. In *Moore v Hughes Helicopter, Inc.* (1983), Moore, the plaintiff, brought a case of race and sex discrimination against her employer. The courts refused to accept her as the class representative on the grounds that, as a Black woman, she had been discriminated against as a Black woman, and so could not adequately represent white women. Crenshaw speculates that the court imagined that she had not been discriminated against 'as a woman', but only as a Black woman. As Crenshaw argues, this logic suggests that the general category 'woman' is implicitly understood as white. So race privilege, the privilege that white women have as white, is taken for granted, and is not counted as having any effect.

In the Moore case, the plaintiff was only allowed to use statistics about Black women to prove her claim that there was racist and sexist discrimination. The sample she was left with was too small for her to effectively make the claim, and the court ruled that there was no proof of discrimination. The problem that the case illustrates is the habit of thinking that sexism must be measured independently of other oppressions. On this way of thinking, sexism against Black women is not recognized: it always looks like something else.

Furthermore, this approach impedes solidarity between Black and white women. As Crenshaw puts it:

> The refusal to allow a multiply-disadvantaged class to represent others who may be singularly-disadvantaged defeats efforts to restructure the distribution of opportunity and limits remedial relief to minor adjustments within an established hierarchy. Consequently, "bottom-up" approaches, those which combine all discriminatees in order to challenge

an entire employment system, are foreclosed by the limited view of the wrong and the narrow scope of the available remedy. If such "bottom-up" intersectional representation were routinely permitted, employees might accept the possibility that there is more to gain by collectively challenging the hierarchy rather than by each discriminatee individually seeking to protect her source of privilege within the hierarchy.[8]

In other words, so long as the only available recourse for discriminatory treatment involves people being allowed to represent only their own small group, people have a disincentive for banding together. In fact, they will end up in competition, trying to protect the limited privileges they have. Crenshaw argues that this helps stabilize the unjust system.

Additionally, Crenshaw points out that Black women have also been prevented from representing Black men in discrimination suits. The third case she discusses, *Payne v Travenol* (1976), is such a case. The plaintiff, a Black woman, was not allowed to represent Black men, but only the women. She won her case for Black female employees, but despite the court finding that there was general racial discrimination, Black men were excluded from compensation. Again, Crenshaw argues, Black women are forced to choose between solidarity (with Black men in this case) and their own interests.

Crenshaw recognizes that her complaints about these cases might seem in tension. In the Graffenreid case, the court refuses to recognize that Black women face a compounded discrimination due to the combination of race and sex. In the other two cases, the courts insist that Black women must be treated as a special case, and not folded into race or sex categories. But it is precisely this sort of simplification that Crenshaw objects to. Insisting that sex and race discrimination work separately obscures the combined effect that Black women suffer. But it is equally problematic to admit that Black women suffer something different to white women and Black men while refusing to recognize that there is also something that Black women have in common with each of those groups. As Crenshaw puts it:

> Black women sometimes experience discrimination in ways similar to white women's experiences; sometimes they share very similar experiences with Black men. Yet often they experience double-discrimination – the combined effects of practices which discriminate on the basis of race, and on the basis of sex. And sometimes, they experience discrimination as Black women – not the sum of race and sex discrimination, but as Black women.[9]

This is what gives rise to the metaphor of the intersection. If someone is hit by a car in an intersection, the injury could have been caused by traffic coming from either direction, and it also could have been caused by traffic from both directions at once.

In the later article, 'Mapping the Margins', Crenshaw expands on her account and explores the complex ways that the intersection of race and sex affect structural, political, and representational aspects of violence against women of colour. As an example of neglect of structural intersectionality, Crenshaw takes US immigration law, which until 1990 required immigrant spouses to be married for two years before they could apply for permanent status. This had the result that women who were battered did not dare seek help in case it undermined their immigration status.

The law was changed to include a waiver, so that women who were battered were treated as an exception. However, the new law required that evidence be provided, precisely the sort of evidence that poor immigrant women of colour were likely to have difficulty obtaining: affidavits from police reports, social workers, schools, psychologists, and so on. If a measure is to be genuinely helpful it needs to recognize the complexities of intersecting oppressions. A woman who is battered and otherwise privileged is much more able to avail herself of opportunities for help than a woman who is battered and also disadvantaged in other ways.

Political intersectionality is what we see when apparent conflicts between group interests meet in the person at the intersection of those groups. Crenshaw discusses the racist stereotyping of Black men as violent, and anti-racist groups' efforts to counteract that stereotype. Crenshaw argues that Black women are sometimes a casualty of that struggle, in that attention to violence against them, particularly domestic violence, is suppressed in the name of fighting racist stereotypes. At the same time, Crenshaw points out, anti-domestic violence campaigns that try to undo the racialized stereotypes of violent abusers by pointing out that middle-class white women are victims too often backfire. These campaigns can end up diverting resources from those who need them most to the white and middle-class victims of domestic abuse. There are no easy answers here. Oppression is complex, and an adequate analysis must be willing to address complexities and apparent paradoxes.

Crenshaw also examines the way that rape law functions and the way that rape law reform has worked. As I discuss in Chapter 6, rape law has historically been focussed on the rights of men rather than the rights of women. As Crenshaw puts it, the law has traditionally divided women into good women (who can be raped) and bad women (who cannot). Black women come pre-packaged as bad women.[10] Rape law has also been catastrophic for Black men. The popular construction of rape involves a Black offender and a white victim, and that idea has been used to terrorize Black men through police and legal harassment as well as through extra-legal measures, such as lynching.

Crenshaw argues that harmful stereotypes about race and sexuality mean that the rape of Black women is taken less seriously than the rape of white women. But there is a further problem: Black women victims are sometimes marginalized *because of* the struggle to undo the racism inherent in our understandings of rape and the application of rape law. Crenshaw uses the example of Mike Tyson, who was accused of rape by a Black woman, Desiree Washington. Tyson was defended and supported by many prominent Black leaders, but no-one spoke up for Washington. Another example is that of Anita Hill, who accused Judge Clarence Thomas of sexual harassment in the hearings for his appointment to the Supreme Court. Thomas famously argued that this was a 'high tech lynching', thus arguing that the attack on him was racism rather than well grounded. Anti-racist forces mobilized behind Thomas. But would that have been possible if the victim was white? As a Black woman, Hill was not a 'perfect victim', and was powerless to make herself heard.

As well as structural intersectionality and political intersectionality, there is also what Crenshaw terms 'representational intersectionality'. Crenshaw discusses the mechanisms by which representation in the media, in pop culture, and so on can disadvantage people in intersecting ways. The obscenity case against the rap group 2 Live Crew serves as an illustration.

The prosecution claimed to be concerned with misogyny, but, as Crenshaw points out, it is not hard to see that the real motive wasn't to prevent victimization of Black women, but rather to target Black artists. Crenshaw argues that the prosecution was racist, but that the lyrics are indeed misogynistic. This complexity was missed in the court case, which polarized the debate between those who argued for obscenity on grounds of misogyny and those who argued that the case was a racist witch hunt. Crenshaw argues that we need to have both discussions, that even if rap is a distinctively African American cultural tradition, we need to think about whether it oppresses Black women.

Recognizing privilege

One of the important lessons of intersectionality is that it is easy to ignore privilege, or to take privilege as the neutral state rather than recognizing that privilege works to propel the privileged forward just as oppression holds the oppressed back. Crenshaw's Moore and Payne cases are used to criticize standard legal approaches to discrimination as failing to recognize privilege. She explains that discrimination law assumes that a decision (about promotion or hiring, for example) is only unjust if someone would have been promoted, *but for* their race or sex. This takes for granted that these decisions are generally fair and just. Crenshaw argues that that is not the case: those who are being hired and promoted are the most privileged, and the least privileged do not even get a look in. So, the most privileged white women may be able to show that they would have been promoted but for their sex, but someone who is in multiple categories of disadvantage is so far from the rewards and benefits that she cannot point to one factor that explains her failure.

Crenshaw offers a second metaphor to make this vivid. She asks us to imagine a basement containing all the people who are disadvantaged on the basis of characteristics such as race, sex, class, and so on. These people are stacked up so that at the bottom are those who are in multiple categories, and at the top, standing on their shoulders, are the people who only fall into one category. The people at the top are brushing the ceiling, which is actually the floor of the room above. In the room above are those who suffer no categorial disadvantages: nothing about them is a target of unjust discrimination. The people in the privileged room allow some from below to crawl up. But they want to be fair, so they will only allow those who would have been in the upper room, 'but for the ceiling'. Of course, that only applies to those who are at the top of the stack below. Those at the bottom cannot claim that the ceiling was stopping them: they were nowhere near the ceiling.

These points about privilege are also made by Elizabeth Spelman, in her 1988 book, *Inessential Woman*. Spelman's book is an examination of the way that white middle-class privilege has dominated feminist thought in a way that is invisible to those who have that privilege. Spelman does not use the phrase 'intersectionality', but hers is an argument about intersectionality: she points out that we cannot assess the effects of race and gender independently, and she rejects the idea that there is some essence of womanhood that all women share. Spelman, like Crenshaw, argues that trying to isolate gender as a cause of oppression leads to ignoring the other privileges of those whose gender we focus on.

Examples like this [examples that show different axes of oppression combine in complex ways] might suggest that we can get the clearest picture of how women are oppressed "as women" if we focus on the lives of women who are subject only to sexism and not to any other forms of oppression. We then don't have to look at a woman's race or class in order to understand how she is being treated as a woman. But this idea is preposterous: while a woman's being white, for example, is not the cause of or occasion for her being systematically subject to violence, it has everything to do with how she is treated.[11]

The overall effect of ignoring privilege is that discrimination law, in both its design and its application, benefits those who are the most privileged out of the disadvantaged group. Of women, middle-class women, of Black people, middle-class Black men. Again, imagining that discrimination works on a single axis ignores Black women. Crenshaw argues that the tendency to frame issues in terms of a single axis understanding of oppression, and to design interventions on that basis, is extremely widespread across different areas of life.

Identity

As I said, intersectionality is not primarily a theory of subjective identity, it is a theory of the structural categories that are imposed upon us, and how they interact in complex ways. For example, being British may not be an essential part of what I feel is important about myself, but if that is relevant to the society that I am in, then that is part of my structural identity, and can be a source of oppression. So the question arises, what is the most effective political response? Should we stop talking about categories of race and sex and nationality on the grounds that they are not morally relevant? There are good reasons not to do that. For a start, we need to talk about the history of these oppressive categories, and the causal effects that persist. The fact that someone is racialized in a particular way still matters, even if we think it shouldn't. It matters because that person has faced and will face disadvantages, and the oppression is only predictable and comprehensible if we retain the traditional categories.

Crenshaw points out that there are ways to reclaim the categories, because the problem is not usually with the categories themselves, but with the characteristics and values that are associated with them. The classic example is 'queer', originally a pejorative, reclaimed as a proud self-naming. And of course, it is not just the word that is reclaimed, it is the category. The point is to subvert the values that the heteropatriarchy accords the category, and to say that being queer is positive. As Crenshaw puts it, "At this point in history, a strong case can be made that the most critical resistance strategy for disempowered groups is to occupy and defend a politics of social location rather than to vacate and destroy it."[12]

A difficulty arises, however, when we consider intersectionality. Retaining traditional categories of race and sex is in tension with the analysis of intersectional oppression, which points out that the categories of race and sex seem monolithic, but the reality is that oppression varies in very fine-grained ways. Why should a poor woman of colour fighting for immigration status and minimum wage think that she has any shared experience with a well-off white woman academic who is fighting for her right to be paid as much as her male colleagues?

Some feminists, Naomi Zack, for example, argue that too much focus on intersectionality can undermine feminist solidarity and lead to fragmentation of identity.[13] Zack worries that the category of woman loses its force, and that there is no possibility for an inclusive feminism. She argues that those at the intersection are limited to only their own feminisms, that the logic of intersectionality implies that Black women can speak only for themselves, and that white women can speak only for themselves. Zack urges the need for an account of the commonality of women.

As Elizabeth Spelman argues, it is very difficult to give an account of something that all women have in common given that there are so many differences between women. There is no 'nugget' of pure womanness. Judith Butler adds a further worry, that any account of what women have in common becomes a normative account, an account of what women *should* be. Butler points out that this is inevitably exclusionary, leading to a problematic identity politics, where some people are excluded from the category 'woman'. These two issues, the commonality problem (or 'particularity' problem as it is sometimes known) and the normativity problem, stand in the way of any simple descriptive account of what 'womanness' is.[14]

Ann Garry takes up the issue of how we should think of the category 'woman' given the fact of intersectionality.[15] She discusses Maria Lugones' account of intersectional identity. Lugones, like Zack, thinks that taking intersectionality into account leads to dissolving the traditional categories. Unlike Zack, Lugones thinks that this is positive step. Lugones argues that in order to avoid an account of someone's identity as fragmented, where the race and the gender must be seen as logically separate entities, we must posit many different genders. So Latina women have a different gender from white women, and so on.[16] This is the conclusion that Zack worries about, that in order to avoid fragmentation at the intra-personal level, we have to accept fragmentation of the gender category 'woman'.

Garry proposes that we think of the gender category 'woman' as a family resemblance category. In that way, to identify as a woman is not to claim some essential property that overlaps completely with all other women, but only to claim membership of a broad category. The family resemblance approach has also been defended by Natalie Stoljar, who, like Zack, worries that feminists need a unified account of woman in order to justify feminist political action. On Stoljar's account, being a woman is a matter of having a sufficient number of characteristics from a cluster. Thus there is no commitment to a nugget of womanness, and the view can avoid the commonality and normativity problems.

One way to understand the move towards a family resemblance view is to think in terms of moving the discussion away from subjective identity and focussing instead on solidarity. If we think of woman as a broad category, there is no tension with intersectionality, and solidarity is possible. This is what Crenshaw suggests in 'Mapping the Margins'. Crenshaw argues that in order for reclaiming the traditional race and gender categories to be effective, we have to acknowledge the multiple dimensions of identity. We must see the traditional categories of race, gender, and so on, as *coalitions*. That is, we must adapt our own use of the structural category. Her point is that we should see ourselves as allied to those in social categories that overlap with our own.

Alison Bailey expands on this notion of a coalition in her critique of Zack. Bailey appeals to Bernice Johnson Reagon's 1981 speech 'Coalition Politics and the Turning of the Century'. Johnson Reagon makes a distinction between 'home' and 'coalition' from an activist's point of view. Home is the place where you are with other members of your intersection, where you can recharge. Coalition building work is where you work with others in the larger group to build a coalition through differential privileges and varied experience. It is not home, and it is not comfortable: it is challenging and difficult. Zack's mistake, Bailey argues, is to focus on the 'home' part of the equation, and to think that that is the aim of intersectionality theory: to give everyone their home. Bailey argues that we need to see both home and coalition building as working together: "if we understand intersectionality as one way of bringing to the surface tensions between women that have prevented coalition building in the past, then intersectional tools can be understood as a necessary part of coalition building rather than as fragmenting." [17]

Another way to put Bailey's point is in terms of the difference between structural identity and subjective identity. Insofar as we are talking about structural identity, intersectionality need not impede solidarity: structural identity can be a coalition. But subjective identity cries out for unity in a way that structural identity does not. Consider the example of Gay Pride. Reclaiming an identity such as 'gay' or 'queer' need not be a matter of subjective identity. Gay Pride *as a political movement* is a way of subverting the values imposed on an artificial category, of rejecting the dominant interpretations. As such, Gay Pride can include many different sub-categories, as the acronym LGBTQ+ indicates. However, subjective identity is not a coalition, it is indivisible. To be a bisexual Latinx is different to being an Asian lesbian. But having one's own subjective, complex identity that is different to other people's does not rule out sharing a structural identity for political purposes.

Solidarity

Solidarity is primarily a political stance rather than a question of identity or commonality. Solidarity is a necessary political attitude, as the Combahee River Collective Statement declares:

> Although we are feminists and Lesbians, we feel solidarity with progressive Black men and do not advocate the fractionalization that white women who are separatists demand. Our situation as Black people necessitates that we have solidarity around the fact of race, which white women of course do not need to have with white men, unless it is their negative solidarity as racial oppressors. We struggle together with Black men against racism, while we also struggle with Black men about sexism.

Or, as bell hooks puts it,

> Women do not need to eradicate difference to feel solidarity. We do not need to share common oppression to fight equally to end oppression. We do not need anti-male sentiments to bond us together, so great is the wealth of experience, culture and ideas we have to share with one another. We can be sisters united by shared interests and beliefs, united in our appreciation for diversity, united in our struggle to end sexist oppression, united in political solidarity. [18]

Many feminists have pointed out that recognizing difference, far from undermining solidarity, is crucial for robust solidarity. Elizabeth Spelman points out that the real danger is not that recognizing difference will undermine solidarity, rather, ignoring differences is the real danger, as the concerns of the more privileged will end up taking precedence over the concerns of the less privileged. Feminists such as Audre Lorde and Kimberlé Crenshaw also argue that it is recognition of difference that leads to proper solidarity. As Lorde puts it in her well known paper, 'The Master's Tools',

> As women, we have been taught either to ignore our differences, or to view them as causes for separation and suspicion rather than as forces for change. Without community there is no liberation, only the most vulnerable and temporary armistice between an individual and her oppression. But community must not mean a shedding of our differences, nor the pathetic pretence that these differences do not exist.[19]

This does not deny that recognizing difference can be painful. As I pointed out above, one of the lessons of intersectionality is that privilege can go unrecognized, and that it should not be accepted as the neutral position, the measure of oppression. Related to this is a practical conclusion: privileged women must be willing to confront their own privileges and relinquish them. Crenshaw uses the example of Sojourner Truth to illustrate the point: In 1851, Sojourner Truth spoke at the Women's Rights Conference in Akron, Ohio. Crenshaw tells us that white women who were present did not want Truth to speak, worrying that the focus on race and the horrors of slavery would detract from the struggle for women's emancipation. Crenshaw quotes Truth's words:

> Look at my arm! I have ploughed and planted and gathered into barns, and no man could head me – and ain't I a woman? I could work as much and eat as much as a man – when I could get it – and bear the lash as well! And ain't I a woman? I have born thirteen children, and seen most of 'em sold into slavery, and when I cried out with my mother's grief, none but Jesus heard me – and ain't I a woman?

Crenshaw goes on:

> By using her own life to reveal the contradiction between the ideological myths of womanhood and the reality of Black women's experience, Truth's oratory provided a powerful rebuttal to the claim that women were categorically weaker than men. Yet Truth's personal challenge to the coherence of the cult of true womanhood was useful only to the extent that white women were willing to reject the racist attempts to rationalize the contradiction – that because Black women were something less than real women, their experiences had no bearing on true womanhood. Thus, this 19th-century Black feminist challenged not only patriarchy, but she also challenged white feminists wishing to embrace Black women's history to relinquish their vestedness in whiteness.[20]

Crenshaw's point is that in an oppressive system, one weapon of power is the fragmentation of resistor groups. And in particular, oppressive systems can reinforce the status quo by threatening the privilege of the more privileged within the oppressed groups in order to prevent them from banding together with those at a less privileged intersection. White feminists must be willing to give up the benefits of white supremacy, the benefits of standing by white men, in order to stand in solidarity with Black women.

Summary

There are various misunderstandings about what intersectionality is. Intersectionality is not the same as inclusivity, and it is not primarily a theory of subjective identity. I take it to be a framework for illuminating an important aspect of oppression, that different axes of oppression interact to create new oppressions.

Crenshaw's analysis in terms of discrimination law illuminates the concept and the way that it applies to Black women in America. Crenshaw examines various cases. In one sort of case, the particular kind of discrimination that Black women face is ignored because the court refuses to recognize anything other than sexism (and there is no apparent sexism against white women, so they conclude there is no sexism) and racism (and there is no apparent racism against Black men, so they conclude there is no racism). In the other sort of case, the opposite happens. The courts refuse to see that Black women suffer racism, because whatever discrimination Black women suffer they must suffer as Black women, not as Black. And the courts refuse to see that Black women suffer sexism, because whatever discrimination they suffer must be suffered as Black women, not as women. The issue in the background is the same: white women are taken to represent women, and Black men are taken to represent Black people. Black women are marginalized.

Considering intersectionality illuminates the various ways that privilege is taken for granted. For example, as Crenshaw's basement metaphor illustrates, we should not define sexism by asking whether someone would have been promoted but for their sex. That would ignore the other privileges that have worked to get them into a position where they might be considered for promotion. If we fail to recognize privilege, only the most privileged will benefit from anti-discrimination measures.

It is also important to make a distinction between structural identity and subjective identity. A structural identity is imposed, although it can be reclaimed and celebrated. Structural identities need not be unified, and so can accommodate intersectionality: a structural identity can be a coalition. The question of how to reconcile complex intersectional personal identities with the need for solidarity, and an account of structural identities that are broad enough to be politically useful, may be harder to resolve.

One worry about seeing things in terms of intersectionality is that it makes solidarity between members of a group more difficult. To recognize the special circumstances of Black women might appear to alienate them from both their gender and their racial groups. However, as many Black feminist theorists have pointed out, if intersectional oppression is a reality, it is important to recognize it, and true solidarity requires a clear vision of difference as well as similarity. Solidarity is not always easy. Solidarity requires recognizing one's own privileges, and, more demandingly, being willing to give them up. It requires communicating with people who are different from oneself, and working to break through internalized prejudices.

Notes

1 Cooper, *A Voice from the South by a Black Woman of the South*, p.134.
2 The Combahee River Collective Statement.
3 Cooper, 'Intersectionality', p.390.

4 Collins, *Fighting Words: Black Women and the Search for Justice*.
5 Alexander-Floyd, 'Disappearing Acts: Reclaiming Intersectionality in the Social Sciences in a Post-Black Feminist Era'.
6 Bilge, 'Intersectionality Undone: Saving Intersectionality from Feminist Intersectionality Studies', p.413.
7 Collins, *Fighting Words: Black Women and the Search for Justice*, p.211.
8 Crenshaw, 'Demarginalizing the Intersection of Race and Sex: A Black Feminist Critique of Antidiscrimination Doctrine, Feminist Theory, and Antiracist Politics', p.145.
9 Op. cit., p.149.
10 Crenshaw, 'Mapping the Margins: Intersectionality, Identity Politics, and Violence Against Women of Color', p.1271.
11 Spelman, *Inessential Woman: Problems of Exclusion in Feminist Thought*, pp.14-15.
12 Crenshaw, 'Mapping the Margins: Intersectionality, Identity Politics, and Violence Against Women of Color', p.1297.
13 Zack, *Inclusive Feminism: A Third Wave Theory of Women's Commonality*.
14 Butler, *Gender Trouble*.
15 Garry, 'Intersectionality, Metaphors, and the Multiplicity of Gender'.
16 Lugones, 'Heterosexualism and the Colonial/Modern Gender System'.
17 Bailey, 'On Intersectionality, Empathy, and Feminist Solidarity: A Reply To Naomi Zack', p.26.
18 hooks, 'Sisterhood: Political Solidarity Between Women', in *Feminist Theory: From Margin to Center*, p.67.
19 Lorde, 'The Master's Tools Will Never Dismantle the Master's House', in *Sister Outsider: Essays and Speeches*, p.112.
20 Crenshaw, 'Demarginalizing the Intersection of Race and Sex: A Black Feminist Critique of Antidiscrimination Doctrine, Feminist Theory, and Antiracist Politics', pp.153-154.

Further reading

Collins, Patricia Hill and Bilge, Sirma (2020) *Intersectionality*. Polity Press. (In-depth examination of the theory and practical implications of intersectionality).
Crenshaw, Kimberlé Williams (2021) *On Intersectionality: Collected Writings*. The New Press (collected writings of the last 20 years).
Moraga, Cherrie and Anzaldua, Gloria (eds.) (2015) *This Bridge Called My Back: Writings by Radical Women of Color*. Kitchen Table/Women of Color Press. (Essays and poems exploring intersectional oppression).

9 Ideology, false consciousness, and adaptive preferences

"Men do not want solely the obedience of women, they want their sentiments. All men, except the most brutish, desire to have, in the woman most nearly connected with them, not a forced slave but a willing one, not a slave merely, but a favourite. They have therefore put everything in practice to enslave their minds. The masters of all other slaves rely, for maintaining obedience, on fear . . . The masters of women wanted more than simple obedience, and they turned the whole force of education to effect their purpose. All women are brought up from the very earliest years in the belief that their ideal of character is the very opposite to that of men; not self-will, and government by self-control, but submission, and yielding to the control of others."

John Stuart Mill, *The Subjection of Women*

Chapter overview: This chapter begins with an explanation of the notion of ideology. I then cover various attempts to define false consciousness, looking at the sense in which it is false, its effects, and G.A. Cohen's defence of functional explanation. I examine the difference between theories of false consciousness and theories of adaptive preferences, and explore various accounts of adaptive preferences, including Serene Khader's and Martha Nussbaum's. Finally, I look at Sally Haslanger's account of ideology critique.

Introduction

A puzzling thing about oppressive systems is that it is very common for members of the oppressed group to accept the system and collude with it. This is what Ann Cudd calls 'oppression by choice'. The victims of oppression internalize the ideology that supports their own oppression – they don't see it as oppression. The point of talking about false consciousness is to show that these people are misled in some way, that there is still oppression.

The terms here are used in slightly different ways by different writers. I will be fairly broad in my usage, distinguishing between the beliefs and values of the subject, which I will call 'false consciousness' or 'ideological consciousness' on the one hand, and the (false or problematic) system of beliefs and values that they subscribe to, which I will refer to as 'ideology'. In other words, ideology and false consciousness are two sides of the same coin. As I use the term (fairly standardly), 'ideology' is always pejorative; it does not refer to true or harmless beliefs and value systems.

I also discuss 'adaptive preferences' in this chapter. Adaptive preferences are preferences formed in poor choice conditions. Like false consciousness, adaptive preferences can serve the oppressive system. So, for example, a woman under patriarchy may have a strong preference for being slender, and spend a lot of time and effort thinking about her body shape. But this, arguably, is an adaptive preference: she prefers that because the oppressive system has limited her horizons. Sandra Lee Bartky calls the enjoyment that women feel in conforming to patriarchal beauty standards 'repressive satisfactions': such satisfactions are real, but they contribute to oppression.[1]

The problem is that it is not easy to distinguish ideological beliefs or preferences from authentic ones. Someone who chooses to conform to feminine beauty norms may insist that her choice is her own, that her decisions are fully autonomous, and that to question that is to patronize her. It is very hard to resolve a disagreement about the origin of her choices. The surface facts do not resolve the issue – the content itself is not necessarily problematic, and the circumstances are not obviously coercive.

Another putative case of false consciousness that illustrates this point is the backlash against feminism by women. Ironically, this is sometimes motivated by apparently feminist concerns. Feminism is rejected on the grounds that women need to stand up for themselves, and not play the victim. This may include accepting allegedly factual claims (there is no gender pay gap, or violence against women is exaggerated) and norms (feminist philosophy is not academically respectable, or affirmative action policies are unfair). The debate here can seem intractable, with each side thinking the other is not seeing things clearly. The feminists think the anti-feminists are in the grip of false consciousness, and the anti-feminists think the feminists are simply deluded.

The challenge is how to define the notions of ideology and false consciousness so that they are robust, and not simply a charge to be made against anyone with a different outlook. Most philosophers writing on the topic agree that it is characteristic of false consciousness that it is encouraged and reinforced by a social system, and, in turn, reinforces that social system. We have the attitudes about gender that we do because we are products of a gendered system. Those attitudes are then reinforced by that very system. This is a familiar idea from Marx's analysis of capitalism. Marx did not have a fully worked out theory of ideology and false consciousness, but the ideas are important in Marxist theory. Part of the explanation for the resilience of the exploitative capitalist system is that the working classes themselves have internalized the value system that legitimates their oppression. Similarly, we can explain the persistence of gender inequality, which is bad for both men and women, by pointing out that both men and women have internalized a value system that legitimates this inequality. This very general account of false consciousness is enough to give a good sense of what it is and why it is a useful idea, but we need a more thorough analysis.

Ideology

Before I get on to accounts of false consciousness and adaptive preference I will explain what I mean by ideology. In brief, ideology is a belief system that supports an oppressive system. I'll come back to how it supports it – for now I want to give some examples and clarifications in order to lay the groundwork for accounts of false consciousness.

Ideologies are multi-faceted, consisting of factual claims, explanatory stories, norms, value systems, and so on. Ideologies can also include subtle accounts of what is important, what is worthy of attention, what is 'normal', and what is 'Other' (as Simone de Beauvoir puts it). A central site of ideology is gender. Traditional gender roles may include allegedly factual claims (women are more nurturing and less rational then men; little boys are rougher than little girls) and norms (women ought to stay at home with children; women ought to be slender, and dress a certain way; women ought to be gentle). One of the major ideological norms of gender roles is heterosexuality: heteronormativity, as it has come to be known, dictates that only heterosexual relationships are natural and permitted.

As I discuss in the chapters on pornography, sex work, and sexual violence, there is a deep patriarchal ideology about the nature of sexuality. Again, this is partly a matter of accepting alleged factual claims about sex (women have a lower sex drive than men; women are less visually aroused than men) and norms (women ought not to make the first move; women ought to please men). These narratives serve the patriarchy by disguising the fact that violence is used to keep women in their place. Sexual harassment is portrayed as being a result of the out of control libidos of powerful men, an understandable (if regrettable) side effect of too much masculine energy. Men like Harvey Weinstein are seen as bad apples, the men who couldn't curb their sexuality in quite the right way. But this is a story that hides what feminists take to be a more sinister reality, that sexual harassment and rape are structural, they serve a purpose. They are mechanism of oppression.

Tommie Shelby argues that ideology tells a story that is superficially coherent.[2] Ideology provides a general picture of what Black people are like, what women are like, and so on, and we can often recognize that apparently positive stereotypes (like being good at sport or dancing) are the flip side of a much more serious negative stereotype (like lacking intelligence and dignity). Thus the supposedly flattering views of relevant group members turn out to be part of a picture that, *overall*, is negative. This is the point of Marilyn Frye's birdcage analogy (from Chapter 7): if you look at one bar, it is hard to see why it is restrictive; you need to look at how the bars work together to form a cage.[3]

However, it is worth stressing that ideology is often inconsistent and self-contradictory. One story about women is that they are weak and delicate, another is that rape is not a big deal to them. Women ought to be attractive and sexually available, but women ought to be chaste. It is not hard to see why there would be such holes in the plot: ideology springs up in fairly random ways, it is not designed in advance, and it is bound to be patchy. If it was too patchy, it would be too obviously false, and would not survive. But there is no reason to think it must be seamless.

Sometimes, though, what looks like inconsistency may not be not inconsistent if we look at the ideological story in a more fine-grained way. Ideology, like oppression in general, works intersectionally. Race, class, ability, and so on affect what the ideological narrative says: stories about Black women's sexuality are different to stories about white women's sexuality. Ideology may also cover up differences. As Angela Davis points out, the idea of a woman as housewife, which emerged in the nineteenth century, applied to a very narrow segment of women.

> The reality of women's place in nineteenth-century U.S. society involved white women, whose days were spent operating factory machines for wages that were a pittance, as surely as it involved Black women, who laboured under the coercion of slavery. The "housewife" reflected a partial reality, for she was really a symbol of the economic pros- perity enjoyed by the emerging middle classes . . . Although the "housewife" was rooted in the social conditions of the bourgeoisie and the middle classes, nineteenth-century ideology established the housewife and the mother as universal models of womanhood.[4]

So, superficial coherence may hide random incoherence, or complex and insidious fictions which are a functioning part of an ideology. Ideology can make irrelevant differences seem relevant, as classic racist and sexist ideology does, and it can also ignore differences that are relevant, as the model of woman as housewife does. Ideology tells a story that suits the existing power structures. As Davis argues about the ideology of the housewife, this nine- tenth-century model of womanhood then justified low wages for women in the workforce, as women who worked were framed as being outside of their natural sphere.

Pieces of ideology often seem to be supported by the evidence. Take claims about innate gender differences (which I talked about in the introduction to the book). These ideas have some apparent scientific backing, and so it can seem respectable to accept them. The difficult issue here is that in order to convince someone that these claims are false, it is necessary to argue that they are part of a web of ideological beliefs, and that scientists themselves are taken in by the ideology. At that point the task becomes intimidatingly large. As critics of Marx's account of ideology say: it proves too much; it begins to seem as though the charge of false consciousness can be applied to any claim that is disagreed with. We need an account of false consciousness that distinguishes respectable authentic beliefs from ideological ones.

Defining false consciousness: Truth and justification

It seems plausible that a necessary condition for a belief to be a case of false consciousness is that it is false. However, the situation is not quite that straightforward. Tommie Shelby argues that racist ideology contains both obviously false and less obviously false elements. The same is true for sexist ideology. It was once thought that a woman's uterus could break free and wander around her body, causing emotional outbursts (hysteria). That's obviously false, but it is much harder to refute claims about innate differences between men and women, or the cause of the gender pay gap. Shelby stresses that much ideology is a *distortion* rather than an outright falsehood. Because there is just a distortion, our ability to coordinate ourselves on the basis of these half-truths is not impeded, and of course, it is easy to avoid the whole truth. If we don't look too closely, our experience confirms our ideological beliefs about what women are like. We look around and see that women do the bulk of the childcare and that when men do it they are less competent. This makes it easy to carry on thinking that men are innately ill-suited to childcare.

Shelby acknowledges that false ideological beliefs are sometimes false in fairly subtle ways: they are distortions, rather than outright falsehoods. Others point out that ideological beliefs can be *true*. Sally Haslanger focusses on the way that ideology permeates our social lives, and so creates a 'looping effect'. If we think of things as being a certain way, that can be self-fulfilling, for both objects and people. If we have Phillips head screwdrivers, we will make more Phillips head screws, and then we will keep making Phillips head screwdrivers.[5] When men objectify women, they believe that women are well suited to be objects, but they also make it the case that women are objects in some sense (they make it the case that women are treated as objects) and this provides more (apparent) evidence that women really are suited to being treated as objects. In other words, ideology and false consciousness are involved in social construction: the way that we create and embellish social reality so as to suit our purposes.[6]

Another reason not to think that false consciousness must be false is that we may sometimes come to true beliefs through a mechanism that makes them look like a case of false consciousness. Imagine that a despotic ruler induces fear and compliance in the citizens by convincing them that the world is on the brink of disaster. Perhaps the world really is on the brink of disaster, but that doesn't make the citizens' beliefs rational.

It seems, then, that we should not try to make falsity part of the definition of false consciousness. Intuitively, the defining feature of false consciousness is the way that the beliefs are formed. To put it very simply: some of our beliefs come about in ways that justify those beliefs, that is, we have good reasons for those beliefs. But other beliefs come about through problematic mechanisms, such as wishful thinking, fear, carelessness, or brainwashing. False consciousness seems to be in the category of beliefs that come about in the wrong way. So we need an account of what goes wrong in the formation of false consciousness.

Jon Elster, Denise Meyerson, and Ann Cudd all appeal to empirical accounts of bad mechanisms in their work on this topic.[7] The point of drawing on empirical work is to show that we form beliefs in non-rational ways, and that evidence resistance is a well-documented fact of everyday life. Elster and Meyerson both rely heavily on Nisbett and Ross's work in experimental psychology. Nisbett and Ross show that we are prone to many irrationalities and errors. For example, for good evolutionary reasons, we rely heavily on heuristic reasoning (reasoning that takes short cuts), which is very vulnerable to error.

Cudd draws on a wide body of literature in social psychology. She emphasizes the role of groups and group formation, as oppression is a group phenomenon; it is not about individuals oppressing each other. Cudd relies on social identity theory, which postulates that our identity is heavily invested in our social identity, which explains our tendencies to form 'in-groups' and treat all others as 'out-groups', and our acceptance of stereotypes. These human tendencies may be good evolutionary strategies overall, but they are not rational, and can result in us accepting false or distorted beliefs and values. Social psychology can explain why we fall into error, and how we create social constructs that justify themselves through a looping effect, but are morally problematic.

It is important to stress that false consciousness is not merely badly formed beliefs. It is more than that. As I said in my initial characterization of false consciousness, it is a belief system that props up an unjust social system. Compare two different unjustified beliefs that one might have, both formed by the heuristic devices of reading the newspapers and trusting your peers. First, take the claim that lactic acid build-up causes muscle ache. Scientists now think that this is not the case, in fact lactic acid is a fuel. Despite that, the idea that lactic acid build-up is a problem persists.[8] The lactic acid misconception is certainly socially reinforced; it is 'common knowledge'. However, it does not perpetuate any sort of social system. Contrast a belief about the natural roles of men and women. It is easy to see how this belief comes about in a similar way to a belief about lactic acid causing muscle ache. But the belief about natural roles does perpetuate a social system.

Thus we need an account of what effects false consciousness must have in order to count as false consciousness, in particular, how false consciousness contributes to oppression.

Defining false consciousness: Effects

A belief about lactic acid has little or no impact on our everyday lives, on our dealings with each other. But beliefs about what men and women are like, or what roles they ought to inhabit, affect the way we build our social world. The point about ideology in the political sense is that it contributes to an unjust social system - it becomes a mechanism of oppression. As Angela Davis points out in the example discussed above, the idea of woman as housewife serves to justify exploitation of women in the workforce. The ideological beliefs help to prop up the unjust social order. That's what distinguishes ideology from harmless fiction and innocent mistakes.

Shelby analyzes racist ideology in detail, showing that ideas about racialized groups serve to legitimize their poor treatment. Slavery in the New World was justified by beliefs about the inherent inferiority of Black people. Cruel treatment was made permissible by a view that Black people were not fully human, did not have the same capacities as white people, and were inherently lazy and deceitful. Post civil rights era racist ideology is more subtle but just as pernicious.[9] These false and distorted beliefs and values support the racist system.

The same point applies to sexist ideology. Patricia Hill Collins' account of the controlling images of Black women is an account of racist and sexist ideology working to justify oppression.[10] Feminist writers on pornography argue that pornography is ideology that legitimizes the subordination of women. Ideas about what women are like, what their talents and weakness are, reinforce prescribed gender roles. Prescribed roles justify unfavourable treatment for those who step outside of their allotted role.

Stability is crucial for ideology to have the effect of maintaining existing power relations. Shelby points out that ideology can 'do its dirty work' through various means: through legitimization, but also through other stabilizing mechanisms, like making the situation seem natural and inevitable (reification), or metaphysical mystification (for example, making it seem as though the situation is commanded by a deity). There are often many different stories overlapping and supporting each other in an ideological system. So, oppressive systems disguise themselves, and people do not recognize them for what they are, but take them to be fair, natural, and right. The point about maintaining oppressive systems distinguishes false consciousness from other forms of cognitive error, and shows what is pernicious about it. These stereotypes rationalize oppression, and thus play a stabilizing role that is essential to false consciousness.

So far I have argued that in order to count as false consciousness, a badly formed belief system must have the effect of stabilizing an unjust system. This is a definitional point: if we are to call something false consciousness, it should be distinguished from other forms of error. But I have said nothing about *why* false consciousness has that effect. One sort of view is that no further explanation is needed here. We tend to these errors, and they have bad effects, end of story. The point of talking about individual mechanisms is to provide 'microfoundations' as Elster puts it.[11] The basic idea is that individuals have tendencies which result in and perpetuate macro level systems of oppression. They form groups, and identify with those groups, they want to be comfortable, they want to maintain a view of themselves as decent, and of the world as just. In Elster's view, this is all we need to say.

Other theorists think that there is more to the story, that part of the explanation for false consciousness is precisely that it stabilizes the oppressive system. In this view, ideology maintains power relations through inducing a distorted picture of the world, and that is why some people have a distorted view.

Defining false consciousness: Genetic origin and functional explanation

The relatively uncontroversial claim about the origin of ideological beliefs is that they come about or are maintained because people are unaware of the oppressive system and their place in it. This is how Shelby understands it. As Shelby says, "The claim that ideologies are accepted because of class based false consciousness constitutes the *genetic* component of our conception of ideology. It is this feature of ideologies that underwrites the Marxian idea that ideologies have socioeconomic *causes* in addition to their oppressive social effects."[12] The idea is that unawareness of the true social relations leads people to accept a distorted picture of reality. People may think that they are being rational, but actually they are swayed by fear, or a desire to rationalize their situation, or some other bad mechanism. As Engels says, "Ideology is a process accomplished by the so-called thinker consciously, it is true, but with a false consciousness. The real motive forces impelling him remain unknown to him . . . he imagines false or apparent motives".[13]

However, there is a more ambitious version of the genetic claim. The ambitious version says that ideological beliefs occur *because they are useful* for maintaining the social order. Note that talking about the 'function' of ideological beliefs prejudices things in this direction. There is a difference between the effect something has and its function. A rain shower makes people wet, but that is not normally described as a function, because there is no designer with a plan, it just happens.

The idea that false consciousness comes about *because* it helps preserve an oppressive system is puzzling. (Here is what is not puzzling: the existence of false consciousness helps preserve the oppressive system). Compare manufactured objects: the function of an axe explains why axes exist (we made axes to chop wood). Sometimes, oppressive systems are closely controlled and monitored, and can be compared to axes as a functional system designed by people. In Margaret Atwood's Gilead, the anti-feminist dystopia she creates in *The Handmaid's Tale*, false consciousness is deliberately induced to create stability. It is particularly useful for an oppressive system to have members of the oppressed group on board, and compliance is rewarded. Members of the oppressed group have a certain authority when it comes to saying whether the oppression is oppression, and if *they* say there is no problem, then it is more convincing. In Gilead, the first line of enforcement is chiefly undertaken by the 'aunts', women complicit in the regime. As Atwood argues in the voice of the anthropologist at the end of the book, "no empire imposed by force or otherwise has ever been without this feature: control of the indigenous by members of their own group."[14]

But oppressive systems are not usually like axes, in that they are not designed and controlled. On the surface, the ambitious version of the genetic claim looks like the claim that the system itself has a plan, to keep the people deceived in order to continue to exist. But of course, systems are not conscious, they do not have plans.

G.A. Cohen defends the idea of functional explanation by appealing to cases in the natural world. He agrees that oppressive systems are not conscious beings, driven to seek their own survival.[15] So, if they tend to survive, it must be that there is some account of how their success-giving features work, some 'elaborated explanation' as Cohen calls it. Natural selection and deliberate planning are both elaborated explanations – they make sense of how the effect (for function) can be the cause of the entity existing. It makes sense to say that birds have hollow bones *in order to fly*, not because they or anyone else had a plan. Rather, hollow bones enable flying, and that's why birds survive. It makes sense to say that large-scale production happens because it is efficient: in that case, the owners of the means of production deliberately do what will result in more profit.

Cohen argues that versions of the natural selection explanation can be applied to oppressive systems, but his aim is not to give a fully worked out story about the mechanisms of survival of oppressive systems. His point is to rehabilitate functional explanation as a sort of explanation, and to demystify claims like the claim that false consciousness comes about and persists because it helps maintain the oppressive system. Cohen argues that we do not need to fill in the details, we are justified in positing the existence of some functional explanation or other. We should look around at the oppressive system and be suspicious.

Cohen's account of functional explanation has been thoroughly examined and criticized by Marxist theorists and critics, including Jon Elster. Elster is skeptical of what he calls, 'consequence explanations', and takes their attractiveness to be a form of 'obsessional search for meaning':

> In everyday life – in politics, in the family or at the work-place – one constantly encounters the implicit assumption that any social or psychological phenomenon must have a meaning or significance that explains it: there must be some sense or some perspective

in which it is beneficial for someone or something – and these benefits also explain the presence of the phenomenon.[16]

The worry, pressed by Elster and others, is that there is no way to make sense of the manner in which an oppressive system is self-maintaining. Elster objects that the feedback mechanism for survival of organisms, natural selection, does not apply to social systems. Elster insists that we should stick to psychological explanations, and avoid mystical appeal to structure.

However, it could be argued that these two things are not fully distinct. Psychological mechanisms are affected by structures. The main purpose of powerful individuals may be to make money, or to build and keep power for themselves rather than to preserve patriarchy overall. We do not have to say that their purpose is simple. And we need not say that their aims are direct or well-focussed. It may be that successful, powerful people are not fully con-sciously aware of what they need to do to manipulate people, but they are highly responsive to what will effectively indoctrinate. The explanatory power in this story is just that there are individual people who work to induce false consciousness in others, and that they are successful.

Take, as an example, ideals of feminine beauty, and what Sandra Lee Bartky calls the fashion-beauty complex.[17] Women are harmed, both physically and economically (by expen-sive products, by anorexia, by leaky breast implants, by liposuction gone wrong, by sore backs, and deformed feet), and in more complex ways, as Susan Bordo argues.[18] Bordo's analysis of beauty standards links them directly to oppression. She argues that feminine beauty as slenderness is a symbolic capitulation to male power, a commitment to obedience, and an unthreatening form of femininity. So why do women do it? Because women are sys-tematically told that their value is in their looks. This has been part of patriarchal systems for hundreds of years. Mary Astell, writing in 1694 ('A Serious Proposal to the Ladies') argues that if women are valued only for their looks they will come to value themselves in that way:

> When a poor Young Lady is taught to value her self on nothing but her Cloaths, and to think she's very fine when well accoutred. When she hears say that 'tis Wisdom enough for her to know how to dress her self, that she may become amiable in his eyes; to whom it appertains to beknowing and learned; who can blame her if she lay out her Industry and Money on such Accomplishments.[19]

It is not difficult to argue that women internalize beauty norms. The question is, who ben-efits? Beauty is a massive distraction: a woman who is having her hair and nails done is not overthrowing the patriarchy. And of course, there are people making money. There are rooms full of people designing careful and sophisticated advertising campaigns – campaigns that get women to think that looking a certain way is absolutely required, and yet create an illu-sion that the choice to try to look that way is liberated and liberating. Advertising campaigns do not come from diffuse and accidental sources, they come from groups of individuals.

The fashion-beauty complex may not be aimed directly at the subordination of women, and, indeed, it has some interest in women's freedom. It is important that women have a disposable income, for example. But it is also important that women feel obliged to spend it on their appearance. So it serves the interests of the fashion-beauty complex for women to think that their appearance is one of the most important things about them. Is it coincidence that that is indeed part of our ideology about gender? It doesn't seem a huge stretch to apply a functional explanation here. Women think that appearance is paramount because it serves the interests of the fashion-beauty complex that they do so.

False consciousness vs adaptive preferences

Some accounts of adaptive preference are focussed on individual irrationality rather than social conditions. Jon Elster, for example, is concerned to explain why preferences formed in response to limited choice conditions are not autonomous. He argues that we have a tendency to reduce dissonance between our desires and what we can attain, and so we (irrationally) downgrade unattainable options. His broader point is that theories like preference utilitarianism miss something important, because they do not take account of the way in which preferences are formed.[20]

However, the notion of adaptive preferences, like the notion of false consciousness, can be useful in explaining 'oppression by choice': the situation where people seem to voluntarily choose oppressive options. Feminist adaptive preference theorists examine the ways that people's preferences are warped by oppressive systems. For example, a woman may prefer to be thin than to eat healthily. As with false consciousness, an account of what is wrong with that sort of preference is needed.

Feminist theories of adaptive preferences are not generally committed to discussing adaptive preferences *as opposed to* false consciousness. Accounts of adaptive preference, such as Serene Khader's and Martha Nussbaum's, usually encompass beliefs and value systems as well as desires.[21] In that sense, their theories are aiming to do the same work as the accounts of false consciousness I discuss earlier in the chapter. They aim to understand how people can internalize the values of systems that oppress them, and how to pin down the difference between those states of mind which result from internalization of oppression and those which are autonomous.

The major difference between the two sorts of theory (other than the obvious difference between a focus on beliefs and a focus on preferences) is that accounts of adaptive preferences are typically motivated by immediately practical concerns. In particular, adaptive preference theorists ask the question, 'how can we justify intervening in people's lives when their expressed preference suggests that they do not need or welcome intervention?' Of course, preferences may be expressed under duress, and may not reflect desires. But sometimes, people seem to genuinely prefer, or desire, options that perpetuate their own oppression. The question is: what does justice require? Should we respect the preference, or override it?

This is a problem for liberalism. Liberals generally say that it is wrong to interfere with someone except to prevent harm to others. So liberals tend to accept that even self-destructive preferences should be respected. But adaptive preferences seem different; they do not strike us as worthy of respect in the same way. So it is important to give an account of adaptive preferences that makes sense of the way in which they are not eligible for respect as other preferences (even self-destructive ones) are.

Both Nussbaum and Khader have a very immediately practical aim in mind, to determine how best to intervene in the lives of women in poverty. Women in poverty are in paradigmatic limited choice situations, and so are very likely to have adaptive preferences. They may prefer to stay married to abusive men, to remain uneducated, and even to engage in genital mutilation. But the issues involved in determining which preferences are adaptive here are complex. How can Western feminists avoid cultural imperialism, imposing their own values inappropriately? On the one hand, it is important to respect the autonomy and cultural differences of third world women. On the other hand, we should not use that as an excuse for inaction. I discuss some of these issues in Chapter 1, on the challenges of global feminism. Here, I focus on the definition of adaptive preference.

Accounts of adaptive preferences

It is worth explaining what is meant by 'preference' in this context. I am following standard usage, construing preference as a desire, not as a belief about what is desirable or good. So, it is not a cognitive state, it is a 'conative' one: a motivational state. It is also worth clarifying that preference and choice are not the same when we talk about adaptive preferences. Some economists use the term 'preference' so that it is equivalent to choice: whatever an agent chooses is what they prefer. This is one sense of preference: preferences as 'revealed preferences'. If I choose to give you my money rather than my life, obviously there is a sense in which that is what I prefer. But there is another sense for 'preference', which is closer to *desire*. I may choose something that I do not have a preference for, on this usage. The relevant sense of preference here is the desire sense. An adaptive preference is one where the agent takes herself to be choosing something that she really wants.

As I say, if we are to claim that a preference is 'adaptive' and therefore not necessarily to be honoured, we need an account of what is wrong with that preference: what prevents it from being autonomous. There are two different ways to define non-autonomous preferences: procedural (or content neutral) accounts, such as Jon Elster's and Marilyn Friedman's,[22] and substantive accounts, such as Martha Nussbaum's and Serene Khader's. Procedural accounts define adaptive preference in terms of the mechanism of preference formation; substantive accounts define adaptive preference at least partly in terms of the content of the preference, i.e. what the preference is a preference for.

Nussbaum criticizes Elster's procedural account of adaptive preferences, and argues that a substantive account is necessary to do the work of criticizing preferences formed in oppressive conditions. Elster's central example is the fox in the fable, who cannot have the grapes, so he decides they are sour and that he does not want them anyway. This is not a deliberate strategy of the fox's, rather, it happens to him, it is a 'behind the back' process. Elster contrasts preferences that are formed involuntarily with preferences that are reflectively formed or, at least, approved of as part of a deliberate effort to shape one's own character. Elster argues that a preference is properly autonomous only if the agent has other options. The fox, in the sour grapes story, does not have the option to have the grapes, and so his preference against them is not a fully autonomous preference.[23] Nussbaum points out that adaptive preference formation can sometimes be a *good* thing when we have no choice anyway, as, for example, an unfulfillable preference to be a great opera singer. It is better for the agent to drop that preference. This leads Nussbaum to focus on the agent's flourishing as the central issue in saying what is wrong with adaptive preferences. The problem with preferences formed in oppressive conditions is primarily that they are bad for the agent.

But, of course, we do not want to rely on a narrow or parochial account of flourishing. Both Nussbaum and Khader are committed to an objective account of human flourishing. Nussbaum argues that there are several important capabilities that humans should have, and that these apply to all humans everywhere (see the whole list on p.17–18 in Chapter 1). If someone does not have these capabilities, an injustice has been done, even if that person's preferences do not favour the capabilities. Nussbaum's idea is not that people must avail themselves of the capabilities: a woman might be free to take paid employment, but choose not to, or be free to go without a veil, but choose to wear one. The important point is the capacity: what we are able to do and be. Nussbaum's argument is about preferences regarding the conditions for capabilities. If someone chooses to deprive themselves of one of the basic capabilities, there is something problematic about that preference.

Sometimes, because of entrenched ideologies, women end up with no positive preferences to have a capability, or even preferences *not* to have a capability. Women sometimes end up thinking that their bodies are not really theirs to control, or that they should not be educated, or vote, or have independent jobs, or own property. These are adaptive preferences according to Nussbaum's theory, and policy-makers should be cautious about taking them into account.

Khader agrees with Nussbaum that it is essential to the definition of an adaptive preference that it impedes flourishing. But it is also essential that the preference is imposed on the agent in some way, that it is not her own. Khader points out that if we drop either condition, the case no longer strikes us as an adaptive preference case. A woman who decided to learn to read just because everyone else is does not have a fully autonomous preference, but it is not an adaptive preference. And someone who has many options and is clear-sighted but decides to engage in a dangerous sport is impeding her own flourishing, but it does not seem like an adaptive preference, because it is the agent's own autonomously formed preference.[24]

Khader argues that the crucial point is that the preferences were formed in circumstances not conducive to flourishing, and would not have been formed had the circumstances been better. So, her complete definition is that an adaptive preference is detrimental to the agent's flourishing and is causally related to the poor circumstances in which it was formed. As Khader puts it, "The problem with adaptive preferences is not just that social conditions influence them; it is that *bad* social conditions influence people to form preferences that are *bad for them*."[25]

Khader cautions against being too quick to make judgments about adaptive preferences, particularly in third world contexts. Sometimes, women make choices that have a superficial appearance of adaptive preferences, but are in fact rational in the situation. A woman might choose not to take up an opportunity for education, for example. In those cases, intervention in the circumstances of choice (for example, providing better childcare options) would change people's choices, and the question of unjustified intervention does not arise. As Uma Narayan puts it, sometimes what looks like an adaptive preference may be a case of 'bargaining with the patriarchy'.[26] I discuss these issues in more detail in Chapter 1.

Ideology critique

Sally Haslanger approaches the issue of false consciousness from a different angle. She is interested in how to critique 'social knowledge': our knowledge of social constructions. Haslanger emphasizes that there is something true in many of the beliefs that we ordinarily think of as being false consciousness: the knower has correctly identified a social norm. Thus it is not obvious how to criticize the belief. For example, we 'know' that high heels are attractive on women, or that it is rude to push past someone in the bus queue.

In an early paper on the topic Haslanger focusses on the limits of epistemic critique.[27] She starts by distinguishing between different approaches one might take to a claim like 'crop tops are cute' uttered by a 13-year-old girl. For Haslanger, as the parent, this is objectionable: she thinks that crop tops inappropriately sexualize young girls. But her daughter has correctly identified the fashion norms of her age group: cute girls wear crop tops, dorks wear ordinary tops. How can we analyze the claim so as to capture the ways in which both parent and daughter are correct? Haslanger rejects an objectivist approach, which would say simply that it is false that crop tops are cute. That is an important piece of social knowledge, and we want to capture that. Haslanger also rejects subjectivism: the issue is not simply a disagreement in taste between the kids and the adults.

Haslanger goes on to consider 'the framework reading' according to which there is a sense in which the cute/dork dichotomy is valid, and yet a sense in which it is not. Believing in and talking about the distinction can make it true, and it would be bad for it to reified. So we should not believe in the distinction. But Haslanger worries that the framework reading says that there is an epistemic reason to believe that crop tops are cute, and a moral reason not to. She would like to make sense of an epistemic reason not to believe that crop tops are cute. Haslanger is compelled by the thought that there must be a sense in which there are epistemic reasons to believe *both* that crop tops are cute, and that they are not.

Haslanger's solution appeals to a very complex semantic theory, which I will not explain in great detail. In brief, her idea is that we need to use a sort of relativism that she calls 'milieu relativism'. According to milieu relativism, the correct standards of assessment are relative to our milieus. The kid is in a different milieu to the adults. In the kid's milieu, crop tops are cute. In the adults', they are not. Parents and daughter have the same context of use, but different contexts of assessment. They genuinely disagree because they are talking about the same thing, but their disagreement is, in a sense, faultless, because they are using different standards of assessment.

This makes better sense of something like the framework reading: from within the parents' milieu, the dichotomy can be understood, but should be rejected. So, the parents see that it makes sense from the daughter's point of view but refuse to engage with it: "they are refusing to collaborate in the collective definition of cuteness".[28]

Haslanger admits that this leaves us with a problem. We want to be able to critique the daughter's milieu. Her standards, which mandate clothing that inappropriately sexualizes young girls, are not the right standards. We want to change the daughter's milieu, to bring her around. With children, who grow up, that sometimes happens. But we do not have much reason to be optimistic that other adults, whose standards we think are problematic, will come around simply through exposure to other milieus. Haslanger is skeptical that we can appeal to epistemic warrant: she thinks we have no purely epistemic standard for preferring one milieu over another. (It is worth reminding ourselves that Haslanger is talking about social knowledge here, the sort of knowledge that is constructed socially and so depends on our invented norms. There is no external fact to check it by.)

Haslanger's own solution, in the paper described above and in later work,[29] is to stress the importance of critique from the inside, to look for common ground from which to criticize cultural practices. Haslanger stresses that the looping effect can make a particular structure seem natural and inevitable, and because ideology is connected to our identity, moral critique, even if apt, can easily backfire. Nonetheless, it is possible to push back, and to create new systems and new meanings. And those who are negatively affected by aspects of ideology are well-placed to recognize injustices that others will be blind to. This, ideally, gives rise to social movements, and social movements aim to get everyone to recognize that a bad system, one they may have benefited from, is unjust.

Clare Chambers argues that Haslanger puts too much importance on epistemological critique. The only possible critique, Chambers argues, is moral. We need to look at the bad values that are inherent in some milieu standards, and critique on a normative basis. Chambers says,

> we are looking for normative facts that do not depend on a particular culture or ideology for their truth-value. Facts and judgements that depend on a culture for their truth include statements like "crop tops are cool" or "high heels are sexy" or "pale skin is beautiful". These will be true in some cultures and false in others. Normative facts and judgements are not like this.[30]

Chambers argues that we need to appeal to a robust normative theory to critique a social milieu, and we need to argue that the social relations that result from the milieu are unjust.

Summary

Oppressive systems are sometimes maintained by the internalization of ideology by both the oppressed and oppressor groups. But it is not easy to give an account of what counts as ideology, or when a belief or value system is false consciousness. There are less and more ambitious ways of defining false consciousness. On the less ambitious sort of account, there are two major conditions: the beliefs must be defective, that is, not related to evidence in the right way, and the belief system must perpetuate oppression. These conditions are cashed out in different ways by different writers, and although in the literature they apply primarily to false consciousness, understood as belief systems, they could equally be applied to adaptive preferences: the desires that we acquire as a result of our position in an oppressive system.

The more ambitious account of false consciousness claims that it is not coincidental that false consciousness exists and perpetuates oppression; it exists *because* it benefits the ruling classes. This is controversial because it seems to involve a claim about the effect of something being simultaneously its cause, which is impossible. But, as G.A. Cohen points out, this sort of explanation, which he calls functional explanation, is not mysterious in other domains. In biology, the fact that a species has a useful feature explains why the species has come about and persists. But we need to point to the mechanism – for example, in the case of species, the mechanism is natural selection. It is not obvious that that mechanism applies in the case of oppressive systems.

The issues for adaptive preference are similar, but the focus of the literature has been much more on political questions than conceptual ones. The question that has exercised writers on the topic of adaptive preferences has been, how can we justify disregarding the preferences of apparently competent adults? If their preferences are flawed in some way, not fully autonomous, or not in line with their real interests due to bad circumstances of formation, then we might be justified in interfering, even from a liberal point of view.

Finally, the project of ideology critique is especially challenging when we focus on cases where there is no way to say that the beliefs are epistemically flawed. If the beliefs in question are beliefs about our own social world, about what is cool or funny or cute, we do not have an independent realm from which to critique them. Haslanger argues that in that case we need to find common ground to provide an internally accessible critique.

Notes

1 Bartky, *Femininity and Domination*.
2 Shelby, 'Ideology, Racism, and Critical Social Theory'.
3 Frye, 'Oppression', in *The Politics of Reality*.
4 Davis, *Women, Race, and Class*, p.229.
5 Haslanger, 'Culture and Critique'.
6 Haslanger, 'On Being Objective and Being Objectified', in *Resisting Reality: Social Construction and Social Critique*.
7 Cudd, *Analysing Oppression*; Elster, 'Belief, Bias and Ideology', in *Sour Grapes: Studies in the Subversion of Rationality*; Meyerson, *False Consciousness*.
8 www.nytimes.com/2006/05/16/health/nutrition/16run.html.
9 Shelby, 'Ideology, Racism, and Critical Social Theory', pp.175–176.
10 Collins, 'Mammies, Matriarchs and Other Controlling Images', in *Black Feminist Thought: Knowledge, Consciousness, and the Politics of Empowerment*.
11 Elster, 'Belief, Bias and Ideology', in Sour Grapes, p.143.
12 Op. cit., p.183.
13 Engels, *Letter to Mehring*, in Marx and Engels, *Selected Correspondence*, p.459.
14 Atwood, *The Handmaid's Tale*, p.320.
15 Cohen, *Karl Marx's Theory of History: A Defence*.
16 Elster, 'Sour Grapes', in *Sour Grapes: Studies in the Subversion of Rationality*, p.102.
17 Bartky, *Femininity and Domination*.
18 Bordo, *Unbearable Weight: Feminism, Western Culture, and the Body*.
19 Astell, *A Serious Proposal to the Ladies*, p.69.
20 Elster, 'Sour Grapes', in *Sour Grapes: Studies in the Subversion of Rationality*.
21 Khader, *Adaptive Preferences and Women's Empowerment*; Nussbaum, *Women and Human Development: The Capabilities Approach*.
22 Friedman, *Autonomy, Gender, Politics* (discussed in Chapter 1).
23 Elster, 'Sour Grapes', in *Sour Grapes: Studies in the Subversion of Rationality*.
24 Khader, *Adaptive Preferences and Women's Empowerment*, pp.47–48.
25 Op. cit., p.20.
26 Narayan, 'Minds of their Own: Choices, Autonomy, Cultural Practices, and Other Women', p.421. The phrase comes from Deniz Kandiyoti's article with the same name.
27 Haslanger, 'But Mom, Crop-Tops *are* Cute: Social Knowledge, Social Structure, and Ideology Critique', in *Resisting Reality: Social Construction and Social Critique*.
28 Op. cit., p.423.

29 See especially, Haslanger, 'Culture and Critique'.
30 Chambers, 'II–Ideology and Normativity', p.183.

Further reading

Fanon, Frantz (1979) *Black Skin White Masks*. Paladin. (Fanon was a psychiatrist, but takes a very philo-
  sophical approach to exploring racism and false consciousness).
Meyer, Diana Tietjens (2002) *Gender in the Mirror: Cultural Imagery and Women's Agency*. Oxford
  University Press. (Catalogues and critiques a range of harmful ideological gender imagery).
Oshana, Marina (ed.) (2015) *Personal Autonomy and Social Oppression*. Routledge. (Collection of essays
  focussed on making sense of autonomy in conditions of oppression).
Stanley, Jason (2015) *How Propaganda Works*. Princeton University Press. (A lengthy and detailed
  account of how propaganda undermines democracy, focussed on the United States).

10 Objectification

"All women live in sexual objectification the way fish live in water."

Catharine MacKinnon, *Toward a Feminist Theory of the State*

Chapter overview: In this chapter I examine the nature of objectification, looking at the ideas of Simone de Beauvoir, Rae Langton, Martha Nussbaum, and Nancy Bauer. I consider whether objectification can be morally neutral. I also discuss objectification in images and art, the male gaze, and the challenges posed by the idea of self-objectification.

Introduction

The idea of objectification is roughly the idea that a person is seen as an object instead of as a person. Feminist philosophers are interested in the concept because it seems that women are objectified all the time. In particular, as Andrea Dworkin and Catharine MacKinnon have argued, women are *sexually* objectified – they are seen as objects for the sexual gratification of men, not as people with choices and preferences about sex. Women are sexually objectified in representation (in pornography, in advertising, in film, in art) and in real life, when they are wolf whistled at, or ogled, or touched without consent (up to and including sexual assault and rape).

In one sense, the idea of objectification is very broad, simply referring to any treatment that does not respect the full humanity and agency of a person. In this sense women are objectified in the gendered division of labour; in the way that they are seen as wives and mothers above all else; and in the way that they are treated as reproductive machines. Women are sexually objectified in pornography and as prostitutes; they are objectified by being assaulted and raped; they are objectified by the ideological stories about them; they are objectified by being ignored and silenced, and so on. The question then is whether there is something at the root of all these forms of sexist treatment that properly deserves the name 'objectification', or, alternatively, whether there is an interesting narrower use of the term.

Simone de Beauvoir uses the idea in a very broad sense, but she certainly thinks that there is something useful and meaningful in the claim that women are seen as and treated as objects. Famously, according to Beauvoir, one is not born, but becomes a woman.[1] For Beauvoir, one of the essential features of women's oppression is the ideology of womanhood, the way that 'woman' is socially constructed. Beauvoir argues that women are not allowed the full subjectivity that men are – because men are the subject, they define what woman is, and so she is 'the Other'. Women are 'immanent', conceived of as essentially embodied, limited, and defined by material reality. Men trap women in this role, saving for themselves the possibilities of freedom, of being 'transcendent' in Beauvoir's terminology. Women are forced into passivity, though of course they are ambivalent, seeking freedom, and in some sense knowing they are not the passive objects that the world tells them they are.

According to Beauvoir, women have a certain nature and role imposed on them, a role that is essentially in the world of things, and this is the root of their oppression. Hence the general applicability of the idea of objectification. Women are objects. As Beauvoir puts it in one passage describing ideals of feminine beauty, "The ideal of feminine beauty is variable; but some requirements remain constant; one of them is that since woman is destined to be possessed, her body has to provide the inert and passive qualities of an object." Beauvoir goes on to catalogue the ways in which ideals of beauty restrict women, both actually and symbolically:

> Customs and fashions were often applied to cut the feminine body from its transcendence: the Chinese woman with bound feet could barely walk, the Hollywood star's painted nails deprived her of her hands; high heels, corsets, hoops, farthingales, and crinolines were meant less to accentuate the woman's body's curves than to increase the body's powerlessness. Weighted down by fat or on the contrary so diaphanous that any effort is forbidden to it, paralyzed by uncomfortable clothes and rites of propriety, the body thus appeared to man as his thing.[2]

Beauvoir's is not a strict analysis of the term 'objectification'. But we can see how the term is appropriate for what she means, and how it is intelligible. Nancy Bauer argues that to look for more from the term is to distort its meaning. Bauer argues that the broad idea of sexual objectification as used by feminist theorists is incredibly useful. When we have a grasp of the concept we can see that there is sexual objectification everywhere: it is a crucial conceptual resource. As Bauer puts it, the term was coined as part of a shift in how to understand the world.

> According to this shift, *in a context in which women experience widespread, systematic, diachronic, structural disadvantages*, certain ways of perceiving and representing women tend to cause women direct and indirect material and psychological harm. Once you participate in this shift, the term *sexual objectification* will come to have purchase for you. It will "light up" the relevant phenomena . . .[3]

Bauer thinks that analysis of the concept beyond that is futile, and will miss what is interesting about objectification.

Bauer criticizes both moralized and non-moralized accounts of the concept. (On the moralized concept, to objectify someone is morally bad by definition, on a non-moralized account, it may not be). Catharine MacKinnon and Sally Haslanger both attempt to analyze objectification as an essentially problematic notion.[4] Martha Nussbaum, by contrast, and to some extent Rae Langton too, attempt to give a morally neutral account of objectification.[5]

There is a sense in which there is really no dispute here. MacKinnon and Haslanger are interested in talking about a problematic thing they see, and label, objectification. But Nussbaum has a different starting point: her aim is to think about the various ways that people can treat other people as objects. Some of these ways can be problematic, but there is no reason to think that *all* these ways are. Nussbaum agrees that certain ways of instrumentalizing people can be harmful, and expands on that in a later article, but that is not her main focus in her discussion of objectification.

There is a parallel here with different ways of talking about pornography. Dworkin's and MacKinnon's discussion of pornography (see Chapter 4) starts by defining pornography as depicting subordination of women. But, of course, there might be other sorts of sexually explicit material that are not morally problematic. Dworkin and MacKinnon are focussed on the problematic thing, and aim to illuminate what is problematic about it. Similarly here, we might focus on the problematic thing and try to illuminate what is bad about it, or we might focus on understanding different ways of treating people like objects.

The neutral account of objectification

Nussbaum starts her account of the concept of objectification by considering several passages from a range of texts that describe or exemplify something that looks like objectification. Nussbaum is careful to point out that we need not take the attitude described as the author's attitude but should focus on the implied author, the stance the narrative as a whole takes. In *Ulysses*, James Joyce portrays Molly's lust for Boylan in a certain way, but we need not think that Joyce shares her attitude. By contrast, the pornography of 'Laurence St Clair' (a pseudonym) is full of degrading sexual objectification, and there is no apparent distance between the author and the objectifying attitude. Nussbaum's point is that these different texts are very different: some are offensive, some are not, some describe an offensive attitude, some do not.

Nussbaum understands objectification to be a 'cluster concept'. There are various ways of treating a person as an object, which can appear singly or overlapping. We should not look for necessary and sufficient conditions, rather, for something to count as objectification is for it to have enough of these features, and what counts as enough may vary from context to context. Nussbaum distinguishes between various kinds of objectification:

1. Instrumentality: The objectifier treats the object as a tool of his or her purposes.
2. Denial of autonomy: The objectifier treats the object as lacking in autonomy and self-determination.
3. Inertness: The objectifier treats the object as lacking in agency, and perhaps also in activity.
4. Fungibility: The objectifier treats the object as interchangeable (a) with other objects of the same type, and/or (b) with objects of other types.

5. Violability: The objectifier treats the object as lacking in boundary integrity, as some-thing that it is permissible to break up, smash, break into.
6. Ownership: The objectifier treats the object as something that is owned by another, can be bought or sold, etc.
7. Denial of subjectivity: The objectifier treats the object as something whose experience and feelings (if any) need not be taken into account.[6]

According to Nussbaum, all of these are familiar ways of treating objects, and intuitively play some role in the feminist idea of objectification. A person objectifies someone else when they treat someone in the ways that are usually appropriate for treating objects. However, the conditions that determine whether it is appropriate to treat a person, or even an object, in one or more of these ways are complex and hard to pin down. As Nussbaum points out, even with objects, there can be limits on what is morally acceptable. Sometimes we should not treat objects as violable, for example.

In her search for what is problematic about objectification, Nussbaum focusses on denial of autonomy and instrumentalizing, which often go hand in hand, and can lead to other forms of objectification. As Nussbaum explains,

> a certain sort of instrumental use of persons, negating the autonomy that is proper to them as persons, also leaves the human being so denuded of humanity, in the eyes of the objectifier, that he or she seems ripe for other abuses as well – for the refusal of imagina-tion involved in the denial of subjectivity, for the denial of individuality involved in fun-gibility, and even for bodily and spiritual violation and abuse, if that should appear to be what best suits the will and purposes of the objectifier. The lesson seems to be that there is something especially problematic about instrumentalizing human beings, something that involves denying what is fundamental to them as human beings, namely, the status of beings as ends in themselves. From this one denial, other forms of objectification that are not logically entailed by the first seem to follow.[7]

So for Nussbaum, denial of autonomy and instrumentalization are core notions in the femi-nist account of objectification: denying someone's autonomy, and treating them merely as an instrument for one's ends, are acceptable ways to treat actual objects but are not generally appropriate for persons. They exemplify the sort of disrespect and disregard that is central to the feminist worry.

Nussbaum puts most weight on the notion of instrumentalization, saying that treating some-one else merely as a means to one's own ends is always problematic. This is a very Kantian view. Kant famously argues that we must always treat humanity as an end in itself (though it is agreed that that is not easy to interpret), and that it is never permissible to use someone as a mere means. Contemporary Kantians argue, and this is what Nussbaum thinks too, that we can use people as a mere means so long as that is not our primary way of viewing them – in other words, we can use people as a means but not as a 'mere' means. A lot hangs on 'mere' in this account. Nussbaum thinks that using a lover's stomach as a pillow is acceptable, even though one is using them as a means. Presumably, then, one is not using them as a mere means. The claim then is that the sort of objectification that tends to be problematic is instrumentalization.

Nussbaum goes on to discuss the various other sorts of objectification with reference to her literary examples, and argues that it is not obvious that they are all always problematic. In some of the cases, something that is clearly objectification in one of the seven senses she identifies can be construed as healthy and respectful. Her underlying point is that sometimes we can revel in the animalistic aspects of ourselves, and we do not always need to inhabit full personhood.

For example, in her discussion of the sex scenes in *Lady Chatterley's Lover*, Nussbaum analyzes the way that the lovers reduce each other to body parts. Nussbaum says that the intense focussing on the bodily parts is what makes the sex between Lady Chatterley and her lover so wonderful:

> Why is Lawrentian objectification benign, if it is? We must point, above all, to the complete absence of instrumentalization, and to the closely connected fact that the objectification is symmetrical and mutual – and in both cases undertaken in a context of mutual respect and rough social equality. The surrender of autonomy and even of agency and subjectivity are joyous, a kind of victorious achievement in the prison-house of English respectability. Such a surrender constitutes an escape from the prison of self-consciousness that, in Lawrence's quite plausible view, seals us off from one another and prevents true communication and true receptivity.[8]

Nussbaum's main argument is that in the right context, a good and joyful sex life may include almost any of these forms of objectification.

According to Nussbaum, forms of objectification other than instrumentalization can all be morally acceptable:

> there seems to be no other item on the list that is always morally objectionable. Denial of autonomy and denial of subjectivity are objectionable if they persist throughout an adult relationship, but as phases in a relationship characterized by mutual regard they can be all right, or even quite wonderful in the way that Lawrence suggests. In a closely related way, it may at times be splendid to treat the other person as passive, or even inert. Emotional penetration of boundaries seems potentially a very valuable part of sexual life, and some forms of physical boundary-penetration also, though it is less clear which ones these are. Treating-as-fungible is suspect when the person so treated is from a group that has frequently been commodified and used as a tool, or a prize; between social equals these problems disappear, though it is not clear that others do not arise.[9]

Rae Langton agrees that objectification is usefully seen as a cluster concept. Langton suggests various supplements to Nussbaum's account that are relevant to feminist thinking about objectification. First, she adds three items: reduction to body parts, reduction to appearance, and silencing, that is, treating the person as if they cannot speak. (This is not quite the same idea as the silencing discussed in Chapter 13: treating someone *as if* they cannot speak is not quite the same as making it the case that they cannot speak). Langton argues that these features, although not necessary conditions, are often present in the cases that feminists worry about, and help to distinguish cases of objectification from other ways of disregarding people's actually important characteristics as persons. For example, Langton describes a burglar, who certainly treats the person he burgles as violable, fungible, non-autonomous, merely instrumentally valuable, and so on, but this is not objectification in the interesting sense.

Langton also develops a more detailed account of what is involved in autonomy denial. Nussbaum thinks that autonomy denial can be benign, but she acknowledges that, along with instrumentalization, with which it is often conjoined, it is frequently problematic. As Nussbaum describes it, autonomy denial is a matter of treating someone as if they lack autonomy and self-determination. Langton argues that there are complexities here: there are various different things we may mean when we say that someone treats another as if they do not have autonomy.

First, Langton distinguishes between believing that someone is not autonomous (non-attribution of autonomy) and autonomy violations. These can come apart. A doctor may see her patient as lacking autonomy, but treat her with care and respect. On the other hand, problematic autonomy denial may essentially affirm the existence of autonomy while violating it. For example, in sadistic rape, the rapist wants the woman to say no: he wants her to use her autonomy to refuse, and he wants to violate her autonomy by ignoring her refusal.

This is important because it captures a sort of objectification that is problematic in pornography. There is a somewhat paradoxical element of pornographic narratives, given the feminist claim that they are objectifying. The women are often portrayed as *choosing* the degradation they endure, and as enjoying it. Langton uses the example of the film *Deep Throat*. In that film, the actor Linda Lovelace is portrayed as autonomous, as a "Liberated Woman in her most extreme form, taking life and sex on her own terms".[10] Langton argues that this autonomy affirmation is compatible with autonomy violation. First, Linda Lovelace's account of the making of the film reveals that the real life actor suffered a great deal of autonomy violation. She was raped and beaten into submission. But additionally, Langton argues, the portrayal of women as choosing according to pornographic standards is a sort of autonomy denial: "this autonomy-affirmation serves autonomy-denial, a false vision of autonomy being, after all, among the most potent enemies of autonomy."[11] The fellatio depicted in *Deep Throat* was not realistically pleasurable for the woman, but it was taken as being so. Langton cites Catharine MacKinnon on the real-world effects of the film: increased incidences of throat rape and unwanted deep throat sex.

In other words, the feminist critique of objectification in pornography is compatible with recognizing that the women are portrayed as autonomous. This is congruent with MacKinnon's argument about pornography: that it tells a distorted story about what women are and what they are for, and that when people believe this story, women are harmed.

The moralized account of objectification

Some feminist philosophers offer accounts of objectification that start from the premise that objectification is problematic, and indeed, at the root of sexist oppression. "Objectification is an injury right at the heart of discrimination: those who can be used as if they are not fully human are no longer fully human in social terms; their humanity is hurt by being diminished", as Andrea Dworkin puts it.[12]

Sally Haslanger, developing Catharine MacKinnon's view, argues that objectification involves seeing something as an object for the satisfaction of one's desire. Furthermore, it involves seeing that thing as having a nature that makes it desirable in the way that it is desired, and enables it to satisfy that desire. We see a cow as made of meat, and delicious, and there to be eaten.[13]

But more importantly, and this is what captures the essential wrong in objectification, when someone objectifies, they have the power to enforce their way of seeing things. They do not objectify 'in their head' but in the real world. To use the cow analogy again: we think of cows as meat, as suitable for eating, and then we make them into meat.

Part of both MacKinnon's and Haslanger's story is that objectification involves a sort of illusion. Objectification is entrenched by the illusion of naturalness: part of the successful objectification of women is that the idea that this is how things really, *naturally* are is built into it. As Haslanger puts it,

> if men desire submission, then in objectifying women men view women as having a nature which makes them (or, under normal circumstances, should make them) submissive, at the same time as they force women into submission. The illusion in successful objectification is not in the reports of its consequences – the women who have been forced to submit do submit; the illusion is in, so to speak, the modality of such claims – women submit *by nature*.[14]

In its general shape, this sounds very similar to Beauvoir's account. Objectification is ideological: there is a pervasive mythology about what women are.

Returning then to the moralized account of objectification, we can distinguish between various different accounts of what exactly is problematic. As we saw, Nussbaum argues that the wrong at the heart of objectification is usually autonomy denial, or instrumentalization. Langton implicitly identifies autonomy denial as the major problem. Timo Jütten defends the MacKinnon–Haslanger style view, which he characterizes as 'the imposition view'. The phrase captures the way that objectification is an imposition of social meaning on women.[15]

Jütten objects to Nussbaum's 'mere instrumentalization' account that the question of whether something is instrumentalization focusses too much on the transaction between two people, and on the question of whether one is using the other as a mere instrument. A man might have sex with someone in an instrumentalizing way, but, Jütten argues, that doesn't capture the objectification in the situation. The objectification is structural; it is in the general understanding of women as the sexual servants of men.

According to Jütten's account of the imposition model, to be objectified is to be socially constructed as something to be used sexually. There are obvious harms here, harms we have discussed at length in this book. Women's freedom and opportunities are severely restricted. Jütten draws on work by David Velleman to add a more general account of the harm of having a social meaning imposed on one. Velleman argues that we need to be seen as 'self-presenting' agents – we need to be seen as people who have made a choice about how others see us. That is more important than any particular choice about how we are seen, it is a way of demonstrating that we are autonomous, that we are directing our own lives.

Women are limited in how they are permitted to self-present. As Jütten points out, our self-presentation relies on shared understandings, on the story we present about ourselves being intelligible to others. The roles that women can inhabit are limited if they start beyond a certain suite of stereotypical roles. They are unintelligible. This is a familiar point from Patricia Hill Collins' account of 'controlling images' of Black women, or the idea of 'role traps' discussed in Chapter 7 on sexism and oppression.

Not being free to present as a self-presenter damages autonomy, and equal social standing. As Jütten puts it,

> sexual objectification is a threat to women's autonomy, because it invites men (and other women) to see them as sex objects whose worth is defined by men's sexual interests, rather than as self-presenting autonomous agents who make claims on their own behalf and have the right to be recognized as such agents. This threat to autonomy differs from more obvious threats to individual acts of self-determination, but it is at least as serious as these threats, because it attacks women's social standing as autonomous agents that grants them the right to self-determination in the first place. Of course, once women's social standing as autonomous agents is undermined, they also become vulnerable to interference with individual acts of self-determination, because it becomes more difficult to demand respect for their autonomy.[16]

Objectifying images

One pervasive feature of modern life is objectifying images of women. It seems that everywhere you look, women are represented as sex objects, as body parts, as beautiful dolls, as non-persons in one way or another. Kathleen Stock identifies three common tropes in these images: women-as-bodies, women-as-animals, and women-as-duplicates. Less common tropes include women-as-children (as when grown women are shown in childish poses, biting their nails, knees together, and feet splayed) and women-as-insensate objects, for example a naked woman as a table. We might add others, for example, women-as-corpses (perhaps starting with the dead but beautiful Laura Palmer in *Twin Peaks*, and recurring in crime dramas with alarming frequency).

Stock's question is whether it is possible to give a unifying account of the objectification in these various images. Stock suggests that these images are all 'mind-suppressing': they represent the woman as if she doesn't really have a mind. Stock argues that this can be obvious, as when only body parts are shown, but it can also be more insidious: "Mind-suppression may also be conveyed by more subliminal features: for instance, across a wide range of images, men's faces tend to be represented as proportionately larger than that of women, with consequences for viewer's relative ratings of intelligence of the represented subjects."[17]

Stock argues that mind-suppressing images of women lead us to perceive women as being without minds, or at least less 'minded' than men. Stock labels this perceiving as 'seeing-as'. It is not just that we think of the women in the picture that way, we see them as being that way, just as we might see a cloud as an elephant, or see a tree as a sycamore. Furthermore, Stock argues, and backs this up with reference to empirical research, if we are exposed to a lot of images like that, we end up more likely to see real women in that way. Stock cites work by Rudman and Mescher that shows that men who objectify women in the ways described above, seeing them as animals or objects, are more likely to have negative attitudes towards rape victims.[18]

For women, being seen primarily as bodies, or sexual objects, is damaging. There is the possibility that exposure to objectifying images makes men more likely to rape women. But aside from that, there are the harms of not being taken seriously (which I discuss in Chapters 12 and 13), as well as psychological harms that are more directly related to objectification. Stock cites empirical work by social psychologists, showing that anticipation of the male gaze, that is, anticipating being seen in mind-insensitive ways, causes women to feel self-conscious and ashamed of their bodies. There is a significant cognitive load associated with dealing with the male gaze, and women perform less well in other tasks as a result.

Stock claims that this account of seeing-as is causally prior to the various forms of treating someone as an object identified by Nussbaum and Langton. One treats a person as an object because one sees them as an object. Relatedly, this account helps explain why objectifying images are morally problematic in a simple and compelling story. They are morally problematic because they cause harm.

This account echoes the critique of pornography by Catharine Mackinnon and others. Pornography, and other objectifying images of women, tell a story about what women are like. By some mechanism or other, men come to believe that story, and that affects their behaviour – perhaps making them more likely to ignore and disbelieve women, to treat them as sex objects, and even to rape them. Women know that men believe the story, and may also internalize it themselves.

Anne Eaton examines objectification in art, in particular the female nude, and asks what might be problematic about female nudes from a feminist perspective. Eaton agrees with MacKinnon, that the basic problem with objectification is that it eroticizes male dominance. Eaton thinks that this critique can be extended to female nudes in art, even when it is undeniably great art. As Eaton summarizes the basic argument:

> Women's subordination has several sources and components, one of the most significant being the sexualization of traditional gender hierarchy; that is, the way in which dominance and related active traits are eroticized for males whereas the contraries are eroticized for females. Insofar as it makes male dominance and female subordination sexy, the female nude is one important source of this eroticization and in this way is a significant part of the complex mechanism that sustains sex inequality.[19]

Eaton gives an account of the various ways in which the painting or sculptures of naked women objectify women – not just the subject of the art, but women in general. First, women are often portrayed as objects. Take the famous picture by Man Ray, *Le Violon d'Ingres* (1924, Getty Collection). An image of a woman's naked back has the f-holes of a stringed instrument imposed onto the narrowest part of her upper back, suggesting that her body is the body of a violin.

Then there is a related set of features that Eaton identifies as common in art throughout history. Rape and violation of women is often portrayed as erotic. Body parts, and particularly erogenous zones, are often foregrounded, and the female subject is posed in a vulnerable or passive position. Her passivity and powerlessness are themselves eroticized. Eaton mentions the theme of the 'nymph and satyr', which appears countless times throughout centuries of art.

Eaton also discusses the way that female nudes are portrayed as essentially fungible, in Nussbaum's terminology. Female nudes are not shown with personality, their faces are often identical from painting to painting and within one painting, as the popular modernist theme of 'bathers' illustrates – an opportunity to portray a crowd of naked female forms.

Eaton points out that female nudes often appear alongside clothed men, as in Manet's *Le Dejeuner sur l'herbe* (1863, Musée d'Orsay, Paris). The men are portrayed as doing things – talking, painting, thinking – and the woman is gratuitously naked, just sitting there, being gazed upon by the viewer. This is a frequent set-up, the nude woman among clothed men, an object to be gazed at. Sometimes, she is seen gazing upon herself, and this, as Eaton quotes John Berger as saying, both objectifies women and condemns them for it.[20]

Eaton argues that although not all female nudes in art objectify, the vast majority do, and this is what justifies the generalization. There are some that do not: Eaton discusses Artemisia Gentileschi's *Susanna and the Elders* (1610, Pommersfelden). This subject is a common one, and most paintings show Susanna bathing naked, about to be attacked by the Elders (who plan to rape her). Most of these paintings objectify Susanna, showing her as voluptuous and appealingly vulnerable. Gentileschi's version shows Susanna as an agent, not as passive, but as resisting, not as an object, but as a person experiencing peril. Her naked body is not idealized, but painted as it would look, contorted at an awkward angle.

Crucial to Eaton's argument is that these paintings do not just objectify the woman who is the subject, but *all* women. Her basis for that claim is that nudes are almost always generic and idealized. They are generic in the sense discussed above: they are not identifiable as individual women, but are types. They are idealized according to the beauty standards of the time they were painted in. Thus they present women as objects of sexual desire, not as agents. They invite the male gaze.

Eaton spends some time explaining what the 'male gaze' means. It is not merely the empirical fact of men looking. As Eaton explains:

> To say that a work embodies *the male gaze* is to say that it calls upon its audience to "see" (whether literally or figuratively) the woman represented – in this case the unclothed female body – as primarily a sex object. To describe this "way of seeing" as "male" is not to claim anything about how all, or even most, men respond to such pictures; rather, it is to note that this is the "way of seeing" proper to someone in the masculine social role, a role which, it should be noted, is avowedly heterosexual.[21]

Women can turn the male gaze on themselves. As Eaton says,

> The narcissism that results from this learned obsession with our appearance and sexual attractiveness itself becomes a theme of the genre . . . The nude is not just a sight for the masculine gaze; she is a thing to be looked at *even by herself*, although always evaluated through masculine eyes. As art historian John Berger astutely puts the point, "A woman must continually watch herself. She is almost continually accompanied by her own image

of herself. Whilst she is walking across a room or whilst she is weeping at the death of her father, she can scarcely avoid envisaging herself walking or weeping. From earliest childhood she has been taught and persuaded to survey herself continually."[22]

Eaton concludes that art can be like pornography, in portraying women in a way that eroticizes male domination and female submission, and causes harm to women in various ways. The fact that art has aesthetic value does not detract from this criticism. On the contrary, it may make the harmful power of art more potent: "The female nude not only eroticizes but also aestheticizes the sexual objectification of women, and it does so from on high."[23] In other words, we take art to be important and authoritative, and to be immune from feminist criticism.

Self-objectification

While feminist philosophers talk about objectification, it seems that real women, some of them self-described feminists, are brushing it off. As is documented in various recent books, there seems to be a feminist-inspired attempt to embrace sexual objectification, to turn it into something empowering.[24] What should feminist philosophers say about that?

Reclaiming or repurposing identities is a complex and difficult business. The most successful examples in Western culture are in queer culture, where modes of dress and speech, and of course the word 'queer' itself, have been successfully reclaimed, and put to use as positive and politically useful aspects of identity. But there are clearly aspects of the ways that oppressed groups are characterized that cannot be appropriated – they are negative and harmful all the way down. For example, it seems obvious that feminism cannot reclaim the idea of women as hysterical and make it into something positive and politically useful. Sexiness is more tempting – after all, sex is an important part of human life, and as we saw in the discussion of pornography in Chapter 4, it is important to make room for a light-hearted approach. That seems to be the driving force behind the current popularity of pole dancing for fitness, or sexy selfies posted on Instagram.

The feminist philosophers' general view on the possibility of reclaiming objectification is pessimistic. Instead, feminist philosophers argue, what is going on here is self-objectification. There are different ways that women might self-objectify. There are incentives to comply, and failing to comply to norms of feminine beauty attracts penalties. Excellence at meeting the standards for feminine beauty and sexiness attracts rewards (though also of course, as Marilyn Frye points out, women are in a double bind: they are punished for conforming to feminine appearance norms as well as for rebelling against them). So long as the rewards are sufficient, it can make sense from a pragmatic point of view to successfully make oneself into an object that will be desired by men. This is rational self-objectification.

But there is also a sort of self-objectification that is a form of false consciousness. Sometimes, women take on the values of the system that oppresses them in all sincerity. This is easy to see in the case of ideals of feminine beauty. Sandra Lee Bartky discusses this at length in her account of the repressive satisfactions involved in meeting the demands of the fashion-beauty complex. Bartky appeals to Beauvoir's account of women as being caught between two views of themselves, as objects for male sexual attention on the one hand, and as free and rational beings on the other. According to Beauvoir, 'narcissism', the focus on the self as object, is a way of escaping the pressures of being both objectified and free to struggle against the objectification. It is easier to simply allow oneself to be the object.

Bartky identifies the particular way in which the fashion-beauty complex works on insecurities as the source of its effectiveness in persuading women to buy into it. She points out that the fashion-beauty complex must constantly make women feel that they are not good enough, that they are not meeting the ideal. Thus narcissism is "infatuation with an inferiorized body".[25] Bartky compares the internalization of beauty norms to religious practice: "Body Care rituals are like sacraments; at best, they put a woman who would be lost and abandoned without them into what may feel to her like a state of grace".[26]

Bartky's account explains what is pleasurable, and a relief about succumbing to self-objectification. But as Heather Widdows argues, the ever more sophisticated system goes further than that. Stringent beauty ideals are imposed, and, further, they are normalized, made ethical and obligatory. *Of course* we comply. But this is not bargaining with the patriarchy, complying in order to avoid penalties (though that happens too). Part of the essential narrative is that we do this out of our own free will. As Widdows puts it,

> To remove body hair, to purchase breast implants, to wear high heels has to be "for me!" To claim that it is "for me!" in the liberal context, is the correct and acceptable narrative. Like the "to be normal" narrative, "I chose it, I'm doing it for me!" is the only acceptable reason for action.[27]

But there is still something puzzling about this, particularly in the case of sexual self-objectification. Nancy Bauer relates conversations with her female students, who report their sex lives as liberating and fun, but as chiefly involving unreciprocated oral sex on men. Bauer believes them when they say that this is enjoyable: she accepts that the sense of power and the success of being desirable are deeply pleasurable. But as Bauer points out, there is a tension between the way that young women see themselves as agents, the equals of men, and the way that they seem to make themselves into sex toys for men. And this is a tension they sometimes feel themselves, as when the 'hook-up hangover' kicks in: the boy doesn't call, or when a young woman finds that she has "slid irrevocably over the line, which is as sharp and fateful as ever, from babe-hood into slut-dom."[28]

Bauer argues that Beauvoir's account of self-objectification solves this puzzle. On Beauvoir's view, as I say, women are both a subject and an object. This is true for all human beings, but it is different for women than it is for men, as women are powerfully objectified by men. Women are discouraged from taking an active role, from taking on their subjectivity, and struggling against object status. And this makes object status even more tempting, and not just irrationally so, but rationally. To put it in existentialist terms, the call of self-objectification is not bad faith. It is not mere laziness.

Bauer quotes Beauvoir as saying, "To decline to be the Other, to refuse to be a party to the deal – this would be for women to renounce all the advantages conferred upon them by their alliance with the superior caste."[29] Bauer's point is that giving up objectification, refusing the pleasures of self-objectification, is a genuine sacrifice: it does not merely require courage to see oneself as one really is, but courage to give up an already scant and unreliable privilege. This is not intended as a version of the 'bargaining with the patriarchy' story, although part of the point is to explain that it is possible to have both views of oneself at once and to feel the tension between them. This is a false consciousness story, in that women have genuinely internalized the norms of objectification. The point is that internalizing those norms is seductive.

Bauer does not think that the pleasures of self-objectification are real or stable, and in the end she thinks we should give them up. But the reasons to give up self-objectification are not just self-regarding. Self-objectification is obviously complicity in sexist oppression. It might be a particularly insidious kind, if we think of Langton's account of autonomy denial. One way that women are portrayed in pornography is as autonomously choosing things that degrade and subordinate them. As Langton argues, this false view of autonomy is a way of denying autonomy and can result in autonomy violations. Women are presented as voluntary sex objects, which justifies treating them as sex objects. By the same argument, self-objectification presents a false view of autonomy, and as it is self-presented, it is even more likely to be persuasive than the false views presented in pornography.

Summary

There is a very general sense in which women are objectified, and the chapters of this book are a catalogue of the forms that objectification takes. But some philosophers have attempted to give a more precise account of what objectification is.

One influential account is Martha Nussbaum's morally neutral account of objectification. She starts by listing seven ways that we treat objects and do not generally treat persons. If we treat persons in these ways, we are 'objectifying' in a technical sense. But, as Nussbaum points out, and as other philosophers object, this does not capture what is wrong with objectification – some forms of objectification can be benign in the right context.

An alternative approach starts with the feminist's moralized concept of objectification: that thing, whatever it is, that is done to women and is harmful. Catharine MacKinnon and Sally Haslanger both argue that objectification is a way of imposing an account of what women are and what they are for – in particular, women are seen as, and so become, objects for the sexual use of men.

We often talk about objectifying images. Feminist philosophers give various accounts of what it is for an image to be objectifying. Kathleen Stock argues that an objectifying image is one that portrays women as if they do not really have minds, and that this in turn encourages men to think of them that way. Anne Eaton focusses on how high art can be objectifying. She argues that objectifying images are not any less so just through being great art, and indeed can be more so, as they have extra authority.

Finally, self-objectification is the phenomenon of taking oneself to be an object, and presenting oneself in the objectified ways. This can be seen either as a form of rational response to the penalties and rewards of patriarchy, or as internalized false consciousness.

Nancy Bauer argues from Simone de Beauvoir's framework that it is a bit of both – the high penalties for rejecting objectification explain partly why it is so tempting to self-objectify.

Notes

1 Beauvoir, *The Second Sex*, p.283.
2 Op. cit., pp.210–211.
3 Bauer, 'What Philosophy Can't Teach Us about Sexual Objectification', in *How To Do Things with Pornography*, p.28.
4 MacKinnon, *Towards a Feminist Theory of the State*, Haslanger, 'On Being Objective and Being Objectified' in *Resisting Reality: Social Construction and Social Critique*.
5 Nussbaum, 'Objectification'; Langton, 'Autonomy-Denial in Objectification' in *Sexual Solipsism: Philosophical Essays on Pornography and Objectification*.
6 Nussbaum, 'Objectification', p.257.
7 Op. cit., p.265.
8 Op. cit., p.275.
9 Op. cit., p.290.
10 Langton, 'Autonomy-Denial in Objectification', in *Sexual Solipsism*, p.237.
11 Op. cit., p.240.
12 Dworkin, 'Against the Male Flood: Censorship, Pornography, and Equality', pp.30–31.
13 Haslanger, 'On Being Objective and Being Objectified', in *Resisting Reality: Social Construction and Social Critique*.
14 Op. cit., p.66.
15 Jütten, 'Sexual Objectification'.
16 Op. cit., p.38.
17 Stock, 'Objectification, Objectifying Images and "Mind-Insensitive Seeing-As"', p.300.
18 Op. cit., p.307.
19 Eaton, 'What's Wrong with the (Female) Nude?', p.270.
20 Op. cit., p.290.
21 Op. cit., p. 293.
22 Op. cit, p.294, quoting Berger, *Ways of Seeing*, p.46.
23 Op. cit., p.307.
24 See e.g. Natasha Walter's *Living Dolls: The Return of Sexism* and Ariel Levy's *Female Chauvinist Pigs: Women and the Rise of Raunch Culture*.
25 Bartky, 'Narcissism, Femininity and Alienation', in *Femininity and Domination*, p.40.
26 Op. cit., p.41.
27 Widdows, *Perfect Me: Beauty as an Ethical Ideal*, p.201.
28 Bauer, 'Beauvoir on the Allure of Self-Objectification', in *How to Do Things with Pornography*, p.46.
29 Op. cit., p.49; Beauvoir, *The Second Sex*, p.10.

Further reading

Bartky, Sandra-Lee (1990) *Femininity and Domination: Studies in the Phenomenology of Oppression*. Routledge. (Collection of essays exploring women's oppression, in particular by the 'fashion-beauty complex').
Bordo, Susan (1993) *Unbearable Weight*. University of California Press. (Classic analysis of women's relationship to their bodies under patriarchal oppression).
Cahill, Ann J. (2011) *Overcoming Objectification: A Carnal Ethics*. Routledge. (Analysis of objectification with a strong post-modern influence).
Young, Iris Marion (2005) *On Female Body Experience: "Throwing Like a Girl" and Other Essays*. Oxford University Press. (Collection of essays on bodily experience, including the classic 'Throwing Like a Girl').

11 Consent

"A little still she strove, and much repented, And whispering 'I will ne'er consent' – consented."

Lord Byron, *Don Juan*

Chapter overview: I briefly cover the legal history of consent and the problematic default supposition that women consent to sex unless there is force. I explain the conditions that are commonly thought to undermine consent: coercion and deception. I then examine problems with the traditional model of consent, including that it makes it difficult to determine a *mens rea* in rapists. I examine new models of consent: affirmative consent, negotiation, and consensus.

Introduction

Understanding consent is particularly important to feminists because sexual violence against women is widespread, and yet convictions for sexual assault and rape are low across the world. This is sometimes because rapists are not caught, or not prosecuted, but sometimes it is because the law deems that a woman has consented when, in fact, she did not. As feminist legal theorists argue, historically, the law has accepted a problematic and sexist account of what consent is.

Rape law reform in the Anglo-American legal system began in the 1970s.[1] Until then, it was usual for rape to be defined as sexual intercourse that was non-consensual and involving the use of force. The persistent idea that the only 'real' rape is the sort where a stranger jumps out of the bushes and physically attacks and overpowers his victim is related to the force requirement in law. The idea is that rape is essentially violent, a terrible and unusual crime, committed by individual wicked men, rather than something that is common and perpetrated by ordinary men. The feminist claim that rape is possible between acquaintances, or on a date, was not taken seriously until relatively recently (see Chapter 6 for a more general discussion of rape and sexual assault). The legal presumption in non-violent cases was that the woman had consented. Hence the force requirement: if force could be proved, non-consent was proved.

The force requirement has been relaxed in the Anglo-American legal system. Either rape is defined in terms of non-consent, or the force requirement is interpreted to mean 'force or coercion'. But it is not easy to give an account of the conditions that undermine consent. We need an account, both of what sort of pressure is undermining, and how much is needed to undermine consent.

Some undermining conditions are widely agreed on. First, valid consent requires that the person consenting has certain capacities and is able to use them. So, someone who is a child, or severely mentally ill, cannot consent at all. Hence the 'age of consent': the idea is that below a certain age, consent to sexual intercourse is simply not possible – the child does not have the capacities to understand what they are consenting to. And for those who have the capacities, it is essential that they are able to use those capacities. If someone is asleep or unconscious, or under the influence of drugs or alcohol, they cannot consent at all. A person may be able to say the words, but if her capacities are sufficiently impaired, this will not be valid consent.

Second, if consent is coerced, it is not valid. This raises thorny issues, as the notion of coercion is not transparent: What counts as coercion? What sort of threat can undermine consent? A case where someone is threatened with serious violence is clear enough, but what about cases where someone is threatened with emotional harm? Or, what should we say about cases where a woman feels that she should have sex because of all the social pressures on her, pressures to be pleasing to men, to not make a fuss, to put the man's sexual pleasure above her own?

Considering the complexities in understanding, valid consent leads to a different issue. If it is not clear what undermines consent, it may not be clear to the person asking for consent. What should the law say about *mens rea* in such cases, the 'guilty mind' of someone who thought he had consent but did not have consent at all, or did not have valid consent? If our myths about sex and consent have it that women welcome forcible seduction, for example, how is a man to know when a woman is consenting? On the one hand, it seems that there can be genuine confusion over whether someone has consented, and that if someone has made an innocent mistake they should not be held responsible. On the other hand, if the explanation for the confusion is the many misconceptions about what consent looks like, and when women are likely to consent, it seems that mistakes about consent are often deeply sexist, and possibly not innocent. If a man claims that he thought she was consenting because she allowed him to buy her dinner, we may understand *why* he made the mistake without thinking that it exonerates him.

It appears that, politically and practically, we need clear guidelines for what counts as consent. This thought has guided many US educational institutions in their response to Title IX requirements. Title IX of the Education Amendments Act (1972) is an anti-discrimination policy that aims to ensure that state-funded educational establishments do not exclude anyone on discriminatory grounds. In 2011, the Department of Education issued guidelines about how to interpret Title IX, including a requirement that universities pursue investigative and disciplinary proceedings to prevent sexual harassment and assault. These guidelines have since been overturned by the Trump administration, and Title IX's implications are currently (in 2020) being reviewed by the Department of Education. But it remains the case that many universities and colleges have developed their own consent policies, in which they lay out the conditions for what counts as consent, often demanding that consent be a clear and verbal 'yes'. This has the advantage of making consent clear and unequivocal, but there may be downsides, as we will see below.

Before I start on the main issues, I will briefly mention a debate in the literature on consent that I will not spend time on. There are two different ways to think of consent: as a state of mind (the attitudinal account), or as an action that is performed (the performative account). On the attitudinal account, to consent is to make some internal determination, 'yes, I will'. Others might not be able to tell that someone has consented. Imagine for example, that Juan asks if he can borrow a pen, and Aya thinks to herself, 'yes, that is fine, I will let him borrow my pen', but for some reason does not speak. According to the attitudinal view, she has consented. On the performative view, she has not consented until she has made some publicly accessible declaration, words, or deeds, that convey to Juan that she consents.

Although philosophers and legal theorists have argued about which view is correct, that disagreement is not central to the main issues about consent that I will focus on in this section. Even if we prefer the attitudinal account for some purposes, it is clear that in the legal context (including quasi legal situations, such as university tribunals), some sort of evidence of consent is required. In the end, the line between what counts as evidence of consent and what counts as consent may not be of much practical importance.

Legal history: Force

The justification for the force requirement was that a reasonable woman would resist 'to her utmost'. Resistance is what indicates sincere refusal. If she did not resist to her utmost – if for example, she succumbed under mere *threat* of violence – that counted as valid consent. As feminist legal theorists point out, this defines a 'reasonable woman' as someone who prefers possible death and certain serious physical harm to being raped. But that does not seem reasonable. As Susan Estrich argues in her influential critique of rape law, judges have often ruled that there was no rape on the grounds that there was no force in cases where it is very clear that the victim felt, very reasonably, totally overpowered by her assailant.[2] She may not have tried to fight him, but only because she knew that fighting would be hopeless and, furthermore, dangerous.

It is fairly obvious that force undermines consent, and this is why legal systems have used force as an indicator that there was no consent. In fact, as the legal application of the force requirement implies, it is not simply that force *undermines* consent. The point is that when there is force there has usually been no consent at all. Thus force is taken as evidence of non-consent. But, obviously, there can be cases where a woman appears to consent or, at least, acquiesces because there is a threat of force.

In both UK and US law, the force requirement is now understood to include threat of force. It is fairly clear that a credible threat of serious violence undermines consent (that is to say, that when a woman consents in the face of a serious threat, her consent is not valid). However, what counts as a threat is controversial. Courts have often required an actual explicit threat of physical violence. But, as Estrich argues, that is to take a very limited point of view. A woman can feel threatened by the perceived possibility or likelihood of violence, even when there is no explicit threat. Again, we need an account of what a reasonable woman would find threatening. Estrich argues that US courts have expected women to be extraordinarily tough in their assessment of what counts as a serious enough threat. Because the standard is so demanding, actual women, who are terrorized and cowed by the power that their rapist has over them, do not count as reasonable women, and do not secure convictions. As Estrich points out, we should take into account the reality of men's power and physical superiority in judging what a reasonable woman would take to be a threat of force.

Even if we can come up with a good account of what counts as a serious enough threat of force, there is another problem. Arguably, threat of physical force is not the only thing that undermines consent. Feminists have argued that we need an account of coercion that goes beyond threat of force. Intuitively, there are threats that are serious enough to count as undermining consent that do not threaten physical violence, but rather, psychological, emotional, or even financial harm.

Coercion

Here is a rough definition of coercion: an agent is coerced if they are made to feel they have to do something because of the way the projected consequences are stacked. The paradigmatic case is when someone threatens something bad, whether violence or some other consequence. In that case we have a clear coercer, who intends to get their victim to act in a certain way, and uses a threat to do so. But there is philosophical disagreement about which of those conditions are necessary for a case to count as coercion: about whether offers as well as threats could be coercive, about whether the coercer must intend to coerce, and about how high the stakes must be. These questions are relevant in cases of sexual coercion, where the situation is extremely complicated.

Sarah Conly agrees that we should see coercion as being broader than threat of physical harm. She cites an example of an actual legal case, where a foster father threatened his foster daughter with return to the detention centre if she did not have sex with him. He was not found guilty of rape, as there had been no threat of violence. But the threat of hardship here seems sufficient to undermine her consent. However, what should we say about a case where someone gives in to persuasion and has sex they do not really want to have? Conly argues that although there are lots of cases of illegitimate pressure without the threat of physical violence, we cannot rule that all cases where pressure has been applied are cases where the consent was not genuine. In the context of sexual relationships, certain kinds of pressure are legitimate.

Conly proposes that we should see coercion as illegitimate pressure: a threat that the threatener is not entitled to make. Conly offers cases where, although pressure may be quite severe, it is legitimate, such as a case where a person explains to their partner that if there is to be no sex in the relationship, he will leave. His partner is under pressure to have sex, but, Conly argues, that is legitimate pressure: it is within one's rights to expect to have sex within a romantic relationship. Contrast cases where the threat is extortion or blackmail: these are not legitimate threats; the threatener is not entitled to make them. The contentious question is, what about the in-between cases? The cases where pressure is complex, for example, the pressure a woman feels to have sex after a date the man has paid for, where she has drunk too much and flirted, and where the man evidently feels that she has promised him sex?

Conly thinks that ordinary forms of seduction and persuasion are morally permissible, even when they result in an agent consenting to something against her better judgment. As Conly puts it, someone may "coax, cajole, wheedle, importune, harangue, berate, and browbeat another into doing their bidding."[3] But that does not mean that they have raped someone, just as it would not mean that they have robbed someone if they coaxed, cajoled, and so on, until that person handed over their money. Conly's approach accepts that people can make bad decisions without any failure of autonomy. Conly's point is that women should be treated as adults, capable of making up their own minds and owning their mistakes.

Conly's view is positioned in opposition to the view taken by Catharine MacKinnon and others, that women face a form of coercion in the social conditions of patriarchy (I discuss this in more detail in the chapter on sexual violence). Scott Anderson criticizes Conly's argument for underplaying the social forces that back up the persuasions and seductions she thinks are morally permissible.[4] Anderson argues that our cultural norms of seduction are morally dubious, depending on the familiar sexist ideology about male and female sexualities. Furthermore, he argues, there are all sorts of pressures on women to conform to sexist norms, to fit in, to be accommodating, popular, and so on. And of course, the threat of force is often implicit, even when not explicit, just through the general physical strength differences between men and women.

One important upshot of discussions of what counts as coercion is that in a world structured by gender hierarchy, it is not easy to draw a sharp line between sex that is morally problematic in some way and rape. As Nicola Gavey argues, there is a grey area, an area where women themselves feel ambivalent, and although do not think they have been raped, are not comfortable with the sexual transaction.[5] As Ann Cahill puts it, there can be unjust sex, which is not rape, but is not morally innocent.[6] (See Chapter 6 for more on this.)

A different distinction arises when we think about the responsibility of the perpetrator. In one sort of case, an individual applies pressure on someone in order to have sex with them. They may cajole, plead, threaten, promise, and so on (it may or may not be classifiable as coercion). In these cases, the rape or unjust sex is perpetrated by a particular person with bad motivations. But there might be another sort of case, where consent is problematic without there being a deliberate manipulation. If our ideas about seduction and sexual norms are deformed by ideology, it is conceivable that the man may quite innocently make mistakes about his partner's enthusiasm. I come back to that below in the section on *mens rea*.

Deception

Deception is generally held to undermine consent. If someone lies about the nature of the act, that is a clear case of deception, and both legally and morally it is uncontroversial that consent is undermined. If a doctor tells a woman that he is performing a medical procedure and in fact is doing something purely for his own sexual gratification, her consent is not genuine. If someone impersonates someone else, for instance, a twin brother impersonates a woman's husband in order to have sex with the woman, then, again, both morally and legally it is clear that consent is undermined.

However, it is less obvious what we should think about cases where the deception concerns something that is not immediately related to the act. For example, a would-be seducer might lie about his sexual history, his job, his nationality or religion, his eating habits, and so on. There is a sense in which his partner has consented to sex and a sense in which she has not. The seducer, in deceiving her, has not entirely taken over her decision about whether to have sex, but he has certainly interfered with it.

Intuitively, some lies are more important than others. If someone lies about whether or not they have a sexually transmitted disease, or about who they are, the interference with the other's decision seems major enough to undermine consent. Whereas a lie about being a doctor, or about one's natural hair colour, does not seem important enough to render the consent invalid. However, it will be hard to say what makes the difference between the cases. Tom Dougherty argues that we should not try to arbitrate which of these lies is important or significant enough to undermine consent.[7] Rather, we should simply take what would matter from the other person's point of view as decisive. If an issue would be a 'deal-breaker', that is, if for example, the other person would not have had sex had they known that the seducer was not in fact a vegetarian, then we should take it that consent is undermined.

One problem with this view is that it allows trivial, esoteric, and even immoral deal-breakers to count as consent undermining. Imagine that someone deceives someone else about their natural hair colour, or takes a couple of years off their age. It is unlikely, but not impossible, that natural hair colour, or a precise age, is very important for someone. Yet it is not at all obvious that consent is undermined by something so trivial, even if it was important to the person concerned. Similarly, the case of immoral deal-breakers does not elicit clear intuitions. Imagine that someone omits to mention that they have gay parents to a partner. That would be a deal-breaker for a homophobic partner, but homophobic preferences seem too unreasonable to have the normative power to undermine consent.

Of course, lying itself might be a deal-breaker, but that is not Dougherty's point. His point is that the thing lied about might be a deal-breaker. Dougherty goes so far as to argue that the deception need not be deliberate: if the issue is a deal-breaker for one party, and they are not aware of it at the time of consent, their consent is undermined. This implies that we have a duty to find out about and to disclose potential deal-breakers before having sex with someone. If it turns out that there was a deal-breaker, the sex was non-consensual. And as Bromwich and Millum point out in their critique of Dougherty, on a view like this, it might even be the case that *subsequent regret* is a deal-breaker.[8] In other words, if it is the case that someone's consent to sex is undermined because they would not have consented had they known their partner was a natural brunette and not a natural blonde, so their consent might be undermined because they would not have consented had they known that they would regret the sex later.

The overall worry is that a view like Dougherty's asks too much from consent. On this sort of view, consent is only valid if the person would still have consented if they had known everything there is to know, if they were thinking clearly, and so on. The reality is that people consent to things in less than ideal situations all the time, and we sometimes consent to things against our better judgment. A parent might consent to a child going on a sleepover because the parent is exhausted. A teacher might consent to an extension because she doesn't feel like arguing. A landlord might consent to expensive renovations because at that moment she is more afraid of being sued than of overstretching herself. In these circumstances, we normally think that the consent is valid, even if the agent is not happy with their decision. Of course, saying that consent is not undermined is different to saying that consent cannot be retracted. The parent might say, 'I'm sorry, I have changed my mind'. That is different to saying, 'I was very tired when I made the decision so my consent was not valid'.

Consent and condescension

This takes us back to an issue that is in the background of Conly's discussion: how paternalistic should we be in defining the conditions that undermine consent? That is, to what extent should we focus on what we think is really good for the person as opposed to what they actually say? It is true that women are often pressured or coerced into sex. And coercion undermines consent. But not all the non-ideal conditions of a decision undermine consent. Surely women can make bad decisions, hasty ones, and lazy ones, and yet still be bound by those decisions? Women are competent adults.

Dougherty's view errs on the side of paternalism. For him, consent is very fragile; it is easy to disrupt and dominate someone. If that is how we think of consent, valid consent to sex will be much rarer than we think. And not just rarer than sexist judges think, it would be rarer than most feminists think. This leads to back to Conly's problem. There are no sharp lines dividing cases where consent genuinely does seem to be vitiated from cases where the seducer may be behaving unjustly, badly, or like a jerk, but the other person has consented. In other words, as Conly's paper illustrates, it is very difficult to define coercion. The same issues apply to accounts of the sort of deception that undermines sex.

Janet Halley argues that current laws and Title IX regulations about rape and sexual assault go too far in the direction of trying to protect women from unwanted sex.[9] Halley argues that threat of force is a clear vitiation of consent, but that other pressures that might make women consent to sex they do not really want, such as social compliance, and pressures that may make women regret sex they did consent to, such as moral concerns, do not vitiate consent. Halley argues that the law should not punish men for women's bad decisions, and it should not incentivize retroactive decision-making – it should not encourage women to think that they can always press charges later.

Another problem with erring too far on the side of paternalism is that it risks devaluing consent. If consent is often invalid, why even bother with consent? Some feminists have embraced this conclusion. Catharine MacKinnon, for example, argues that "Rape should be defined as sex by compulsion, of which physical force is one form. Lack of consent is redundant and should not be a separate element of the crime".[10] Her proposal, essentially, is that we should focus directly on compulsion, and not worry too much about when compulsion is compatible with apparent consent. MacKinnon, unlike Halley, thinks that social forces can be a form of compulsion.

Responsibility and *mens rea*

Criminal liability requires a '*mens rea*': a guilty mind. If rape is non-consensual penetration, the perpetrator must be aware that the victim does not consent, or at the very least must be reckless as to the possibility that she does not. But if it is difficult to tell whether someone is consenting, then someone might make a mistake. Heterosex in a patriarchal culture is confusing and complex. Men are encouraged to seduce, and forcible seduction is normalized. As Susan Estrich puts it:

> At its simplest, the dilemma lies in this: If nonconsent is essential to rape (and no amount of force or physical struggle is inherently inconsistent with lawful sex), and if no sometimes means yes, and if men are supposed to be aggressive in any event, how is a man to know when he has crossed the line? And how are we to avoid unjust convictions?[11]

Estrich's question is not entirely sincere – she is describing the way that she thinks the legal system works. In her view, the Anglo-American legal system is designed, above all, to protect innocent men from false accusations.

Current UK law has it that a person is guilty of an offence of rape if there is penetration, no consent to penetration, and the person does not reasonably believe that there is consent. In other words, an honest belief in consent is not sufficient to undermine culpability, the belief must be reasonable. This has not always been the situation. In the famous case of *DPP v Morgan* (1976), a man told his friends that they could go to his house and have sex with his wife, that she would struggle and refuse, but that her resistance was just part of her fun. The original court convicted on the grounds that although the defendants believed they had consent, their belief was unreasonable, and that was upheld in an appeal. A later review in the House of Lords argued that the law says that an *honest* belief in consent is a sufficient defence, but that the belief was so patently unreasonable in this case that it could not have been an honest belief. So, the House of Lords' view was that the law says that an honest belief in consent is enough for an acquittal, even if it is unreasonable.

The importance of an 'honest belief' is that someone who makes an innocent mistake is not guilty of bad motivations. Contrast recklessness, which is a clear *mens rea*. If someone is acting recklessly, they know that there is a risk of harm, and are choosing to take that risk. They are culpable in a clear way. But someone who does not know that there is a risk of harm, who sincerely believes that the woman is consenting, seems to be innocent, even though a harm has been done. The harm is 'not their fault'. Douglas Husak and George Thomas argue that we should indeed countenance the possibility of 'rape without rapists'.[12] They argue that our social conventions are such that non-verbal signals can communicate consent, and that part of our convention is that women are sometimes taken to mean 'yes' when they say 'no'. Thus it is possible for men to be non-culpably mistaken about consent. Husak and Thomas accept the feminist premise that sex and consent are confusing in a world where women are not believed, but they focus on the problem of the innocent man.

Antony Duff, by contrast, argues that mistakes about consent are never really innocent. Duff argues that someone might 'honestly believe' that the woman consents, but nonetheless be culpable. Duff says:

[the mistaken view that we should always judge the defendant on the facts as they believe them to be] assumes that an unreasonable belief can never manifest anything worse than stupidity or negligence; whereas a man who forces intercourse on a non-consenting woman in the unreasonable belief that she consents manifests not just stupidity or negligence, but a reckless indifference to her consent which justifies convicting him of rape.[13]

This motivates a change in the law from a standard of honest belief to a reasonable belief standard. In Duff's view, a false belief in consent is always unreasonable in a sense that implies culpability, and so the man should be convicted of rape.

Duff argues that, given what sex is, a highly emotional and intimate act, to not realize that the partner is not consenting *must* involve some sort of blameworthy indifference. He argues that consent is not a prerequisite to sex, but an essential part of it. Various other writers have made similar points. David Archard, objecting to Husak and Thomas's argument that there can be reasonable mistakes about consent, argues that it is not reasonable to rely on consent conventions when it comes to sex.[14] Sex is complex, and high stakes, so the onus is on the agents involved to make sure that there is explicit consent. Lois Pineau argues that sexual encounters should be communicative and respectful, and a man who is not approaching the question of consent in that mode is at the very least guilty of reckless indifference or wilful ignorance if he mistakenly believes he has consent.[15] Similarly, Marcia Baron argues that an unreasonable mistake about consent always involves a 'tainted mind': an agent who does not pay enough attention to the issue of consent is guilty of not caring enough about consent.[16]

There are two different issues here. One argument is that it is simply not possible to proceed with non-consensual sex without, at some level, knowing that something is wrong. If consent is not immediately clear, then to proceed would be reckless, and there would be culpability, or blameworthiness, in an obvious way. One objection to that is that sexist ideology may go so deep that men *can* make genuine and serious mistakes about consent. For example, they may expect consent to be ambiguous (as norms of feminine modesty require), or they may be so deep in sexist ideology that they think that consent is not terribly important. In that case, it is not clear whether there is culpability.

The other issue concerns the law. Some feminists, including Estrich, argue that we should radically alter the way that we understand *mens rea* in rape cases. The question is, what is the law trying to do? Estrich argues that the law is historically and currently focussed on protecting men, both in insisting on the force requirement (if there was force, the man is definitely culpable, but if the women did not resist, the law presumes the man is innocent) and in the way that *mens rea* standards are understood. Catharine MacKinnon argues likewise that the concern with *mens rea* elevates the importance of the man's guilt or innocence and relegates the harm done to the woman to a secondary issue.

Feminists argue that rape law needs to shift from being chiefly concerned with protecting innocent men to being concerned with protecting women from rape. Estrich argues that rather than judging *mens rea* by a standard that takes into account that men are inclined to take a 'no' as a 'yes', the law should work on the assumption that 'no' means 'no'. She agrees that it is possible that a man could be mistaken about that, but she argues the law should focus on the woman's non-consent here, not the man's understanding of the situation. As she puts it, "In holding a man to such a standard of reasonableness, the law signifies that it considers a woman's consent to sex to be significant enough to merit a man's reasoned attention."[17]

In the actual world, given sexist norms about what women might mean when they say 'no', it can be difficult to decide whether someone consents. This leads to a question about how ideal sexual communication would take place, and a related question about how that should be enforced in law and other policy, such as university compliance with Title IX regulations.

Redefining consent: Affirmative consent

One new model of consent that has been enshrined in some law and university Title IX regulation is known as 'affirmative consent'. This model thus insists that permissible sex requires a clear and unambiguous 'yes'. Stephen Schulhofer, for example, argues that the law should protect sexual autonomy, and so should ask for affirmative consent. He argues that sexual contact should always be preceded by clear and unambiguous verbal or non-verbal signalling of permission.[18] Nicholas Little argues that only an affirmative consent standard can achieve the aim of moving away from the presumption of consent until there is refusal. On an affirmative consent standard, the onus is on the man to prove that there was consent, rather than on the woman to prove that there was not.[19]

One of the first such policies was the Antioch College Consent policy. The code, introduced in 1990 and still applied, lays out what students should look for in consent.[20] Alan Soble has several objections to such a policy, but his main objection is that such a policy would undermine sexual pleasure by destroying spontaneity.[21] The policy states that consent must be unambiguous and continuous, obtained afresh at each new stage in a sexual encounter. However, as Eva Feder Kittay points out, the Antioch policy does *not* require verbal agreement. It requires verbal agreement when the participants do not know each other well.[22] Most affirmative consent proposals do not require verbal expression of consent in all circumstances: consent can be expressed in other ways. As Schulhofer puts it, a requirement of verbal consent would "impose a degree of formality and artificiality on human interactions in which spontaneity is especially important."[23]

Michelle Anderson objects to the affirmative consent standard, a version of the 'Yes Model' as she terms it, precisely on the grounds that affirmative consent can be non-verbal. Because it allows consent to be non-verbal, it relies on the man's interpretation of events:

> At its core, the Yes Model relies on a man's ability to infer actual willingness from a woman's body language. Yet study after study indicate that men consistently misinterpret women's nonverbal behavior. They impute erotic innuendo and sexual intent where there is none. Any theory that relies on a man's ability to intuit a woman's actual willingness allows him to construct consent out of stereotype and hopeful imagination.[24]

In other words, Anderson thinks that the affirmative consent model is vulnerable to the same worry that some feminists have about *mens rea* standards. In a patriarchal society, men see consent where there is none. Or, at the very least, men fail to see that there is duress. Furthermore, Anderson argues, consent to heavy petting is often taken to be indicative of consent to sex, but in some circumstances, and this is particularly important in the context of the risks of sexually transmitted disease or pregnancy, heavy petting is a substitute for penetration, not consent to it. Thus Anderson thinks that the idea of non-verbal affirmative consent is not useful. It leaves too much space for misunderstanding.

Anderson recognizes that a requirement for verbal communication might be seen as a killjoy. She addresses that by pointing out briskly that AIDS killed the romance of uncommunicative sex a long time ago. Her point might be put in a more nuanced way. We have been inculcated with an idea of romance as spontaneous and sometimes shockingly unexpected. So, it is not surprising that communicative sex seems unromantic. But the old tropes of romance are deeply problematic, and so we will need to adjust, as we did to AIDS.

Another objection to affirmative consent standards comes from Jacob Gersen and Jeannie Suk.[25] They are objecting to the various policies put in place by US universities in order to comply with Title IX. Gersen and Suk argue that there are serious risks in the creep of what they call 'the sex bureaucracy'. Gersen and Suk are concerned that non-criminal proceedings in universities are applying problematic definitions of consent and sexual assault, and that they are interfering in people's sex lives way beyond the issue of consent. Their worry might be put in terms of the difference between rape and unjust sex. As they see it, universities, in their keenness to comply with Title IX, are inflating the notion of consent so that 'consent' is not enough: what is needed is fully enthusiastic consent. They are legislating sex itself, not just rape and sexual assault.

As Gersen and Suk put it,

> As nonconsent became the distinguishing feature of illegal sex, schools, parents, advocacy organizations, and the government gave commonsense advice: if there is any ambiguity about consent, stop. Don't take the absence of a no to mean consent. Out of an abundance of caution, avoid ambiguity, get a yes, and avoid the cliff of nonconsent and sexual assault. In short order, however, the extra-cautious strategy of steering clear of the cliff became the new legal definition of consent.[26]

Again, we are back to the problem about what counts as vitiating consent. On the one hand, we do not want to say that mere passive acquiescence or any 'yes' at all counts as consent. On the other hand, it is possible to consent to sex that is not desired for its own sake. Adults consent to things they are less than fully enthusiastic about all the time. Gersen and Suk are pointing out that affirmative consent standards can be taken too far, and can veer into criminalizing unenthusiastic sex, which is not the same as non-consensual sex.

Redefining consent: Negotiating consent

There is something odd about the traditional framing of consent, as many feminists have argued. On the traditional framing, men ask for sex, and women respond with consent or refusal. This view entrenches a gender norm according to which men ask permission to use women's bodies. Women are not seen as desiring sex or as initiating it, and in being cast in the passive role, the responder, their agency is minimized. Ideally, we want a more egalitarian account of what goes on in a permissible sexual encounter.

Michelle Anderson proposes a new way of thinking about what makes sex permissible, which moves away from the notion of consent, and requires instead that there has been an open-ended negotiation. Anderson argues that feminist interventions in consent law have not solved the basic problem, that women are not seen as fully agential. She distinguishes between two feminist models of consent, the 'No Model' and the 'Yes Model'.[27] Both are an improvement on the traditional view, that the only sort of rape is by force, but, Anderson argues, both are flawed. The No Model, which Estrich proposes, insists that when a woman says 'no', she has refused, and that it is never permissible to proceed. The point of the No Model is to overturn the assumption that women sometimes mean 'yes' when they say 'no', and to move away from the excessive concern with the possibility that the man has made an innocent mistake. Although this is a step forward, it doesn't deal with cases, which Anderson argues are not uncommon, where the woman is too traumatized to manage to say no. Silence does not mean yes. Anderson also objects to the Yes Model, as I explain earlier in the chapter. She thinks that a non-verbal 'yes' is too easily misinterpreted.

Anderson proposes legal reform that moves away from consent, and instead requires negotiation and genuine communication. Anderson argues that the law should define 'negotiation' as an open discussion in which partners can come to a free and autonomous agreement. In this, she is echoing Lois Pineau's argument. Pineau proposes that we should see consent on a communicative model, more like a real conversation than a contract. On the standard legal account, according to Pineau, consent is seen on a contractual model, and consent is assumed unless there is a vigorous act of refusal. But on the communicative model, as Pineau sees it, it would not be reasonable for a man to believe the woman is consenting if the encounter has not been properly communicative. As Pineau puts it, "On the old model of aggressive seduction we sought evidence of resistance. But on the new model of communicative sexuality what we want is evidence of an ongoing positive and encouraging response on the part of the plaintiff."[28]

The negotiation model, as Anderson understands it, requires clear *verbal* signals. As I said above, Anderson is fairly robust in her insistence that, at least in a first encounter, verbal communication is crucial. But she recognizes exceptions: "Most negotiations regarding specific activities that are to occur in the future happen verbally, of course. Language is ordinarily required to clarify one's desires over time; however, an established custom between two people of engaging in mutually desired behavior in a certain way may itself constitute a negotiation."[29]

In a more recent account of negotiation around sex, Quill Kukla recognizes that communication around sexual activity is complex, and argues that we need a richer set of accepted linguistic tools. As Kukla points out, sex sometimes starts with a request, and subsequent consent, but there are other useful notions, such as invitations, gift offers, and promises.[30] Kukla argues that the focus on consent is unhelpful given that good sex requires a continuous and complex agreement. Kukla urges that education about 'consent' is broadened to include a wider vocabulary of sexual interaction, particularly the use of safe words, which allow the participant to signal an end to the sexual framework, in which communication is often indirect and ambiguous.

Redefining consent: Consensus

John Gardner takes very seriously the worry that traditional models of consent are asymmetric, that one person has something done to them, and this person is usually the woman. The traditional model allows a crude reading of what consent is, just a formal necessity, that once obtained, can be forgotten. As Gardner puts it, this reinforces the sexist ideology of predatory men:

> it legitimises their antediluvian view of sex as something which men, when they get lucky, get to do to women, and access to which women are (unfortunately) allowed to ration – but which women are rationing using a system that can (fortunately) be 'gamed', so that canny men with enough 'charm' can in effect get access on demand. And by legitimating that view of sex, the ideology quite possibly adds to the bitterness of these already embittered 'charmers' and compounds their misogyny. Why are women still denying them their rightful access when they, so to speak, did everything they were meant to? Why don't women surrender to their charms?[31]

Gardner accepts that it is possible to consent to sex that one is not very enthusiastic about, but those are not the ideal cases. Gardner's enquiry is therefore focussed on what goes on in the ideal cases of sex – not morally ideal, but humanly, or sexually ideal – where the sex is the best sort of sex. Gardner's radical conclusion is that in some cases, consent is not a necessary condition for morally permissible sex.

Gardner replaces the notion of consent with something he suggests we could call 'consensus'. This proposal shares something in common with both the affirmative consent model and the negotiation model. Gardner argues that we should see sex as a sort of teamwork. Teamwork requires ongoing agreement between the parties. This kind on ongoing agreement should be distinguished from a performative agreement to *begin* the teamwork. Teamwork can begin without that, as when two people, or a group of people, spontaneously start working together. But teamwork requires that the team members are on board throughout the process, and this is not consent, but rather, consensus. Affirmative consent supporters go wrong in insisting that *consent* must be ongoing and continuous. Gardner's point is that the thing that must be ongoing and continuous in good sex is consensus.

Summary

One important philosophical issue concerning consent is, what undermines consent? It is clear that threat of force undermines consent. It is harder to give an account of what further conditions undermine consent. The law recognizes coercion and deception, but both of these are very broad terms, encompassing a wide variety of different things. Coercion certainly includes threat of serious force, but it is not clear whether it includes 'ordinary seduction' under conditions of patriarchy. Some philosophers, such as Sarah Conly, argue that ordinary seduction is not coercive, even if it persuades someone into sex they regret. Others, such as Scott Anderson, argue that men have huge social and physical pressures on their side, and that we need to understand coercion as being structural as well as individual.

Familiar sexist myths about men and women and sex, the narratives of patriarchal ideology, mean that it might not always be easy for men to tell when a woman has consented to sex. Criminal conviction requires a *mens rea*, that is to say, that the defendant has a 'guilty mind'. In the case of rape, that means that the defendant must have known that there was no consent in order for a conviction to be made. But if men can easily make mistakes about consent, it might seem that there is rape without rapists. Feminists have resisted this conclusion, arguing that mistakes about consent generally are culpable, and that in any case, the law must prioritize the protection of women, rather than men.

Some feminists want to move away from non-consent as the standard for rape, or to give a new account of what consent must be. The traditional account of consent seems to enshrine a norm where men ask for permission and women give it or not. Ideally, we should see sexual consent as something more egalitarian. On a more egalitarian model, the correct standard for morally (and legally) permissible sex might not be whether the women refused, or even whether she affirmatively consented, but whether or not the sex was engaged in in a truly communicative and mutually agreed on way.

Notes

 1 See the Women's Law Project Report, 'Rape and Sexual Assault in the Legal System'.
 2 Estrich, 'Rape'.
 3 Conly, 'Seduction, Rape, and Coercion', p.115.
 4 Anderson, 'Sex Under Pressure: Jerks, Boorish Behavior, and Gender Hierarchy'.
 5 Gavey, *Just Sex? The Cultural Scaffolding of Rape*.
 6 Cahill, 'Unjust Sex vs. Rape'.
 7 Dougherty, 'Sex, Lies, and Consent'.
 8 Bromwich and Millum, 'Lies, Control, and Consent: A Response to Dougherty and Manson'.
 9 Halley, 'The Move to Affirmative Consent'.
10 MacKinnon, *Toward a Feminist Theory of the State*, p.245.
11 Estrich, 'Rape', p.1095.
12 Husak and Thomas, 'Date Rape, Social Convention, and Reasonable Mistakes'.
13 Duff, *Intention, Agency and Criminal Liability: Philosophy of Action and the Criminal Law*, p.171.
14 Archard, '"A Nod's as Good as a Wink": Consent, Convention, and Reasonable Belief'.
15 Pineau, 'Date Rape: A Feminist Analysis', p.239.
16 Baron, 'I Thought She Consented'.
17 Estrich, 'Rape', p.1104.
18 Schulhofer, *Unwanted Sex: The Culture of Intimidation and the Failure of Law*.
19 Little, 'From No Means No to Only Yes Means Yes: The Rational Results of an Affirmative Consent Standard in Rape Law'.
20 https://antiochcollege.edu/campus-life/sexual-offense-prevention-policy-title-ix/.
21 Soble, 'Antioch's "Sexual Offense Policy": A Philosophical Exploration'.
22 Kittay, 'AH! My Foolish Heart: A Reply to Alan Soble's "Antioch's 'Sexual Offense Policy'"': A Philosophical Exploration'.
23 Schulhofer, *Unwanted Sex*, p.272.
24 Anderson, 'Negotiating Sex', p.1406.
25 Gersen and Suk, 'The Sex Bureaucracy'.
26 Op. cit., p.931.
27 Anderson, 'Negotiating Sex'.
28 Pineau, 'Date Rape: A Feminist Analysis', p.240.
29 Anderson, 'Negotiating Sex', p.1425.
30 Kukla, 'That's What She Said: The Language of Sexual Negotiation'.
31 Gardner, 'The Opposite of Rape', p.70.

Further reading

Alcoff, Linda Martín (2018) *Rape and Resistance*. Polity Press. (Survivor-focussed account of the harms of rape and how to speak about it).

Estrich, S. (1987). *Real Rape*. Harvard University Press. (Expanded version of the arguments discussed in this chapter).

McGregor, Joan (2005) *Is It Rape? On Acquaintance Rape and Taking Women's Consent Seriously*. Ashgate. (Presents a feminist approach to the legal theory of rape).

Schaber, Peter and Müller, Andreas (eds.) (2018) *The Routledge Handbook of the Ethics of Consent*. Routledge. (Collection of articles on a wide range of issues about consent).

Wertheimer, A. (2003) *Consent to Sexual Relations*. Cambridge University Press. (Thorough philosophical analysis of consent).

12 Knowledge and ignorance

"It is a common sentence that Knowledge is power; but who hath duly Considered or set forth the power of Ignorance?"

George Eliot, *Daniel Deronda*

Chapter overview: This chapter examines feminist arguments about the nature of knowledge. I discuss the need for objectivity and rationality, and Longino's argument that science is not value free, as well as the parallel argument for naturalized epistemology. I go on to discuss standpoint theory, motivated ignorance, epistemic injustice, and other forms of epistemic oppression.

Introduction

Epistemology is concerned with knowledge and ignorance: with what counts as knowledge, how knowledge can be acquired, and what counts as justification. If epistemology is just a matter of examining objective norms, then there is no room for feminist concerns. Traditionally, that is how epistemology has been conceived: as a value-free enterprise, guided by objective norms of enquiry. The classic postulate is that knowledge is justified true belief. Epistemologists then think about possible counterexamples, almost always based on the possibility that an individual is misled in some way. Cultures, groups, and social context are not taken to be relevant.

Feminist accounts of epistemology and philosophy of science are not accounts of a feminine way of knowing. It is worth stressing again what I said in the introductory chapter: that feminist epistemology, like feminist philosophy in general, is not a methodology. It is simply a subject matter. The subject matter is the possible tendency of intellectual enquiry to marginalize women. The methodology here is usually that of social epistemology, which need not be feminist at all (and is not in its early incarnations). Social epistemology is the project of looking at the social aspects of knowledge production, the way that social structures and social groups affect how knowledge is acquired, and what counts as knowledge.

One early contribution to feminist epistemology is Lorraine Code's 1981 self-described 'exploratory' paper, 'Is the Sex of the Knower Epistemologically Significant?' In that paper she raises doubts about the then ubiquitous and still common idea that women have different cognitive capacities to men. She argues that differences in knowledge are socially caused, that apparent different capacities are socially conditioned. Nonetheless, she argues, those differences become real. If a woman's environment constrains her, her capacities will be stunted. Furthermore, if men are in charge of 'conceptual structuring' (what Miranda Fricker later calls 'hermeneutical resources'[1]), there may be ways that women are excluded. Women's experience of the world is very different to men's, and so, Code suggests, women may well acquire different knowledge. These ideas have all been taken up in recent literature and I examine them further below.

Feminists urge us to examine the social context of scientific and intellectual enquiry, looking at the social situation of the knower, and the way that that affects what and how they know. Our so-called knowledge may in fact be deeply affected by biases in the modes of enquiry. Furthermore, knowledge and ignorance play important roles in power relations, and yet philosophical enquiry into what knowledge and ignorance are has rarely focussed on that. A feminist epistemology, or feminist philosophy of science, aims to understand these concepts and these phenomena in the context of a patriarchal power system.

Objectivity

Lorraine Code worries about the methodological tendency of traditional epistemology to see the knower in an entirely atomistic way, and in some of her remarks, she (along with some other feminist writers) suggests that feminist epistemology should problematize rationality and objectivity as masculine ideals. It would be remiss of me not to mention this strand of feminist epistemology. However, I will not spend time exploring it further. My own view, as I said in the introductory chapter, is that we need those ideals in order to argue *against* sexism. As Louise Antony neatly puts it,

> Critics [of objectivity] charge either that the concept of "objectivity" serves to articulate a masculine or patriarchal viewpoint (and possibly a pathological one), or that it has the ideological function of protecting the rights of those in power, especially men. But how is it possible to criticize the partiality of the concept of objectivity without presupposing the very value under attack? Put baldly: If we don't think it's good to be impartial, then how can we object to men's being partial?[2]

Sally Haslanger offers one account of how this mistake comes about. Haslanger's argument comes into her account of objectification, which I discuss in Chapter 10. Part of Haslanger's point is that there is an illusion of objectivity in objectification, but that we should not think that objectivity is *bound up* with objectification. This is a mistake that Haslanger sees in MacKinnon's work, but it appears elsewhere too. The basic error is to think that because the idea of objectivity is sometimes weaponized, feminists should eschew it altogether.

Haslanger argues that objectifying views of women have a pretence of objectivity. The (man) objectifier has more social power than the person he objectifies, and he uses his power to impose qualities on the objectified. Because he is powerful, he creates reality: in the end, there is an important sense in which the woman really does have those qualities. Women have a social role, and that social role is enforced. Patriarchal power can do more than just say that women are sex objects: it can make them into sex objects. So now the objectifier can say, 'look! From an objective standpoint she has these qualities, so, objectively, she is really like that.' In other words, the patriarchy makes claims about what is objectively true – that women really are the way the ideology says they are – and in doing that, they are using the power of the idea of objectivity.

Haslanger wants us to be careful not to conflate the stance of objectivity with this misuse of it. We should debunk this false claim of naturalness. The reasoning here is not properly objective, because it ignores the fact that the qualities in question were produced by the circumstances, and are not natural. As Haslanger says, "observed regularities do not support the claim that women are, by nature, submissive. Straightforward empirical research would appear to show that many of the features the objectifier attributes to women 'by nature' are a product of contingent social forces."[3] The objectifier blocks this objection with what is, in effect, bluster. They insist that they had nothing to do with it, that they are taking a properly objective view of the evidence.

So, there is no need to think of objectivity as essentially masculine, or a tool of patriarchy. In fact, we need to use the concept of objectivity in the right way, and use it to undermine the bad arguments behind patriarchal ideology.

Neutrality

One might think that feminist thinkers who are wedded to objectivity and rationality should also be wedded to the idea that science and other knowledge-seeking enterprises should proceed in a value-free way. In the traditional view, good science is independent of social forces and works in a realm of pure reason and experiment. If that is right, we just need to rid enquiry of problematic bias and aim for neutrality. However, feminist philosophers have argued that science, and knowledge more generally, can never be value-free, and that it is important from a feminist point of view to recognize that.

Helen Longino makes a distinction between constitutive values and contextual values: the former are the norms that govern scientific enquiry, such as, what counts as a good explanation, or a simple explanation.[4] No-one denies that these values are necessarily part of scientific enquiry. Philosophers of science spend a good deal of time trying to figure out the best account of these values. The values that are thought to be eliminable are 'contextual values': the ethical and political values in the background of enquiry, for example, views about animal rights, gender equality, and so on. Longino argues that these values are not eliminable, but that this does not make for bad science.

The crux of Longino's argument is that scientific enquiry depends on a dynamic interplay of observation and experiment, and, crucially, background assumptions. Without background assumptions, there is not enough to get us from evidence to hypothesis. So, for example, red spots on a child's stomach constitute evidence of measles given the background belief that measles causes red spots. This raises the question, how do we settle on which background beliefs are acceptable? As Longino points out, it is tempting to say that we should go with the background beliefs that are best supported by the evidence. But of course, we would need more background beliefs to get from the evidence to the background beliefs, and regress threatens.

Longino argues that science cannot exclude unsupported background beliefs: to insist that all background beliefs are supported is to insist that a theory is self-supported, and that allows no progress. We need to take some background beliefs for granted. Thus it is impossible to exclude contextual values. We can exclude the obvious cases (the sort of bad science about gender critiqued by Cordelia Fine, which I discussed in the introduction to the book), but there may be much more subtle bias in our background beliefs.

This gives rise to a dilemma. If scientific knowledge is produced in a biased way, and value-laden enquiry is unavoidable, what can be done? It seems impossible to get unbiased knowledge. Longino herself argues that scientific enquiry is steeped in a pervasive assumption of sexual essentialism. As she says, "The feminist scientist, or the radical scientist, cannot simply try to be sensitive to the noxious values embedded in some research programs or try to avoid ideology by sticking to the data. 'Letting the data suggest' is a recipe for replicating the mainstream values and ideology that feminist and radical scientists reject."[5] Unsurprisingly, there are echoes of the challenges of ideology critique here (see Chapter 9). How do we escape from the feedback loops that confirm and further entrench the biased background assumptions?

Longino's solution is to appeal to the social and interactive nature of scientific knowledge. She argues that we need to see science as social enquiry, something that necessarily involves input from numerous people. Enquirers need to take science as a collective endeavour, in which criticism is standard and background assumptions are questioned. Longino argues that a multiplicity of individuals produces a balance of outlooks that form a basis for linking evidence and hypotheses. This is what gives us 'objectivity': objectivity is the property of the group perspective, not the individual's perspective.

As critics of Longino have pointed out, the idea that interaction will produce better outcomes is very optimistic. Problematic ideologies are often further entrenched by being shared in a community, and come to have the air of objectivity, but are no less problematic for that. Of course, Longino is not imagining mere shared agreement, she is imagining vigorous discussion and disagreement, and open-minded participants engaging in 'transformative criticism' as she calls it. Objectivity, according to this view, is a thoughtful inter-subjectivity.

The conclusion that bias is an ineliminable feature of enquiry is also implied by W.V. Quine's 'naturalized epistemology', as feminist epistemologists have pointed out. Quine argues against a foundationalist picture, according to which knowledge builds up from certainty at the base: no such certainty is available. Epistemology should instead be focussed on the empirical study of knowers. In order to make progress, there will be things that we must take for granted, and there will sometimes be biases. Louise Antony argues for the feminist potential of a naturalized epistemology, and suggests a solution to what she calls 'the paradox of bias'.[6] The problem, as she puts it, is how do we know the difference between good biases and bad biases?

Antony argues that we should investigate that actual acquisition of knowledge, and we should see if it leads to truth.

We know that human knowledge requires biases; we also know that we have no possibility of getting a priori guarantees that our biases incline us in the right direction. What all this means is that "biasedness" of biases drops out as a parameter of epistemic evaluation. There's only one thing to do, and that's the course always counselled by a naturalized approach: We must treat the goodness or badness of biases as an empirical question.[7]

Antony relies on a robust objectivism about truth, arguing that biases are good if they lead us to truth, and bad if they lead us to falsehood. We can accept that our knowledge of the truth is limited without having to give up on the idea that some things are true and others are not. As she says, the whole point of feminist analysis of these things is to show that sexist biases are wrong because they lead to false views about women. Thus we can critique the racist and sexist assumptions behind some research projects: they are based on falsehoods, and they lead to more falsehoods.

Standpoint theory

The aim of standpoint theory is not to give an account of knowledge (it is consistent with various accounts), but rather to critique the way that knowledge plays a part in oppression. Standpoint theory starts from the observation that different standpoints, or perspectives, produce different knowledge, and emphasizes the value of the knowledge of the oppressed. Being in a certain social position gives one access to knowledge that the powerful do not have. In most respects being oppressed is a disadvantage, including epistemically: the oppressed are deprived of knowledge and deprived of the opportunity to share their knowledge. However, standpoint theorists point out that there may also be an epistemic advantage. What a member of an oppressed group experiences can give them knowledge that is not available to members of the dominant group. Furthermore, understanding the situatedness of knowledge gives tools for critique and transformation.

It is important to stress that standpoint theory is not committed to epistemic relativism. The claim is not that knowledge differs depending on social position, such that the knowledge that women have is just different to the knowledge that men have. Rather, the situated knowledge claim is that social position can open up experience, and thus evidence. Women might just know more than men about what it is to be oppressed, because they have more evidence. Black women might know more than white women, because they have experienced something that is invisible to white women. As bell hooks puts it,

> Black women . . . often have a lived experience that directly challenges the prevailing classist, sexist, racist social structure and its concomitant ideology. This lived experience may shape our consciousness in such a way that our world-view differs from those who have a degree of privilege (however relative within the existing system). It is essential for the continued feminist struggle that black women recognize the special vantage point our marginality gives us.[8]

Moreover, as Alison Wylie argues, it is important that two common misconceptions are cleared up.[9] First, the claim that women (or some other group) have an epistemic standpoint is not an essentialist claim. It is not the claim that there is a feminine way of thinking. Second, standpoint theory is not committed to the view that those in an oppressed group automatically know more. Of course they sometimes know less.

Standpoint theory has its roots in Marx's account of the relationship between the workers and the capitalists. Both are in the grip of false consciousness, a set of beliefs and values that serves to maintain the status quo. For the capitalists, there is a possibly wilful ignorance about the injustices inherent in the situation. The idea that the standpoint of the worker might be an epistemically advantageous one comes from Marxist theorist Lukács. He points out that for the workers, there is a tension, for although they are inculcated with the ideology that tells them that their situation is natural and just, they also experience, and understand at some level, their exploitation.

Most feminist standpoint theory aims to go beyond merely analyzing the effects of social location. Standpoint theory is a political theory as well as an epistemological one: the aim is to use understanding of structural situatedness as a tool to critique the injustices in hierarchical systems. Nancy Hartsock, one of the first feminist standpoint theorists, argues that women's experiences of work and care are very different to men's given the traditional gendered division of labour. She argues that men experience the world as a more competitive and combative place than women do. Women's labour tends to be more grounded and more immediately productive.[10] Hartsock's point is not that one standpoint is more true or more accurate. Her point is that we need to recognize that there are those different perspectives if we are to make progress on understanding patriarchal power structures. She is not concerned to identify a 'feminine' standpoint, but a feminist one, one that recognizes different experiences in order to critique them.

Sandra Harding's argument has the same aim: the point of standpoint theory is as a tool to fight oppression; it is not primarily an account of knowledge. She says,

> The adequacy of standpoint projects is to be judged by the success of the practices they legitimate rather than the truth or verisimilitude of representations of nature and social relations. (Recollect that the success of practices has always been the ultimate test of the adequacy of scientific claims.) Do they in fact produce more accurate, comprehensive, rationally justifiable, and politically useful knowledge for the exploited group to which they are accountable?[11]

Patricia Hill Collins stresses the need to think of the 'interlocking' (intersectional) nature of oppressions.[12] She discusses the experience of Black women working as domestic labourers in white families. They have a special vantage point, the 'outsider within'. They are privy to the secrets of the white families they work for, because they are treated as if they are not really there, not listening, not understanding. Collins argues that Black women in the academy (she is talking about academic sociology in particular) have a similarly epistemically privileged position, in that they have experienced a racist world first hand, and so can see the flaws and privileges that go unnoticed in the paradigms and methods of a discipline. The idea of the 'outsider within' has been influential in work on standpoint theory, capturing, as it does, a complex but familiar phenomenon.

In sum then, standpoint theory is based on a situated knowledge thesis, which is itself uncontroversial: different social positions produce different evidential situations. But the notion of a 'standpoint' goes further than that. A standpoint is a politically aware vantage point, from where the oppressive structures that create situated knowledge can be understood and critiqued. One way to put this is to say that it is a technical way of understanding the point of 'consciousness raising': reaching feminist consciousness is achieving a standpoint.

Motivated ignorance

Many philosophers, including Marilyn Frye writing about gender, and Charles Mills writing about race, argue that ignorance of the dominant group about the oppressed group is cultivated, and socially supported. Sometimes ignorance is not just accidental, a case of missing evidence. Sometimes it is more like *ignoring*, as Frye puts it.[13] Charles Mills discusses what he calls 'white ignorance' as a 'group based cognitive handicap'.[14] He argues that social structures and ideas create a sort of filter. White people perceive things through a lens that distorts reality, from the erasure of Black history, to the inability of the white person to see through the racist concepts that structure their perceptions.

Mills finds a wide awareness and many non-technical discussions of the phenomenon in fiction and non-fiction outside of academic philosophy (including in works by James Baldwin and W.E.B. Du Bois and Ralph Ellison's novel, *The Invisible Man*). Mills aims to present a formalized account of white ignorance as part of a structure of white supremacism.[15] As Mills puts it, this is a special sort of ignorance, an ignorance that is "militant, aggressive, not to be intimidated, an ignorance that is active, dynamic, that refuses to go quietly – not at all confined to the illiterate and uneducated but propagated at the highest levels of the land, indeed presenting itself unblushingly as knowledge".[16]

Mills examines the various mechanisms by which ignorance comes about and is maintained. Mills looks at a variety of ways that our beliefs are formed, including perception, conception, memory, testimony, and motivational group interest. He points out that all are subject to distortions. Take perception for example. What we perceive is already infused with the concepts we have picked up from our social milieu. To use an example that is not Mills': according to an apocryphal story, the British Labour politician Peter Mandelson asked for a serving of what he thought was guacamole in a fish and chip shop. It was mushy peas. The story, although not true, was widely circulated, because it seemed so very plausible that Mandelson would not have recognized mushy peas, that his social milieu was so far from the milieu of fish and chip shops.

We perceive the world with concepts ready-made, and our concepts embody hierarchies (they are 'ideological', in Marxist terms). Mills uses the example of the concept of a 'savage'. The concept of a savage is purely ideological; it is there to justify power relations, not to reach truth. Mills argues that along with the obviously racist terms and concepts, there are more subtle cases. Take 'colour-blind' ideology, the idea that it would be good to ignore race altogether. In fact, this maintains racist hierarchy, in making whiteness neutral and ignoring past discrimination.

Mills goes on to talk about how collective memory is carefully managed so as to maintain power structures. What we remember and what we forget are part of a narrative about who we are. We tend to forget the non-white victims. White history books sanitize past racial injustices. So when we think about current inequality, we forget that it can be traced to past injustice. Narratives about the current high levels of poverty among Native Americans and African Americans ignore the past: "the denial of the extent of Native American and black victimization underwrites the whitewashed narrative of discovery, settlement, and building of a shining city on the hill."[17]

Next, Mills discusses the role of testimony, which I come back to below in examining the phenomenon that Miranda Fricker terms 'epistemic injustice'. Mills and Fricker both argue that social status affects how reliable one is taken to be as a knower, and as a witness. Mills uses real life history to illustrate the point: for example, in the time of slavery, Black people were not seen as able to testify against white people in court, and so if the only witnesses to a white person's crime were Black, there could be no trial. Mills points out that there is long history of the voices of people of colour being ignored, suppressed, and disbelieved so that the ignorance of the privileged can be maintained. Mills argues that we should not think of motivated irrationality as being something that only happens on an individual basis, we should also recognize it on a group level.

These conceptual tools, as Mill recognizes, can be applied to other areas, including male ignorance, the ignorance of men about the reality of women's lives. Mills argues that it is crucial that we understand and work to undermine this sort of ignorance, but it will not be easy. "The white delusion of racial superiority insulates itself against refutation. Correspondingly, on the positive epistemic side, the route to black knowledge is the self-conscious recognition of white ignorance (including its black-faced manifestation in black consciousness itself)."[18] I discuss related issues in the chapter on false consciousness and ideology.

Epistemic injustice

Fricker covers some of the same ground in her 2007 book, *Epistemic Injustice*, but focusses on the particular case of testimonial injustice. Fricker uses the fictional example of Herbert Greenleaf, from Patricia Highsmith's novel *The Talented Mr Ripley* to illustrate her central point. The character of Herbert Greenleaf consistently discounts the views of Marge, the young woman who would have become his daughter-in-law had his son not been murdered. Marge is actually correct about the identity of the murderer, but Greenleaf repeatedly ignores her insights. He is unable to see Marge as a credible witness: he cannot believe that she has grasped something that he, a man, has not grasped.

Fricker argues that there is a particularly *epistemic* injustice here: "The idea is to explore testimonial injustice as a distinctively epistemic injustice, as a kind of injustice in which someone is *wronged specifically in her capacity as a knower*."[19] Fricker starts with an account of power. First, she discusses 'social power': the capacity we have to influence how things go in the social world. Social power depends on our social identity, and that is related to how seriously we are taken as knowers and testifiers. Fricker argues that the system of different levels of social power is backed up by explicit and implicit stereotypes. Some people seem fit for power and influence, others don't – and not just because of their individual characteristics, but because of the stereotypes we apply to them: their group membership. Our 'identity prejudices' get in the way of our believing some people – those that we see through the filter of our stereotypes.

Fricker makes a distinction between two sorts of injustice. The first is testimonial injustice, which involves a systematic identity prejudice resulting in a 'credibility deficit': the person is not believed, although the evidence points to their credibility. Fricker also points out that some people are believed more than they should be: they are given a credibility excess. Fricker thinks that a credibility excess is not usually harmful, whereas a credibility deficit involves serious harms. First, Fricker argues that there is a particularly epistemic harm. She argues that testimonial injustice can undermine the person's very personhood. It undermines their status as a knower by denying their ability to share knowledge. Being able to have and share knowledge is part of being a reasoner, which is essential to being a rational being. So epistemic injustice denies personhood.[20]

Fricker expands on primary harm of epistemic injustice in Chapter 6 of her book, where she puts it in terms of 'epistemic objectification'. (I examine the general idea of objectification in Chapter 10). Fricker draws on Edward Craig's account of what it is to take someone as a 'good informant'. She expands on one of Craig's remarks, in which he says that taking someone to be a good informant is treating them as a fellow subject with a common purpose, rather than as an object from which information can sometimes be extracted. Fricker characterizes the harm of epistemic injustice as epistemic objectification:

> [the victim] is ousted from the role of participant in the co-operative exercise of the capacity for knowledge and recast in the role of passive bystander – a role in which, like objects, he is able to exercise no greater epistemic capacity than that of featuring in potentially informative states of affairs. The moment of testimonial injustice wrongfully denies someone their capacity as an informant, and in confining them to their entirely passive capacity as a source of information, it relegates them to the same epistemic status as a felled tree whose age one might glean from the number of rings.[21]

More obviously, there are also practical and psychological harms. Another of Fricker's literary examples is a vivid illustration of practical harms. The character of Tom Robinson in Harper Lee's *To Kill a Mockingbird* is wrongly accused of rape and is sent to prison, where he is shot and killed by the prison guards. The evidence of his innocence was overwhelming, but as a Black man, he was not believed. The case of Marge from *The Talented Mr Ripley* serves as an example of the psychological harm that can result from epistemic injustice. After repeatedly being ignored and dismissed, Marge begins to lose confidence in herself, and finds it harder and harder to keep on an even keel emotionally. Fricker describes this as loss of epistemic confidence.

The second kind of injustice is hermeneutical injustice. Society marginalizes some categories of people, so that their experiences do not feed into 'interpretive resources'. As a result, society's interpretive resources are inadequate to deal with their experiences. To put it more simply, there are things the dominant group does not understand, and has no words for, because the people for whom those understandings and words would be useful lack social power. Sometimes no-one has the hermeneutical resources, and sometimes the hermeneutical resources are developed by the oppressed group, and resisted by the dominant group.

The classic example here is of sexual harassment. Fricker discusses the case of Carmita Wood, who was employed as an administrator at Cornell University in the 1970s. She was sexually harassed by her boss to a point where her physical and mental health was impacted, and she quit her job. She was denied unemployment benefit because she was unable to name the issue, far less make a formal complaint against her boss. At that point in time, there was no term for the phenomenon. It wasn't until Wood began discussing what had happened with other women, and they realized that they needed to name the problem, that the term 'sexual harassment' was coined.[22] Until then, there was what Fricker terms a hermeneutical gap: as Fricker explains it, Wood was unable to express herself or even to articulate the issue to herself, because the collective hermeneutical resources did not include the concept of sexual harassment.

Both testimonial injustice and hermeneutical injustice could be seen as forms of silencing. Silencing, which I examine in Chapter 13, is the term used for a situation where a group is systematically prevented from communicating. There are lots of different ways that people can be silenced, and a lot of work has been done in categorizing and analyzing different mechanisms. Both systematic credibility deficit, and lack of hermeneutical resources, are ways that women are prevented from communicating and thereby silenced.

Fricker's account of epistemic injustice has been enormously influential, and has given rise to much discussion and critique. One common objection is that, as Fricker presents it, it looks as though testimonial injustice is a matter of individuals not believing each other. But, as with hermeneutical injustice, the deeper problem is that our society has built up a powerful ideology about race and gender, in which women are not fit testifiers.

What we think about the nature of the problem affects what solutions make sense. Various philosophers have argued that Fricker puts too much stress on individuals, both in her account of the nature of testimonial injustice and in her suggestion that corrective virtues can ameliorate the problems. Fricker argues that we should cultivate corrective virtues. In the case of testimonial injustice, we need to be aware of our own likely prejudices and compensate for them. Fricker suggests that we can acquire the virtue of testimonial justice even if we are in the grip of residual prejudices. There is also a virtue of hermeneutical justice: the (corrective) virtue of being alert to "the possibility that the difficulty one's interlocutor is having as she tries to render something communicatively intelligible is due not to its being nonsense or her being a fool, but rather to some sort of gap in collective hermeneutical resources".[23]

Elizabeth Anderson argues that this emphasis on individual solutions does not address the scale or nature of the problem.[24] Anderson points out that what we know about implicit bias (what Fricker calls residual or internalized prejudice) suggests that it is not easily accessible to us. We cannot simply correct our mistakes, as most of the time we are not aware that we are making them. Second, individual effort may not address certain structural epistemic injustices that may have locally innocent (non-prejudicial) causes, but require structural remedies. For example, education develops competence, and good writing is a sign of education. So it is not irrational to downgrade the credibility of those with bad grammar. But it can be unjust: poor people are more likely to have bad grammar. Downgrading their credibility excludes those groups (who may also be part of other disadvantaged groups) even further from discourse. Anderson focusses on structural solutions, for example, integrated schooling, that will decrease the distance between groups and reduce marginalization.

José Medina, in his 2013 book, *The Epistemology of Resistance*, aims to give an account of the ways that we can solve the problems of epistemic injustice. One criticism he has of Fricker's account is that she focusses on the harms done to the individual by credibility deficit. Medina points out that we should also take into account harms to the person who makes the mistake, and to others who are affected. For example, one can harm oneself by granting others who are unlike oneself a credibility excess, while granting those who are like oneself a credibility deficit. And one can harm others by giving a false impression about credibility levels.[25] Medina points out that credibility excesses and deficits are intimately related. It is not a zero sum game, but it is similar to one. We tend to attribute credibility hierarchically.

Medina also argues that granting too much credibility can be worse than granting a credibility deficit, although in a different way. First, Medina agrees with Fricker that being the subject of a credibility excess can result in epistemic vices. Medina admits that practical harms befall those who suffer a credibility deficit more than those who receive an excess, but argues that the hermeneutically privileged are *epistemically* worse off than the oppressed group. He says,

> while women socialized in a culture that gives them very limited sexual agency . . . have a hard time making sense of their desires and pleasures, it is in fact the men who are epistemically worse off in the long run, because they . . . inhabit the sexist perspective comfortably, without any resistance or epistemic friction, speaking and listening through it with arrogance, laziness and closed-mindedness.[26]

Medina's point here is (as he acknowledges) a point from standpoint theory. His claim is that the hermeneutical disadvantage can result in an epistemic advantage – the man feels no friction, and so is not able to improve his knowledge. The woman, because of her experiences, does feel friction, and according to Medina, epistemic friction is what prompts us to open our minds to new ideas. Medina cautions against romanticizing the oppressed (this has been a criticism of standpoint theory, that it over-valorizes the perspective of the oppressed). Rather, Medina's thought is that being comfortable is epistemically disadvantageous.

These questions about harms done bring us back to one of Fricker's central claims, that testimonial injustice harms the subject 'in her capacity as a knower', that it is a particularly *epistemic* harm. Looking at Medina's point that sexist men are epistemically worse off than women, the question arises: how does epistemic harm compare to more familiar sorts of harm? The idea that one is *harmed* in a simply epistemic sense as compared to being harmed in the way that members of oppressed groups are typically harmed – being imprisoned, attacked, raped, killed, and so on – is not easy to get a grip on.

Other forms of epistemic oppression

Several philosophers have argued that there are various other forms or sub-forms of epistemic oppression. Kristie Dotson distinguishes between 'testimonial quieting', and 'testimonial smothering'.[27] Testimonial quieting is what happens when a person speaks and there is no uptake. Dotson starts with Jennifer Hornsby's insight, that testimony is not just one person speaking, it is a communication, a two-way thing, and requires that the audience listen and respond in good faith.[28] If the audience is not willing to reciprocate in this way, testimony falls flat. Dotson says that it is 'epistemic violence' when an entire group is deprived of this reciprocity due to the 'pernicious ignorance' (ignorance that is harmful) of the audience.

Dotson argues that one form of epistemic violence is enacted against Black women when, as is 'normal' in the US, they are not taken seriously as knowers. Drawing on the work of Patricia Hill Collins, Dotson argues that the controlling stereotypes that are applied to Black women prevent them being taken seriously as knowers. Collins identifies various 'controlling images' of Black women that are pervasive in the US context. I discuss the phenomenon of controlling images, or 'roles traps', in the chapter on sexism and oppression. The basic idea is that members of oppressed groups are seen though a limited set of stereotypes, and their behaviour is interpreted accordingly. Seen through the lens of these controlling images, Black women are not credited with competence or knowledge.[29] Dotson terms this 'testimonial quieting'. Black women as a group are not taken seriously as knowers because of pernicious ignorance about them.

'Testimonial smothering' occurs when the speaker recognizes or suspects the pernicious ignorance of her audience, and pre-emptively silences herself. Dotson argues that this sort of self-censorship is coerced, not voluntary. The speaker recognizes that she will not be taken seriously, and when the content of what she might say is risky in some way, she realizes that she cannot, or would much rather not, speak. Dotson uses an example discussed by Cassandra Byers Harvin. Harvin, who is Black, is asked by a white woman what she is working on. When Harvin replies, 'raising black sons in this [US] society', the women responds by asking 'how is that different to raising white sons?' The question reveals an ignorance of and hostility towards concerns about racial injustice in the US, and Harvin sees that there is no value in continuing the conversation. Dotson labels this a particular sort of microaggression: a 'microinvalidation'. Given the riskiness of the subject matter, the potential for upset and for reinforcing negative stereotypes, this is a conversation that Harvin cannot have. This is an example of testimonial smothering.

Testimonial smothering is distinct from what Fricker calls 'pre-emptive testimonial injustice'. Fricker points out that people who are subject to the identity prejudices of others often suffer pre-emptive testimonial injustice: they are not asked in the first place, at least about anything controversial or important. So, although their opinions may be solicited and they may be believed about mundane everyday things ('did you buy flour at the grocery store?'), they would not be asked to speak about anything that would touch on or threaten the oppressive system in which that person is oppressed.

Another area of discussion concerns hermeneutical injustice. Several philosophers have pointed out that hermeneutical gaps are not always gaps for all groups. Rebecca Mason takes up the example of Carmita Wood, and points out that Wood sought out a consciousness raising group, and she and the other women discussed the case with a clear understanding of what had happened.[30] They could understand their own situation, and did in the end articulate it. The problem was that there was no name for it, and that powerful men would not listen. This, Mason says, is not hermeneutical injustice in Fricker's sense, but deliberate (and blameworthy) ignorance.

Gaile Pohlhaus makes a similar point.[31] She starts with standpoint theory, arguing that the situatedness of the knower, and particularly her position in a power structure, affects what she knows. Someone who is powerless must be aware of the concerns of the powerful; she has an interest in anticipating the way that others might become a threat to her. Those in the powerful position do not have this sort knowledge of the less powerful, because they do not have any motivation to acquire such knowledge. Pohlhaus characterizes the phenomenon that Fricker calls 'hermeneutical injustice' as a tension between the situated knower's need to make sense of the world she experiences, and the epistemic resources that are available to do so. A marginalized knower is likely to find that the resources developed by the dominant group do not adequately describe her experiences.

Pohlhaus points out that marginalized groups often develop their own epistemic resources, but that the dominant group, because of the way that the power imbalance affects what they need to know, is not interested. Pohlhaus (like Hartsock and Harding before her) thinks that members of the dominant group can come to understand the situation of the oppressed, but that it is hard work and requires a practical engagement – it is not just a theoretical exercise. Furthermore, as Pohlhaus points out, the marginalized group may not welcome the dominant group's use of their epistemic resources, or may (justifiably) be unwilling to help members of the dominant group reach consciousness.

However, Pohlhaus points out that, often, the dominant group does not even try to do better, and, indeed, dismisses the hermeneutical resources of marginalized groups. "We also see this happen when those situated dominantly dismiss the viability of such arduously honed concepts like 'white privilege,' 'date rape,' or 'hetero normativity.'"[32] This is the phenomenon she calls, 'wilful hermeneutical ignorance'. Dotson, developing the view, calls it 'contributory hermeneutical injustice'.[33] Both Dotson and Pohlhaus argue that members of the dominant group have a clear interest in remaining ignorant here: they do not want the comfort of their privilege disrupted, and so the ignorance is motivated ignorance.

As Pohlhaus points out, this pattern of the dominant group dismissing the epistemic resources of another group is played out in academic philosophy too. The very idea of feminist philosophy has taken a long time to reach respectability. It is not so long ago that to say you were doing feminist philosophy in Anglophone academia was instantly to be dismissed as non-serious, as not doing 'proper philosophy'. We can also see the issues that are being discussed here reflected in our cultural battles over terms such as 'woke' and 'microaggression', which are met with a term specially devised to discredit any complaint about offence: the insult, 'snowflake'. The internet is a battleground, where members of oppressed groups can quickly be reminded of the resilience of the hermeneutical resources of the dominant group.

Both Nora Berenstain and Emmalon Davis have recently identified 'epistemic exploitation' as an important form of epistemic oppression.[34] For example, a Black student in a white society, or a Black professor, is supposed to be an expert on the Black experience, and to educate her white contemporaries about all aspects of race. The primary harm here is a sort of Othering: the agent is not seen as a regular epistemic agent, but as something exotic. She is accorded a credibility excess in one realm, her perceived area of expertise, which is the group she belongs to, but not in others. The secondary harm is the burden, the fact that she must do a lot of extra work to know the things she is supposed to know, and to explain them. As Berenstain points out, there is a classic double bind here. If she refuses to explain, she will be shunned, and if she agrees to explain, she is taking on a heavy epistemic and emotional burden.

The idea of epistemic exploitation appears earlier in the literature. As Audre Lorde puts it,

> Black and Third World people are expected to educate white people as to our humanity. Women are expected to educate men. Lesbians and gay men are expected to educate the heterosexual world. The oppressors maintain their position and evade their responsibility for their own actions. There is a constant drain of energy which might be better used in redefining ourselves and devising realistic scenarios for altering the present and constructing the future.[35]

Uma Narayan also explores epistemic exploitation in her discussion of the roles that are assigned to third world women in Western academic contexts.[36] Narayan identifies a tendency for third world women (including immigrants and visitors) to be assigned certain social roles, and then to be understood through those roles. Narayan refers to these roles as the 'Emissary', the 'Mirror', and the 'Authentic Insider'. All these roles function as a way of limiting what women can say, as their words are pre-filtered by role expectations. The Authentic Insider is the one that is relevant to epistemic exploitation. Narayan describes a demand for third world women to represent their culture, to deliver information to Westerners who are thirsty for knowledge of the Other culture. But the role is not an easy one. Appearing to fail in the role invites disapproval. But additionally, the role is very circumscribed: the speaker can speak on the assigned topic, but is not taken to be a fully competent interlocutor:

> Being in such situations feels like participating in some sort of "ritual of diversity", where the "Insider" has the instrumental role of "speaking difference" but is not seen to have her own stakes in hearing a rich range of responses and criticisms that would enable her to refine, rearticulate or defend her account. In short, to be an "Authentic Insider" sometimes results in not being treated as an "authentic scholar" who has the abilities and training to respond constructively to criticism and to defend her views.[37]

Summary

Feminist explorations of knowledge and ignorance point out the relevance of sexist oppression to accounts of knowledge. This does not mean abandoning objectivity, or positing a special feminine way of knowing. The point is rather to build on existing accounts of knowledge and knowledge acquisition in a way that does not marginalize women, and to point out ways in which knowledge and ignorance function as part of power structures.

The goal of entirely value-free enquiry seems unrealistic to many epistemologists. Helen Longino argues that although neutrality is an impossible goal in scientific enquiry, we can improve on current practices by including more perspectives, and by recognizing that science is essentially a social project. Longino argues that objectivity is a property of group enquiry, not individual enquiry. Louise Antony takes a different approach, arguing that we should focus on empirical investigation of the effect of different biases, and that will tell us which are helpful and which are not.

Standpoint theory argues that the position of the knower might be relevant to what she knows: a person in an oppressed position has a different, and in some ways superior, perspective on the world. Correlatively, those in a position of power might be ignorant of the nature of the oppressive world they inhabit, and, of course, sometimes this ignorance is wilful ignorance. Philosophers like Charles Mills have stressed that this sort of ignorance should be understood as structural, it is systemic, and part of the way that oppressive systems perpetuate themselves. The knowledge of members of an oppressed group is ignored and marginalized.

Miranda Fricker argues that we can think of some of these problems as distinctly epistemic harms. She focusses on testimonial injustice, the way that members of an oppressed group are not listened to, and hermeneutical injustice, the way that the concepts in use in an oppressive society are designed by and for the privileged. Fricker argues that these have the effect of undermining the subject's agency. She is epistemically objectified, seen as an object, not a full epistemic subject.

Since the publication of Fricker's book in 2007, there has been a rich thread of discussion and additions to the catalogue of epistemic harms discussed by Fricker. Concepts such as testimonial quieting, testimonial smothering, wilful hermeneutical injustice, and epistemic exploitation are all distinct and useful notions, capturing different aspects of epistemic oppression.

Notes

1 Fricker, *Epistemic Injustice*: *Power and the Ethics of Knowing*.
2 Antony, 'Quine as Feminist: The Radical Import of Naturalized Epistemology', p.114.
3 Haslanger, 'On Being Objective and Being Objectified', in *Resisting Reality: Social Construction and Social Critique*, p.70.
4 Longino, *Science as Social Knowledge: Values and Objectivity in Scientific Inquiry*.
5 Op. cit., p.218.
6 Antony, 'Quine as Feminist: The Radical Import of Naturalized Epistemology'.
7 Op. cit., p.142.
8 hooks, *Feminist Theory: From Margin to Center*, p.16.
9 Wylie, 'Why Standpoint Matters'.
10 Hartsock, *Money Sex, and Power: Toward a Feminist Historical Materialism*, pp.234-235.
11 Harding, 'Standpoint Theories: Productively Controversial', p.195.
12 Collins, 'Learning from the Outsider Within: The Sociological Significance of Black Feminist Thought'.
13 Frye, 'In and Out of Harm's Way', in *The Politics of Reality*.
14 Mills, 'White Ignorance'.
15 He first discusses it in *The Racial Contract* (1997), and reworks the ideas in an article in *Race and Epistemologies of Ignorance* (2007). A revised and updated version appears in his recent collection of essays, *Black Rights/White Wrongs: The Critique of Racial Liberalism*.
16 Mills, Epigraph to 'White Ignorance', p.13.
17 Mills, 'White Ignorance', p.31.
18 Op. cit., p.19.
19 Op. cit., p.20.
20 Op. cit., p.44.

21 Op. cit., pp.132–133.
22 Fricker, *Epistemic Injustice: Power and the Ethics of Knowing*, pp.149–150. Fricker takes the example from Susan Brownmiller's discussion in *In Our Time: Memoir of a Revolution*, pp. 280–281.
23 Op. cit., p.169.
24 Anderson, 'Epistemic Justice as a Virtue of Social Institutions'.
25 Medina, *The Epistemology of Resistance: Gender and Racial Oppression, Epistemic Injustice, and Resistant Imaginations*, pp.60–61.
26 Op. cit., p.73.
27 Dotson, 'Tracking Epistemic Violence, Tracking Practices of Silencing'.
28 Hornsby, 'Disempowered Speech', p.134.
29 Collins, *Black Feminist Thought: Knowledge, Consciousness, and the Politics of Empowerment*, pp.72–81.
30 Mason, 'Two Kinds of Unknowing'.
31 Pohlhaus, 'Wrongful Requests and Strategic Refusals to Understand'.
32 Op. cit., p.722.
33 Dotson, 'A Cautionary Tale: On Limiting Epistemic Oppression'.
34 Berenstain, 'Epistemic Exploitation'; Davis, 'Typecasts, Tokens, and Spokespersons: A Case for Credibility Excess as Testimonial Injustice'.
35 Lorde, 'Age, Race, Class and Sex: Women Redefining Difference', in *Sister Outsider: Essays and Speeches*.
36 Narayan, *Dislocating Cultures: Identities, Traditions and Third World Feminism*.
37 Op. cit., p.149.

Further reading

Alcoff, Linda and Potter, Elizabeth (eds.) (1993) *Feminist Epistemologies*. Routledge. (Collection of early writings on feminist epistemology).
Antony, Louise and Witt, Charlotte (eds.) (2002) *A Mind of One's Own: Feminist Essays on Reason and Objectivity* (2nd ed.). Westview. (Collection of articles by well-known philosophers working in the analytic tradition).
Grasswick, Heidi (ed.) (2011) *Feminist Epistemology and Philosophy of Science: Power in Knowledge*. Springer. (Collection of original essays on themes in feminist epistemology and philosophy of science).
Harding, Sandra (ed.) (2004) *The Feminist Standpoint Theory Reader*. Routledge. (Collection of classic articles).
Kidd, Ian James, Medina, José, and Pohlhaus Jr., Gaile (eds.) (2017) *Routledge Handbook of Epistemic Injustice*. Routledge. (Collection of essays criticizing and developing ideas of epistemic injustice).
Sherman, Benjamin R. and Goguen, Stacey (eds.) (2019) *Overcoming Epistemic Injustice: Social and Psychological Perspectives*. Rowman & Littlefield. (Collection of essays criticizing and developing ideas of epistemic injustice).

13 Speech acts and silencing

> "When it comes to silencing women, Western culture has had thousands of years of practice."
>
> Mary Beard, *Women & Power: A Manifesto*

Chapter overview: In this chapter I cover the philosophy of language inspired approach to silencing presented by Rae Langton and Jennifer Hornsby. I start with Langton's speech act approach to MacKinnon's claim that pornography is subordination. I go on to examine the idea that silencing can be understood as illocutionary disablement. I examine whether the speech acts analysis can shed light on the conflict between free speech rights of women and some pornographic speech. Finally, I explore Mary Kate McGowan's taxonomy of different sorts of silencing.

Introduction

The notion of silencing first appears in analytic feminist philosophy as a move in arguments about pornography. The traditional feminist worry about pornography is that it harms women in some way, the idea being that there is some causal route to women being disrespected, having lower status, and being victims of sexual and violent crimes (I talk about these arguments in Chapter 4 on pornography). The traditional response from opponents is that there is some sort of right to pornography, in particular, a free speech right.

Feminists such as Catharine MacKinnon have responded that pornography doesn't just harm women, it *silences* them.[1] When women try to refuse sex, their refusals are inert, they cannot make themselves heard. So, the feminist argument is that the free speech right cannot be deployed to defend pornography, as pornography prevents women from exercising their right to free speech. This argumentative move explains the initial impetus to talk about silencing, but feminist accounts of silencing now go far beyond discussions of pornography.

There are various different sorts of silencing, and there are also various different accounts of how each sort works. The first sort of silencing is literal silencing. Someone can be threatened, or gagged, so through coercion or force they literally cannot speak. There is a parallel here with discussions about coercion in rape, in that it is not always easy to define coercion. Threat of force is not the only way to coerce. If that is right, then it is difficult to determine what counts as silencing. And of course, this is particularly vivid in the case of sexual refusal, as the chapters on rape and consent show: it is very difficult to know when someone's sexual refusal was silenced, and when the responsibility for lack of refusal is with the agent.

Feminist philosophers have focussed a lot on the silencing of sexual refusal, the way in which women's refusal ends up being ineffective. But it is worth pointing out that there are many different realms where women are silenced. I mentioned one account of literal silencing in the previous chapter, under the description 'testimonial smothering'. Kristie Dotson argues that there are some circumstances under which people censor themselves because of the dangers of speaking from certain positions about 'risky' topics, such as race.

The notion of hermeneutical injustice that I covered in the previous chapter is very closely related to literal silencing. There, the claim is not that women are cowed into literal silence, but that the available linguistic tools do not allow them to say what they want or need to say. Jennifer Hornsby talks about this as 'ineffability'. Hornsby focusses on the way that language gets subverted, so that meanings and senses that were previously available are no longer available. She talks about how words like 'socialism' have come to have an entirely negative valence. Another of her examples is the word 'quota' in the context of affirmative action. She argues:

> The word "quota" has come to be associated with a narrowly defined political agenda. As used by the American right, a consequence understood as accruing to a practice described as imposing quotas is that the practice is unfair or unreasonable. You might think that a certain school should have a certain proportion of children from its immediate neighborhood; but it may be difficult to express that thought publicly otherwise perhaps than by representing yourself as a dangerous liberal (or perhaps by engaging in such circumlocution as is bound to detract from the main message).[2]

The second major category of silencing identified in the silencing literature is the sort where people speak, but they are not listened to, or not taken seriously. There are various accounts of how this sort of silencing might work. Miranda Fricker describes the way that women are not listened to as 'testimonial injustice'. In particular, women suffer a 'credibility deficit' – they are believed less than they should be. Fricker favours seeing the silencing of sexual refusal as an extreme form of testimonial injustice: "the dehumanizing sexual ideology is such that the man never really *hears* the woman at all – her utterance simply fails to register with his testimonial sensibility."[3]

Third, is the sort of silencing identified by Rae Langton and Jennifer Hornsby (separately) as 'illocutionary silencing'.[4] The idea is that social position can prevent people from being able to do things with their words. Just as some people are in a position to give orders and some people are not, they argue, women are not in a position to make sexual refusals. A woman refuses sex, but her refusal does not work; she cannot make herself understood. It is not just that this particular hearer does not take her seriously, it is rather that the possibility of doing what she wants to with her words has been foreclosed.

The contrast between the epistemic injustice account and the illocutionary account of silencing is quite subtle. In broad terms, the idea of epistemic injustice is that women are not listened to, not taken seriously, not believed. The focus there is on the hearer, on the way that prejudicial stereotypes get in the way of taking women as full epistemic agents, capable of knowing and sharing knowledge. Women's words do not have the effect they should. The point of talking about illocutionary silencing is to focus in on how the conditions of patriarchy sometimes mean that there is no way for a woman to be heard. To put it very simply, language is based on conventions, and being understood depends on those conventions allowing understanding. If our conventions work so as to rule out certain things being said by certain speakers, those speakers are silenced, no matter how clear their words are.

Speech act theory

I will briefly sketch Langton's and Hornsby's accounts of how J.L. Austin's speech act theory might be relevant to debates about pornography and silencing. First, we need the basic architecture, the three-way distinction between locution, perlocution, and illocution. A locution is just the content, the meaning of a sentence. So, the locution 'the cat is on the mat' is just about where the cat is, and uttering that sentence is performing the locutionary act of conveying information about where the cat is.

However, as we know from everyday life, when a sentence is uttered, it can have different effects depending on context. Imagine the mat has a cup of hot tea on it. Then, uttering that sentence might alarm the hearer: the cat is about to knock over a hot cup of tea. The perlocutionary act here is one of alarming the hearer. Speaking can *do* things as well as saying things. A perlocutionary act can vary according to how the hearer is disposed. We can imagine that the same locution could alarm one person, and amuse another. We often rely on perlocution to get people to do what we want (to pick up the cat, for example), but perlocutionary effects can be unpredictable.

Finally, an utterance can do something in a special sort of way. Sometimes a speech act can directly do something. For example, some speech acts are promises, some are acts of marrying, or signing something into law, or naming someone. Of course, certain conditions have to be met. For example, in order to marry someone, you have to have the right sort of authority, be in the right sort of licensed place, and the subjects have to be legally allowed to marry each other. Austin calls these 'felicity conditions'. So long as the felicity conditions are met, an illocutionary act can marry, name, promise, and so on. An illocutionary act is much more proscribed by conventions than a perlocutionary act.

In her influential 1993 article, 'Speech Acts and Unspeakable Acts', Langton uses the idea of an illocutionary speech act in two different ways. Langton is picking up on and defending two claims of Catharine MacKinnon's, that pornography is the subordination of women, and that it silences women. First, she argues that pornography itself can be an illocutionary speech act, an act of subordinating women. Second, Langton argues that women's illocutionary speech act of refusal is disabled in patriarchal societies: when women try to refuse, it does not work. Hence, women are silenced. That is my main focus in this chapter, but first I will briefly explain Langton's subordination argument.

Subordination

Langton argues that pornography is a speech act, which may sound odd. Pornography is usually pictures, or moving images, and it is not literally speech. However, Langton's point is that pornography says something, it has a meaning. It presents women, and sexuality, as being a certain way. The issue of whether pornography is an illocutionary speech act, that is, whether it can directly do something as well as saying something, hangs on whether the felicity conditions are met. According to Austin, felicity conditions are typically set by conventions or rules, typically require the right intention from the speaker, and typically require uptake from the hearer. Marriage is a very clear example. Most states have legal rules about marriage, which vary from jurisdiction to jurisdiction, but usually involve restrictions on who can perform marriages (a licence is required), and often on where a marriage can take place. There are also rules about who can get married: usually the participants must be unmarried adults. In some places, same sex marriage is permitted, and in others it is not. But it is not enough that the rules are followed: a successful marrying event requires the right sort of intention from the speaker and the hearer. The speaker must intend to be performing a marriage (if the speaker is rehearsing the words, it would not be a marriage, it would not be the same illocutionary act). And there must be uptake from the hearer: the hearer must hear and understand what is going on.

Langton argues that it is clear that there are speech acts that can subordinate. She uses speech acts of apartheid, such as a sign that says 'whites only', as an example. This sign both says something about racial groups (it ranks them hierarchically), and it makes it the case that some people are excluded. In Austin's terms, it has both a verdictive function, and an exercitive function: it both gives a verdict and it changes people rights. As Langton stresses, for an illocution to be verdictive or exercitive, the speaker must have the right sort of authority. The need for authority to perform an exercitive illocution is illustrated by the case of marriage: only someone with the right legal authority can marry people. To see the same is true for verdictive illocutions, think about a judge. The judge pronounces the guilty verdict, and the judgment *stands* in an important way. Contrast the tabloid press pronouncing the guilty verdict, which may have important perlocutionary effects (it may make it less likely the defendant will get a fair trial), but does not have the illocutionary effect that the judge's verdict does, of rendering the defendant legally guilty (whether he is actually guilty or not).

Langton claims that pornography is an illocutionary speech act, one that has verdictive and exercitive power, to rank women as sex objects, and to endorse the degradation of women and legitimate sexual violence. Langton argues that although pornography is not as clear a case as speech acts of apartheid, it nonetheless meets enough of the felicity conditions to count as an illocutionary act of subordination. She points out that although reactions to pornography vary, women do take themselves to be ranked and subordinated by it, so there is enough of the necessary uptake. She admits that pornographers probably do not intend to subordinate – their main purpose is to make money – but this may be a non-necessary condition if pornography can be shown to be close enough to paradigmatic illocution in other ways.

One important and controversial felicity condition for an illocution is the authority of the speaker. If pornography has verdictive and exercitive power, it must have authority. Langton argues that pornography has the right sort of authority to pass judgment on women in the way that it does. It does not have official authority of course, but not all authority is official. Langton argues that although pornography does not have official authority, it has authority where it counts:

> What is important is whether it is authoritative in the domain that counts – the domain of speech about sex – and whether it is authoritative for the hearers that count: people, men, boys, who in addition to wanting "entertainment" want to discover the right way to do things, want to know which moves in the sexual game are legitimate. What is important is whether it is authoritative for those hearers – one way or another – who seem to learn that violence is sexy and coercion legitimate.[5]

Much of the debate since the publication of the original article has focussed on the question of authority. Leslie Green, for example, argues that pornography is low status speech, it is not taken seriously enough to have authority.[6] Langton replies that if the view of women promulgated by pornography is efficacious – if enough people accept it – then that is sufficient for it to have authority. This sort of line is supported by Ishani Maitra, who argues that authority can be gained even when it is not part of any official set of rules. People can gain authority by taking it, and if others do not object, they have it.[7]

This raises a question that has important ramifications for the account of pornography as an illocution. As Nancy Bauer and Louise Antony both argue, the sort of authority that is required for an exercitive illocution is the power to instantaneously make something the case.[8] What pornography does is not so much to instantly change the status of women, but to influence men to think about women a certain way. That, of course, contributes to the subordination of women, but that is not to say that it directly subordinates. As Bauer puts it, "One might be tempted to think that pornography virtually inevitably makes people see the world in a certain way. But even that is simply to say that is has a certain very strong perlocutionary force."[9] Antony puts the point in terms of a distinction between power and authority. Antony is happy to grant that pornography has power to change people's attitudes, but, she says, this is not a story about authority, but about power.

This focus on speech acts may strike the reader as puzzling. The question is, what is it adding to the debate about pornography? Some critics, including Nancy Bauer and Lorna Finlayson, argue that the complex discussion of speech acts is a distraction from the really important issues. Finlayson makes this point in strong terms in her discussion of the speech act approach, arguing that it is a mistake to 'fetishize' Austin's work, and to render the debate about pornography abstract and overly technical. Finlayson argues that MacKinnon's argument that pornography subordinates and silences women is perfectly coherent as it stands, and it does not need to be analyzed in terms of speech act theory. As Finalyson puts it, "it seems clear enough that by identifying porn with subordination (rather than following the more usual practice of identifying it as a cause of subordination), MacKinnon is making a claim about the intimacy, immediacy, and systematicity of the relationship she sees between pornography, on the one hand, and violence and discrimination against women, on the other. That is not empty, nor is it mysterious."[10] Bauer and Finlayson both think that the idea of silencing is useful, but that we should take it as a causal consequence of pornography (and other aspects of sexist culture).

A final point to make is that, as Langton agrees, these issues about the effects and powers of pornography do not lead directly to any conclusions about whether or not pornography should be restricted or censored. As I discuss in Chapter 4, there are various different possible answers to questions about how to respond to the harms of pornography. Perhaps, as Langton suggests, what we need to do is undermine the authority of pornographers, for example, with sensible and sensitive sex education in schools. Perhaps what we need is more feminist pornography. I discuss some of these possibilities in Chapter 4, and will leave them aside here.

Silencing

The second role that the notion of illocution plays in the feminist account is in trying to understand what goes wrong with women's sexual refusals. In some cases of rape, assault, or harassment, the man clearly understands that the woman is refusing, but he deliberately ignores that. This is the paradigmatic case of rape. But it seems that sometimes the woman refuses, or tries to, and it falls on deaf ears. Rae Langton and Jennifer Hornsby aim to make sense of this by talking about the way that language works in general, and the way that women are disempowered in language use as in other things.

Both Langton and Hornsby take it that refusal is an illocutionary speech act. A refusal is an exercitive: it should change the rights and permissions of the person refused. If someone is refused, they do not have the right to continue. A successful refusal thus has to meet Austinian felicity conditions. The person must have the right sort of authority (over her own body, in this case), and the parties must have the right sort of intentions and grasp of what is going on. But, very often, something about the social conditions that women are in means that the felicity conditions are not met, their refusals misfire.

Langton puts this in terms of uptake failure: women attempt the illocution of refusal, and there is systematic uptake failure.[11] Uptake is one of Austin's felicity conditions for successful illocution. Without uptake, there is no illocution. Hornsby puts it slightly differently, pointing out that communication requires reciprocity: that the speaker and the hearer are willing to try to understand each other. If that reciprocity is missing, then illocution fails, the person who tries to refuse has not refused.[12] Women suffer illocutionary disablement, as Langton puts it.

Langton and Hornsby need to explain how it could come about that women are not able to perform the illocutionary act of refusal. They both argue, echoing MacKinnon's views, that women, and particularly women's sexuality, is widely misrepresented in pornography and culture more generally. As Hornsby puts it,

> It requires some explaining, of course, how there could be circumstances in which a word that is suited for refusal cannot be used to perform a perfectly good illocutionary act of refusing. But this is easily explained if we believe that embedded within the social practices in which our speech actions happen is an unwritten code of behaviour.

> I mean a code according to which men have uncontrollable sexual urges; women who do not behave and dress with great circumspection are ready and willing to gratify those urges, but will feign unwillingness, whether through decency, or through deceitfulness, or through a desire to excite. If the idea were widespread that this is how men are and how women conduct themselves, and if the code informed men's expectations, then situations in which the reciprocity of intention and recognition required for a woman to refuse a man were lacking would be common. A woman confronted by a man with sex on his mind could not (successfully) refuse him by saying "No".[13]

The underlying argument here is the one that I discuss at length in Chapter 4 about the problematic causal effects of pornography. But of course, we do not need to think of pornography as the only contributor to a societal illusion about sex and sexuality. There is a whole interconnected mesh of sexist ideas and ideology that permeates our language conventions and our social world in general. It is possible to theorize about the mechanisms of silencing separately from the social causes. In putting these issues into a new framework, Langton and Hornsby hope to shed new light on the mechanisms of oppression.

There is a huge literature in response to the speech act approach, and, interesting as it is in its own right, it can be difficult to tease out what is relevant from a feminist point of view and what is primarily of interest to philosophers of language. For example, one question that may seem pointlessly technical is that of whether uptake failure means that there was no illocution. Langton and Hornsby, following Austin, argue that uptake is a necessary condition for a successful illocution. Daniel Jacobson objects that uptake is not a necessary condition for a successful illocution. Jacobson thinks that to say that uptake is necessary is "to hold the performance of an illocutionary act hostage to the perversity of one's audience".[14]

Alexander Bird agrees with Jacobson.[15] He argues that illocutions like refusal occur, and are felicitous, even if there is no uptake. He gives the example of a warning sign: if a burglar sees the sign and does not take it seriously, he cannot complain that he was not warned about the dogs when he is later attacked. He was warned. The warning was a successful illocution, even though there was no uptake. Bird argues that it is perlocution, not illocution to which uptake is essential: one has not had the effect of shocking, amusing, or defaming unless there is uptake. He thinks that when there is uptake failure of refusal, there is a successful illocution but perlocutionary frustration.

Mari Mikkola defends Langton's and Hornsby's view by using the Morgan case (also discussed in Chapter 11).[16] In that case, the defendant told a group of three young men, whom he had just met and been drinking with, that they could have sex with his wife. He told them that she would resist, but that it was just for show, and she was in fact consenting. The woman gave very clear signs of refusing (screaming 'no', shouting for her 11-year-old son to call the police, and so on), but the men ignored it and forced her into sex. Mikkola argues that this is a case where refusal was not possible. Mikkola also argues that it is very implausible to say that the woman's refusal was successful but was not taken seriously.

This example illustrates the fact that Jacobson's worry, that the performance of an illocutionary act is hostage to the perversity of one's audience, points to the real issue: the performance of a refusal *is* hostage to the perversity of one's audience. At least, it is when refusal fails systematically because of an audience's perversity. Langton makes clear that we should make a distinction between uptake failure that is esoteric, a one off, and uptake failure that is systematic. The former does not undermine the illocution, but the latter does. Intuitively, if uptake failure is widespread and unavoidable, then it makes sense to say that it is not possible to successfully perform that illocution.

This is not handing power to the oppressor: the oppressor already has the power, and we must recognize that. And this is the heart of the matter: women's refusal not being understood *is important*, and when it is systematic, we have to try to see what is going wrong. So it is reasonable to say that women's illocution fails, rather than say that there is a successful illocution which fails in its perlocutionary effect. And quite possibly, the philosophy of language framing is helpful in understanding the broader issues.

Silencing and free speech

Let's return to the question of free speech, and how the illocutionary disablement analysis might help with that debate. Even if we grant that women's refusals are not always effective and that we can trace this to social conditions, including pornography, there remains a question about whether women's right to free speech has been undermined. Sometimes, we cannot do things we would ideally be able to do, but no rights have been violated. As Ronald Dworkin complains, the silencing argument is based on the "unacceptable proposition: that the right to free speech includes a right to circumstances that encourage one to speak, and a right that others grasp and respect what one means to say."[17] In a similar vein, in response to Langton, Daniel Jacobson argues that liberal free speech principles, such as John Stuart Mill's, mandate against restrictions on the basis of content, but do not go further than that.[18] They do not (Jacobson argues) mandate 'freedom of illocution', the right to be able to do things with words.

Langton and Hornsby, in a co-authored response to Jacobson, argue that Mill's account of the value of free speech does not exclude illocutionary speech acts. Of course, Mill wants to exclude some perlocutions and illocutions, as they can be harmful. As Langton points out, her own initial argument about pornography as an illocution was that it is a very problematic illocution. But that leaves open that some illocutions might be included in the general justification for free speech, which includes the idea that people should be allowed to communicate to each other. If women cannot perform some illocutions, they are being prevented from communicating.

Caroline West, addressing Dworkin's objection, argues that the sort of silencing that feminists are talking about is indeed the sort that constitutes a free speech violation.[19] West agrees that a liberal right to free speech does not include a right to conditions that would enable one in feeling brave enough to speak. That is too demanding on the audience. On the other hand, of course there are restrictions on what an audience can do: the audience cannot threaten the speaker into silence. That would clearly be a violation of the right to free speech. As West admits, it is not easy to draw a line here. What should we say about an audience that makes faintly menacing noises? But West is prepared to agree with Dworkin and other critics that right to free speech is not the right to circumstances that encourage one to speak.

West is also in agreement with Dworkin that the right to free speech is not a right that others grasp and respect what one says. One might be saying something too complex, or something the audience is not interested in, or something the audience is hostile to. A non-receptive audience is not ideal, but it is not a violation of free speech rights.

However, West argues that the case of illocutionary silencing is different. She presents an example designed to show that we do have a right that other agents do not undermine our ability to make ourselves understood. She asks us to imagine a dictator who wants to silence dissenters. Instead of more traditional methods, he puts a meaning scrambler in the heads of all citizens so that they systematically fail to understand what the dissenters say. West argues that the dictator is violating the dissenters' right to free speech. The point is not simply that we have a right to be understood – there are all kinds of reasons we might not be understood – the point is that others have a duty not to prevent us being understood. So if pornography (and that's a serious 'if' on West's view) prevents women's refusals being understood, it is a violation of women's right to free speech.

West's argument echoes the account that Hornsby presents in her original article on these topics, which is framed as a reply to Dworkin on the pornographers' right to free speech. Dworkin admits that drowning someone out violates their right to free speech. Hornsby argues that the illocutionary speech act analysis of silencing shows how women are drowned out.

Types of silencing

As I said above, there are various things that count as silencing: preventing someone from speaking at all, letting them speak but ignoring or dismissing them, and preventing their words from being able to do anything. The distinction between the second and third types is not always very sharp, and that becomes even more evident when we examine in more detail how silencing works.

Mary Kate McGowan distinguishes between various mechanisms of silencing, focussing on the silencing of sexual refusal.[20] She agrees with Langton that refusal is an illocutionary speech act. McGowan identifies four types of silencing: failure to recognize intention to refuse; authority silencing, which is failure to recognize that the speaker has the authority to refuse; sincerity silencing, which is when the hearer thinks that the speaker does not really mean what she says; and recognition silencing, when the hearer thinks that the speaker's true feelings are not reflected in her refusal, and so it is not a valid refusal.

Much of the time, both Langton and Hornsby seem to focus on the failure to recognize intention to refuse. As Hornsby puts it, "a woman may mean to refuse, but be unable successfully to refuse, because a condition of her having successfully refused – that she be recognized as attempting to refuse – is not satisfied."[21] As McGowan understands it, the failure here is a failure of communication rather than a failure of illocution, but the upshot is the same: the woman's refusal is not effective. This captures the sense in which refusal is 'unspeakable': the woman can go through performance of a refusal but cannot communicate it. Her refusal systematically misfires.

But Langton also talks about what McGowan calls authority silencing. For example, she says,

> A woman who prohibits sexual advances . . . has authority within the local domain of her own life, her own body. If she cannot prohibit, cannot refuse, the authority is absent. If she is disabled from speaking refusal, it is a sign that her body is, in a sense, not her own. If pornography prevents her from refusing, then pornography destroys her authority as it twists her words.[22]

There is also sincerity silencing, which is when the hearer thinks that the speaker does not really mean what she says. Jennifer Hornsby sometimes veers towards a sincerity approach. In discussing the remarks of a judge who claimed that women do not always mean 'no' when they say 'no', she says,

> He hoped to create a presumption of the woman's having been insincere; and if she had been insincere, then indeed there would not have been any act of refusal on the woman's part. Where such a presumption is in place, the demands on the audience lapse, and it becomes impossible for a speaker with however much sincerity she actually utters "No" to be taken to refuse . . .[23]

As part of his objection to the idea that illocutions of refusal fail, Bird appeals to a sincerity reading of the failure of sexual refusal. His point is that there has been a refusal, and it is taken as a refusal, but it is not taken seriously. On Bird's view, the intended perlocutionary effect has failed, but not the illocution. Mikkola points out that if someone refuses but does not mean it, their refusal has not misfired; rather, they are abusing the illocution.[24] She admits that that can happen, and she agrees with Bird that abuses are not failed illocutions. She argues, however, that there are also cases where an attempted refusal genuinely misfires, where the conditions do not allow communication of an intention to refuse. This case highlights the very fine line between perlocutionary and illocutionary failure: if we understand silencing as sincerity silencing, it is not obvious which category it falls into. The line between being taken to be 'refusing insincerely' and 'not refusing' is not easy to draw.

We could also categorize Lois Pineau's view as being a version of sincerity silencing. Pineau argues that our myths about rape have it that women do want sex but feel that they shouldn't, so (according to the myth) they want to be raped in order to take the responsibility of the decision to have sex off their shoulders. Thus their refusals are taken as insincere. This illustrates the way that rape myths can be conceptualized as a form of silencing.

In the fourth sort of silencing, recognition silencing, the hearer thinks that the speaker's true feelings are not reflected in her refusal, and so it is not a valid refusal. With recognition silencing, the man recognizes that there is an intention to refuse, but does not think that the intention is well formed or stable, and thinks that he knows better what will be good for the woman. We can see how this sort of silencing is suited to an analysis in terms of testimonial justice: what is going on here is that the woman is not being taken seriously as a knower of her own desires and decisions.

Another sort of silencing, or partial silencing, that is closely related to illocutionary silencing is identified by Quill Kukla as 'discursive injustice'. Kukla describes the phenomenon whereby women's speech acts are taken to have a different force from the intended force. An order, for example, may be taken as a request, or an assertion. Something that is intended to convey information may be taken as an expression of emotion. Kukla's point is that those in socially disadvantaged positions do not have the same ability to mobilize language conventions that the powerful do. This is not exactly silencing but it is importantly related. Women do not get to use language the way that men do, and thus sometimes cannot do what they want with their words. In Kukla's story, uptake is not simply a yes or no thing, it is complicated, and uptake can be distorted by the social position of the speaker.

As McGowan points out, these different accounts of the way that uptake failure happens affect how we should think of possible causal connections to pornography. As I show in Chapter 4, the task of demonstrating that pornography causes harm is not easy. We can see these detailed accounts of silencing as fitting in to the project of understanding a complex causal story.

Silencing and responsibility

One counterintuitive consequence of the view that women's refusals are silenced is that it seems that a man who presses on with sex has done nothing wrong at all, and there was no rape. Daniel Jacobson, Alexander Bird, and Nellie Wieland all point out that if men do not understand women's intention to refuse, then it looks as though the responsibility of the man is, at the very least, diminished.[25]

We should separate three different sorts of question: first, the question of what the law should say; second, the question of the harm done to the woman; and third, the question of whether the man himself is fully blameworthy. The answer to the first question depends on exactly how we think about *mens rea*, which I discuss in Chapter 11 on consent. There is certainly no obvious reason to say that there was no crime. Mari Mikkola raises the issue of law in her defence of the Hornsby–Langton view, and points out that if there really are conventions whereby when women say 'no' they are taken to mean 'yes', then the law must be reformulated to take that into account.

The second question is the question that Langton and Hornsby answer in their response to Jacobson.[26] First, lack of refusal is not the same as consent. But more importantly, it doesn't matter what the man thought about the situation: if a woman's attempted refusal has had no effect, she has been raped. There is a clear harm, regardless of what the man thought he was doing.

The third question is the tricky one. It is conceivable that a man in the grip of sexist ideology might genuinely and sincerely believe that the woman who is saying 'no' to him means 'yes', and if that is the case it is not a simple matter to say what is blameworthy about his proceeding. As Wieland puts it, it seems that the man has been 'interpretively disabled'. It is not his fault that he misinterprets the woman's attempted refusal.

This worry is related to a problem that I examine in Chapter 11. The problem is that someone who is deeply in the grip of sexist ideology may have an honest belief in consent, even when there was none, and so may not have a clear *mens rea*. The answer given by legal theorists and feminist philosophers in that field is that someone who proceeds with sex when there is in fact no consent must be guilty of recklessness. Consent is so important that you should not take any risks at all. In their response to Wieland, Ishani Maitra and Mary Kate McGowan make a similar move. They argue that sexual contact brings special responsibility to make sure that all parties are consenting.

> Even if pornography causes its viewers to make mistakes about women's communicative intentions, this is insufficient to diminish their responsibility for such mistakes. Just as responsible driving requires attention to detail and sufficient care, so too does responsible sexual behaviour. One really ought to be very careful when forming beliefs about sexual consent, since errors in this domain can result in immense harm.[27]

Summary

The idea that women are silenced is a powerful one. Feminist philosophers have analyzed various sorts of silencing and ways that silencing can happen. First, women are sometimes prevented from speaking at all. Second, women might be allowed to speak, but their words are not taken seriously. Third, is illocutionary silencing, introduced by Jennifer Hornsby and Rae Langton. Their account of illocutionary silencing aims to capture the idea that women cannot do things with their words. Feminist philosophers have focussed on the silencing of sexual refusal, and on the way that pornography might play a role on silencing.

Langton has an additional argument which I also cover in this chapter, that pornography subordinates women, not indirectly, but directly, by fiat, as it were. This is a different argument to the silencing argument, but uses the same tools from Austin's speech act theory. The idea is that pornography is an authoritative illocutionary speech act which rules that women are subordinate.

The silencing argument works by explaining how women's illocutionary speech acts, particularly of sexual refusal, can fail. On the original Hornsby–Langton line, the point is that the social position of women means that men do not recognize women's intention to refuse, and so one felicity condition – uptake - is not met. Mary Kate McGowan points out that there are various ways we can understand the mechanism, including sincerity silencing, authority silencing, and recognition silencing.

Accounts of silencing are partly motivated by a concern to rebut the argument that pornographers have a right to free speech. The rebuttal works by pointing out that if pornography undermines women's right to free speech, there is no free speech argument for pornography. The argument that women are systematically silenced in not being able to do what they intend to do with the words addresses some worries about this rebuttal. The feminist claim is not just that the conditions for women's speaking are non-ideal; it is that women are prevented from communicating.

Once we take seriously the possibility that women's sexual refusals are silenced, we face an apparently counterintuitive result: it is not obvious that men who misunderstand refusal are culpable. As various writers have argued, this certainly doesn't imply that there was no rape, and does not have clear implications for the legal system. But it does raise a problem about blameworthiness, just as the general fact of pervasive sexist ideology does.

Notes

1 See especially MacKinnon, 'Francis Biddle's Sister', in *Feminism Unmodified*, and her later work *Only Words*.
2 Hornsby, 'Disempowered Speech', p.135.
3 Fricker, *Epistemic Injustice*, p.140.
4 Langton, 'Speech Acts and Unspeakable Acts', in *Sexual Solipsism: Philosophical Essays on Pornography and Objectification*; Hornsby, 'Speech Acts and Pornography'.
5 Langton, 'Speech Acts and Unspeakable Acts', in *Sexual Solipsism*, p.45.
6 Green, 'Pornographies'.
7 Maitra, 'Subordinating Speech'.
8 Bauer, 'On Philosophical Authority', in *How to Do Things with Pornography*; Antony, 'Be What I Say: Authority Versus Power in Pornography,' in *Beyond Speech*.
9 Bauer, 'How To Do Things with Pornography', in *How to Do Things with Pornography*, p.80.
10 Finlayson, 'How to Screw Things with Words', p.784.
11 Langton, 'Speech Acts and Unspeakable Acts', in *Sexual Solipsism*.
12 Hornsby, 'Speech Acts and Pornography'.
13 Op. cit., p.42.
14 Jacobson, 'Freedom of Speech Acts? A Response to Langton', p.74.
15 Bird, 'Illocutionary Silencing'.
16 Mikkola, 'Illocution, Silencing and the Act of Refusal'.
17 Dworkin, 'Women and Pornography', p.38.
18 Jacobson, 'Freedom of Speech Acts? A Response to Langton'.
19 West, 'The Free Speech Argument Against Pornography'.
20 McGowan, 'On Multiple Types of Silencing'.
21 Hornsby, 'Speech Acts and Pornography', p.42.
22 Langton, 'Speech Acts and Unspeakable Acts', in *Sexual Solipsism*, pp.58-59.
23 Hornsby, 'Speech Acts and Pornography', p.42.
24 Mikkola, 'Illocution, Silencing and the Act of Refusal'.
25 Jacobson, 'Freedom of Speech Acts? A Response to Langton'; Bird, 'Illocutionary Silencing'; Wieland, 'Linguistic Authority and Convention in a Speech Act Analysis of Pornography'.
26 Langton and Hornsby, 'Free Speech and Illocution'.
27 Maitra and McGowan, 'On Silencing, Rape, and Responsibility', p.171.

Further reading

Maitra, Ishani and McGowan, Mary Kate (eds.) (2012) *Speech and Harm: Controversies Over Free Speech*. Oxford University Press. (Collection of essays on harmful speech in various contexts).
McGowan, Mary Kate (2019) *Just Words: On Speech and Hidden Harm*. Oxford University Press. (Sustained argument for the view that speech is harmful when it enacts norms prescribing harm).
Mikkola, Mari (2019) *Pornography: A Philosophical Introduction*. Oxford University Press. (Clear introduction to the debates about pornography, with a focus on speech act accounts of silencing).

Glossary

Note: some of the definitions that I use are contested, and, in particular, there are often slightly different uses of the terms that are pejorative. I define the terms as I use them. It should also be noted that I discuss some of these terms, and alternative accounts, in more detail in the relevant chapters.

Adaptive Preference a preference that is formed because of poor choice conditions rather than through independent processes. An adaptive preference feels to the subject like a genuine <u>autonomous</u> preference, but is in fact formed because of outside influences and may not be conducive to flourishing.

Affirmative Action policies that aim to increase representation of under-represented groups. There are many different policies under this umbrella, e.g. quotas, lower barriers for candidates in the under-represented group, using group membership as a tie breaker, and targeted recruitment.

Affirmative Consent an understanding of valid consent that takes it to require a clear and unambiguous (though not necessarily verbal) 'yes'.

Analytic Philosophy a loose term, used to refer to the style of philosophy generally practised in the English-speaking world. The style is characterized by a focus on logical argument, concept analysis, and minimal guesswork or speculation. Often contrasted with <u>Continental philosophy</u>. This is a loose contrast, there are many areas of overlap.

Autonomy self-rule, self-determination. The term is usually used in a psychological sense, to distinguish acting on reasons and motives that are one's own from being unduly influenced by someone else or being in the grip of <u>false consciousness</u>, or <u>adaptive preferences</u>, for example.

Bargaining with the Patriarchy to be distinguished from <u>adaptive preferences</u>, to bargain with the patriarchy is to see in a clear-eyed way that a bad choice situation means that it is rational to choose an option that would not otherwise be chosen. E.g. a woman might choose to appear meek so as to avoid aggression.

Birdcage Analogy Marilyn Frye's image to illustrate the necessity of seeing the whole picture to understand sexist <u>oppression</u>. If you look at one bar of the cage it might not look restrictive; you have to look at the whole thing to see how it restricts. It may look as though women are advantaged by some aspects of <u>patriarchy</u> (e.g. they are the default custodian in a divorce), but if we look at the bigger picture we see that women suffer from being the default parent.

Capabilities   Nussbaum's word for the capacities that she thinks essential to human flourishing, which all people should be able to exercise.

Care Ethics   an account of ethical thinking developed by feminist thinkers. It is characterized by a focus on personal connections as opposed to impartial considerations.

Coercion   manipulation of choice (including <u>consent</u>) by pressuring the agent.

Commodification   treating something as though it can be bought and sold. This may be appropriate, as with objects such as cars, but may be problematic in other cases, as with people's bodies, or with things such as knowledge, art, and so on.

Communitarianism   a normative political theory that stresses the importance of communities, and argues for rights and protections for communities (in contrast to the usual approach, which makes individuals the locus of rights). Popular in the 1980s but largely out of fashion now.

Consent   the act of agreeing to or permitting something.

Consequentialism   a theory in normative ethics that says, roughly, that the right action is the one that has the best consequences. Different accounts of what the best consequences are make for different consequentialist theories. Commonly contrasted with <u>deontology</u> and <u>virtue ethics</u>.

Continental Philosophy   a style of doing philosophy that has developed from nineteenth-and twentieth-century traditions in continental Europe, broadly understood as including writers such as Hegel, Schopenhauer, and Nietzsche, the <u>Frankfurt School</u>, and twentieth-century French thinkers such as Sartre, Foucault, and Deleuze. Usually contrasted with <u>analytic philosophy</u>, although this is not a sharp distinction. Continental philosophy tends to appeal more to lived experience and involves more imaginative creation than analytic philosophy.

Critical Theory   theory aimed at understanding and ending oppression. Originally used to refer to the approach of the <u>Frankfurt School</u> (philosophers and sociologists working at the Institute for Social Research in Frankfurt in the middle years of the twentieth century). Now it is mostly used in a wider sense to refer to any theory that aims for social transformation.

Deontology   a theory in normative ethics that says, roughly, that right action involves obeying certain principles, for example, 'do not lie'. Different accounts of what the principles are make for different deontological theories. Commonly contrasted with <u>consequentialism</u> and <u>virtue ethics</u>.

Double Bind   the situation where someone will be disapproved of (or worse) if they obey certain norms or rules, but also if they disobey. So they can't win.

Epistemic Injustice   an injustice that stems from underestimating someone's capacities as a knower. According to Fricker's account, there are two main kinds: <u>testimonial injustice</u> and <u>hermeneutical injustice</u>.

Epistemology   the philosophical study of knowledge, looking at the nature and structure of knowledge, how it is acquired, what justification is, and so on.

Essentialism   a view about something that takes there to be an essence (some essential properties) of the thing in question. E.g. essentialism about gender says that there is some essential womanness in being a woman.

Exercitive (speech act)   a sort of <u>illocutionary speech act</u> that grants or removes permissions. E.g. a 'No smoking' sign.

False Consciousness   a state of having internalized the values of the oppressor.

Felicity Conditions   the conditions that must be in place in order for an <u>illocutionary speech act</u> to work as it is supposed to. E.g. the speaker must have the right sort of authority.

Femininity   the package of traits associated with women as a <u>gender</u>. Usually used by feminists to refer to the traits associated according to patriarchal norms, e.g. gentleness, meekness, emotional intelligence, lack of rationality, and so on.

Frankfurt School   philosophers and sociologists working at the Institute for Social Research in Frankfurt in the middle years of the twentieth century, including Horkheimer, Adorno, Marcuse, and Habermas. They developed an approach to political theory, known as <u>critical theory</u>, that was aimed at social change.

Gaslighting   a way of misleading and manipulating someone in order to persuade them that bad treatment is merely imagined or exaggerated.

Gender   the social categories of man and woman. In the patriarchal system, gender is taken to be binary and strictly related to sex. In an alternative system, gender may come apart from sex and need not be binary.

Gendered Division of Labour   a stable social arrangement where jobs and activities are divided up according to gender.

Generic   a generalizing statement, such as 'women are nurturing'. It is important to interpret generics carefully: they may not imply that all the individuals have the property, and they may not imply that they have the property innately.

Harm Principle   Mill's principle that the only reason for interfering with someone is to prevent harm to others. Mill adds the anti-paternalist principle, that someone's own good is not a reason for interfering with them.

Hermeneutical Injustice   a kind of <u>epistemic injustice</u>, namely, the situation that arises when a society lacks the conceptual resources (understanding and/or language) to express something that affects the subject in a problematic way.

Heteropatriarchy   a <u>patriarchal</u> system in which heterosexuality is socially enforced. Most feminists using the term 'patriarchy' take it for granted that heterosexism is one of the patriarchal norms.

Heterosex   a term for sexual intercourse in a heterosexual framework.

Heterosexuality   in a thin sense, this is a sexual preference of males and females for each other, as opposed to same sex preference. Feminists often argue that heterosexuality is not just a sexual preference, but a social system enforced by <u>patriarchy</u> (or 'heteropatriarchy').

Hierarchy   a system with several levels organized in order of importance. Used in feminism to refer to social structures that privilege some people over others.

Identity   there are many uses of this term in philosophy. In this book I use it to refer to the way a person is categorized. There are two senses, <u>structural identity</u> (how a person is categorized by society) and <u>subjective identity</u> (how a person sees themselves).

Identity Politics   the name given to political efforts that are centered around a structural identity, e.g. race. Has been used as a pejorative, but need not be.

Ideology   a system of beliefs, values, and norms that supports a dominant group in maintaining power.

Illocutionary Speech Act   a speech act that can instantaneously 'make it so'. E.g. an illocutionary speech act can marry two people, or name a ship, or make a promise. As soon as the words are uttered in the right conditions, the situation has changed accordingly.

Implicit Bias   a psychological tendency to favour or disfavour certain groups that the holder is not aware of having.

Intersectionality   a theory about the way that different axes of oppression intersect and produce unique forms of oppression. E.g. the form that oppression of Black women takes is not fully expressible in terms of adding the racist oppression of Black men and the sexist oppression of white women.

Liberal Feminism   a broad approach that takes the tenets of political liberalism (particularly the harm principle) seriously as a starting point.

Male Gaze   the mode of looking at women as passive sex objects. Usually used in the context of a claim that women are depicted in art and media in anticipation of the male gaze.

Marginalization   the process of excluding and disempowering people from particular social groups and making the nature of the group appear to justify that treatment.

Marital Rape Exception   the law that says that forced sex within marriage is not a crime.

Masculinity   the package of traits associated with men as a gender. Usually used by feminists to refer to the traits associated with men by patriarchal norms, e.g. strength, intelligence, emotional resilience, and so on.

Microaggression   an apparently small action, possibly unintentional, that contributes to oppression by marking the person as inferior.

Misogyny   hatred of women as expressed in systemic ways. Related terms 'misogynoir' (applies to Black women) and transmisogyny (applies to trans women) capture the potential intersectionality of misogyny.

Moralism   a view that stakes a fairly extreme and inflexible moral position, usually based on traditional morality, and then insulates that particular moral judgment from criticism and reflection.

Multiculturalism   can refer simply to the existence of different cultural groups but is usually used to refer to a normative view, often a policy of allowing and encouraging different ethnic and cultural groups to maintain their distinct customs, religions, etc. within a nation state.

Naturalism about Ethics   the view that it is possible to make sense of ethics without appealing to anything supernatural.

Necessary and Sufficient Conditions   a common way of describing and distinguishing between different aspects of a definition or theory about something, but it can also be used to talk about conditions for a permission or other action. A necessary condition is a condition that is essential for the thing to be the thing it is (e.g. a necessary condition for a shape to be a square is that it has four sides). A sufficient condition is a condition that is enough (e.g. a sufficient condition for a shape to be a square is that it has four sides the same length). It is generally agreed that it is possible to analyze some things, particularly complex social phenomena, without giving necessary and sufficient conditions.

Norm a rule or guideline. The term usually refers to an informal rule that is socially created and enforced. E.g. a norm of queuing at bus stops.

Normative Theory a theory about how things should be, as opposed to a theory about how things are (a descriptive theory). E.g. standpoint theory is a normative theory in that it aims to ameliorate as well as understand oppression.

Objectification treating someone as an object.

Objectivism the view that there is something independently true in the relevant domain, e.g. objectivism about morality says that some moral claims are true. Objectivism is not committed to any particular account of what makes the claims true; it can be fairly modest. Usually contrasted with subjectivism and relativism. Most of the feminists discussed in this book accept that there are objective moral truths, or universal values, as Nussbaum calls them.

Oppression a situation of unjust domination.

Othering treating, or talking to or about someone in a way that indicates that they are not from the dominant group, and are unknown or unknowable to members of the dominant group. To think of someone as 'Other' is to ignore their shared humanity and focus instead on what makes them different, and this is subtly used to downgrade their interests.

Paternalism the policy of interfering with a person for their own good, e.g. motorcycle helmet laws.

Patriarchy literally means the rule of the father, but used by feminists to refer to a social and political system in which being a man is necessary to be deemed qualified for power and authority.

Perlocutionary (speech act) 'perlocutionary' refers to the effects of a speech act, thus a perlocutionary speech act is the utterance understood in terms of its effects. E.g. a speech act of frightening the listener.

Privilege unearned advantage, such as advantages based on race, class, or sex.

Rape Culture the normalization of rape in a culture.

Rape Myths sexist myths about the nature of rape, e.g. that women welcome it, or that the only real rape is stranger rape.

Relativism the view that there is no independent truth of the matter, that correctness is relative to some set of standards. For example, a relativist about morals thinks that moral claims are only true relative to an arbitrary set of standards, e.g. society's moral traditions.

Roe v Wade the 1973 legal case that established the legality of abortion in the USA.

Self-objectification participation in one's own objectification by objectifying oneself, usually as a matter of false consciousness rather than autonomous choice.

Sexism discrimination against women on grounds of sex.

Sexual Harassment unwanted harmful sexual attention, usually in a professional context.

Social Construction a social construction is something that has evolved or been created through social processes. Social construction often piggybacks on something that is itself mind-independent (e.g. age is partly socially constructed insofar as different ages are imbued with social meaning, as in the case of 'being a teenager'). Social constructions are no less real for being socially constructed, although they should be easier to change than brute objects. Feminists are interested in the social construction of gender roles, and in arguing that they have been constructed in problematic ways.

Solidarity   the political stance of expressing shared values and willingness to share struggle with people in different situations.

Standpoint   according to standpoint theory, the position from which one can critique the hierarchical system that creates different social and epistemic vantage points.

Standpoint Theory   a theory in feminist epistemology that points out that different social situations produce different knowledge and that this can be developed in a politically aware and active 'standpoint'.

Stereotype   a widely accepted template for how someone in a certain group will behave, feel, look, and so on. Usually used in a negative sense, both in that stereotypes tend to be derogatory, and in that it is harmful to have a stereotype applied to one.

Structural Explanation   an explanation that appeals to social and legal systems to explain the phenomenon. Feminists usually argue that we need structural explanations to make sense of gender inequality. For example, the explanation for the gender pay gap should appeal to social and legal systems, such as divorce laws, maternity policies, and so on, rather than simply individual choices.

Structural Identity   the category that an individual is placed in by society, for example, being a refugee is a structural identity, as are racial categories. Structural identity can overlap with subjective identity, but it need not.

Subjective Identity   the sense of their own identity that an individual agent feels. A subjective sense of identity is contrasted with an identity that is imposed by someone else.

Subjectivism   the view that correctness in a certain area is a matter of the individual's point of view. For example, a subjectivist about art thinks that aesthetic value depends entirely on the individual.

Testimonial Injustice   A kind of epistemic injustice, namely, failing to recognize someone's testimony (their report about how things are) as truthful and/or important.

Title IX   the 1972 US law mandating equal opportunity for women in public education. Recent efforts to prevent sexual assault and harassment on US campuses have focussed on the application of Title IX regulations.

Trafficking   forcing someone into selling sexual services against their will, often through kidnapping and imprisoning them.

Universal Values   see objectivism.

Verdictive (speech act)   a sort of illocutionary speech act that announces a verdict. E.g. 'foul!', declared by the umpire.

Virtue Ethics   A philosophical account of normative ethics, such that the centrally important ethical notion is virtue, e.g. courage, or generosity. Different accounts of what the virtues are make for different theories. Commonly contrasted with deontology and consequentialism.

Bibliography

Abramson, Kate (2014) 'Turning up the Lights on Gaslighting'. *Philosophical Perspectives* 28: 1-30.

Ahmed, Leila (1992) *Women and Gender in Islam: Historical Roots of a Modern Debate*. New Haven, Conn.: Yale University Press.

Alcoff, Linda Martín (1991) 'The Problem of Speaking for Others'. *Cultural Critique* 20: 5-32.

Alcoff, Linda Martín (2018) *Rape and Resistance*. Cambridge: Polity Press.

Alexander-Floyd, Nikol (2012) 'Disappearing Acts: Reclaiming Intersectionality in the Social Sciences in a Post-Black Feminist Era'. *Feminist Formations* 24(1): 1-25.

Anderson, Elizabeth (1993) *Value in Ethics and Economics*. Cambridge, Mass.: Harvard University Press.

Anderson, Elizabeth (2006) 'Recent Thinking about Sexual Harassment: A Review Essay'. *Philosophy and Public Affairs* 34(3): 284-312.

Anderson, Elizabeth (2012) 'Epistemic Justice as a Virtue of Social Institutions'. *Social Epistemology* 26(2): 163-173.

Anderson, Michelle J. (2005) 'Negotiating Sex'. *Southern California Law Review* 78: 1401-1438.

Anderson, Michelle J. (2016) 'Marital Rape Laws Globally: Rationales and Snapshots Around the World', in Kersti Yllö and M. Gabriela Torres (eds.) *Marital Rape: Consent, Marriage, and Social Change in Global Context*. Oxford: Oxford University Press.

Anderson, Scott A. (2002) 'Prostitution and Sexual Autonomy: Making Sense of the Prohibition of Prostitution'. *Ethics* 112(4): 748-780.

Anderson, Scott A. (2005b) 'Sex Under Pressure: Jerks, Boorish Behavior, and Gender Hierarchy'. *Res Publica* 11(4): 349-369.

Anthias, Floya and Yuval-Davis, Nira (1992) *Racialized Boundaries: Race, Nation, Gender, Colour and Class and the Anti-Racist Struggle*. Oxford: Routledge.

Antony, Louise (1993) 'Quine as Feminist: The Radical Import of Naturalized Epistemology', in Louise Antony and Charlotte Witt (eds.) *A Mind of One's Own: Feminist Essays on Reason and Objectivity*. Boulder: Westview Press, 185-226.

Antony, Louise (2012) 'Different Voices or Perfect Storm: Why Are There So Few Women in Philosophy?' (Report). *Journal of Social Philosophy* 43(3): 227-255.

Antony, Louise (2017) 'Be What I Say: Authority Versus Power in Pornography', in Mari Mikkola (ed.) *Beyond Speech*. Oxford: Oxford University Press.

Antony, Louise (2020) 'Feminism Without Metaphysics or a Deflationary Account of Gender'. *Erkenntnis* 85(3): 529-549.

Archard, David (1997) '"A Nod's as Good as a Wink": Consent, Convention, and Reasonable Belief'. *Legal Theory* 3(3): 273-290.

Astell, Mary (2003) (first published 1697) *A Serious Proposal to the Ladies: Parts I and II*, Patricia Springborg (ed.) Toronto: Broadview Press.

Atwood, Margaret (2010) (first published 1985) *The Handmaid's Tale*. New York: Vintage Books.

Austin, J.L. (1975) *How To Do Things with Words*, 2nd ed. Cambridge, Mass.: Harvard University Press.

Bailey, Alison (2009) 'On Intersectionality, Empathy, and Feminist Solidarity: A Reply To Naomi Zack'. *Journal for Peace and Justice Studies* 19(1): 14-36.

Baron, Marcia W. (2001) 'I Thought She Consented'. *Philosophical Issues* 11 (1):1-32.

Bartky, Sandra Lee (1990) *Femininity and Domination*. Oxford: Routledge.

Bauer, Nancy (2015) *How to Do Things with Pornography*. Cambridge, Mass.: Harvard University Press.

Beauvoir, Simone de (2011) (first published 1949) *The Second Sex*, Constance Borde and Sheila Malovany-Chevallier (trans.) New York: Vintage Books.

Beebee, Helen and Saul, Jennifer (2011) 'Women in Philosophy in the UK: A Report by the British Philosophical Association and the Society for Women in Philosophy UK', www.bpa.ac.uk/uploads/2011/02/BPA_Report_Women_In_Philosophy.pdf.

Benhabib, Seyla (1999) 'The Liberal Imagination and the Four Dogmas of Multiculturalism'. *Yale Journal of Criticism* 12(2): 401-413.

Berenstain, Nora (2016) 'Epistemic Exploitation'. *Ergo: An Open Access Journal of Philosophy* 3: 569-590.

Bettcher, Talia Mae (2014) 'Trapped in the Wrong Theory: Rethinking Trans Oppression and Resistance'. *Signs* 39(2): 43-65.

Bilge, Sirma (2013) 'Intersectionality Undone: Saving Intersectionality from Feminist Intersectionality Studies'. *Du Bois Review* 10(2): 405-424.

Bird, Alexander (2002) 'Illocutionary Silencing'. *Pacific Philosophical Quarterly* 83(1): 1-15.

Bordo, Susan (1993) *Unbearable Weight: Feminism, Western Culture, and the Body*. Berkeley: University of California Press.

Brake, Elizabeth (2012) *Minimizing Marriage: Marriage, Morality, and the Law*. Oxford: Oxford University Press.

Brennan, Jason and Jaworski, Peter M. (2016) *Markets Without Limits: Moral Virtues and Commercial Interests*. New York: Routledge.

Bridges, A.J., Wosnitzer, R., Scharrer, E., Sun, C., and Liberman, R. (2010) 'Aggression and Sexual Behavior in Best-Selling Pornography Videos: A Content Analysis Update'. *Violence Against Women* 16(10): 1065-1085.

Brighouse, Harry and Wright, Erik Olin (2008) 'Strong Gender Egalitarianism'. *Politics and Society* 36(3): 360-372.

Brison, Susan J. (1998) 'The Autonomy Defense of Free Speech'. *Ethics* 108(2): 312-339.

Brison, Susan J. (2003) *Aftermath: Violence and the Remaking of a Self*. Princeton, NJ: Princeton University Press.

Brison, Susan (2016) *Remarks in Boston Review Forum on The Logic of Misogyny*, http://bostonreview.net/forum/logic-misogyny/susan-j-brison-susan-j-brison-responds-kate-manne.

Brod, Harry (1988) 'Pornography and the Alienation of Male Sexuality'. *Social Theory and Practice* 14(3): 265-284.

Bromwich, Danielle and Millum, Joseph (2018) 'Lies, Control, and Consent: A Response to Dougherty and Manson'. *Journal of Ethics* 128(2): 446-461.

Brownmiller, Susan (1975) *Against Our Will: Men, Women and Rape*. New York: Simon & Schuster.

Brownmiller, Susan (1999) *In Our Time: Memoir of a Revolution*. New York: Dial Press.

Burgess-Jackson, Keith (ed.) (1999) *A Most Detestable Crime: New Philosophical Essays on Rape*. New York: Oxford University Press.

Butler, Judith (1990) *Gender Trouble*. Oxford: Routledge.

Butler, Judith (1997) *Excitable Speech: A Politics of the Performative*. Oxford: Routledge.

Cahill, Ann J. (2001) *Rethinking Rape*. Ithaca, N.Y.: Cornell University Press.

Cahill, Ann J. (2014) 'Recognition, Desire, and Unjust Sex'. *Hypatia* 29(2): 303-319.

Cahill, Ann J. (2016) 'Unjust Sex vs. Rape'. *Hypatia* 31: 746-761.

Calhoun, Cheshire (1994) 'Separating Lesbian Theory from Feminist Theory'. *Ethics* 104(3): 558-581.

Calhoun, Cheshire (2002) *Feminism, the Family, and the Politics of the Closet: Lesbian and Gay Displacement*. Oxford: Oxford University Press.

Calhoun, Cheshire (2009) 'The Undergraduate Pipeline Problem'. *Hypatia* 24(2): 216-223.

Califia, Pat (1995) *Public Sex: The Culture of Radical Sex*. Jersey City, N.J.: Cleis Press.

Cameron, Deborah and Frazer, Elizabeth (2007) 'On the Question of Pornography and Sexual Violence: Moving Beyond Cause and Effect', in Drucilla Cornell (ed.) *Feminism and Pornography*. Oxford: Oxford University Press, 218-239.

Card, Claudia (1991) 'Rape as a Terrorist Institution', in R. Frey and C. Morris (eds.) *Violence, Terrorism, and Justice*. Cambridge: Cambridge University Press, 296-319.

Card, Claudia (1996) 'Against Marriage and Motherhood'. *Hypatia* 11(3): 1-23.

Chambers, Clare (2017a) 'II–Ideology and Normativity'. *Aristotelian Society Supplementary Volume* 91: 175-195.

Chambers, Clare (2017b) *Against Marriage: An Egalitarian Defense of the Marriage-Free State*. Oxford: Oxford University Press.

Chartered Institute of Insurers, (2016) 'Risk, Exposure and Resilience to Risk in Britain Today: Women's Risks in Life – An Interim Report', www.cii.co.uk/media/7461333/risks_in_life_report.pdf.

Code, Lorraine (1981) 'Is The Sex of the Knower Epistemologically Significant?' *Metaphilosophy* 12(3-4): 267-276.

Cohen, G.A. (1978) *Karl Marx's Theory of History: A Defence*, Oxford: Clarendon Press, Oxford University Press/Princeton, N.J.: Princeton University Press.

Collins, Patricia Hill (1985) 'Learning from the Outsider Within: The Sociological Significance of Black Feminist Thought'. *Social Problems* 33(6): S14–S32.

Collins, Patricia Hill (1990) *Black Feminist Thought: Knowledge, Consciousness, and the Politics of Empowerment*. Oxford: Routledge.

Collins, Patricia Hill (1998) *Fighting Words: Black Women and the Search for Justice*. Minneapolis: University of Minnesota Press.

Combahee River Collective Statement (1977). Reprinted in Keeanga-Yamahtta Taylor (ed.) (2012) *How We Get Free: Black Feminism and the Combahee River Collective*. Chicago: Haymarket Books.

Conly, Sarah (2004) 'Seduction, Rape, and Coercion'. *Ethics* 115(1): 96-121.

Cooper, Anna Julia (1988) (first published 1892). *A Voice from the South by a Black Woman of the South*. New York: Oxford University Press.

Cooper, Brittney (2016) 'Intersectionality', in Lisa Disch and Mary Hawkesworth (eds.) *The Oxford Handbook of Feminist Theory*. Oxford: Oxford University Press.

Crenshaw, Kimberlé Williams (1989) 'Demarginalizing the Intersection of Race and Sex: A Black Feminist Critique of Antidiscrimination Doctrine, Feminist Theory, and Antiracist Politics'. *University of Chicago Legal Forum* 1989: 139-167.

Crenshaw, Kimberlé Williams (1991) 'Mapping the Margins: Intersectionality, Identity Politics, and Violence against Women of Color'. *Stanford Law Review* 43(6): 1241-1299.

Crenshaw, Kimberlé Williams (1993) 'The 2 Live Crew Controversy'. Originally published in *Stanford Law Review* 1241(1993) 20-52. Extract reprinted in Drucilla Cornell (2007)(ed.) *Feminism and Pornography*. Oxford: Oxford University Press, 218-239.

Criado Perez, Caroline (2019) *Invisible Women: Exposing Data Bias in a World Designed for Men*. London: Penguin.

Cudd, Ann (2006) *Analysing Oppression*. Oxford: Oxford University Press.

Davis, Angela Y. (1983) *Women, Race, and Class*. New York: Vintage Books.

Davis, Emmalon (2016) 'Typecasts, Tokens, and Spokespersons: A Case for Credibility Excess as Testimonial Injustice'. *Hypatia* 31(3): 485-501.

de Marneffe, Peter (2009) *Liberalism and Prostitution*. Oxford: Oxford University Press.

Dines, Gail (2010) *Pornland*. Boston, Mass.: Beacon Press.

Dotson, Kristie (2011) 'Tracking Epistemic Violence, Tracking Practices of Silencing'. *Hypatia* 26(2): 236-257.

Dotson, Kristie (2012) 'A Cautionary Tale: On Limiting Epistemic Oppression'. *Frontiers: A Journal of Women's Studies* 33(1): 24-47.

Dougherty, Tom (2013) 'Sex, Lies, and Consent'. *Ethics* 123(4): 717-744.

Duff, R.A. (1981) 'Recklessness and Rape'. *Liverpool Law Review* 3: 49-64.

Duff, R.A. (1990) *Intention, Agency and Criminal Liability: Philosophy of Action and the Criminal Law*. Oxford: Blackwell.

Dustin, Moira and Phillips, Anne (2008) 'Whose Agenda Is It?: Abuses of Women and Abuses of "Culture" in Britain'. *Ethnicities* 8(3): 405-424.

Dworkin, Andrea (1974) *Woman Hating*. New York: Penguin.

Dworkin, Andrea (2000) 'Against the Male Flood: Censorship, Pornography, and Equality', in Drucilla Cornell (ed.) *Oxford Readings in Feminism: Feminism and Pornography*. Oxford: Oxford University Press, 19-44.

Dworkin, Ronald (1985) *A Matter of Principle*. Oxford: Oxford University Press.

Dworkin, Ronald (1993) 'Women and Pornography'. *New York Review of Books*, 21 October.

Eaton, A.W. (2007) 'A Sensible Antiporn Feminism'. *Ethics* 117(4): 674-715.

Eaton, A.W. (2012) 'What's Wrong With the (Female) Nude? A Feminist Perspective on Art and Pornography', in Hans Maes and Jerrold Levinson (eds.) *Art and Pornography: Philosophical Essays.* Oxford: Oxford University Press, 229-253.

Elster, Jon (2016) *Sour Grapes: Studies in the Subversion of Rationality.* Cambridge: Cambridge University Press.

English Collective of Prostitutes (2016) 'Report of the Prostitution Law Review Committee on the Operation of the Prostitution Reform Act 2003', https://prostitutescollective.net/wp-content/uploads/2016/10/report-of-the-nz-prostitution-law-committee-2008.pdf.

Estrich, Susan (1986) 'Rape'. *Yale Law Journal* 95(6): 1087-1120.

Fausto-Sterling, Anne (2000) *Sexing the Body.* New York: Basic Books.

Fine, Cordelia (2010) *Delusions of Gender.* London: Icon Books.

Finlayson, Lorna (2014) 'How to Screw Things with Words'. *Hypatia* 29(4): 774-789.

Firestone, Shulamith (1970) *The Dialectic of Sex: The Case for Feminist Revolution.* New York: William Morrow and Co.

Flanigan, Jessica and Watson, Lori (2019) *Debating Sex Work.* Oxford: Oxford University Press.

Fricker, Miranda (2007) *Epistemic Injustice: Power and the Ethics of Knowing.* Oxford: Oxford University Press.

Friedman, Marilyn (2003) *Autonomy, Gender, Politics.* New York: Oxford University Press.

Frye, Marilyn (1983) *The Politics of Reality.* Trumansburg, N.Y.: Crossing Press.

Frye, Marilyn (1992) *Wilful Virgin.* Freedom, CA: The Crossing Press.

Gardner, John (2018) 'The Opposite of Rape'. *Oxford Journal of Legal Studies* 38: 48-70.

Garry, Ann (2011) 'Intersectionality, Metaphors, and the Multiplicity of Gender'. *Hypatia* 26(4): 826-850.

Gauthier, Jeffrey (2011) 'Prostitution, Sexual Autonomy, and Sex Discrimination'. *Hypatia* 26(1): 166-186.

Gavey, Nicola (2005) *Just Sex? The Cultural Scaffolding of Rape.* New York: Routledge.

Gersen, Jacob and Suk, Jeannie (2016) 'The Sex Bureaucracy'. *California Law Review* 104: 881.

Geuss, Raymond (1981) *The Idea of a Critical Theory: Habermas and the Frankfurt School.* Cambridge: Cambridge University Press.

Gheaus, Anca and Robeyns, Ingrid (2011) 'Equality Promoting Parental Leave'. *Journal of Social Philosophy* 42(2): 173-191.

Goldman, Emma (1934) *Living My Life.* New York: Knopf.

Green, Leslie (2000) 'Pornographies'. *Journal of Political Philosophy* 8(1): 27-52.

Hacking, Ian (1999) *The Social Construction of What?* Cambridge, Mass.: Harvard University Press.

Haines, E.L., Deaux, K., and Lofaro, N. (2016) 'The Times They Are a-Changing . . . Or Are They Not? A Comparison of Gender Stereotypes, 1983-2014'. *Psychology of Women Quarterly* 40(3): 353-363.

Hale, Sir Matthew (1971) (first published 1736) *The History of the Plea of the Crown.* London: Professional.

Halley, Janet (2016) 'The Move to Affirmative Consent'. *Signs* 42(1): 257-279.

Handley, Ian M., Brown, Elizabeth R., Moss-Racusin, Corinne A., and Smith, Jessi L. (2015). 'Gender-Biased Evaluations of Gender-bias Evidence'. *Proceedings of the National Academy of Sciences* 112(43): 13201-13206.

Harding, Sandra (2009) 'Standpoint Theories: Productively Controversial'. *Hypatia* 24(4): 192-200.

Harris, Luke Charles and Narayan, Uma (1994) 'Affirmative Action and the Myth of Preferential Treatment: A Transformative Critique of the Terms of the Affirmative Action Debate'. *Harvard Journal of Ethnic and Racial Justice* (formerly *Harvard Blackletter Law Journal*) 11: 1-35.

Hartsock, Nancy C.M. (1983) *Money, Sex, and Power: Toward a Feminist Historical Materialism.* Boston: Northeastern University Press.

Haslanger, Sally (2012) *Resisting Reality: Social Construction and Social Critique.* Oxford: Oxford University Press.

Haslanger, Sally (2017) 'Culture and Critique'. *Aristotelian Society Supplementary Volume* 91(1): 149-173.

Holroyd, Jules and Saul, Jennifer (2018) 'Implicit Bias and Reform Efforts in Philosophy'. *Philosophical Topics* 46(2): 71-102.

hooks, bell (1982) *Ain't I a Woman: Black Women and Feminism.* London: Pluto Press.

hooks, bell (2000) (first published in 1988) *Feminist Theory: From Margin to Center,* 2nd ed. London: Pluto Press.

Hornsby, Jennifer (1993) 'Speech Acts and Pornography'. *Women's Philosophy Review* 10: 38-45.

Hornsby, Jennifer (1995) 'Disempowered Speech'. *Philosophical Topics* 23: 127-147.

Hurd, Heidi M. (1996) 'The Moral Magic of Consent'. *Legal Theory* 2(2): 121-146.

Hursthouse, Rosalind (1991) 'Virtue Theory and Abortion'. *Philosophy and Public Affairs* 20(3): 223-246.

Husak, Douglas and Thomas, George (1992) 'Date Rape, Social Convention, and Reasonable Mistakes'. *Law and Philosophy* 11: 95-126.

Jacobson, Daniel (1995) 'Freedom of Speech Acts? A Response to Langton'. *Philosophy and Public Affairs* 24(1): 64-78.

Jaggar, Alison (1973) 'Abortion and a Woman's Right to Decide'. *Philosophical Forum* 5(1): 347.

Jaggar, Alison M. (2005) '"Saving Amina": Global Justice for Women and Intercultural Dialogue'. *Ethics and International Affairs* 19(3): 55-75.

Jaggar, Alison M. (2009) 'Transnational Cycles of Gendered Vulnerability: A Prologue to a Theory of Global Gender Justice'. *Philosophical Topics* 37(2): 33-52.

Jenkins, Katharine (2017) 'What Women Are For: Pornography and Social Ontology', in Mari Mikkola (ed.) *Beyond Speech: Pornography and Analytic Feminist Philosophy*. Oxford: Oxford University Press.

Jensen, Robert (2007) *Getting Off: Pornography and the End of Masculinity*. Cambridge, Mass.: South End Press.

Jütten, Timo (2016) 'Sexual Objectification'. *Ethics*, 127(1): 27-49.

Kandyoti, Deniz (1988) 'Bargaining with the Patriarchy'. *Gender and Society* 2(3): 274-290.

Kanter, Rosabeth Moss (1977) *Men and Women of the Corporation*. New York: Basic Books.

Khader, Serene J. (2011) *Adaptive Preferences and Women's Empowerment*. Oxford: Oxford University Press.

Khader, Serene J. (2013) 'Identifying Adaptive Preferences in Practice: Lessons from Postcolonial Feminisms'. *Journal of Global Ethics* 9(3): 311-327.

Kimmel, Michael (2008) *Guyland: The Perilous World Where Boys Become Men*. New York: Harper.

King, Deborah (1986) 'Multiple Jeopardy, Multiple Consciousness: The Context of Black Feminist Ideology'. *Signs* 14: 42-72.

Kipnis, Laura (2018) *Unwanted Advances: Sexual Paranoia Comes to Campus*. New York: Harper.

Kittay, Eva Feder (1997) 'AH! My Foolish Heart: A Reply to Alan Soble's "Antioch's 'Sexual Offense Policy'": A Philosophical Exploration'. *Journal of Social Philosophy* 28(2): 153-159.

Klaassen, Marleen J.E. and Jochen, Peter (2015) 'Gender (In)equality in Internet Pornography: A Content Analysis of Popular Pornographic Internet Videos'. *The Journal of Sex Research* 52(7): 721-735.

Koenig, Anne M. and Eagly, Alice H. (2005) 'Stereotype Threat in Men on a Test of Social Sensitivity'. *Sex Roles: A Journal of Research* 52(7-8): 489-496.

Kukla, Quill (2014) 'Performative Force, Convention, and Discursive Injustice'. *Hypatia* 29(2): 440-457. Published under 'Rebecca Kukla'.

Kukla, Quill (2018) 'That's What She Said: The Language of Sexual Negotiation'. *Ethics* 129: 70-97. Published under 'Rebecca Kukla'.

Langton, Rae (2009) *Sexual Solipsism: Philosophical Essays on Pornography and Objectification*. Oxford: Oxford University Press.

Langton, Rae and Hornsby, Jennifer (1998) 'Free Speech and Illocution'. *Legal Theory* 4(1): 21-37.

LeDoeuff, Michelle (1989) *The Philosophical Imaginary*, C. Gordon (trans.). Stanford: Stanford University Press.

Lee, Lorelei (2019) 'Cash/Consent: The War on Sex Work'. *N+1 Magazine*, https://nplusonemag.com/issue-35/essays/cashconsent/.

Leslie, S.-J., Cimpian, A., Meyer, M., and Freeland, E. (2015) 'Expectations of Brilliance Underlie Gender Distributions across Academic Disciplines'. *Science* 347(6219): 262-265.

Levin, Ira (1972) *The Stepford Wives*. New York: Random House.

Levy, Ariel (2005) *Female Chauvinist Pigs: Women and the Rise of Raunch Culture*. New York: Free Press.

Little, Margaret Olivia (1999) 'Abortion, Intimacy, and the Duty to Gestate'. *Ethical Theory and Moral Practice* 2(3): 295-312.

Little, Nicholas (2005) 'From No Means No to Only Yes Means Yes: The Rational Results of an Affirmative Consent Standard in Rape Law'. *Vanderbilt Law Review* 58(4).

Longino, Helen (1980) 'Pornography, Oppression, and Freedom: A Closer Look', in Laura Lederer (ed.) *Take Back The Night*. New York: William Morrow.

Longino, Helen (1990) *Science as Social Knowledge: Values and Objectivity in Scientific Inquiry*. Princeton, N.J.: Princeton University Press.

Lorde, Audre (1984) *Sister Outsider: Essays and Speeches*. Trumansburg, N.Y.: Crossing Press.

Lugones, María (2007) 'Heterosexualism and the Colonial/Modern Gender System'. *Hypatia* 22(1): 186-209.

Lukács, György (1971) (first published 1923) *History and Class Consciousness: Studies in Marxist Dialectics*, Rodney Livingstone (trans.). London: Merlin Press.

Mac, Juno and Smith, Molly (2018) *Revolting Prostitutes*. London: Verso.

MacKinnon, Catharine (1979) *Sexual Harassment of Working Women: A Case of Sex Discrimination*. New Haven: Yale University Press.

MacKinnon, Catharine (1987) *Feminism Unmodified*. Cambridge, Mass.: Harvard University Press.

MacKinnon, Catharine (1989a) *Toward a Feminist Theory of the State*. Cambridge, Mass.: Harvard University Press.

MacKinnon, Catherine (1989b) 'Sexuality, Pornography, and Method: Pleasure under Patriarchy'. *Ethics* 99: 314-346.

MacKinnon, Catharine (1993) *Only Words*, Cambridge, Mass.: Harvard University Press.

MacKinnon Catharine (2011) 'Trafficking, Prostitution, and Inequality'. *Harvard Civil Rights - Civil Liberties Law Review* 46(2): 271-309.

MacKinnon, Catharine and Dworkin, Andrea (1997) *In Harm's Way: The Pornography Civil Rights Hearings*. Cambridge, Mass./London: Harvard University Press.

Maitra, Ishani (2012) 'Subordinating Speech', in Ishani Maitra and Mary Kate McGowan (eds.) *Speech and Harm: Controversies Over Free Speech*. Oxford: Oxford University Press.

Maitra, Ishani and McGowan, Mary Kate (2010) 'On Silencing, Rape, and Responsibility'. *Australasian Journal of Philosophy* 88(1): 167-172.

Manne, Kate (2017) *Down Girl: The Logic of Misogyny*. Oxford: Oxford University Press.

Markowitz, Sally (1990) 'Abortion and Feminism'. *Social Theory and Practice* 16(1): 1-17.

Marx, Karl and Engels, Frederick (1846) *The German Ideology*. Reprinted in *Collected Works* Vol. 5 (1976). London: Lawrence and Wishart.

Marx, Karl and Engels, Frederick (1975) *Selected Correspondence*. Moscow: Progress.

Mason, Rebecca (2011) 'Two Kinds of Unknowing'. *Hypatia* 26(2): 294-307.

May, Larry and Strikwerda, Robert (1991) 'Fatherhood and Nurturance'. *Journal of Social Philosophy* 22(2): 28-39.

McGowan, Mary Kate (2009) 'Debate: On Silencing and Sexual Refusal'. *The Journal of Political Philosophy* 17(4): 487-494.

McGowan, Mary Kate (2017) 'On Multiple Types of Silencing', in Mari Mikkola (ed.) *Beyond Speech*. Oxford: Oxford University Press.

McGregor, Joan (2005) *Is It Rape? On Acquaintance Rape and Taking Women's Consent Seriously*. Farnham: Ashgate.

McGregor, Joan (2011) 'The Legal Heritage of the Crime of Rape', in *Handbook on Sexual Violence*. Oxford: Routledge, 69-89.

McLeod, Carolyn (2008) 'Referral in the Wake of Conscientious Objection to Abortion'. *Hypatia* 23(4): 30-47.

McLeod, Carolyn (2020) *Conscience in Reproductive Health Care: Prioritizing Patient Interests*. Oxford: Oxford University Press.

Medina, José (2013) *The Epistemology of Resistance: Gender and Racial Oppression, Epistemic Injustice, and Resistant Imaginations*. Oxford: Oxford University.

Meyerson, Denise (1991) *False Consciousness*. Oxford: Clarendon Press.

Mikkola, Mari (2011) 'Illocution, Silencing and the Act of Refusal'. *Pacific Philosophical Quarterly* 92(3): 415-437.

Mikkola, Mari (2016) *The Wrong of Injustice: Dehumanization and Its Role in Feminist Philosophy*. New York: Oxford University Press.

Mikkola, Mari (ed.) (2017) *Beyond Speech*. Oxford: Oxford University Press.

Mill, John Stuart (1859) *On Liberty*. Reprinted in *On Liberty and the Subjection of Women* (2006) Alan Ryan (ed.). London: Penguin Classics.

Mills, Charles (1997) *The Racial Contract*. Ithaca, N.Y.: Cornell University Press.

Mills, Charles (2007) 'White Ignorance', in Shannon Sullivan and Nancy Tuana (eds.) *Race and Epistemologies of Ignorance*. Albany: State University of New York Press, 11–38.

Mills, Charles (2017) *Black Rights/White Wrongs: The Critique of Racial Liberalism*. Oxford: Oxford University Press.

Morton, Jennifer M. (2019) *Moving Up Without Losing Your Way: The Ethical Costs of Upward Mobility*. Princeton, N.J.: Princeton University Press.

Moss, P. and Deven, F. (2015) 'Leave Policies in Challenging Times: Reviewing the Decade 2004-2014'. *Community, Work & Family* 18(2): 137-144.

Moss-Racusin, Corinne A., Dovidio, John F., Brescoll, Victoria L., Graham, Mark J., and Handelsman, Jo (2012) 'Science Faculty's Subtle Gender Biases Favor Male Students'. *PNAS* 109(41): 16474-16479

Narayan, Uma (1997) *Dislocating Cultures: Identities, Traditions and Third World Feminism*. Oxford: Routledge.

Narayan, Uma (2002) 'Minds of Their Own: Choices, Autonomy, Cultural Practices, and Other Women', in Louise Antony and Charlotte Witt (eds.) *A Mind of One's Own: Feminist Essays on Reason and Objectivity*, 2nd ed. Boulder, Colo.: Westview Press.

Nisbet, Richard and Ross, Lee (1980) *Human Inference: Strategies and Shortcomings of Social Judgment*. Upper Saddle River, NJ: Prentice Hall.

Noddings, Nel (1986) *Caring: A Feminine Approach to Ethics and Moral Education*. Berkeley: University of California Press.

Norlock, Kathryn (2011) 'Update on Women in the Profession', committee memo, available at the website of the APA Committee on the Status of Women under 'Data on Women in Philosophy', www.apaonlinecsw.org.

Nussbaum, Martha (1995) 'Objectification'. *Philosophy and Public Affairs* 24(4): 249-291.

Nussbaum, Martha (1999) *Sex and Social Justice*. Oxford: Oxford University Press.

Nussbaum, Martha (2001) *Women and Human Development: The Capabilities Approach*. Cambridge: Cambridge University Press.

Okin, Susan Moller (1989) *Justice, Gender and the Family*. New York: Basic Books.

Okin, Susan Moller (1994) 'Gender Inequality and Cultural Differences'. *Political Theory* 22(1): 5-24.

Okin, Susan Moller (1998) 'Feminism and Multiculturalism: Some Tensions'. *Ethics* 108(4): 661-684.

Okin, Susan Moller (1999) *Is Multiculturalism Bad for Women?*, with Joshua Cohen, Matthew Howard and Martha Nussbaum Princeton University Press.

Pateman, Carole (1988) *The Sexual Contract*. Stanford: Stanford University Press.

Phillips, Anne (2007) *Multiculturalism without Culture*. Princeton, NJ: Princeton University Press.

Pierce, Chester (1970) 'Offensive Mechanisms', in Floyd B. Barbour (ed.) *The Black Seventies*. Boston: Porter Sargeant, 265-282.

Pilipchuk, Miranda (2019) 'Good Survivor, Bad Survivor: #MeToo and the Moralization of Survivorship'. *APA Newsletter on Feminism and Philosophy* 19: 5-12.

Pineau, Lois (1989) 'Date Rape: A Feminist Analysis'. *Law and Philosophy* 8(2): 217-243.

Pohlhaus, Gaile Jr. (2011). 'Wrongful Requests and Strategic Refusals to Understand', in Heidi E. Grasswick (ed.) *Feminist Epistemology and Philosophy of Science: Power in Knowledge*. Dordrecht: Springer, 223-240.

Pohlhaus, Gaile Jr. (2012) 'Relational Knowing and Epistemic Injustice: Toward a Theory of Willful Hermeneutical Ignorance'. *Hypatia* 27(4): 715-735.

Radin, Margaret (1987) 'Market Inalienability'. *Harvard Law Review* 100(8): 1849-1937.

Rawls, John (1971) *A Theory of Justice*, Cambridge, Mass.: Harvard University Press.

Rich, Adrienne (1980) 'Compulsory Heterosexuality and Lesbian Existence'. *Signs* 5(4): 631-660.

Rini, Regina (2018) 'How to Take Offense: Responding to Microaggression'. *Journal of the American Philosophical Association* 4(3): 332-351.

Rossi, Clio Magnum (2017) 'Not About the Heart of Darkness: Whoring as a Profession at the End of Capitalism'. *Whores of Yore*, www.thewhoresofyore.com/sex-worker-voices/not-about-the-heart-of-darkness-whoring-as-a-profession-at-the-end-of-capitalism-by-clio-magnum-rossi.

Ruddick, Sara (1989) *Maternal Thinking: Toward a Politics of Peace*. New York: Ballantine.

Rudman, L. and Mescher, K. (2012) 'Of Animals and Objects'. *Personality and Social Psychology Bulletin*, 38(6): 734-746

Satz, Debra (1995) 'Markets in Women's Sexual Labor'. *Ethics* 106(1): 63-85

Saul, Jennifer (2014) 'Stop Thinking So Much About "Sexual Harassment"'. *Journal of Applied Philosophy* 31(3): 307-321.

Schouten, Gina (2019) *Liberalism, Neutrality, and the Gendered Division of Labor*. Oxford: Oxford University Press.

Schulhofer, Stephen J. (2000) *Unwanted Sex: The Culture of Intimidation and the Failure of Law*. Cambridge, Mass.: Harvard University Press.

Schultz, Vicki and Hoffman, Allison (2006) 'The Need for a Reduced Workweek in the United States', in Judy Fudge and Rosemary Owens (eds.) *Precarious Work, Women, and the New Economy: The Challenge to Legal Norms*. Portland, Oregon: Hart, 131.

Sen, Amartya (1993) 'Capability and Well-being', in Martha Nussbaum and Amartya Sen (eds.) *The Quality of Life*. Oxford: Clarendon Press, 30-53.

Shelby, Tommie (2003) 'Ideology, Racism, and Critical Social Theory'. *The Philosophical Forum* 34: 153-188.

Sherwin, Susan (1991) 'Abortion Through a Feminist Ethics Lens'. *Dialogue* 30: 327-342.

Shrage, Laurie (1989) 'Should Feminists Oppose Prostitution?' *Ethics* 99(2): 347-361.

Singer, Peter (1972) 'Famine, Affluence, and Morality'. *Philosophy and Public Affairs* 1(3): 229-243.

Singer, Peter (1979) *Practical Ethics*. Cambridge, Mass.: Cambridge University Press.

Soble, Alan (1997) 'Antioch's "Sexual Offense Policy": A Philosophical Exploration'. *Journal of Social Philosophy* 28(1): 22-36.

Spelman, Elizabeth (1988) *Inessential Woman: Problems of Exclusion in Feminist Thought*. Boston: Beacon Press.

Spivak, Gayatri Chakravorty (1988) 'Can the Subaltern Speak?'. *Die Philosophin* 14(27): 42-58.

Steele C.M. and Aronson, J. (1995) 'Stereotype Threat and the Intellectual Test Performance of African Americans'. *Journal of Personality and Social Psychology* 69(5): 797-811.

Steinpreis, R.E., Anders, K.A., and Ritzke, D. (1999) 'The Impact of Gender on the Review of the Curricula Vitae of Job Applicants and Tenure Candidates: A National Empirical Study'. *Sex Roles* 41: 509.

Stock, Kathleen (2018) 'Sexual Objectification, Objectifying Images, and "Mind-Insensitive Seeing-As"', in Anna Berqvist and Robert Cowan (eds.) *Evaluative Perception*. Oxford: Oxford University Press.

Stoljar, Natalie (1995) 'Essence, Identity and the Concept of Woman'. *Philosophical Topics* 23: 261-293.

Superson, Anita (1993) 'A Feminist Definition of Sexual Harassment'. *Journal of Social Philosophy* 24 (1): 46-64.

Tarrant, Shira (2016) *The Pornography Industry*. Oxford: Oxford University Press.

Thomson, Judith Jarvis (1971) 'A Defense of Abortion'. *Philosophy and Public Affairs* 1: 47-66.

Thomson, Judith Jarvis (1973) 'Preferential Hiring'. *Philosophy and Public Affairs* 2(4): 364-384.

Threadcraft, Shatema (2016) *Intimate Justice: The Black Female Body and the Body Politic*. Oxford: Oxford University Press

Tooley, Michael (1972) 'Abortion and Infanticide'. *Philosophy and Public Affairs* 2(1): 37-65.

Walter, Natasha (2010) *Living Dolls: The Return of Sexism*. London: Virago.

Warren, Mary Anne (1973) 'On the Moral and Legal Status of Abortion'. *The Monist* 57(1): 43-61.

Watson, Lori (2019) '#MeToo?' *APA Newsletter on Feminism and Philosophy* 19: 20-23.

West, Caroline (2003) 'The Free Speech Argument Against Pornography'. *Canadian Journal of Philosophy* 33(3): 391-422.

Widdows, Heather (2018) *Perfect Me: Beauty as an Ethical Ideal*. Princeton, NJ: Princeton University Press.

Wieland, Nellie (2007) 'Linguistic Authority and Convention In a Speech Act Analysis of Pornography'. *Australasian Journal of Philosophy* 85(3): 435-456.

Women's Law Project Report (Tracy, Carol E., Fromson, Terry L., Gentile Long, Jennifer, and Whitman, Charlene Aequitas) (2012) 'Rape and Sexual Assault in the Legal System', https://womenslawproject. org/wp-content/uploads/2016/04/Rape-and-Sexual-Assault-in-the-Legal-System-FINAL.pdf.

World Economic Forum (2018) 'The Global Gender Gap Report', www3.weforum.org/docs/WEF_ GGGR_2018.pdf.

Wylie, Alison (2003) 'Why Standpoint Matters', in R. Figueroa and S. Harding (eds.) *Science and Other Cultures*. New York: Routledge.

Young, Iris Marion (1990) *Justice and the Politics of Difference*. Princeton, NJ: Princeton University Press.

Young, Iris Marion (2009) 'The Gendered Cycle of Vulnerability in the Less Developed World' in Debra Satz and Rob Reich (eds.) *Toward a Humanist Justice: The Political Philosophy of Susan Moller Okin*. Oxford: Oxford University Press.

Young, Iris Marion (2011) *Responsibility for Justice*. Oxford University Press.

Zack, Naomi (2005) *Inclusive Feminism: A Third Wave Theory of Women's Commonality*. Lanham, MD: Rowman and Littlefield.

Zack, Naomi (2007) 'Can Third Wave Feminism Be Inclusive? Intersectionality, Its Problems, and New Directions', in Linda Alcoff and Eva Feder Kittay (eds.) *The Blackwell Guide to Feminist Philosophy*. Oxford: Blackwell, 193-207.

Zheng, Robin (2019) 'Women, Work, and Power: Envisaging the Radical Potential of #MeToo'. *APA Newsletter on Feminism and Philosophy* 19: 29-35.

Index

abortion 11, 53, 55, 56; foetus's right to life 54, 57-58, 61-62; moral right to 58-63; practical issues 63-65; virtue ethics 61-62
Abrams, Kathryn 113
Abramson, Kate 133
Ackerly, Brooke 26
adaptive preferences 24-27, 151-166
addiction model of sexual violence and pornography 79-80
Advertising Standards Authority, UK 73
affirmative action 43-46, 50, 125, 126, 213
affirmative model of consent 190-191, 193
age of consent 182
agency, category of gender stereotypes 35-36; ambivalent agency in sex 109
Ahmed, Leila 23
AIDS 191; see also HIV
Alcoff, Linda Martín 21, 22, 24, 107-108
Alexander-Floyd, Nikol 140
Amnesty International 20, 99
Anderson, Elizabeth 95, 97, 113, 192, 205-206
Anderson, Michelle 190-191
Anderson, Scott 94-95, 111, 193
Anthias, Floya 44
anti-abortion movements 65
anti-immigrant sentiment 24
Antioch College Consent policy 190
Anti-Slavery International 99
Antony, Louise 7, 8, 197, 199-200, 210
apartheid and subordinating speech acts 215
appearance, reduction to 171
Archard, David 189
Aronson, Joshua 38
art, objectification in 175-177

Astell, Mary 123, 159
attitudinal and performative consent 183
Atwood, Margaret 158
Austin, J.L. 214-217, 223
'authentic insider' 21, 129, 209
authority and pornography 215-216
authority silencing 220-221, 223; see also silencing
autonomy: and abortion 63-65; and adaptive preferences 24-27; men and housework 35; and oppression 129; sexual 190
autonomy denial, as a form of objectification 169, 170, 172, 173

bad sex 109-111; see also unjust sex
Bailey, Alison 146-147
Bakke, Allan 45
Baldwin, James 202
'bargaining with the patriarchy' 25, 26, 162, 178, 179
Baron-Cohen, Simon 6-7
Bartky, Sandra Lee 152, 159, 177-178
basement analogy 144, 149
Bauer, Nancy 168-169, 178-180, 216-217
BDSM (Bondage-Discipline, Dominance-Submission, Sadomasochism) 85
Beard, Mary 212
beauty: fashion-beauty complex 159-160; female beauty norms 152, 159, 168, 177-178
Beauvoir, Simone de 10, 132, 153, 168, 173, 177-178, 180
Benhabib, Seyla 18
Berenstein, Nora 208, 209
Berger, John 176-177

Bettcher, Talia Mae 126

bias: and epistemology 199-200, 210; implicit
37-38, 205

Bilge, Sirma 140

biological differences between men and women 2-3

Bird, Alexander 218, 221, 222

birdcage analogy 127

Black feminism 15, 34, 49; and intersectionality
139, 140

Blackstone, Sir William 105

body parts: objectification 175-176; reduction to 171

Bordo, Susan 159

Brake, Elizabeth 50

Brennan, Jason 92

Brighouse, Harry 46-47

Brison, Susan 73, 107, 135

Brod, Harry 75-76, 127-128

Bromwich, Danielle 186

Brownmiller, Susan 101, 107, 108, 118

Bundy, Ted 80

Burke, Tarana 115, 116

Butler, Judith 146

Byron, Lord 181

Cahill, Ann 104, 108, 110, 118

Calhoun, Cheshire 39, 49-50

Cameron, Deborah 79-80

capabilities approach 17-18, 25-26, 28, 162

capitalism 128, 129, 152; worker-capitalist
relationships 201; *see also* Marx, Karl

care 33-52

care ethics 6, 8

Catholic Church and abortion 54

Center for Reproductive Rights 53

'Central Park Jogger' 103

Chambers, Clare 50, 164

child abuse 72, 102

child care, community-based 49, 50

choice: and adaptive preferences 24-27; free
choice 132

class and sexual violence 102

clitoris 103-104

Code, Lorraine 197

coercion 213; coerced marriage 22; coercion
condition for oppression 130; and consent 182,
184-185; sex work 88-90

Cohen, G.A. 158, 164-165

Collins, Patricia Hill 44, 50, 75, 102, 129, 139, 140,
156-157, 201, 207

colonialism 19-20

colour-blind ideology 124, 202

Combahee River Collective Statement 139, 147

commodification: of labour 24; of sexual labour
94-95

communicative model of consent 192

communion category of gender stereotypes 35, 36

confirmation bias 36, 79

Conly, Sarah 111, 184-185, 187, 193

Connellan, Jennifer 7

conscientious refusal, right of 64-65

consciousness raising 26-27, 202, 207-208

consent 110, 114, 118, 181-195, 222, 223; affirmative
model of 190-191, 193; attitudinal and
performative consent 183; and coercion 182,
184-185; and deception 185-187; and force
182-184; negotiation model of 103, 191-192;
responsibility and *mens rea* 188-190, 194;
sexual history evidence 106; unwanted sex
110-111; *see also* rape; sexual assault; sexual
refusal; sexual violence

contraception 55, 62; practical issues 64-65

contractual model of consent 192

controlling images 129, 156, 174, 207, 209; *see also*
role traps

Cooper, Anna Julia 14, 139

Cooper, Brittney 139

copycat model of sexual violence and
pornography 79-80

Craig, Edward 204

credibility deficit 204, 206, 213

credibility excess 204, 206

Crenshaw, Kimberlé 15, 72, 102-103, 139-146, 148

Criado Perez, Caroline 3

criminalization of sex work 87, 93, 96-99

'crisis of masculinity' 128

critical race theory 124

Cudd, Ann 39, 130, 134, 151, 155-156

culture 18; cultural differences 18; cultural
imperialism 22, 129; cultural practices and
multiculturalism 22-24; cultural relativism 16,
22; cultural respectability norms 129

Daly, Mary 19

Davis, Angela 49, 62, 107, 139, 154, 156

Davis, Emmalon 208
Deaux, K. 35, 36
deception and consent 185-187
decriminalization of sex work 88, 92-100
Deep Throat 172
deference, gendered 133
DeGraffenreid v General Motors (1976), USA
    141, 142
de Marneffe, Peter 95-97
'developing world' terminology 15
'different voices model' 7, 8
Dines, Gail 76
discursive injustice 221-222
domestic labour 41-42; and socialisation
    of children 35; third world women 42;
    transnational markets in 43
domestic violence 102; and culture 19, 20; and
    racist stereotyping 143; and US immigration
    law 142-143
Dotson, Kristie 206-207, 213
double bind 126-127, 132, 135, 177, 209
Dougherty, Tom 186
dowry murder 19, 20
DPP v Morgan (1976) 188, 218
dress codes, for women 22
drugs, legalization of 91
Du Bois, W.E.B. 202
Duff, Anthony 188-189
'dupes of patriarchy' 24, 26
Dworkin, Andrea 69-71, 73, 75-77, 89, 124, 134, 135,
    167, 169, 172
Dworkin, Ronald 45, 73, 219, 220

Eaton, Anne 78, 81, 175-177, 179
economic deprivation and oppression 131
Eliot, George 196
Ellison, Ralph 202
Elster, Jon 155, 157-161
emotional labour 42
End Violence Against Women Coalition (EVAW) 106
Engels, Friedrich 157
epistemic friction 206
epistemic oppression 206-209
epistemology 132, 196-197, 209-210; 'epistemic
    exploitation' 208-209; epistemic humility 18-21;
    epistemic injustice 133, 203-206, 214; epistemic
    objectification 204; epistemic oppression

206-209; epistemic violence 207; feminist
    196-199; motivated ignorance 202-203; and
    neutrality 198-200; and objectivity 197-198,
    209-210; social context of 197; standpoint
    theory 200-202, 206, 208, 210
erotica 69, 77; *see also* pornography
essentialist argument, sex work 92, 94-97,
    99-100
Estrich, Susan 105, 183, 184, 188, 192
eugenics programs 54-55
Evans, Ched 106
EVAW (End Violence Against Women Coalition) 106
evidence, in rape and sexual assault cases
    105-106, 114-115
exploitation: epistemic 208-209; and
    oppression 129

Fair Food Program, Latin America 117
false accusations of rape/sexual assault 114-115
false consciousness 12, 24, 132, 151-166, 177, 179, 201
family resemblance approach 146
family work, gendered division of 33; and the
    gendered cycle of vulnerability 40-50
Farley, Lin 111
fashion-beauty complex 159-160, 178
fatherhood 40; parental leave 46-48, 50
Fausto-Sterling, Anne 9
feedback loops 9-10, 155-156, 164, 199
felicity conditions 214, 215, 217, 223
female beauty norms 152, 159, 168, 177-178
female nudes, in art 175-177
femininity 10, 113, 116, 153, 159, 168, 189
Feminist Porn Awards 81
feminist pornography 71, 81-82
Fey, Tina 36
Fight Online Sex Trafficking Act (FOSTA), USA 88
Fine, Cordelia 6-8, 37, 199
Finlayson, Lorna 216-217
Finstad, Liv 96
Firestone, Shulamith 49
Flanigan, Jessica 92
force 213; and consent 181-184; forced marriages
    22; forced sterilization 49, 54-55; forcible
    seduction 104, 115, 182, 188; utmost resistance
    law 104-105, 118, 182-184
FOSTA (Fight Online Sex Trafficking Act), USA 88
Foucault, Michel 128

France 23

Frazer, Elizabeth 79-80

freedom of speech: and pornography 72-73, 77, 212, 220, 223; and silencing 219-220

Freud, Sigmund 103, 104

Fricker, Miranda 197, 203-208, 210, 213

Friedan, Betty 14

Friedman, Marilyn 25, 161

Frye, Marilyn 37, 44, 124-126, 128, 130, 131, 134, 153, 177, 202

functional explanation 158-159, 164-165

fungibility, as a form of objectification 169, 172, 176

Gardner, John 193

garment industry 27-28

Garry, Ann 81, 146

gaslighting 133, 134

Gauthier, Jeffrey 95

Gavey, Nicola 109-111, 185

Gay Pride 147

gender: biological differences between men and women 2-3; gendered division of labor 33-50, 201; metaphysics of 10, 146-147; and sex 9-11, 126; as social construction 9-10, 104

gender gap: 2018 Global Gender Gap Report (World Economic Forum) 2

gender pay gap 4, 41

gender stereotypes *see* stereotypes

generics 7-8

genital cutting 22, 25, 26

Gentileschi, Artemisia 176

Gersen, Jacob 191

Gheaus, Anca 46-47

Gilligan, Carol 5-6

Ginsberg, Ruth Bader 53

Global Alliance Against Traffic in Women 99

Global Commission on HIV and the Law 99

Global Network of Sex Work Projects 99

Goldman, Emma 76

Green, Leslie 216

group rights *see* rights

Hacking, Ian 9

Haines, E.L. 35, 36

Halbertal, Moshe 22

Hale, Lord Matthew 105, 114-115

Halley, Janet 109, 115, 187

Handmaid's Tale, The (Atwood) 158

Harding, Sandra 201, 208

harm: harm condition for oppression 130; harm principle 56, 72, 90; of objectification 172-174, 179; of pornography 73-81, 90, 217-218, 222

Harris, Charles Luke 45-46

Harris v McRae 63

Hartsock, Nancy 201, 208

Haslanger, Sally 10, 130, 155, 163-165, 169, 173, 179, 197-198

health care systems, structural racism in 3

health and survival, gender gap in 2

hermeneutical injustice 204-205, 207-208, 210, 213

heteronormativity 50-53, 104, 116, 153; *see also* heterosex; heterosexuality

heterosex 108-110, 118, 188; *see also* heteronormativity; heterosexuality

heterosexuality 10, 41-42, 49, 75-76, 86, 95, 102, 104, 107-111, 116, 118, 127, 153, 176, 188, 208; and the family 49-50; *see also* heteronormativity; heterosex

Highsmith, Patricia 203, 204

Hill, Anita 143

HIV 91; *see also* AIDS

Hochschild, Arlie 41

Hoffman, Allison 48

Hoigard, Cecilie 96

Holroyd, Jules 37-38

hooks, bell 1, 15, 34, 35, 48-50, 107, 139, 147, 200

Hornsby, Jennifer 69, 74, 207, 213, 214, 217-223

hostile environments and sexual harassment 112, 113

housewife, ideology of 154-156

Human Rights Watch 99

humility, epistemic 18-21

Hursthouse, Rosalind 61, 66

Husak, Douglas 188, 189

hysteria 9, 154

IAT (Implicit Association Test) 38

identity: and intersectionality 145-147; politics 44, 146; and self-objectification 177-179

ideology 131-132, 151-166, 199

ignorance 196-197; motivated 202-203; pernicious 207; 'wilful hermeneutical ignorance' 208; *see also* epistemology

illocution 214; failure of 221

illocutionary silencing 213-220, 223

images, objectifying 174-177
Imam, Ayesha 20
immigration law 142-143
immigration law, US 142-143
'impermissible sacrifice principle' 63
Implicit Association Test (IAT) 38
implicit bias 37-38, 205
imposition model 173
inclusive feminism 146
inclusivity 139, 149
ineffability 213
inegalitarian pornography 70, 71, 79, 81; *see also* pornography
inertness, as a form of objectification 169
injustice: epistemic 133, 203-206, 214; hermeneutical 204-205, 207-208, 210, 213
instrumentality, as a form of objectification 169, 170, 172, 173
International Labour Organization 99
intersectionality 3, 10-12, 15-16, 34, 87, 138-150, 154, 201
intersex people 9
Invisible Man, The (Ellison) 202
Irigaray, Luce 108

Jacobson, Daniel 218-219, 222
Jaggar, Alison 20, 21, 28, 42-43, 63
Jarvis, Judith 43
Jaworski, Peter 92
Jenkins, Katharine 80-81
Jensen, Robert 68, 70
Johnson Reagon, Bernice 146-147
Joyce, James 169
Jütten, Timo 173, 174

Kaczyński, Jarosław 54
Kanter, Rosabeth Moss 129
Kant, Immanuel 170
Khader, Serene 15, 26-27, 160-162
Khattak, Saba Gul 42
Kimmel, Michael 76
kin work 42
Kipling, Rudyard 88
Kipnis, Laura 109, 110, 115
Kittay, Eva Feder 190
Know My Name (Miller) 101, 103
knowledge 196-197; *see also* epistemology

Kohlberg, Lawrence 5
Kukathas, Chandran 22
Kukla, Quill 192, 221-222
Kymlicka, W. 23

labour: commodification of 34; *see also* domestic labour
Lady Chatterly's Lover (Lawrence) 71, 171
Langton, Rae 69, 74, 171-172, 175, 179, 213-220, 222, 223
lap dancing 85
Laude, Jennifer 87
'Laurence St Clair' 169
law: abortion law 53, 54, 63, 64; immigration 142-143; marriage 46; and morality 55-56; pornography law 78; and rape 104-106, 118, 143, 181-184, 187-190
Lawal, Amina 20
Lawrence, D.H. 71, 171
Lee, Harper 204
Lee, Lorelei 89
Leonard, Gloria 69
lesbians and the family 49-50, 72
Leslie, Sarah Jane 39
Levin, Ira 135
liberal feminism and sex work 90-93, 96, 99
liberalism 17, 41, 71, 90, 160
literature, sexism and misogyny in 79
Little, Margaret 58, 61-62, 66
Little, Nicholas 190
locution 214
Lofaro, N. 35, 36
Longino, Helen 77, 198-199, 209-210
Lorde, Audre 6, 139, 148
Lovelace, Linda 172
Lukács, G. 201
Lust, Erika 81
lying and consent 185-187; *see also* deception

Mac, Juno 89, 98-99
MacKinnon, Catharine 63, 66, 69-71, 73, 75-77, 79, 80, 95, 97, 104, 108, 111, 112, 115, 118, 167, 169, 172, 173, 175, 179, 185, 187, 189, 197, 212, 214, 216
'mail order brides' 43
Maitra, Ishani 216, 223
male gaze 175, 176
male ignorance 203

Mandelson, Peter 202
Manet, Edouard 176
Manne, Kate 115, 124, 134–136
Margalit, Avishai 22
marginalization, as a form of oppression 128–129
marginalized groups: epistemic resources 208
marital rape exception 5, 105, 118
Markowitz, Sally 63
marriage 46, 50, 215; laws 46
Marx, Karl 12, 34, 76, 128, 129, 152, 158, 201
masculine identified women and sexual
    harassment 116
masculinity 40, 86, 95, 98, 116; 'crisis of' 128; and
    pornography 75–76
Mason, Rebecca 207–208
masturbation 71, 77; *see also* pornography
May, Larry 40
McGowan, Mary Kate 220–223
McGregor, Joan 105
McLeod, Carolyn 64–65
Me Too/#MeToo 103, 115–118
Mead, Margaret 33
Medar-Gould, Sindi 20
Medina, José 206
mens rea 188–190, 194, 222
Mescher, K. 175
metaphor of the intersection 142
Meyerson, Denise 155
microaggressions 129, 207, 208; as a mechanism
    of oppression 132–133; and misogyny 134
'microinvalidations' 207
Mikkola, Mari 218, 221, 222
Milano, Alyssa 115
milieu relativism 163
Miller, Chanel 101, 103
Mill, John Stuart 56, 72, 90, 151, 219, 220
Mills, Charles 202–203, 210
Millum, Joseph 186
MindGeek 82
mind-suppression 174
miscarriages 65
misogyny 12, 69, 79, 123–137, 144
'modest objectivism' 16
Moore v Hughes Helicopter, Inc (1983), USA
    141–142, 144
moral development 5
moralistic arguments 86, 90, 91, 93, 94

morality and law 55–56
moral relativism 16
morning after pill 55, 65
mother-blaming cliché 80
motherhood 62–63; parental leave 46–48, 50;
    and technology 49
multiculturalism 22–24
Muslim feminism 23

Narayan, Uma 18–20, 22–25, 28, 29, 45–46, 117,
    162, 209
narcissism 178
National Black Feminist Organization 54
National Sexual Violence Resource Center 114, 115
'naturalized epistemology' 199
negotiation model of consent 103, 191–192
neutrality and epistemology 198–200, 209
Nisbett, Richard 155
Noddings, Nel 6
'No Model' of consent 192
non-binary people 11, 86
Nordic model of sex work 87, 97–100
#notallmen 8
nurturing 7–8, 40
Nussbaum, Martha 17–18, 25–26, 28, 90–93, 95,
    160–162, 169–171, 173, 175, 176, 179
nymphomania 103

Obama administration 114
objectification 132, 155, 167–180, 197
objectivity 6; and epistemology 197–198, 209–210
obscenity 71–72, 143–144; *see also* pornography
obscenity law 71
offence and pornography 72–73
Okin, Susan 22–24, 29, 40–42, 46, 48, 50
'old boy networks' 46
Open Society Foundations 99
oppression 12, 123–137, 151, 153, 200–202, 206–209
orgasm, female 103–104
Othering 20, 22, 129, 132, 153, 168, 178–179, 208
'outsider within' 201
ownership, as a form of objectification 170

parental leave 46–48, 50
partial silencing 221–222; *see also* silencing
Pateman, Carole 95
paternalism: and consent 187; and sex work 97

patriarchy 10, 76, 123-124, 126, 153; 'bargaining with the patriarchy' 25, 26, 162, 178, 179; definition 3; and epistemology 198; and men 126-128; 'prisoners of patriarchy' 24; and sexual violence 5
Payne v Travenol (1976), USA 142, 144
people seeds analogy 59, 60
perlocution 214, 215, 218, 221
pernicious ignorance 207
personhood and the right to life 57-59
Phillips, Anne 23
Pierce, Chester 132
Pilipchuk, Miranda 117
Pineau, Lois 189, 192, 221
Pohlhaus, Gaile 208
police procedures and sexual violence 106
policy and sex work 93, 96-99
political intersectionality 143; *see also* intersectionality
political lesbianism 50
political power, gender gap in 2
Pornhub 68-69
pornography 4-5, 68-84, 156, 169, 172, 175, 212, 214-218, 220, 222, 223; definitions of 69-71; feminist 71, 81-82
powerlessness, as a form of oppression 129
pregnancy 60-62; *see also* abortion; reproductive rights
'prisoners of patriarchy' 24
privilege: condition for oppression 130; and intersectionality 144-145, 149
product design, sexism in 3
professional extortion 95
prostitution 5, 34; *see also* sex work
psychological differences between men and women 6-7, 197

queer identity 145, 147, 177
Quine, W.V. 199

R. v Butler (1992), Canada 71
race: critical race theory 124; and 'epistemic exploitation' 208-209; and the gendered division of labour 48-49; and sexual harassment 117; and sexual violence 102-103, 107
racialised differences in women's labour 34

racial segregation 131
racism 6; and child welfare policy 130-131; discrimination cases in law 141-142; epistemic violence 207; and forced sterilization 49, 54, 55; Me Too movement 116; and obscenity laws 72, 143-144; and pornography 75, 116; racial segregation 131; racist ideology 154, 156, 202-203; racist stereotypes 102-103, 117, 129-130, 138, 143, 153, 174, 207, 214; and rape law 143; rape and sexual violence 102-103, 107, 143; and reproductive rights 62; and respectability 129; and sex work 89; structural racism in health care systems 3
Radin, Margaret 94, 97
RAINN (Rape, Abuse & Incest National Network) 102, 106
rape 101-103, 130, 153, 191, 194, 213; consent as means of avoidance 110; false accusations 114-115; as a form of oppression 131; in law 104-106, 118, 143, 181-184, 187-190; marital 5, 105, 118; and objectifying images of women 175; as part of sexist oppression 107-109; and pornography 74, 75, 78; rape myths 102, 221; *see also* consent
Rape, Abuse & Incest National Network (RAINN) 102, 106
rape and sexual assault in law 105, 106
'rape shield laws' 106
Rapp, Anthony 116
Rawls, John 17, 41
Ray, Man 175
recklessness 188, 223
recognition silencing 220, 221, 223; *see also* silencing
recruitment and hiring: and affirmative action 44, 46; gender-based bias in 37
Regina v Hicklin (1868), UK 71
regulation, of sex work 87, 88, 93, 97-99
relationship ethics 62
relativism 16; cultural 15-16, 22; epistemic 200; milieu 163; moral 15-16; *see also* values
religious clothing, ban on wearing of in France 23
'replication crisis' in social psychology 37
representational intersectionality 143-144; *see also* intersectionality
repressive satisfactions 152, 177
reproductive labour, freedom from 49

reproductive rights 53–67

respectability and cultural norms 129

responsibility 27–28; and consent 188–190, 194; and silencing 222–223

'reverse discrimination' 45; *see also* affirmative action

Rich, Adrienne 49, 50

rights 56–57, 63–65; to abortion 58–61; foetus's right to life 54, 57–58, 61–62; group rights 22, 23; to pornography 72–73, 77, 212, 220, 223; reproductive 53–67

Rini, Regina 132

Robeyns, Ingrid 46–47

Roe v Wade (US) 53, 54, 63, 64

role traps 129, 132, 134, 207; *see also* controlling images

Rossi, Clio Magnum 85

Ross, Lee 155

Ruddick, Sarah 49

Rudman, L. 175

sati (widow immolation) 19–20

Satz, Debra 86, 90–93, 96

Saul, Jennifer 37–38, 113

Schouten, Gina 41, 42, 46, 48

Schulhofer, Stephen 190

Schultz, Vicki 48

Science, Technology, Engineering and Mathematics (STEM) subjects, under-representation of women in 4, 36–39, 125

Searle, John 80

'second shift' 41–42

Section 41 of the Youth Justice and Criminal Evidence Act 1999, 106

seduction: and consent 185; forcible 104, 115, 182, 188

self-objectification 177–179; *see also* objectification

Sen, Amartya 17

SESTA (Stop Enabling Sex Traffickers Act), USA 88

sex 4; bad 109–111; biological 9, 126; commodification of 94; and gender 9–11, 126; male sexuality model of 70, 75; unwanted 109–111; *see also* heterosex

sex crime: and pornography 78; *see also* rape; sexual assault; sexual violence

sexism 3, 12, 123–137, 154, 156–157

sex marking 126

sex therapy, professional 97

sexual assault: in law 104–106; *see also* consent; rape; sexual violence

sexual harassment 111–113, 118, 143, 153; and hermeneutical injustice 205; in male-dominated areas 39; Me Too 115–117; same-sex 116; and segregated labour 42; Title IX, Education Amendments Act (1972), USA 114–115, 118, 182–183, 187, 190, 191

sexual harassment law 111–112

sexual history and 'rape shield laws' 106

sexual history evidence and consent 106

sexuality 5, 103–104

sexual murders and pornography 80

sexual refusal: and silencing 213, 214, 217–223; *see also* consent

sexual revolution, 1960s 75, 76, 109

sexual violence 5, 101–119, 130

sex work 5, 34, 43, 85–100

Shelby, Tommie 153–157

Sherwin, Susan 64, 66

Shrage, Laurie 91, 92, 96

silencing 132, 212–239

sincerity silencing 220, 221, 223; *see also* silencing

Singer, Peter 27, 57

situated knowledge 202

slavery 75, 156

Smith, Barbara 138

Smith, Molly 89, 98–99

'snowflakes' 208

Soble, Alan 190

'social connections model of responsibility' 27–29

social construction 75, 80–81, 104, 118, 163; and gender 9–10

social epistemology 196; *see also* epistemology

social group condition for oppression 130

social identity theory 155–156

socialization: of children and domestic labour 35; differences between men and women 8; of women into gender roles 40–41

'social threat situation' of women 131

solidarity 15, 21; and intersectionality 146–149

Spacey, Kevin 116

'speaking for others' 21

speech acts 212–239

speech act theory 214-219, 223; *see also* silencing
Spelman, Elizabeth 15-16, 144-148
Spivak, Gayatri 20
standpoint theory 200-202, 206, 208, 210
status incongruity theory 36
Steele, Claude 38
STEM (Science, Technology, Engineering and
    Mathematics) subjects: under-representation
    of women in 4, 36-39, 125
Stepford Wives, The (Levin) 135
stereotypes 6, 8, 10, 21, 40, 73, 81, 82; agency and
    communion categories 35-36; and epistemic
    injustice 203-204, 207; in philosophy 39; racist
    102-103, 117, 129-130, 138, 143, 153, 174, 207, 214;
    of sexuality 109; 'stereotype threat' 38-39; *see
    also* ideology; femininity; masculinity
sterilization 49, 54-55
Stock, Kathleen 174-175, 179
Stoljar, Natalie 146
Stop Enabling Sex Traffickers Act (SESTA),
    USA 88
Strikwerda, Robert 40
stripping 85
structural identity 147, 149
subjective identity 147, 149
subjectivity denial, as a form of objectification 170
subordination: causal claim for pornography
    73-80; and silencing 215-217
Suk, Jeannie 191
Superson, Anita 112

Tailhook scandal 39
Talented Mr Ripley, The (Highsmith) 203, 204
Taormino, Tristan 81
Tarrant, Shira 82
teamwork and consent 193
testimony 203; testimonial injustice 203-205,
    207, 210, 213; testimonial quieting 206-207;
    testimonial smothering 206-207, 213
third world women 14-15, 17, 161; as 'dupes of
    patriarchy' 24; and epistemic exploitation 209;
    and epistemic humility 18-21; and the gendered
    division of labour 42
Thomas, George 188, 189
Thomas, Judge Clarence 143
Thomson, Judith Jarvis 43, 57, 58-61
Threadcraft, Shatema 49

Title IX, Education Amendments Act (1972), USA
    114-115, 118, 182-183, 187, 190, 191
To Kill a Mockingbird (Lee) 204
Tooley, Michael 58
totalizing 19
trafficking 85-86, 88-89
trans people 11; sex workers 86-87; trans identity
    126; 'trans panic defence' 87; transphobia 126
Trouble, Courtney 81
Trump, Donald 103, 114, 183
Truth, Sojourner 148
Turner, Brock 103, 115
Twin Peaks 174
2 Live Crew 72, 143-144
2018 Global Gender Gap Report (World Economic
    Forum) 2
Tyson, Mike 143

Ulysses (Joyce) 169
UNAIDS 99
under-representation of women in philosophy
    4, 37
universal values 16-18
universities: Title IX, Education Amendments Act
    (1972), USA 114-115, 118, 182-183, 187, 190, 191
unjust sex 110, 111, 185, 191
unwanted sex 110-111
UN Women 102
uptake failure 217-219, 222, 223
utmost resistance law 104-105, 118, 182-184

Vadala, Candice (Candida Royalle) 81
values: constitutive and contextual 198; objective
    16; universal 16-18; *see also* relativism
veiling 23
Velleman, David 173
violability, as a form of objectification 170, 172
violence 134, 153; epistemic 207; as a form of
    oppression 129-131; in male-dominated areas
    39; in the name of honour 22; as natural
    characteristic of men 8; and pornography 70;
    see also sexual assault; sexual violence
violinist analogy 53, 59
virtue ethics 61-62

Warren, Mary Anne 57, 58, 60
Washington, Desiree 143

Watson, Lori 96, 97, 116
Weinstein, Harvey 115, 116, 153
West, Caroline 219-220
Western culture 18-19, 48
'white ignorance' 202
'white saviour' 20
Widdows, Heather 178
widowhood, as a social construct 10
Wieland, Nellie 222
'wilful hermeneutical ignorance' 208
Williams, Michelle 116
'woke' 208
Wollstonecraft, Mary 4
Women's March on Washington, 2016, 117
Women's Rights Conference, Akron, Ohio (1851) 148
Wood, Carmita 111, 205, 207-208
work 33-52, 131, 201; *see also* domestic labour

Working Women United 111
World Economic Forum, 2018 Global Gender Gap
    Report 2
World Health Organization 91, 99
Wright, Erik Olin 46-47
Wylie, Alison 200-201

'Yes Model' of consent 190-192
Young, Iris Marion 27-29, 42, 45, 50, 128-130, 134
Youth Justice and Criminal Evidence Act 1999,
    Section 41, 106
Youth Justice and Criminal Evidence Act 1999,
    UK 106
Yuval-Davis, Nira 44

Zack, Naomi 146, 147
Zheng, Robin 117

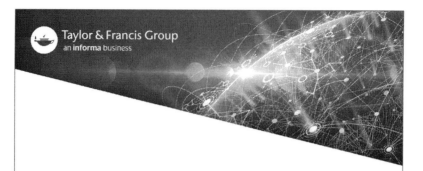